D1249805

Recommended Reference Books

for Small and Medium-sized Libraries and Media Centers

2000

Recommended Reference Books

for Small and Medium-sized
Libraries and Media Centers

2000

Bohdan S. Wynar, editor

2000

Libraries Unlimited, Inc. • Englewood, Colorado

LIBRARIES UNLIMITED, INC.
P.O. Box 6633
Englewood, CO 80155-6633
1-800-237-6124
www.lu.com

Library of Congress Cataloging-in-Publication Data

Main entry under title:

Recommended reference books for small and medium-
    sized libraries and media centers.

    "Selected from the 2000 edition of American
reference books annual."
    Includes index.
    1. Reference books--Bibliography.   2. Reference
services (Libraries)--Handbooks, manuals, etc.
3. Instructional materials centers--Handbooks,
manuals, etc.   I. Wynar, Bohdan S.
II. American reference books annual.
Z1035.1.R435   011'.02   81-12394
ISBN 1-56308-838-X
ISSN 0277-5948

Contents

Introduction

Recommended Reference Books for Small and Medium-sized Libraries and Media Centers (RRB), now in its twentieth volume, is designed to assist smaller libraries in the systematic selection of suitable reference materials for their collections. It aids in the evaluation process by choosing substantial titles in all subject areas. The increase in publication of reference books in the United States and Canada, in combination with the decrease in library budgets, makes this guide an invaluable tool.

Following the pattern established in 1981 with the first volume, RRB consists of book reviews chosen from the current edition of *American Reference Books Annual*. This nationally acclaimed work provides reviews of reference books and CD-ROMs published in the United States and Canada within a single year, along with English-language titles from other countries. ARBA has reviewed more than 50,000 titles since its inception in 1970. Because it provides comprehensive coverage of reference books, not just selected or recommended titles, many are of interest only to large academic and public libraries. Thus, RRB has been developed as an abridged version of ARBA with selected reviews of books suitable for smaller libraries.

Titles reviewed in RRB include dictionaries, encyclopedias, indexes, directories, bibliographies, guides, atlases, gazetteers, and other types of ready-reference tools. General encyclopedias that are updated annually, yearbooks, almanacs, indexing and abstracting services, directories, and other annuals are included on a selective basis. These works are systematically reviewed so that all important annuals are critically examined every few years. Excluded from RRB are regional guides in the areas of biological sciences, travel guides, and reference titles in the areas of literature and fine arts that deal with individual authors or artists. All titles in this volume are coded with letters, which provide worthwhile guidance for selection. These indicate that a given work is a recommended purchase for smaller college libraries (C), public libraries (P), or school media centers (S).

The current volume of RRB contains 526 unabridged reviews selected from the 1,543 entries in ARBA 2000. These have been written by more than 250 subject specialists throughout the United States and Canada. Although all titles in RRB are recommended acquisitions, critical comments have not been deleted, because even recommended works may be weak in one respect or another. In many cases reviews evaluate and compare a work in relation to other titles of a similar nature. All reviews provide complete ordering and bibliographic information. The subject index organization is based upon the 19th edition of the Library of Congress Subject Headings. References to reviews published in periodicals (see page xxi for journals cited) during the year of coverage are appended to the reviews. All reviews are signed.

The present volume contains 37 chapters. There are four major subdivisions: "General Reference Works," "Social Sciences," "Humanities," and "Science and Technology." "General Reference Works," arranged alphabetically, is subdivided by form: bibliography, biography, handbooks, and so on. The remaining three parts are subdivided into alphabetically arranged chapters. Most chapters are subdivided in a way that reflects the arrangement strategy of the entire volume: a section on general works and then a topical breakdown. The latter is further subdivided, based on the amount of material available on a given topic.

RRB has been favorably reviewed in such journals as *Booklist*, *School Library Media Quarterly*, *Journal of Academic Librarianship*, and *Reference Books Bulletin*. For example, *The Book Report* (Jan/Feb 98, p. 47) stated that RRB is "an indispensable purchase for small and medium-sized libraries and one that most librarians rely upon for currency and reliability." The editors continue to strive to make RRB the most valuable acquisitions tool a small library can have.

In closing, I would like to express my gratitude to the contributors whose reviews appear in this volume. I would also like to thank the staff members who have been instrumental in the preparation of this work: Pamela J. Getchell, Shannon M. Graff, and Cari Ringelheim.

Bohdan S. Wynar

Contributors

Stephen H. Aby, Education Bibliographer, Bierce Library, Univ. of Akron, Ohio.

Anthony J. Adam, Reference Librarian, Prairie View A & M Univ., Coleman Library, Tex.

January Adams, Asst. Director/Head of Adult Services, Franklin Township Public Library, Somerset, N.J.

Bev Cummings Agnew, Reference Librarian, Univ. of Colorado Law School Library, Boulder.

Walter C. Allen, Assoc. Professor Emeritus, Graduate School of Library and Information Science, Univ. of Illinois, Urbana.

Donald Altschiller, Reference Librarian, Boston Univ.

Elizabeth L. Anderson, Part-Time Instructor, Lansing Community College, Mich.

Frank J. Anderson, Librarian Emeritus, Sandor Teszler Library, Wofford College, Spartanburg, S.C.

Charles R. Andrews, Dean of Library Services, Hofstra Univ., Hempstead, N.Y.

Susan B. Ardis, Acting Head Science Libraries Division, Univ. of Texas, Austin.

Susan C. Awe, Asst. Director, Univ. of New Mexico, Albuquerque.

Mary A. Axford, Reference Librarian, Georgia Institute of Technology, Atlanta.

Christopher Baker, Professor of English, Armstrong Atlantic State Univ., Savannah, Ga.

Helen M. Barber, Reference Librarian, New Mexico State Univ., Las Cruces.

Daniel C. Barkley, Asst. Director, Government Informations Department, Univ. of New Mexico, Albuquerque.

Craig W. Beard, Reference Librarian, Mervyn H. Sterne Library, Univ. of Alabama, Birmingham.

Sandra E. Belanger, Reference Librarian, San Jose State Univ. Library, Calif.

Carol Willsey Bell, Head, Local History and Genealogy Dept., Warren-Trumbull County Public Library, Warren, Ohio.

George H. Bell, Assoc. Librarian, Daniel E. Noble Science and Engineering Library, Arizona State Univ., Tempe.

Adrienne Antink Bendel, Medical Group Management Association, Lakewood, Colo.

Bernice Bergup, Humanities Reference Librarian, Davis Library, Univ. of North Carolina, Chapel Hill.

Teresa U. Berry, Reference Coordinator, Univ. of Tennessee, Knoxville.

John B. Beston, Professor of English, Santa Fe, N.Mex.

Barbara M. Bibel, Reference Librarian, Science/Business/Sociology Dept., Main Library, Oakland Public Library, Calif.

Terry D. Bilhartz, Assoc. Professor of History, Sam Houston State Univ., Huntsville, Tex.

Richard Bleiler, Reference Librarian, Univ. of Connecticut, Storrs.

Laura K. Blessing, Personnel Librarian, Univ. of Texas, Arlington.

Daniel K. Blewett, Reference Librarian, Cudahy Library, Loyola Univ., Chicago.

Edna M. Boardman, Library Media Specialist, Minot High School, Magic City Campus, N.D.

Bobray Bordelon, Social Science Reference Center, Firestone Library, Princeton Univ. Libraries, N.J.

Georgia Briscoe, Assoc. Director and Head of Technical Services, Law Library, Univ. of Colorado, Boulder.

Simon J. Bronner, Distinguished Professor of Folklore and American Studies, Capitol College, Pennsylvania State Univ., Middletown.

Betty Jo Buckingham, (retired) Consultant, Iowa Dept. of Education, Des Moines.

John R. Burch Jr., Technical Services Librarian, Hagan Memorial Library, Cumberland College, Williamsburg, Ky.

Frederic F. Burchsted, Reference Librarian, Widener Library, Harvard Univ., Cambridge, Mass.

Robert H. Burger, Head, Slavic and East European Library, Univ. of Illinois, Urbana-Champaign.

Ingrid Schierling Burnett, Reference Librarian, Univ. of Southern Colorado Library, Pueblo.

Hans E. Bynagle, Library Director and Professor of Philosophy, Whitworth College, Spokane, Wash.

Joseph L. Carlson, Library Director, Vandenberg Air Force Base, Calif.

Ruth A. Carr, Chief, U.S. History, Local History and Genealogy Div., New York Public Library.

Bert Chapman, Government Publications Coordinator, Purdue Univ., West Lafayette, Ind.

Boyd Childress, Reference Librarian, Ralph B. Draughon Library, Auburn Univ., Ala.

Dene L. Clark, (retired) Reference Librarian, Auraria Library, Denver, Colo.

Paul F. Clark, Assoc. Professor, Pennsylvania State Univ., University Park.

Harriette M. Cluxton, (formerly) Director of Medical Library Services, Illinois Masonic Medical Center, Chicago.

Gary R. Cocozzoli, Director of the Library, Lawrence Technological Univ., Southfield, Mich.

Donald E. Collins, Assoc. Professor, History Dept., East Carolina Univ., Greenville, N.C.

Barbara Conroy, Career Connections, Santa Fe, N.Mex.

Kay O. Cornelius, (formerly) Teacher and Magnet School Lead Teacher, Huntsville City Schools, Ala.

Paul B. Cors, Catalog Librarian, Univ. of Wyoming, Laramie.

Gregory A. Crawford, Head of Public Services, Penn State Harrisburg, Middletown, Pa.

Mark J. Crawford, Consulting Exploration Geologist/Writer/Editor, Madison, Wis.

Milton H. Crouch, Asst. Director for Reader Services, Bailey/Howe Library, Univ. of Vermont, Burlington.

Gregory Curtis, Director, Northern Maine Technical College, Presque Isle.

Donald G. Davis Jr., Professor, Graduate School of Library and Information Science, Univ. of Texas, Austin.

Dominique-René de Lerma, Professor, Conservatory of Music, Lawrence Univ., Appleton, Wis.

Gail de Vos, Adjunct Assoc. Professor, School of Library and Information Studies, Univ. of Alberta, Edmonton.

Barbara Delzell, Vancouver, Wash.

Margaret Denman-West, Professor Emeritus, Western Maryland College, Westminster.

Margaret F. Dominy, Head, Mathematics-Physics-Astronomy Library, Univ. of Pennsylvania, Philadelphia.

Christine Drew, Reference Librarian, Babson College, Wellesley, Mass.

Jean Engler, Reference Librarian, Koelbel Public Library, Englewood, Colo.

Edward Erazo, Head of Reference, Florida Atlantic Univ., Boca Raton, Fla.

Jonathon Erlen, Curator, History of Medicine, Univ. of Pittsburgh, Pa.

Patricia A. Eskoz, (retired) Catalog Librarian, Auraria Library, and Asst. Professor Emeritus, Univ. of Colorado, Denver.

G. Edward Evans, Univ. Librarian, Charles Von der Ahe Library, Loyola Marymount Univ., Los Angeles, Calif.

Elaine Ezell, Library Media Specialist, Bowling Green Jr. High School, Ohio.

Andrew Ezergailis, Professor of History, Ithaca College, N.Y.

Judith J. Field, Senior Lecturer, Program for Library and Information Science, Wayne State Univ., Detroit.

Michael A. Foley, Honors Director, Marywood College, Scranton, Pa.

Lynne M. Fox, Information Services and Outreach Librarian, Denison Library, Univ. of Colorado Health Sciences Center, Denver.

David K. Frasier, Asst. Librarian, Reference Dept., Indiana Univ., Bloomington.

Susan J. Freiband, Assoc. Professor, Graduate School of Librarianship, Univ. of Puerto Rico, San Juan.

David O. Friedrichs, Professor, Univ. of Scranton, Pa.

Ronald H. Fritze, Assoc. Professor, Dept. of History, Lamar Univ., Beaumont, Tex.

Paula Frosch, Assoc. Museum Librarian, Thomas J. Watson Library, Metropolitan Museum of Art, New York.

Sandra E. Fuentes, Public Services Librarian, Vanderbilt Divinity Library, Nashville, Tenn.

Zev Garber, Professor and Chair, Jewish Studies, Los Angeles Valley College, Calif.

Joan Garner, Staff, Libraries Unlimited, Inc.

Pamela J. Getchell, Staff, Libraries Unlimited, Inc.

John T. Gillespie, College Professor and Writer, New York.

Lois Gilmer, Library Director, Univ. of West Florida, Fort Walton Beach.

Barbara B. Goldstein, Media Specialist, Magothy River Middle School, Arnold, Md.

Shannon M. Graff, Staff, Libraries Unlimited, Inc.

Pamela M. Graham, Latin American and Iberian Studies Librarian, Columbia Univ., New York.

Richard W. Grefrath, Reference Librarian, Univ. of Nevada, Reno.

Susan B. Hagloch, Director, Tuscarawas County Public Library, New Philadelphia, Ohio.

Deborah Hammer, Head, History, Travel and Biography Div., Queens Borough Public Library, Jamaica, N.Y.

Gary Handman, Head, Media Resources Center, Univ. of California, Berkeley.

Roland C. Hansen, Readers' Services Librarian, the School of the Art Institute of Chicago.

Kimberley D. Harris, Public Librarian, Newman Riga Library, Churchville, N.Y.

Ann Hartness, Asst. Head Librarian, Benson Latin American Collection, Univ. of Texas, Austin.

Ralph Hartsock, Senior Music Catalog Librarian, Univ. of North Texas, Denton.

Karen D. Harvey, Assoc. Dean for Academic Affairs, Univ. College, Univ. of Denver, Colo.

Fred J. Hay, Librarian of the W. L. Eury Appalachian Collection and Assoc. Professor, Center for Appalachian Studies, Appalachian State Univ., Boone, N.C.

Carol D. Henry, Librarian, Lyons Township High School, LaGrange, Ill.

Diana Tixier Herald, Librarian, Freelance Writer, Grand Junction, Colo.

Mark Y. Herring, Dean of Library Services, Winthrop Univ., Dacus Library, Rock Hill, S.C.

Susan Davis Herring, Reference Librarian, Univ. of Alabama Library, Huntsville.

Janet Hilbun, Student, Texas Woman's Univ., Denton.

Marquita Hill, Cooperating Professor of Chemical Engineering, Univ. of Maine, Orono.

V. W. Hill, Social Sciences Bibliographer, Memorial Library, Univ. of Wisconsin, Madison.

Susan Tower Hollis, Assoc. Dean and Center Director, Central New York Center of the State Univ. of New York.

Leslie R. Homzie, Asst. Reference Librarian, Univ. of Delaware, Newark.

Sara Anne Hook, Assoc. Dean of the Faculties, Indiana Univ., Purdue Univ., Indianapolis.

Shirley L. Hopkinson, Professor, Div. of Library and Information Science, San Jose State Univ., Calif.

Jonathan F. Husband, Program Chair of the Library/Reader Services Librarian, Henry Whittemore Library, Framingham State College, Mass.

Ludmila N. Ilyina, (retired) Professor, Natural Resources Institute, Winnipeg, Man.

Barbara Ittner, Staff, Libraries Unlimited, Inc.

D. Barton Johnson, Professor Emeritus of Russian, Univ. of California, Santa Barbara.

Florence W. Jones, Librarian, Auraria Campus Library, Denver, Colo.

Kelly M. Jordan, Middleburg, Va.

Suzanne Julian, Public Services Librarian, Southern Utah Univ. Library, Cedar City.

Elaine F. Jurries, Coordinator of Serials Services, Auraria Library, Denver, Colo.

Thomas A. Karel, Assoc. Director for Public Services, Shadek-Fackenthal Library, Franklin and Marshall College, Lancaster, Pa.

Dean H. Keller, Assoc. Dean of Libraries, Kent State Univ., Ohio.

Barbara E. Kemp, Asst. Director, Dewey Graduate Library, State Univ. of New York, Albany.

Jackson Kesler, Professor of Theatre and Dance, Western Kentucky Univ., Bowling Green.

Vicki J. Killion, Asst. Professor of Library Science and Pharmacy, Nursing and Health Sciences Librarian, Purdue Univ., West Lafayette, Ind.

Norman L. Kincaide, Citation Editor, Shepard's/McGraw-Hill, Inc., Colorado Springs, Colo.

Bruce Kingma, Assoc. Professor, State University of New York at Albany.

Janet J. Kosky, Mukwonago Community Library, Wis.

Lori D. Kranz, Freelance Editor; Assoc. Editor, *The Bloomsbury Review*, Denver, Colo.

Betsy J. Kraus, Librarian, Lovelace Respiratory Research Institute, National Environmental Respiratory Center, Albuquerque, N.Mex.

Marlene M. Kuhl, Library Manager, Baltimore County Public Library, Reisterstown Branch, Md.

Edward Kurdyla, Staff, Libraries Unlimited, Inc.

Robert V. Labaree, Reference/Public Services Librarian, Von KleinSmid Library, Univ. of Southern California, Los Angeles.

Linda L. Lam-Easton, Assoc. Professor, Dept. of Religious Studies, California State Univ., Northridge.

Binh P. Le, Reference Librarian, Abington College, Pennsylvania State Univ., University Park.

Charles Leck, Professor of Biological Sciences, Rutgers Univ., New Brunswick, N.J.

Hwa-Wei Lee, Dean of Libraries, Ohio Univ., Athens.

R. S. Lehmann, Rocky Mountain BankCard System, Colorado National Bank, Denver.

Polin P. Lei, Assoc. Librarian, Information Services, Arizona Health Sciences Library, Tucson.

Richard A. Leiter, Director, Law Library, Howard Univ., Washington, D.C.

Charlotte Lindgren, Professor Emerita of English, Emerson College, Boston.

Larry Lobel, Virtuoso Keyboard Services, Petaluma, Calif.

Marit S. MacArthur, Reference Librarian, Auraria Libraries, Univ. of Colorado, Denver.

Sara R. Mack, Professor Emerita, Dept. of Library Science, Kutztown Univ., Pa.

Theresa Maggio, Head of Public Services, Southwest Georgia Regional Library, Bainbridge.

Judith A. Matthews, Physics-Astronomy/Science Reference Librarian, Main Library, Michigan State Univ., East Lansing.

John Maxymuk, Reference Librarian, Paul Robeson Library, Rutgers Univ., Camden, N.J.

Peter H. McCracken, Odegaard Undergraduate Library, Univ. of Washington, Seattle.

Dana McDougald, Lead Media Specialist, Learning Resources Center, Cedar Shoals High School, Athens, Ga.

Glenn S. McGuigan, Reference Librarian, Penn State Abington.

Margo B. Mead, Technology Instruction Librarian, Louis M. Salmon Library, Univ. of Alabama, Huntsville.

Michael G. Messina, Assoc. Professor, Dept. of Forest Science, Texas A & M Univ., College Station.

G. Douglas Meyers, Chair, Dept. of English, Univ. of Texas, El Paso.

Robert Michaelson, Head Librarian, Seeley G. Mudd Library for Science and Engineering, Northwestern Univ., Evanston, Ill.

Bogdan Mieczkowski, Professor of Economics, Ithaca College, N.Y.

Seiko Mieczkowski, Cocoa Beach, Fla.

Bill Miller, Director of Libraries, Florida Atlantic Univ., Boca Raton.

Carol L. Mitchell, Southeast Asian Bibliographic Services Librarian, General Library System, Univ. of Wisconsin, Madison.

Terry Ann Mood, Head of Collection Development, Univ. of Colorado, Denver.

Gerald D. Moran, Director, McCartney Library, Geneva College, Beaver Falls, Pa.

Betty J. Morris, Staff, Libraries Unlimited, Inc.

Craig A. Munsart, Teacher, Jefferson County Public Schools, Golden, Colo.

Paul M. Murphy III, Director of Marketing, PMX Medical, Colo.

James M. Murray, U.S. Courts Library, Spokane, Wash.

Joseph Z. Nitecki, Professor Emeritus, School of Information Science and Policy, State Univ. of New York, Albany.

Eric R. Nitschke, Reference Librarian, Robert W. Woodruff Library, Emory Univ., Atlanta, Ga.

Christopher W. Nolan, Head, Reference Services, Maddux Library, Trinity Univ., San Antonio, Tex.

Carol L. Noll, Volunteer Librarian, Schimelpfenig Middle School, Plano, Tex.

David G. Nowak, Asst. Professor and Reference Librarian, Mississippi State Univ. Libraries, Mississippi State.

Marshall E. Nunn, Professor, Dept. of History, Glendale Community College, Calif.

Herbert W. Ockerman, Professor, Ohio State Univ., Columbus.

Berniece M. Owen, Coordinator, Library Technical Services, Portland Community College, Oreg.

Mark Padnos, Humanities Reference Librarian, Mina Rees Library, Graduate School and Univ. Center, City Univ. of New York.

Robert Palmieri, Professor Emeritus, School of Music, Kent State Univ., Ohio.

J. Carlyle Parker, Librarian and Univ. Archivist Emeritus, Library, California State Univ., Turlock.

Gary L. Parsons, Reference Librarian, Florida Atlantic Univ., Boca Raton.

Gari-Anne Patzwald, Freelance Editor and Indexer, Lexington, Ky.

Julia Perez, Biological Sciences Librarian, Michigan State Univ. Libraries, East Lansing.

Glenn Petersen, Professor of Anthropology and International Affairs, Graduate Center and Baruch College, City Univ. of New York.

C. Michael Phillips, Asst. Reference Librarian, Robert Scott Small Library, College of Charleston, S.C.

Phillip P. Powell, Asst. Reference Librarian, Robert Scott Small Library, College of Charleston, S.C.

Ann E. Prentice, Dean, College of Library and Information Services, Univ. of Maryland, College Park.

Pete Prunkl, Freelance Writer, Hickory, N.C.

Jack Ray, Asst. Director, Loyola/Notre Dame Library, Baltimore, Md.

Robert B. Marks Ridinger, Head, Electronic Information Resources Management Dept., Univ. Libraries, Northern Illinois Univ., De Kalb.

Constance Rinaldo, Ernst Magr Library, Museum of Comparative Zoology, Harvard Univ., Hanover, N.H.

Cari Ringelheim, Staff, Libraries Unlimited, Inc.

Anne F. Roberts, Adjunct Professor, School of Education, State Univ. of New York, Albany.

Randy Roberts, Professor of History, Purdue Univ., Ind.

William B. Robison, Asst. Professor, History, Southeastern Louisiana Univ., Hammond.

Deborah V. Rollins, Reference Librarian, Univ. of Maine, Orono.

John B. Romeiser, Professor of French and Dept. Head, Univ. of Tennessee, Knoxville.

Samuel Rothstein, Professor Emeritus, School of Librarianship, Univ. of British Columbia, Vancouver.

Michele Russo, Acting Director, Franklin D. Schurz Library, Indiana Univ., South Bend.

Edmund F. SantaVicca, Librarian, Information Commons, Estrella Mountain Community College Center, Litchfield Park, Ariz.

Ralph Lee Scott, Assoc. Professor, East Carolina Univ. Library, Greenville, N.C.

Robert A. Seal, Univ. Librarian, Texas Christian Univ., Fort Worth.

David Selden, Law Librarian, National Indian Law Librarian, Boulder, Colo.

Ravindra Nath Sharma, Library Director, West Virginia State College, Institute.

Esther R. Sinofsky, Library Media Teacher, Alexander Hamilton High School, Los Angeles, Calif.

Robert M. Slade, Independent Consultant, North Vancouver, B.C.

Steven W. Sowards, Head of Main Reference Library, Michigan State Univ. Libraries, East Lansing.

Jan S. Squire, Reference and Instructional Services Librarian, Univ. of Northern Colorado, Greeley.

Karen Y. Stabler, Head of Information Services, New Mexico State Univ. Library, Las Cruces.

Victor L. Stater, Assoc. Professor of History, Louisiana State Univ., Baton Rouge.

Kay M. Stebbins, Coordinator Librarian, Louisiana State Univ., Shreveport.

Norman D. Stevens, Director Emeritus, Univ. of Connecticut Libraries, Storrs.

John W. Storey, Professor of History, Lamar Univ., Beaumont, Tex.

William C. Struning, Professor, Seton Hall Univ., South Orange, N.J.

Timothy E. Sullivan, Asst. Professor of Economics, Towson State Univ., Md.

Richard H. Swain, Reference Librarian, West Chester Univ., Pa.

Nigel Tappin, (formerly) General Librarian, North York Public Library, Ont.

Martha Tarlton, Head, Humanities and Social Sciences, Univ. of North Texas Libraries, Denton.

Glynys R. Thomas, Sawyer Library, Suffolk Univ., Boston.

Paul H. Thomas, Head, Catalog Dept., Hoover Institution Library, Stanford Univ., Calif.

Peter Thorpe, Professor Emeritus, Univ. of Colorado, Denver.

Linda D. Tietjen, Senior Instructor, Instruction and Reference Services, Auraria Library, Denver, Colo.

Bruce H. Tiffney, Assoc. Professor of Geology and Biological Sciences, Univ. of California, Santa Barbara.

Mary L. Trenerry, Media Specialist, Millard Public Schools, Omaha, Neb.

Dean Tudor, Professor, School of Journalism, Ryerson Polytechnical Institute, Toronto.

Robert L. Turner Jr., Librarian and Asst. Professor, Radford Univ., Va.

Michele Tyrrell, Media Specialist, Arundel Senior High School, Gambrills, Md.

Arthur R. Upgren, Professor of Astronomy and Director, Van Vleck Observatory, Wesleyan Univ., Middletown, Conn.

Phyllis J. Van Orden, Professor, School of Library and Information Science, Seattle, Wash.

Susanna Van Sant, Librarian, Michigan State Univ., East Lansing.

Vandelia L. VanMeter, Professor and Library Director, Spalding Univ., Louisville, Ky.

Graham R. Walden, Assoc. Professor, Information Services Department, Ohio State University, Columbus.

Richard S. Watts, Coordinator, Technical Processing Dept., San Bernardino County Library, Calif.

J. E. Weaver, Dept. of Economics, Drake Univ., Des Moines, Iowa.

Karen T. Wei, Head, Asian Library, Univ. of Illinois, Urbana.

Andrew B. Wertheimer, Librarian, Woodman Astronomical Library, Univ. of Wisconsin, Madison.

Lee Weston, Assoc. Professor/Reference Librarian, James A. Michener Library, Univ. of Northern Colorado, Greeley.

Lucille Whalen, Dean of Graduate Programs, Immaculate Heart College Center, Los Angeles, Calif.

David L. White, Professor, History Dept., Appalachian State Univ., Boone, N.C.

Robert L. Wick, Asst. Professor and Fine Arts Bibliographer, Auraria Library, Univ. of Colorado, Denver.

Agnes H. Widder, Humanities Bibliographer, Michigan State Univ., East Lansing.

Frances C. Wilkinson, Director, Acquisitions and Serials Dept., Univ. of New Mexico, Albuquerque.

Frank L. Wilson, Professor and Head, Dept. of Political Science, Purdue Univ., West Lafayette, Ind.

Mark A. Wilson, Professor of Geology, College of Wooster, Ohio.

Glenn R. Wittig, Director of Library Services, Criswell College, Dallas, Tex.

Bohdan S. Wynar, Staff, Libraries Unlimited, Inc.

Eveline L. Yang, Manager, Information Delivery Programs, Auraria Library, Univ. of Colorado, Denver.

Hope Yelich, Reference Librarian, Earl Gregg Swem Library, College of William and Mary, Williamsburg, Va.

Henry E. York, Head, Collection Management, Cleveland State Univ., Ohio.

Arthur P. Young, Director, Northern Illinois Libraries, Northern Illinois Univ., De Kalb.

Louis G. Zelenka, Jacksonville Public Library System, Fla.

Magda Želinská-Ferl, Professor/Faculty Advisor, Union Institute, Los Angeles, Calif.

L. Zgusta, Professor of Linguistics and the Classics and Member of the Center for Advance Study, Univ. of Illinois, Urbana.

Xiao (Shelley) Yan Zhang, Cataloger, Mississippi State Univ. Library, Mississippi State.

Anita Zutis, Adjunct Librarian, Queensborough Community College, Bayside, N.Y.

Journals Cited

FORM OF CITATION	JOURNAL TITLE
BL	*Booklist*
BR	*Book Report*
C&RL	*College & Research Libraries*
C&RL News	*College & Research Libraries News*
Choice	*Choice*
EL	*Emergency Librarian*
JAL	*Journal of Academic Librarianship*
LJ	*Library Journal*
RBB	*Reference Books Bulletin*
RQ	*RQ*
RUSQ	*Reference & User Services Quarterly*
SLJ	*School Library Journal*
SLMQ	*School Library Media Quarterly*
TL	*Teacher Librarian*
VOYA	*Voice of Youth Advocates*

Part I
GENERAL REFERENCE WORKS

1 General Reference Works

ALMANACS

C, P, S

1. **The Cambridge Factfinder.** 3d ed. David Crystal, ed. New York, Cambridge University Press, 1998. 891p. maps. index. $16.95pa. ISBN 0-521-63770-8.

Divided into broad areas of knowledge, this volume appears to be a hybrid genre containing the best elements of an almanac, a desk encyclopedia, and a mini atlas. Facts are presented regarding the universe, Earth, the environment, natural history, human beings, history, human geography, society, religion and mythology, communications, science and technology, arts and culture, knowledge, and sports and games. The largest section presents profiles of individual nations of the world, indicating time zone, area, population total, history, and so on. Small black-and-white profile maps are included, highlighting major cities and geographical features of each nation.

Although the world chronology ends in 1997, and some of the world records and prizes need to be updated, the majority of information included remains valid and factual. A great deal of the information has been culled from other Cambridge reference tools, and is merely repackaged here in a more portable and condensed version. A full index of some 110 pages supplements the work. This work is recommended for any ready-reference collection, either as a complement to or replacement for other almanacs.—**Edmund F. SantaVicca**

C, P, S

2. **The World Almanac and Book of Facts 2000.** millennium ed. Mahwah, N.J., World Almanac Books; distr., New York, St. Martin's Press, 1999. 1024p. illus. maps. index. $24.95; $10.95pa. ISBN 0-88687-848-9; 0-88687-847-0pa.

For 132 years *The World Almanac and Book of Facts* has been keeping people up-to-date on politics, employment, technology, entertainment, sports, and many other subjects. This millennium edition features new Internet information (including many Websites), up-to-date maps and flags, winners of awards and prizes in 1999, crime statistics, and advances in health and nutrition. Three prominent men of our day contribute essays to this work: Robert Reich writes about technology and tribalism, John Updike lists the 10 greatest works of literature, and Arthur Schlesinger Jr. discusses the most influential people of the 2d millennium. There is a section on memorable quotes of the century, as well as a list of predictions that failed. As always the most important news of the past year is discussed, including the Clinton impeachment trial, the war in Kosovo, and obituaries of the deceased. Because this almanac will find readers among both those fascinated by trivia and those doing important research, this all-encompassing reference source will be a welcome addition to any public, school, or academic library.—**Shannon M. Graff**

BIBLIOGRAPHY

National and Trade Bibliography

International

C

3. **Guide to Microforms in Print 1998: Incorporating International Microforms in Print.** New Providence, N.J., R. R. Bowker, 1998. 2v. $430.00/set. ISBN 3-598-11365-X. ISSN 0163-8386.

The *Guide to Microforms in Print* provides comprehensive information on international microform publications. The form and content of entries in the guide include title, author(s) or editor(s), place of publication, date of publication, collation information, type of microform code, price, ISBN, extra distributor or co-publisher information, further title information, publisher code, and subject classes.

The guide is divided into a subject guide, an index of persons as subject, and an alphabetic index to publishers and distributors. The section on publishers and distributors contains full ordering information for the microforms in the guide. The subject guide provides subject access to international microform publications. The subject classification used in the subject guide is based on Dewey Decimal Classification, with some modified classes that are explained in the foreword to the guide. A finding aid for subject numbers is also included. The index of persons as subject can be consulted when looking for a collection or a nonfiction title dealing with a specific individual.—**Frances C. Wilkinson**

United States

C

4. **Books in Print 1998-99.** 51st ed. New Providence, N.J., R. R. Bowker, 1998. 9v. $525.00/set. ISBN 0-8352-4026-6. ISSN 0068-0214.

The 51st edition contains over 1,449,000 active titles and features over 179,000 new titles and more than 183,000 new ISBNs. Bound in 9 volumes, the set includes 4 volumes arranged by title and 4 by author. The 9th volume is devoted to publisher information and includes names, addresses (including e-mail and Website addresses), and ordering information for all of the publishers mentioned in the author and title volumes. *Books in Print* is also available in several electronic versions—*Books in Print on CD*, online access through American Library Services, CARL, Dialog, DRA, EBSCO Publishing, and others, as listed on page vii in the preface to the 1st volume. Descriptions on how to use this standard title familiar to most libraries are provided on pages ix-xi. Earlier versions of *Books in Print* have been reviewed in previous ARBA editions.—**Bohdan S. Wynar**

Great Britain

C, P

5. **Whitaker's Books in Print 1999: The Reference Catalogue of Current Literature.** New Providence, N.J., R. R. Bowker, 1999. 4v. $700.00/set. ISBN 0-85021-274-X. ISSN 0953-0398.

Published in 4 volumes, *Whitaker's Books in Print* is a standard title in the British book trade with a well-known and long tradition going back to 1874. Joseph Whitaker, creator of *Whitaker's Almanac*, also publishes the *Reference Catalogue of Current Literature* and, since 1968, has maintained the system of Standard Book Numbers. *Whitaker's Books in Print* lists titles published in the United Kingdom and available to the general public through the book trade. English-language titles published in continental Europe are also recorded along with titles that have a sole distributor in the United Kingdom, including American Books.

The current edition contains publishing details for some 887,000 titles from 34,000 publishers. The updating procedures are continuous. Each title that is recorded week by week in the *Bookseller* goes forward to *Whitaker's Books in Print*, including price ranges and deletions of out-of-print titles. The information on several segments of the structure of British bibliography is provided in "Guides to Books Available in the UK and Their Publishers" (pp. 10–11), describing weekly, monthly (the British Bibliography), bimonthly, quarterly, biannually, annual, and multi-year services. *Whitaker's Books in Print* is a standard source for all university and larger public and scientific libraries.—**Bohdan S. Wynar**

BIOGRAPHY

International

C, P

6.   **Abridged Encyclopedia of World Biography.** Farmington Hills, Mich., Gale, 1999. 6v. illus. index. $495.00/set. ISBN 0-7876-3904-4.

This set is an abridgement of Gale's *Encyclopedia of World Biography* (2d ed.; see ARBA 99, entry 23). It provides complete biographical sketches for more than 2,000 well-known individuals and brief sketches on approximately 5,000 others. Each sketch includes key biographical data, such as date and place of birth, date of death (if deceased), nationality, and occupation. The "complete" or lengthier sketches are accompanied by portraits and suggests for further reading.

The encyclopedia is organized into six volumes covering the areas of American history, world history, literature, science and mathematics, arts and entertainment, and social sciences. Each volume contains a master name index, a nationality index, and an occupation index to the entire set.

The stated purpose of this set is to serve as "a comprehensive source of information on over 7,000 of those people who, for their contributions to human culture and society, have reputations that stand the test of time." Its greatest strength is its coverage of contemporary figures, particularly women and minorities. In some cases, this appears to be at the exclusion of prominent earlier figures provided only brief sketches. Because the set seems to be primarily intended for students, it would benefit from the addition of cross-references for names with variant spellings, such as Muammar Al-Gaddafi. One inaccuracy is the substitution of a photograph of Japanese Admiral Togo for a picture of Hideki Tojo. It is apparent that the editorial staff attempted to make the content as up-to-date as possible, given that the sketch on William Jefferson Clinton includes events of the first half of 1999. [R: LJ, 15 Nov 99, p. 58]—**Martha Tarlton**

C, P

7.   **ARBA Guide to Biographical Resources 1986-1997.** Robert L. Wick and Terry Ann Mood, eds. Englewood, Colo., Libraries Unlimited, 1998. 604p. index. $60.00. ISBN 1-56308-453-8.

Inasmuch as biographical information is probably the subject most requested of reference librarians, they will certainly welcome this guide to the most useful collective biographies of the period from 1986 to 1997. As will book selectors, since biographical dictionaries are not only expensive but also often of questionable quality.

The *ARBA Guide* offers 1180 reviews, succinct but critical, of titles that were favorably reviewed in the *American Reference Books Annual* or "selected due to the importance of the work" (p. xvi). The reviews in the guide are all signed (the list of contributors impressive) and, where appropriate, have been updated or otherwise revised. Each entry provides full bibliographical information and includes citations to reviews that have appeared in the standard selection journals such as *Choice* and *Booklist*.

The *ARBA Guide* is divided into two major parts: International and National Biographies and Biographies in Professional Fields; the former is subdivided by geographic area (20), the latter by subject field (24). Thus, for example, readers can find conveniently grouped together collective biographies regarding Romania or the performing arts. Finer classifications can be obtained through the quite comprehensive subject index.

The *ARBA Guide* is a well-made book, featuring large type, generous margins, and a sturdy binding; physically it is a good value for the price. It is textually valuable as well, even for libraries already owning the ARBA volumes from where most of this material has been culled. This compilation will offer a convenient arrangement and useful revision. For libraries lacking ARBA the guide is almost a necessity. [R: Choice, May 99, p. 1587]
—**Samuel Rothstein**

C, P, S

8.   **Chambers Biographical Dictionary.** 6th ed. Melanie Parry, ed. New York, Larousse Kingfisher Chambers, 1997. 2008p. $55.00. ISBN 0-550-16060-4.

This edition of the standard *Chambers Biographical Dictionary* is a valuable and reliable single-volume collection of about 17,300 biographical entries. Previous editions were published in the United States as *Cambridge Biographical Dictionary* (see ARBA 95, entry 25). Recent Cambridge titles and editions have muddied the bibliographic waters.

Although concise and somewhat formulaic, the writing is still intelligent and readable, incorporating some interesting analysis among the facts. Several hundred individuals receive closer scrutiny in larger, boxed biographies, which contain quotes and abbreviated bibliographies. The book's subjects, however, are overwhelmingly male. Parry edited the *Larousse Dictionary of Women* (see ARBA 98, entry 24), and one would think she would be more aware than anyone of remarkable women's lives that belong in this volume. Unfortunately, the entries here are about 87 percent male; a truly comprehensive biographical dictionary needs a better balance.

Chronological coverage is heavily biased toward the present day. Based on death dates, 34 percent of the subjects died in the twentieth century, 19 percent in the nineteenth century, and 19 percent are still living. The remaining 28 percent cover the rest of time, from Adam and Eve to the eighteenth century. Individuals from all disciplines and all fields of enterprise are included, and the volume, although overwhelmingly Anglo-American, includes subjects from other cultures as well.

As a single-volume work, the *Chambers Biographical Dictionary* should be a useful source, but readers seeking more than a paragraph on an individual will likely need to look elsewhere. Its small size and price, plus its extensive, although biased, coverage make it a useful addition to any library.—**Peter H. McCracken**

C

9.   **Encyclopedia of World Biography on CD-ROM.** [CD-ROM]. Farmington Hills, Mich., Gale, 1999. Minimum system requirements: IBM or compatible 386. Double-speed CD-ROM. DOS 5.0. Windows 3.1 or higher. 8MB RAM. 5MB hard disk space. SVGA graphics card and monitor (256 colors). Mouse. $975.00. ISBN 0-7876-2944-8.

Using a myriad of ways to search the database, the *Encyclopedia of World Biography on CD-ROM* provides researchers with information on 7,200 of the "most frequently studied individuals from ancient times to the present." The program reflects the content of the newest edition of the print version, as it incorporates the twentieth-century supplements into one easy-to-use version. Searches can be conducted by entering a name, a subject, a place, a title of a work, or using a timeline; the software also allows for full-text searching and customized searches. Each search results in a list of hits, relevancy ranked. The user is thus immediately provided with cross-referenced information. Photographs accompany the articles.

Installation of the program using the Windows 95 platform was quite simple, and as long as the program will not be used by more than 30 users simultaneously or be used in conjunction with dial-in access, the installer will not have to go through the more tedious "unlock" process. Gale provides for a 30-day review period, but unless a full installation is done (which requires invoice and customer numbers), printing and downloading functions are blocked. Help is provided onscreen, and Gale provides a comprehensive user's manual and help card.

Navigation within the program presented no difficulties; the toolbar is easily understood and uses familiar icons. Entire articles can be printed or the user may print selected text; photographs can be printed without text. Saving text is also familiar; the TXT extension is used for the default. Information regarding correct bibliographic citation is given in the user's manual and on the help card.

The print version of this work has long been a basic resource for reliable biographical information. The CD-ROM version provides an alternative way to provide this information, but unless the library or media center will be networking the product, its cost (about half of the cost of the 19-volume set) may be prohibitive. [R: BR, Sept/Oct 99, p. 86; Choice, Dec 99, p. 684]—**Michele Tyrrell**

C

10.   **Encyclopedia of World Biography Supplement.** Farmington Hills, Mich., Gale, 1999. 561p. illus. index. $99.00. ISBN 0-7876-2945-6. ISSN 1099-7326.

The 1st edition of this encyclopedia was published 25 years ago and the 2d edition was published in 1998 (see ARBA 99, entry 231). This standard work contains information on nearly 7,000 internationally known individuals

who made substantial contributions to our society. It should be noted that the 2d edition includes all entries from the 1st edition and its 3 supplements, with some updating, along with 530 new biographies especially prepared for the 2d edition. This new supplement to the 17-volume set covers 198 new biographies as well as 2 obituary entries for individuals appearing in volumes 1-17. It includes such figures as Tony Blair, the British prime minister, and military figures who died many years ago, such as Walter Bedell Smith (1895–1961), chief of staff to General Dwight D. Eisenhower, and Anne Boleyn, Queen of England (1504–1536). The coverage of important personalities, dead some years ago or alive, will continue in subsequent supplements. [R: BL, 15 Nov 98, p. 610]
—**Bohdan S. Wynar**

United States

C, P
11. **Who's Who in America 1999.** 53d ed. New Providence, N.J., Marquis Who's Who/Reed Reference Publishing, 1998. 3v. index. $549.00/set. ISBN 0-8379-0191-X. ISSN 0083-9396.

This most venerable of the Marquis stable of publications was last reviewed in ARBA in 1996 (see entry 37). That 50th edition included 92,000 entries, whereas the present edition contains approximately 105,000 biographies. The preface states that "selection is based solely on reference value. Individuals become eligible for listing by virtue of their position and/or noteworthy achievements that have proven to be of significant value to society. An individual's desire to be listed . . . [or] wealth or social position [is not sufficient reason for inclusion]." Volume 3 of this edition lists names of the biographees by 38 professional categories as well as by geographic location. However, the geographic list is not completely satisfactory as many individuals do not wish an address to be published. There are a "Retiree Index" and a "Necrology of Biographees." The latter category's entries move to the Who Was Who in America series. Additionally, a new feature of this edition is the inclusion of some enhanced entries in which the biographee provides a description of career accomplishments or family life in his or her own words. More information about avocations is also present. A key biographical reference source, *Who's Who in America* belongs in most libraries.—**Lee Weston**

C, P
12. **Who's Who of American Women 1999-2000.** 21st ed. New Providence, N.J., Marquis Who's Who/Reed Reference Publishing, 1998. 1156p. $259.00. ISBN 0-8379-0424-2. ISSN 0083-9841.

This is the 21st edition of this standard biographical resource, which has been published since 1958. This latest edition contains more than 26,000 entries, slightly less than the 30,000 listed for the 19th and 17th editions reviewed in ARBA 1996 (entry 38) and ARBA 1993 (entry 56). Like other Marquis Who's Who publications, individuals to be included are identified by Marquis staff and a board of advisors, based on "current reference value" and "conspicuous achievement," and information is solicited from each person selected. Each entry gives basic data such as name, occupation, birth date, education, career history, publications, professional activities, awards, and home and office addresses. Although a random check showed that some women whom one might expect to be listed are missing from its pages, this publication belongs on the reference shelf of nearly every library.
—**Susan Davis Herring**

Canada

C
13. **Canadian Who's Who 1999.** [CD-ROM]. Toronto, University of Toronto Press, 1999. Minimum system requirements (Windows version): IBM or compatible. CD-ROM drive. Window 95 or Windows 3.x. Minimum system requirements (Macintosh version): CD-ROM Drive. System 7.0 or later. $195.00; $275.00 (with book).

C
14. **Canadian Who's Who 1999, Volume 34.** Elizabeth Lumley, ed. Buffalo, N.Y., University of Toronto Press, 1999. 1386p. $170.00. ISBN 0-8020-4931-1. ISSN 0068-9963.

Now in its 90th year, *Canadian Who's Who 1999* is still a comprehensive and authoritative source on notable living Canadians. With 1,500 new entries since the last edition, this new edition features 15,000 biographical entries on Canadian elite. Entries feature date and place of birth, education, family history, career information, memberships, creative works, honors, and awards. Influential Canadians from the fields of business, science, politics, government, education, sports, and the arts are featured herein. Libraries will find this a valuable guide for fact-checking names and areas of expertise as well as researching other biographical facts that library patrons might need. *Canadian Who's Who* is also available on CD-ROM and includes the complete text of the paper volume. Searches can be conducted by using a name, address, title, occupation, date of birth, place of birth, or recreation. The two can be purchased together for $275. This standard reference work will be a valuable addition to academic, public, and some special libraries.—**Shannon M. Graff**

DICTIONARIES AND ENCYCLOPEDIAS

C, P, S

15.   Crump, Andy, comp. **The A to Z of World Development.** Wayne Ellwood, ed. Oxford, England, New Internationalist Publications; distr., Sterling, Va., Stylus Publishing, 1998. 293p. illus. maps. $34.95pa. ISBN 1-869847-46-6.

This dictionary of international development provides an overview of the principal issues and concepts preoccupying non-governmental organization (NGO) Third World development activists over the last quarter century in 624 entries. It is a project of the innovative international editorial and graphic design cooperative behind *New Internationalist* magazine. This well-produced reference work lives up to the lively and engaging style of the periodical. It will appeal strongly to school, public, and academic librarians seeking resources on its topic.

Articles are organized alphabetically by title. The writing is straightforward and accessible. Entries range in length from a paragraph to more than a triple-column, 8½-by-11 page. They divide into sections by initial letter. The general contents list these letter sections, while section contents list articles. There is no index. Topics range from people (Willy Brandt, Che Guevara, Mahatma Gandhi) and organizations (Caribbean Development Bank, Grameen Bank) to concepts (ecotourism, genocide) and places (East Timor).

Photographs, charts, tables, graphics, and a map provide lavish illustration. Cross-references are emboldened within entries. A table of comparative statistics by country, with regional and world summary statistics, gives figures, including mortality and life expectancy, per capita GNP, population, proportion of government spending on social issues, and debt servicing as a portion of export earnings. The bibliography lists over 40 United Nations and commercial reference series and works.

Wayne Ellwood is a Toronto-based *New Internationalist* magazine editor. Andy Crump is a Geneva-based ecologist, teacher, writer, photographer, and videographer with extensive experience in development issues. The foreword is by Oxford professor Norman Myers, editor of the *Gaia Atlas of Planet Management*. Endorsing quotes come from the social studies coordinator at the Toronto Board of Education and an Oxford University geographer. This book belongs in most medium-size to large collections. It will be especially attractive to school librarians. [R: Choice, Nov 99, p. 516]—**Nigel Tappin**

S

16.   **DK Concise Encyclopedia.** By John Farndon. New York, DK Publishing, 1999. 512p. illus. maps. index. $16.95pa. ISBN 0-7894-3948-4.

This brief source, designed for children, contains selected basic facts, combined with DK's usual colorful illustrations and photographs, on nine general topics: space, planet earth, the living world, the human body, science and technology, transportation, the world (subdivided by region), people and society, and a history timeline. A reference section concludes the work. Although the occasional error creeps in—for instance a photograph of a Jersey cow is identified as a Guernsey—the brief treatments are commendably succinct and accurate. Although the source is most suitable for a small private collection where children are present, it may also serve as a popular reference or circulating item in a library's juvenile collection.—**Lee Weston**

C, P, S

17. **Encyclopaedia Britannica CD-ROM 1999.** multimedia ed. [CD-ROM]. Chicago, Encyclopaedia Britannica, 1998. Minimum system requirements: IBM or compatible. Four-speed CD-ROM drive. Windows 95, Windows 98, or Windows NT 4.0. 16MB RAM. 80MB hard disk space. SVGA monitor (256 colors). Sound card and speakers. Mouse. Printer recommended. $119.00.

Be assured that the editorial integrity of the venerable *Encyclopaedia Britannica* (EB) is maintained in the 1999 CD-ROM edition. The articles are well written and well edited. The authors of signed articles, in general, possess impressive credentials attesting to their expertise in their fields. Many of the illustrations are nothing short of stunning and they contribute significantly to both the look and utility of the work. As with many multimedia encyclopedias, EB greatly supplements and complements information in the text of articles with information in the multimedia format. Indeed, as with all such encyclopedias, EB on CD-ROM presents certain material in multimedia format that could not be presented equally as well in print format.

Although EB has succeeded in many ways with its integration of text and multimedia to create a valuable and useful reference resource, and learning resource, it has also fallen into the trap of too much reliance on, or belief in, technology. The system just does not live up to expectations set by EB in the hyperbolic marketing and user information. Installation of the work, on a system that exceeded the recommended hardware and software requirements, took more than 20 minutes. The initial screens and navigation designs are attractive but not as easily understandable as they should be. The user guide and other material touts the full-text search capability of the product, even inviting the user to type in very broad and open-ended questions.

Some of the editorial features are nice and adequate, what is expected from any multimedia encyclopedia on the market today. "Spectrum" is similar to Grolier's *Knowledge Tree* and represents the classification of subjects and knowledge in a hierarchical listing. The timeline section was a bit disappointing, although being able to compare two categories side-by-side is worthwhile. The timeline categories, however, might be rethought. Currently they are architecture, literature, medicine, music, religion, science, technology, visual arts, and women's history. The last, while important, does not compare in scope to the other categories and this is shown in the actual listings; many of them are a far stretch for something relating to women and women's achievements, contributions, and so on. This is not the place to debate political correctness versus new approaches to learning, but it is evident that there are some imbalances in approach and coverage. This, of course, is true of all encyclopedias, whether electronic or printed.

EB has the requisite links to the Internet for updates and one feature that is quite interesting, with more appeal for older and more serious users. *Britannica Classica*, part of the "Spotlights" section, presents classic articles from past editions of EB, written by very noteworthy authors, including Albert Einstein, Harry Houdini, and H. L. Mencken.

Encyclopaedia Britannica CD-ROM 1999 is a useful and fact-filled tool, useful for students as a reference work or for learning exercises. If one is going to buy a multimedia encyclopedia, EB, Grolier, World Book, and Encarta offer much the same material in similar fashions and users will not go wrong with any of them. [R: Choice, April 99, p. 1431]—**Edward Kurdyla**

C, P, S

18. **Encyclopedia Americana on CD-ROM.** [CD-ROM]. Danbury, Conn., Grolier, 1998. Minimum system requirements (Windows version): IBM or compatible 386. MPC-rated 150 KB/sec CD-ROM drive. Windows 3.1 or Windows 95. 4MB RAM. 4MB hard disk space. SVGA card & color monitor. Mouse. Windows-supported printer. Minimum system requirements (Macintosh version): 68020 CPU, 16 MHz or faster. 150 KB/sec or higher CD-ROM drive. System 7.0 or higher. 2.5MB RAM. 4MB hard disk space. 12-inch color monitor (256 colors). Macintosh-compatible printer. $179.00. ISBN 0-7172-3404-5.

Suitable for adults and high school students alike, this remarkable reference tool contains the complete and updated text for all 30 volumes of Grolier's *Encyclopedia Americana* as well as *Merriam-Webster's Collegiate Dictionary, Tenth Edition*, Helicon Publishing Company's *Chronology of World History*, the *Dictionary of Science & Technology* from Academic Press, and a software installation program designed to accommodate a variety of systems and platforms. This breadth of scope, coupled with ease of access and change between databases, allows the user to access at least basic information on virtually any topic.

The encyclopedia includes 9 searchable indexes: an article title index (main index), full-text index, bibliography index, contributor index, subject index, geography index, article form index, date index, and maps index. If a user creates notes while using the encyclopedia, an additional user notes index is accessible. The user has the option of choosing one of these indexes from the entry window (available each time one opens the program) or by utilizing an advanced search window that allows users to search multiple indexes and to use Boolean searches. After this initial choice, the user can easily navigate between search results; bookmark, print, or save search results; and make notes regarding particular entries. Another plus is the interface capability with Internet sites through links provided by the editors. Using the other reference tools included is equally easy and straightforward.

Special features included with the set are truncation searching, sentence searching, a subject classification system, field searching, filters, wildcards, proximity searching, and case sensitivity. A brief troubleshooting guide with technical support telephone number and a networking guide are found in the user's guide that accompanies the CD-ROM.

With the usual limitations inherent in a dated, packaged product, this set nonetheless is a valuable complement to any reference collection designed to integrate electronic and print information. Cost savings are another consideration not to be overlooked. [R: BL, 15 Sept 99, p. 284]—**Edmund F. SantaVicca**

S

19. **The New Book of Knowledge.** 1999 deluxe ed. Danbury, Conn., Grolier, 1999. 21v. illus. maps. index. $659.00/set. ISBN 0-7172-0530-4.

The New Book of Knowledge, designed specifically for school-age children in grades 3-8, has long been regarded as one of the top encyclopedias catering to researchers in this age group. With its large print, bright photographs, and easy-to-understand entries, this set will be a popular choice in schools, public libraries, and homes with young children.

The content of this set has been selected by educators and librarians familiar with the unique needs of children as well as familiar with curriculum requirements of schools across the nation. This encyclopedia has the added feature of providing games, illustrations, and activities that will captivate the interest of its intended audience. All articles in the work are signed and each is written by an expert in the field who also writes with the children's interest at heart. The publishers guarantees the accuracy of the articles and illustrations in the preface of the work where it is stated that the book is based on fact, not opinion, and that where there are discrepancies of opinion among experts in the field it is noted in the entry.

The set's accessibility is one its most noted features. It is arranged in alphabetic order. There is an index at the back of each volume (indicated by blue pages), which provides cross-references to the entire set. Furthermore, each volume contains a short section just before the index that provides "dictionary entries," which serve to provide users with short informational terms that may be of interest. The entries also contain important words in bold typeface that will refer readers to other entries in the encyclopedia for further information on that topic. The maps and illustrations throughout the work (often as many as three per page) are designed specifically with children in mind, and many of the illustrations are commissioned specifically for this encyclopedia. A special paperback volume that comes with the set, titled "Home and School Reading and Study Guides," provides a bibliography to other works that may be of interest to young readers. The guide is arranged into primary, intermediate, and advanced categories. New to this 1999 edition is an activities section.

There is no doubt that this encyclopedia will find much use in school libraries, public libraries with a large child clientele, and homes with children. It will give young readers with inquisitive minds just enough of a challenge to continue reading and researching its many pages of worthwhile facts and activities. [R: BL, 15 Sept 99, pp. 294-296]—**Shannon M. Graff**

P, S

20. **World Book: Millennium 2000.** deluxe ed. [CD-ROM]. Chicago, World Book, 1999. Minimum system requirements: IBM or compatible 486 with 100 MHz. Double-speed CD-ROM drive. Windows 95 or Windows NT 4.0. 16MB RAM. 40MB hard disk space. 16-bit sound card. 16-bit color. Mouse. $69.95.

The editors have followed a philosophy similar to that of classroom teaching in structuring this new version. Articles on major topics are designed to give a solid foundation on the topic, to engage the senses through multimedia, to encourage further study through links to other articles and to the Web, to organize thinking through outlines, and to reinforce understanding by posing questions. In addition, all sorts of enhancements and extras pervade this reference tool.

Two major categories divide the homepage: search and browse. The search functions focus on searching for specific topics, an atlas, a dictionary, time frames, and Web links. Browse functions allow one to cruise through various access points, including a series of sites that cover each century of the current millennium. This version contains thousands more articles than are in the print set, as well as basic and full-length video sets, pictures, sound clips, panoramas, accurate maps, simulations, animations, a distance calculator, and a free year of online updates. A series of "Wizards" allow the user to create reports, timelines, charts, Web pages, and quizzes.

As an interactive reference tool, this set offers the user a lot of information at one-tenth the price of the print set. An abridged CD-ROM version is available for almost half the price and the enhanced four–CD-ROM set is available for slightly more money. Perhaps the only aggravation of this two–CD-ROM set is the need to switch discs over and over.

This resource is recommended for high-tech collections whose users can profit from the core information and the enhancements. This is a high-quality work at a reasonable price.—**Edmund F. SantaVicca**

P, S

21.   **The World Book Encyclopedia.** 1999 ed. Chicago, World Book, 1999. 22v. illus. maps. index. $769.00/set. ISBN 0-7166-0099-4.

In an age when multimedia encyclopedias have become standard reference tools it is refreshing and reassuring to use the printed version of *The World Book Encyclopedia*. The 1999 edition, consisting of 22 volumes, some 30,000 articles, more than 28,000 illustrations (some 24,000 in color), and an index with more than 150,000 entries, is a joy to use. The articles are selected for their appropriateness to school curriculum and they are written for age and level appropriateness. The intended audiences include elementary, junior and senior high school students, and the inquisitive adult. The needs of all audiences appear to be met.

World Book engages some 3,700 consultants, advisors, and authors to produce the annually revised set. Most of those 3,700 are recognized or credentialed experts in their areas of study and authorship. The set is as up-to-date as any annual publication can be and, in fact, for most users, it is sufficient. Current events can be monitored in other works (newspapers, television, the Web); the encyclopedia has much historical information that dates very slowly, if at all, and it has value as a complete work, placing each article in context and in relation to others. Encyclopedias are a great example of classification and a great avenue for understanding the body of knowledge and the relative importance of its many components.

Perusing the printed version is an exciting and serendipitous way to discover new facts and knowledge, particularly for young persons and students. Viewing a two-page spread of several articles and illustrations almost forces users to go beyond their immediate information need and learn something new. The printed version can also be read for enjoyment. There is a 64-page article on painting, for example, which contains some 100 illustrations. This is like having a book within a book and for many persons reading a book (a traditional printed volume) is far more enjoyable than reading the equivalent on a computer screen.

Although multimedia encyclopedias have added value of additional information in audio or video formats, the printed work has the added, albeit less tangible added value of being comfortable and inviting. All libraries should have at least one printed multi-volume encyclopedia and *The World Book* should be one of their first choices. [R: BL, 15 Sept 99, pp. 298-300]—**Edward Kurdyla**

P, S

22.   **World Book Multimedia Encyclopedia: Macintosh Edition.** 1999 ed. [CD-ROM]. Chicago, World Book, 1998. Minimum system requirements: Centris 650, 25 MHz 68040 processor. Double-speed CD-ROM drive. Mac OS System 7.1 or higher. 16MB RAM. 42MB hard disk space. 8-bit color monitor. Mouse. $744.00. ISBN 0-7166-8538-8.

With more than 18,000 articles (1,800 of which do not appear in the print set), this multimedia encyclopedia will satisfy introductory research needs on a variety of topics. Also included are some 8,000 illustrations, including maps (20,000 fewer images than the print set). Of these, 300 are unique to the CD-ROM. All maps have been redesigned for enhancement through electronic viewing.

Special features include the addition of two new homework Wizards—the Quiz Wizard and the Web Wizard—in addition to the Report, Chart, and Timeline Wizards of previous editions. A joint venture of World Book and the San Diego Zoo is a new Cyber Safari disc that includes stories, sounds, 360-degree views, facts, and videos regarding zoo habitats and their animal occupants. Access is also provided to the World Book Website, as well as to the 225,000-entry *World Book Dictionary* (see ARBA 98, entry 996, for a review of the print version).

A high-performance search engine and intuitive interface allow the user to access information through "Time Frame," "Just Looking (a browse function)," "Around the World" (map navigation), "Browse Media," and "World Book Online." All of these are in addition to the standard search functions that also provide for Boolean searching.

This is a well-designed, easy-to-use product that should form the base of any home reference collection, as well as the encyclopedia sections of school, public, and college library collections.—**Edmund F. SantaVicca**

DIRECTORIES

P

23.   **African Americans Information Directory 1998-99.** 4th ed. Kenneth Estell, ed. Farmington Hills, Mich., Gale, 1998. 560p. index. $95.00. ISBN 0-8103-9117-1. ISSN 1099-3908.

This standard resource, formerly the *Black Americans Information Directory* (see ARBA 94, entry 407), states this is "a guide to approximately 5,430 organizations, agencies, institutions, programs, and publications concerned with Black American life and culture." More than simply a list of names and addresses of associations, however, this work's 19 sections cite contact and other significant information on awards, colleges and universities, governmental programs, libraries and museums, newsletters and magazines, mass media, religious organizations, scholarships, studies programs, research centers, videos, and Internet databases. The name and subject index, much like that found in the *Encyclopedia of Associations* (see ARBA 99, entries 50 and 51), is an excellent quick resource guide to start any material search. Entries themselves are brief but well organized and easy to read due to the typeface and paper stock quality.

Of special interest is the depth of local reporting found within this text. Rather than focusing entirely on national coverage, this directory includes numerous state and local entries, subdivided by state. Surprisingly for a collection of this size, however, many useful entries are missing altogether (e.g., Black Business Journal Online, the online version of *The Final Call*) or incomplete, but these problems can be resolved with subsequent editions. For its amount of information, this is a major acquisition for most academic and public libraries of any size.

—**Anthony J. Adam**

P

24.   **Guide to American Directories: A Guide to the Major Business, Educational, Scientific, Technical & Professional Directories....** 14th ed. Barry Klein, ed. West Nyack, N.Y., Todd Publications, 1999. 465p. index. $95.00pa. ISBN 0-915344-67-X.

Published for more than 40 years, this guide is intended to assist business and industry in locating new markets for their products and to help organizations, researchers, and those in advertising and public relations to find reliable sources of information. It also purports to aid in finding new sources of products and services. The editors of this new 14th edition have added more than 1,000 new directories (some in new categories) and deleted some 500 that are no longer published. There are close to 200 categories of directories listed alphabetically at the beginning of the volume, covering not only academic, social service, and business-related fields, but also more unusual areas, such as collection agencies and alternative culture, lifestyle, and future research. Although the primary focus is on U.S. directories, some foreign directories are included. These are particularly helpful in fields such as education and government. Entries for each directory typically include title with brief description; number of directories; addresses with telephone, fax, e-mail, and Website information; the cost; whether it is available to the public; and whether a mailing list can be purchased.

Following the main listings are sections titled "Index—Subject" and "Index—Alphabetical," neither of which is a real index. The first simply lists the categories with the titles of the directories included in each category. The second, an alphabetic list of all directories included, would seem to be of little use even if the subject happens to be the first word of the title. For example, the word "environmental" shows 16 directories, but going directly to the category of environment and conservation yields more than 30 directories. Much more helpful would be one subject and keyword index.

In spite of the limitations regarding indexing, the guide contains a lot of information on more than 10,000 directories, many of which cannot be found elsewhere, and is presented in an easy-to-use format. It is recommended particularly for business libraries and large academic and public libraries. [R: Choice, July/Aug 99, p. 1915]—**Lucille Whalen**

C, P
25.   **Toll-Free Phone Book USA 1999: A Directory of Toll-Free Telephone Numbers for Businesses and Organizations Nationwide.** 3d ed. Jennifer C. Perkins, ed. Detroit, Omnigraphics, 1999. 1348p. index. $120.00pa. ISBN 0-7808-0361-2. ISSN 1092-0285.

Toll-Free Phone Book USA 1999 is a useful source with more than 37,000 toll-free telephone numbers, from all carriers, that is geared to the business and professional community but will be equally helpful to the consumer market. The 1999 edition is divided into 3 principal sections, each of which includes the full company, organization, agency, or institution name; its complete mailing address; regular telephone number; toll-free telephone number; fax number; and World Wide Web and e-mail addresses. If the toll-free number is intended for a specific use, the directory describes this use in the listing.

The 1st section is an alphabetic listing by company or association name. The 2d section is a geographic arrangement in which firms and associations are listed by state and then broken down by cities and towns. The 3d section is a classified presentation in which firms and associations appear under an alphabetic (classified) subject listing. The final portion of the volume is an "Index to Classified Headings," which provides the page number for each class heading. The alphabetic listing and the geographic listing also provide the page number for the class heading for the appropriate business or association.

Toll-Free Phone Book USA 1999 provides 3 approaches to locating the toll-free number for a firm or association. The *Business Buyer's Guide: AT&T Toll-Free Directory* (1998 ed.; AT&T, 1998) provides only a yellow-page listing approach and covers only AT&T numbers. This yellow-page listing also provides only city and state, not a full address. Neither directory appears to be 100 percent complete. Of two well-known window manufacturers, Pella Corporation is listed only in *Toll-Free Phone Book USA* and Andersen Corporation is listed only in *Business Buyer's Guide*. Large academic libraries with business collections and large public libraries will wish to acquire both titles.—**Dene L. Clark**

HANDBOOKS AND YEARBOOKS

P
26.   **The New York Public Library Desk Reference.** 3d ed. New York, Macmillan Library Reference/Simon & Schuster Macmillan, 1998. 1040p. illus. maps. index. $34.95. ISBN 0-02-862169-7.

The 1989 edition of this work was reviewed in the 1991 edition of ARBA 91, entry 48, by Susan Baughman, a university librarian at Goddard Library at Clark University. The review of this important reference source created by the New York Public Library was mixed, pointing out some good features along with negatives. The present edition is significantly enlarged and is now published by Macmillan, with a very reasonable price. It has landed on such prestigious best-seller lists as *Publisher's Weekly* and the *New York Times*. This new edition is quite similar to the previous one; it covers thousands of small items arranged under broad subject categories such as the physical world, the biological world, the physical sciences, mathematics, and technology—a total of 26 subject categories. An atlas and a general index conclude the volume. As was pointed out in the previous review, the information is not always accurate (see the section entitled "The World" on p. 929 for information on Ukraine) but in many uses it will answer some basic questions.—**Bohdan S. Wynar**

PERIODICALS AND SERIALS

C

27.   Milton, Suzanne, and Elizabeth Malia. **Index Guide to College Journals.** Lanham, Md., Scarecrow, 1999. 651p. $65.00. ISBN 0-8108-3569-X.

The *Index Guide to College Journals* provides an alphabetic list with indexing information for approximately 16,000 scholarly and popular periodicals that serve undergraduate academic programs. The emphasis is largely on English-language periodicals, although a few foreign-language periodicals are included, and the scope is generally limited to journals that were published in the 1990s. In addition to indexing codes, each journal title entry includes an ISSN number. A total of 48 standard bibliographic sources were consulted for indexing information, including the popular Wilson indexes, Sage abstracting services, *America History and Life*, and *PsycLit*. For each title on the source index list, the compilers have indicated whether it is available electronically.

Reference librarians and students often need to determine the indexing for a periodical in order to verify a bibliographic citation. Although *Ulrich's International Periodicals Directory* (36th ed.; see ARBA 99, entry 74) also provides indexing information, its classified arrangement makes it somewhat cumbersome to use for the purpose. One must first consult the index volume to obtain a page number, then go to the appropriate classified volume for the entry with indexing information. The *Index Guide to College Journals* allows one to obtain indexing information on commonly held periodicals using a simple, alphabetic list. It is highly recommended as a ready-reference source for all academic libraries and is potentially a good resource for larger public library collections.

—**Martha Tarlton**

QUOTATION BOOKS

P

28.   **Dictionary of Contemporary Quotations, Volume 9.** 4th rev. ed. John Gordon Burke and Ned Kehde, eds. Evanston, Ill., John Gordon Burke, 1998. 313p. $55.00. ISBN 0-934272-45-X. ISSN 0360-215X.

As indicated in the introduction, the ongoing purpose of this series of volumes is "to record contemporary quotations which are historically, sociologically, and politically significant." Added to this purpose is the exclusion of quotations from historically significant persons that might have appeared in contemporary media. As volume 9 of the series, this latest compendium serves as a supplement to volumes 5 through 8, with at least 15 percent of the quotations from volume 8 being replaced with new quotations.

The compilers have scanned approximately 175 periodicals and newspapers from 1995 to 1998, the time scope of the current volume. Quotations are arranged in two general alphabetic sections: author and subject. Information provided in the author section includes the name of the speaker, description, annotation (when appropriate), quotation, explanatory amplification, and quotation sources (title, volume, page, and date). In the subject section both speaker and source of publication are indicated.

For students and others needing a ready source of contemporary quotations culled from the leading historical, political, and cultural figures of our times, this work will serve as a beginning. In looking over the quotations, some might suggest questionable use; however, the speaker has significance. Considering the time period involved, it is also curious that the work is full of quotations from the 1970s and 1980s. This volume is recommended as a complement to quotation collections found in standard reference collections. [R: Choice, Nov 99, p. 502]

—**Edmund F. SantaVicca**

Part II
SOCIAL SCIENCES

2

Social Sciences in General

SOCIAL SCIENCES IN GENERAL

P, S

29.   **Social Issues.** Robert D. Benford, ed. New York, Macmillan Library Reference/Simon & Schuster Macmillan, 1998. 942p. illus. index. (Macmillan Compendium). $125.00. ISBN 0-02-865055-7.

Late twentieth-century industrialized societies, like the United States, are confronted by an array of complex social issues and institutional problems. These include poverty and inequality, crime, the evolution/dissolution of the nuclear family, drug abuse, population growth and migration, and race and ethnic relations. Though often experienced as personal troubles, these issues can also be understood as social problems rooted in the structure and functioning of our institutions. As the old sociological example goes: If one person is unemployed, that is a personal problem; if thousands are unemployed, that is a social issue. This 1-volume encyclopedia addresses many of our society's most compelling social issues, presenting some of the best social science insight and research into their causes, functioning, and effects.

The approximately 180 topical essays included here are drawn primarily from the 4–volume *Encyclopedia of Sociology* (see ARBA 93, entry 847) and, in a few cases, the *Dictionary of American History* (see ARBA 97, entry 419). The signed entries are arranged alphabetically by subject and address social institutions (e.g., family, education, work), social problems (e.g., crime, poverty, divorce), social processes (e.g., socialization, urbanization, social change, social movements), and contemporary issues (e.g., affirmative action, religious fundamentalism, terrorism, sexually transmitted diseases). Essays range from two to eight pages in length and are accompanied by extensive bibliographies for further reading. Though overly statistical or theoretical topics are not included, the entries that are here are nonetheless fairly advanced in their treatment of the subjects. A detailed subject/name index provides more than adequate access to the content of the entries.

This encyclopedia would be an excellent starting point for students trying to gain an overview of a subject before developing a paper or class project. Similarly, individuals interested in important policy issues could get a quick understanding of key research and its implications. This is a recommended and affordable purchase for public, school, and academic libraries that do not already own the *Encyclopedia of Sociology*. [R: Choice, July/Aug 99, p. 1929; SLJ, Aug 99, p. 181]—**Stephen H. Aby**

P

30.   Young, T. R., and Bruce A. Arrigo. **The Dictionary of Critical Social Sciences.** Boulder, Colo., Westview Press, 1999. 351p. $50.00. ISBN 0-8133-6672-0.

This dictionary is not neutral; it is written with a "socialist edge," rejects conventional interpretation, and includes words from "socialist, progressive, radical, humanist, and left-liberal thought." Written for North American students, the entries are intended to cover both terms of interest as well as those that they should know about but lack enthusiasm for. Subjects covered include sociology, philosophy, economics, history, social psychology, political science, criminal justice, anthropology, education, theology, and law. Both the emotional and political contents of terms are explored using critical inquiry.

Young and Arrigo have an agenda for this dictionary. They seek to have the words presented move the reader, and by extension, society, toward social justice and social peace. Through critical inquiry the authors hope to "signal what work is left to be done if real peace, authentic justice, and true humanity are to flourish." Cross-references or "pointers" are included for most selections and many *see* references are used for related terms. Biographical entries occur for significant or "important luminaries."

Given the stated purposes of the book, the authors provide some interesting and provocative definitions and descriptions. The goals are lofty and the subject inclusiveness is very broad. As to whether the agenda can be attained is somewhat beyond the scope of standard book reviewing to evaluate. When authors attempt to cover such vast areas of intellectual real estate, it is inevitable that opportunities will exist to point to elements of omission, such as including St. Francis of Assisi but excluding the Jesuits, similarly including homosexuality but excluding homophobia (even though the word is used in the preface). For the clearly stated objectives and value system presented, this dictionary is highly unusual and should be a part of mid-size to large libraries collections. A clear bias is labeled, permitting students easy recognition of a particular point of view.—**Graham R. Walden**

3   Area Studies

GENERAL WORKS

P, S

31. **Fiesta! 2.** Tessa Paul, ed. Danbury, Conn., Grolier, 1999. 16v. illus. index. $265.00/set. ISBN 0-7172-9324-6.

Each of the 16 slim books in this set, titled with a country name, is a resource for middle-grade students who study nations of the world and who like to learn about formal celebrations and cultural traditions. Each cover has a colored picture of an 8– or 10–year–old in traditional dress (for the United States it is western). Inside, an outline map identifies location, and a box contains "first impressions" (basic facts). In each volume there are traditional stories, recipes, songs with music (just the melody), about six words from the country's language, and pictures of items unique to the country (e.g., dishes, clothing, symbols, ritual items). Two crafts for each, which are doable by children under supervision, will make great classroom display items. Religious festivals, central in popular and national celebrations in much of the world, are included, and there is often a box briefly outlining a religion's basic tenets. This set will be a welcome addition to the multicultural studies shelf. Set 1, titled *Fiesta!* (see ARBA 98, entry 1262), has similar material for 16 other countries.—**Edna M. Boardman**

P, S

32. **Lands and Peoples.** Danbury, Conn., Grolier, 1999. 7v. illus. maps. index. $269.00/set. ISBN 0-7172-8021-7.

This set is organized by continent, and the individual volumes by countries. It could be argued that as a whole it deals with neither "lands" (in the sense of geographically, historically, or culturally distinct regions) nor "peoples" (in the sense of language or ethnic groups), but only with modern nation-states. Inasmuch as many current junior high school social studies texts have abandoned the artificially constricting criterion of United Nations membership as the most productive approach to understanding the world we live in, this set will not provide adequate support for students' work outside the classroom. On the other hand, because of its competent entries, written by a battery of capable scholars, its handy summaries of facts and figures, its flags and maps, and its generally representative photographs, it will be of great help to students eager to gather materials efficiently for school reports. All entries include materials on the landscape, language, religion, history, and government; countries deemed significant include topical discussions. If this set is intended for use in teaching beginning library skills, it will certainly serve. But programs that might consider it for use in reinforcing social studies lessons would do well to look elsewhere.—**Glenn Petersen**

C, P

33. Ness, Immanuel. **Encyclopedia of World Cities.** Armonk, N.Y., Sharpe Reference/M. E. Sharpe, 1999. 2v. maps. index. $179.00. ISBN 0-7656-8017-3.

This handy 2-volume encyclopedia covers 132 major world cities. For each city 10 key areas of urban life are explored. Geography, demographics, politics, government, culture, and social issues are discussed in short essays. Each entry also includes a map showing the city's location in relation to other cities within the country and other countries. Statistical charts showing such things as growth rate, education levels, and the population's vital statistics are provided. The introduction gives the user a succinct course in urban development by explaining how the key areas affect a city's growth and development over time and how, in turn, development has impacted such things as health care and education. There is also an explanation of how to interpret statistical data. Five comparative tables make up the appendix. Among them are tables showing population rankings as well as increase and change over time. An alphabetic index and a bibliography are provided.

The encyclopedia does suffer from sins of omission. Examples from the London entry include a lack of any mention of the National Health Service, and only a sketchy description of the British educational system is included. A student looking at the entry may not have the breadth of knowledge that is assumed here. The negatives are balanced by the scope of information, its currency, and the context within which it is presented. Most statistics are from the 1990s, and information as recent as 1998 appears in some entries. Comprehensive information on cities is often hard to find, and this set will fill a need in secondary school and public libraries. [R: BL, 1 May 99, p. 1624; LJ, July 99, p. 83; Choice, Oct 99, p. 315; SLJ, Aug 99, p. 186]—**Marlene M. Kuhl**

P, S

34.   **The World Factbook 1999.** By the Central Intelligence Agency. Herndon, Va., Brassey's (U.S.), 1999. 639p. maps. $39.95. ISBN 1-57488-163-9.

The first review of the original version of this title noted the lack of a hard cover and the absence of an index (see ARBA 84, entry 293). Brassey's has now published the 7th reprint of this title. The cover is hard but indexing has not been added. Earlier reviews of the work (see ARBA 97, entry 80; ARBA 93, entry 105) both mention the availability of the federal government document version at a lower price. The CD-ROM format was reviewed in ARBA 95 (see entry 8) and interestingly the 2 reviewers found the paper tool quicker to use when trying to find "specific factual information." If a library does not participate in the federal documents depository program and anticipates frequent use of the volume, then this Brassey's version is adequate. All others will want to rely on the version from the Government Printing Office.—**Graham R. Walden**

UNITED STATES

General Works

P, S

35.   **Congressional Quarterly's Desk Reference on the States.** By Bruce Wetterau. Washington, D.C., Congressional Quarterly, 1999. 328p. index. $49.95. ISBN 1-56802-444-4.

This volume presents historical information about states, along with information about government, current status, and practices. There are seven chapters: The States, Governorship, Legislatures, Campaigns and Elections, State Courts, State of the States, and What About My State? Chapter 7, "What About My State?—The State Profiles," takes up about 20 percent of the book and gives brief factual information about each one of our 50 states. Various questions are posed and answered. The final question in each chapter, "Where can I find...," cites and annotates various pertinent reference works. Numbered cross-references refer to item numbers within the text, and not to page numbers. So initially it is a little confusing. There are subject and name indexes. Checking under "Abortion," one is referred to item 432, "What did the court rule in *Roe vs. Wade*?" with a brief discussion. Under "*Roe vs. Wade* (1973)" readers are referred to items 418 and 432. Under 418 users find "What proportion of cases the Supreme Court decides affects states?" where *Roe vs. Wade* is mentioned as a controversial case. There is no entry under Wade. Under "Supreme Court" readers get "See also specific cases." There are entries under "Women" but no references there to *Roe vs. Wade*. There is also no entry under "Reproductive Rights," and there are no references to Roe or Wade in the name index. It seems to be a rather superficial treatment of the topic. The preface does not indicate an intended audience, but it seems to be for high school level.—**Frank J. Anderson**

P

36.   Renehan, Edward J., Jr. **Great American Websites: An Online Discovery of a Hidden America.** New York, Osborne/McGraw-Hill, 1997. 470p. illus. index. $24.99pa. ISBN 0-07-882304-8.

In this reference guide, Renehan identifies and cleverly annotates a collection of Websites. Readers can explore categories such as "American Sports," "Architecture," "The Great Outdoors," "Individual Americans," and "Kingdom of Kitsch." However, today one must question the usefulness of printed directories of Websites considering the instability of Web page maintenance. These sites may have short life spans. Yet, all things considered, the author does annotate a number of interesting sites. Some of the sites are clearly biased toward the author's choice in music (folk).

The author includes an overview of the search engines Yahoo! and Alta Vista. This is a nice addition for neophytes to World Wide Web searching.—**Leslie R. Homzie**

Florida

C, P
37.   Philcox, Phil, and Beverly Boe. **The Sunshine State Almanac and Book of Florida-Related Stuff.** Sarasota, Fla., Pineapple Press, 1999. 354p. illus. $16.95pa. ISBN 1-56164-178-2.

This almanac is an informal guide to Florida and is organized in a somewhat haphazard fashion. Chapter titles reflect an assortment of themes, which include animals, people, birds, bugs, health, fish, hobbies, food, house and garden, legal issues, sports, water, weather, wildlife, and vacations. Within the chapters are myriad articles—some of general interest, some humorous, and some strange. A miscellaneous chapter has several articles featuring cemeteries (e.g., early Florida cemeteries, political cemeteries, gravestone rubbings). These are unique articles and contain information of help to genealogical researchers. The first is especially noteworthy in that it contains information concerning burials of slaves and free persons of color during Florida's pioneer days. Elsewhere in the book, readers will find articles that will be ideal for reading out loud from the passenger side of the car, and some contain facts and toll-free telephone numbers for emergencies. A few articles have absolutely nothing to do with Florida. Various contributors to the work have their Internet addresses given so that additional information may be found. Although there is a detailed table of contents in the front of the text, the book could benefit greatly if a full index were added.—**Louis G. Zelenka**

Texas

P, S
38.   **Texas Almanac, 2000-2001.** 60th ed. Mary G. Ramos and Robert Plocheck, eds. Dallas, Tex., Dallas Morning News; distr., College Station, Tex., Texas A&M University Press, 1999. 672p. illus. maps. index. $12.95pa. ISBN 0-914511-28-9.

For ready-reference information on the state of Texas, the *Texas Almanac* has been a standard source since 1857. This 60th edition covers all the usual topics. It begins with a brief statistical profile of the state, including rankings in comparison with other states. This information is followed by a large section individually profiling Texas's 254 counties and supplying such facts as ethnicity, geographical area, climatological information, and economic activities. Another section lists cities and towns of Texas alphabetically under the county where they are located along with their 1998 population. Ghost towns and town name changes are also listed in italics. Detailed information is provided about environment and weather, state and local government, education, agriculture, and business and industry. Special sections provide brief histories of the Texas Rangers, the Texas oil industry, and a short survey of Texas history. An attractive and useful guide to Texas, this edition is billed as the millennium edition. It is too bad that the editors did not wait until 2001 for the true millennium and the 2000 census information in order to use that potent label properly.—**Ronald H. Fritze**

AFRICA

P
39.   DeLancey, Mark W., and Mark D. DeLancey, comps. **Cameroon.** rev. ed. Santa Barbara, Calif., Clio Press/ ABC-CLIO, 1999. 207p. maps. index. (World Bibliographical Series, v.63). $67.00. ISBN 1-85109-301-X.

The 1st edition of this bibliography was published in 1986 when Cameroon's economic future looked promising. By 1994 the country's per capita Gross Domestic Product (GDP) had dropped by almost 50 percent. This change is documented in the selection of titles covering the country's economic development.

The 654 annotated entries are organized into 25 chapters covering the history, geography, politics, and culture of the country. Sources include books, journal articles, and videotapes. Annotations are clearly written and give a comprehensive assessment of a title's contents. Researchers can pick and choose with confidence knowing that the works they select will be pertinent to their needs. The literature and arts and music chapters are outstanding in their breadth of coverage. The literature section contains 47 entries covering fiction, bibliographies, folklore, and essays. There are 64 entries under arts and music covering architecture, specific crafts, fine arts, and traditional and contemporary African music. Particular attention is paid to Cameroon's ethnic groups in these and all sections of the book.

Most titles are in English but given that both French and English are the country's official languages, it is not surprising that a fair number are in French (7 of the 12 archaeology entries are in French). There are title, author, and subject indexes and a substantive introductory essay that gives an overview of Cameroon's history to date.

As with other titles in this series, the information has been carefully selected, usefully annotated, and well organized. The bibliography will provide a good starting point for researchers studying Cameroon as a whole or for those focusing on a specific topic related to the country.—**Marlene M. Kuhl**

C
40.   Harris, Gordon. **Central and Equatorial Africa Area Bibliography.** Lanham, Md., Scarecrow, 1999. 209p. index. (Scarecrow Area Bibliographies, no.18). $58.00. ISBN 0-8108-3606-8.

This highly useful work is the latest in the Scarecrow Area Bibliographies series, which provides access to sources on various regions of the world. The book deals with both Congos, Chad, the Central African Republic, São Tomé and Principe, Equatorial Guinea, Gabon, Rwanda, Burundi, Zambia, and Malawi. The author is a British–based academic librarian with scholarly, consulting, and bibliographic credentials on the region under study.

The series format resembles that of Clio Press's World Bibliographical Series. Both series include lengthy introductory essays on the subject by the compiler. Harris provides a thorough and readable, 32–page bibliographic essay divided into eight subject sections from general works and anthropology to historical and political citations. Sections are further subdivided by state or region. The essay provides a most helpful orientation to the region and its literature.

The bibliography is divided into 12 subsections, 1 for the region as a whole and the rest covering the 11 states. Each subsection is further split by subject. The overview section, for example, has about 50 subheadings, from agriculture and animals to religion and women. The country sections' organization is not alphabetic but geographic, meaning one has to use the contents.

There are 1,763 citations listed. Entries are not annotated. English and French (the main colonial languages) dominate citations, but other European languages appear as well. There is an author index, but no title index. This index refers only to the bibliographic entry; there is no mention of the introductory essay, making the context provided by the essay for some works less easy to access. This is an excellent guide to publications on its region of Africa. Its long introduction may make it of interest to larger public libraries as well as to strictly research institutions.—**Nigel Tappin**

ASIA

General Works

P
41.   Nwanna, Gladson I. **Do's and Don'ts Around the World: A Country Guide to Cultural and Social Taboos and Etiquette: Asia.** Baltimore, Md., World Travel Institute Press, 1998. 254p. $24.95pa. ISBN 1-890605-01-8.

This book is part of a series listing a number of actions and activities that travelers should or should not engage in when traveling to a foreign country. The book consists of a large checklist of the countries in Asia, from Afghanistan to Japan and from China to Indonesia. The checklist indicates whether a number of actions are allowable, are not customary, or are even forbidden. Among the behaviors considered by the author are smoking, eating, and drinking alcohol in public; kissing, spitting, and dancing in public; haggling and giving money to beggars; using a Walkman or possessing a Bible; females drinking or smoking; females wearing lipstick, bikinis, or trousers; and tipping. The book considers each country and includes sections on particular "do's and don'ts," such as whether pedestrians have the right-of-way and the punishment for drug trafficking. "Additional country information," such as safe topics for discussion and whether there is a basic color with negative connotations, is included as well. The book contains much useful information, but its reliability is suspect when the reader is informed that in Pakistan begging is not customary, yet giving money to beggars is. It also states that both "guilty until proven innocent" and "innocent until proven guilty" are the law. The book indicates that spitting in public is not customary in India, which would surprise millions of paan chewers. The book concludes with a useful appendix containing a country-by-country guide to tipping; electricity requirements; telephone dialing codes; banking, business, and shopping hours; and international emergency telephone codes. The book should be used with care.—**David L. White**

China

C, P

42. **Dictionary of the Politics of the People's Republic of China.** Colin Mackerras, with Donald H. McMillen and Andrew Watson, eds. New York, Routledge, 1998. 267p. illus. index. $100.00. ISBN 0-415-15450-2.

Contributed to by 34 China scholars from Australia, Hong Kong, India, Korea, Singapore, and the United States, this dictionary assesses the dynamic nature of Chinese politics from 1978 to 1997. It is aimed at providing students, government, media and business personnel, and nonspecialist academics with useful and accessible information about the People's Republic of China (PRC). The dictionary begins with eight introductory essays, which present an overview history of the PRC, its people and government, ideology, political figures, politics and economy, the region, and the overseas Chinese. This section is followed by the main body of the dictionary, which consists of 114 descriptive topics, alphabetically arranged and carefully chosen in accord with their importance to China's political culture, economy, foreign relations, society, and the political identity of the Chinese people. The signed entries are generally well researched and well written in an essay format, with cross-references at the end of each article. The volume concludes with a selected reading list and an extensive subject index. The Pinyin romanization system is employed throughout the text with the exception of a few names, such a Sun Yat-sen, which has its own established non-Pinyin form. Since more than one-third of the book is devoted to significant persons or events, it would have been useful if the dates were noted immediately following the names and events. It would also have been useful if a glossary of English equivalents of Chinese names or terms was appended for easy reference. This work is suitable for academic and public libraries. [R: LJ, 1 May 98, p. 92]
—**Karen T. Wei**

C, P

43. Perkins, Dorothy. **Encyclopedia of China: The Essential Reference to China, Its History, and Culture.** New York, Facts on File, 1999. 662p. illus. index. (A Roundtable Press Book). $95.00. ISBN 0-8160-2693-9.

This introductory 1-volume reference work contains more than 1,000 entries, arranged alphabetically, on China's past, present, and future. Using an essay-length format to provide up-to-date and comprehensive background information, the encyclopedia has succeeded in offering general readers a source to understand this emerging superpower. The work covers all aspects of the history and culture of China, exploring its geography, population, and lifestyle; religion and popular culture; arts and crafts; literature; performing and martial arts; history; current politics and economics; and foreign relations and trade. The Pinyin romanization system is emphasized in this book but Wade-Giles equivalents are noted and references made. Most entries are also heavily cross-referenced. For example, under the heading "Qing Dynasty" there are more than 100 *see also* references. The book is further enhanced by more than 50 black-and-white photographs and illustrations. A list of suggested readings and an extensive subject index linking concepts, people, and events conclude the volume. The adequate index makes the work extremely easy to use.

A number of similar works have been published in the past 15 years. The competitive *Cambridge Encyclopedia of China* (2d ed.; see ARBA 93, entry 125) is more authoritative but lacks cross-references. Perkins's work is also more current and more adequately indexed. The expensive 3-volume reference set *Information China* (see ARBA 90, entry 121) represents the official view of the Chinese government and is far more extensive in coverage than Perkins's work but desperately needs updates. Finally, *Modern China: An Encyclopedia of History, Culture, and Nationalism* (see ARBA 99, entry 109) begins with the outbreak of the Opium War in

1839 and ends with events up to 1997. Depending on the user's needs, these volumes complement each other well. Perkins's encyclopedia is highly recommended for both academic and public libraries. [R: BL, 1 Feb 99, pp. 995-996; BR, May/June 99, p. 78; Choice, June 99, pp. 1765-1766]—**Karen T. Wei**

Japan

C, P

44.   Eades, J. S., comp. **Tokyo.** Santa Barbara, Calif., Clio Press/ABC-CLIO, 1999. 288p. maps. index. (World Bibliographical Series, v.214). $85.00. ISBN 1-85109-292-7.

Number 214 in the World Bibliographical Series claims the distinction of being the first annotated English-language bibliography of Tokyo. The 1,200 items covering the Edo period to the twentieth century are divided into 27 major sections covering Tokyo's history, such as geography, economy, politics, and culture. Almost all are English titles, although there are a few in French and German. Appropriate fiction, juvenile, and classic reprints are included.

Entries are numbered sequentially and are listed within sections by date of publication. *See* references are used if information on a specific subject is contained in a title whose main entry is located elsewhere. For example, titles on the Pacific War and occupation do not have their own section. Pertinent titles appear under one of the major headings.

Annotations are concise, but give a clear picture of a title's content and perspective. For example, materials printed for the postwar occupation forces and official publications of Tokyo's city government are included. In the geography section, materials published before and after the devastating 1923 earthquake give insight into the significance of the landmark disaster on the city. Painting and woodblock printing are strongly represented by numerous titles on specific artists, including those who specialized in Shunga. Literature and performing arts, both traditional and contemporary, are represented. Pachinko, Karaoke, and Sumo are covered in the popular culture section. Aum Shinrikyo is included with titles on more traditional religions.

The substantive introduction gives a narrative overview of Tokyo's history and geography, and includes tables for area and population by ward and municipality. There are indexes of authors, titles, and subjects, and maps of Central Tokyo and the Tokyo Prefecture.

The comprehensive work will be of value to a range of users. Scholars, secondary and postsecondary students, and general travelers will find it helpful. It will be especially beneficial to those involved in international relations and trade since it offers a broad spectrum of titles that give an in-depth picture of the forces that have shaped one of the world's major cities.—**Marlene M. Kuhl**

P, S

45.   Kamachi, Noriko. **Culture and Customs of Japan.** Westport, Conn., Greenwood Press, 1999. 187p. illus. maps. index. (Culture and Customs of Asia). $45.00. ISBN 0-313-30197-2.

For years, most Japanese leaving the country for a long trip somehow ended up with a copy of Nippon Steel's *Nippon: The Land and Its People.* Now in its 20th edition, it continues to answer a variety of typical questions about Japanese history and culture with facing English and Japanese texts. However, as Japan became more of an economic powerhouse, a number of popular handbooks to understanding Japan for Americans emerged, some by writers whose Japanese knowledge was limited to brief visits and thus were full of whimsical impressions and factual errors. To counter this, "experts" were brought in to create newer guides. *Culture and Customs of Japan* is another example of this trend, written by University of Michigan, Dearborn, professor Noriko Kamachi. The book, although written by a historian, is not an academic one from both a positive angle (in that it is very readable) and a more critical one (there are few footnotes and the four pages of suggested readings are neither descriptive nor evaluative). Indeed, the table of contents reflects the series' aim of introducing Asian culture (religion; literature; art; housing; food; clothing; women, marriage, and family; festivals; entertainment; and social customs) to general Western audiences. From this perspective it could be seen as a cultural counterpart to the CIA country handbook, especially as Kamachi largely relegates post-war political Japan to three pages in the historical introduction. From the perspective of a ready-reference work, *The Kodansha Encyclopedia of Japan* (see ARBA 84, entry 305) or *Japan: An Illustrated Encyclopedia* (see ARBA 94, entry 115) are strongly suggested. Komachi's selection of topics and explanations are a good, readable (junior high and above) introduction to the vanishing world of Japanese traditional culture. If Greenwood comes out with a 2d edition, the editor should not to be afraid of the political aspects and perhaps should choose a less stereotypical cover photograph than the current one of a woman in kimono and bamboo umbrella.—**Andrew B. Wertheimer**

Thailand

C

46.   Smyth, David, comp. **Thailand.** rev. ed. Santa Barbara, Calif., Clio Press/ABC-CLIO, 1998. 226p. maps. index. (World Bibliographical Series, v.65). $91.00. ISBN 1-85109-254-4.

The World Bibliographical Series continues to produce high-quality guides to research literature of the world, and the revised edition of *Thailand* is no exception. The many new and recent entries reflect the considerable growth in English-language scholarship from and about Thailand since the 1986 edition. The compiler demonstrates his knowledge of evolving research trends with the inclusion of new subject categories—"Women and Gender" and "Environment." In addition, the inclusion of works about prostitution, homosexuality, and AIDS, along with the increased number of entries for minorities, modern Thai history and politics, and literature, provides an accurate overview of research and publishing in the field.

Those seeking up-to-date information, especially on the recent economic crisis, can be assured of finding recent publications—many as recent as 1997 and 1998. At the same time, Smyth has not neglected the seminal works that form the foundation of Thai studies. Although the majority of citations refer to published monographs and research papers, the author includes a few dissertation and journal article citations, leaving one to wonder about the criteria for their selection. At a time when computers make it easy to generate endless lists of citations, Smyth's careful selections and his well-written annotations are especially important for those being introduced to the study of Thailand. As with any bibliography, there are omissions. References to CD-ROM and nonprint resources that are increasingly important to the research and teaching community would be a valuable addition. This bibliography not only serves as an excellent guide to the new student of Thailand but also serves to make us aware of the changing nature of scholarship and publishing in area studies. This work is highly recommended for college and research libraries. [R: Choice, Sept 99, p. 122]—**Carol L. Mitchell**

CANADA

C

47.   Gagnon, Alain-G., comp. **Québec.** Santa Barbara, Calif., Clio Press/ABC-CLIO, 1998. 350p. maps. index. (World Bibliographical Series, v.211). $105.00. ISBN 1-85109-290-0.

The World Bibliographical Series' goal is to compile a bibliography of country information for every country in the world. *Québec* is volume 211 of this series. The province of Québec has propelled itself into the national forefront by the Québec Referendum of October 1995 and its active participation in the North American Free Trade Agreement (NAFTA). These two reasons are why the editors decided to include a volume about Québec in its World Bibliographical Series.

The format for this volume is identical to the other country studies volumes. The volume is a bibliography of works about Québec and its people. The succeeding chapters are bibliographies of print, electronic, and nonprint resources categorized by topics. The topics begin with geography and history, moving into social trends, a special chapter on the women of Québec, transportation, education, art and literature, and sports and leisure. It has three separate indexes—author, title, and subject. It has a pen-and-ink map at the end of the book.

This book is recommended to special and academic libraries that have special collections of country information. This will be a valuable handbook for the government libraries that focus on international business and politics.—**Kay M. Stebbins**

EUROPE

Austria

C

48. Mitchell, Michael, comp. **Austria.** rev. ed. Santa Barbara, Calif., Clio Press/ABC-CLIO, 1999. 271p. maps. index. (World Bibliographical Series, v.66). $81.00. ISBN 1-85109-297-8.

Mitchell, a British scholar and translator of German literature, follows a familiar formula in this thorough revision of the World Bibliographical Series volume on Austria that first appeared in 1986 (see ARBA 87, entry 126). Annotated citations cover 793 publications on Austrian history, culture, and society. A table of contents presents 43 topical chapters. There is also a concise introduction to the concept of Austria and an outline map. The volume concludes with author, title, and subject indexes.

Mitchell retains less than 15 percent of the titles in the 1986 edition. He emphasizes current studies; more than one-half of the selections appeared in the 1990s and another one-third in the 1980s. This is both commendable and problematic. Readers will benefit from awareness of recent work, but some key older studies are no longer mentioned. This particularly affects the chapter on history. In the absence of many works written in the 1950s, 1960s, and 1970s, readers may not appreciate the lengthy and hesitant process by which modern Austria emerged from its ambivalent relationship with Germany and with authoritarianism. This revision includes twice as many German-language titles as the 1st edition did—more than 40 percent of the total. This decision enriches many chapters, but assumes familiarity with German. The vast majority of entries describe books. Besides a few articles, periodicals, and maps, Mitchell commendably notes a half-dozen CD-ROM publications and Websites (but does not include URLs for the online versions of some cited newspapers). No other bibliography offers advice to general readers about such a wide range of things Austrian. The ABC-CLIO bibliography on Vienna (see ARBA 99, entry 119) covers the capital city, not the country. The 1986 edition remains useful for its coverage of works published before the 1980s.—**Steven W. Sowards**

Bulgaria

P, S

49. Otfinoski, Steven. **Bulgaria.** New York, Facts on File, 1999. 118p. illus. maps. index. (Nations in Transition). $19.95. ISBN 0-8160-3705-1.

This is another volume in the Nations in Transition series, which is intended for middle school and high school students (see ARBA 99, entry 124, for a review of the volume entitled *Russia*). Bulgaria receives the standard attractive, easy-to-digest treatment. The history and politics of the country is divided into three chapters: prehistory to 1919, 1919 to 1989, and 1989 to the present. Other chapters address the economy, culture, religion, daily life, the cities, and present problems. The concise text is supplemented by photographs, drawings, maps, and biographical sketches (e.g., Simeon I and II, Todor Zhikov, opera singer Ljuba Welitsch, the artist Christo). A chronology of important events and a selective bibliography are useful reference aids. This book is most suitable for public and school libraries; undergraduates will need more substantial resources. [R: BR, May/June 99, p. 78]—**Thomas A. Karel**

Croatia

C, P

50. Carmichael, Cathie, comp. **Croatia.** Santa Barbara, Calif., Clio Press/ABC-CLIO, 1999. 194p. maps. index. (World Bibliographical Series, v.216). $90.00. ISBN 1-85109-285-4.

This comprehensive annotated bibliography of works about Croatia is arranged in broad general subject categories. Most of the books annotated are in English, but several are included that are written in Western European languages and in Croatian and Serbian. In an introductory essay, Carmichael provides a brief history of Croatia from the fifth century to the present day. Aware of political bias that accompanies any publication on

Croatia and Serbia, Carmichael warns that the aura of nationalism conveyed by many of the titles is not unusual for this part of the world, even though it may seem slightly odd or old-fashioned in a greater European context. In order to provide a broad view of the country and its people, she included works that she personally did not agree with and also some that may be considered as anti-Croatian. Her aim was not to take sides, but to present a broad range of information about Croatia.

Like other volumes in this series, the various subject categories that are used to arrange the annotations cover the expected topics of history, geography, language, religion, society, politics, foreign relations, the economy, education, literature, and the arts. In addition, Carmichael provides several topics that are unique to Croatia, such as the national question, minorities, Croatians abroad, and the Croatian War of Independence (1990-1995). This is an excellent source for all levels of users who are looking for up-to-date information about Croatia. Author, title, and subject indexes provide good access to the contents.—**Robert H. Burger**

Former Soviet Republics

C, P
51. **The Territories of the Russian Federation.** London, Europa Publications; distr., Farmington Hills, Mich., Gale, 1999. 286p. maps. index. $95.00. ISBN 1-85743-070-0. ISSN 1465-461X.

The breakup of the Soviet Union in 1989 produced, among other things, a flurry of reference books that provided directories and background surveys of the newly established republics. The best of these sources, David T. Twining's *Guide to the Republics of the Former Soviet Union* (see ARBA 95, entry 166) and *Russia and the Commonwealth A to Z* by Andrew Wilson and Nina Bachkatov (see ARBA 94, entry 525), are now seriously outdated, so this major new publication on Russia is welcome. The volume opens with an introductory essay on the economics of the Russian Federation, with a chronology, statistics, and a government directory. The main portion of the book consists of "territorial surveys" and examines the 89 constituent units of the federation: the autonomous republics, provinces, administrative regions (oblasts), autonomous districts, and federal cities (Moscow and St. Petersburg). For each of these areas brief information on the geography (with a small map), history, and economy are provided, along with a directory of top officials. This will be an extremely useful reference source for students of the region and it nicely supplements *The Newly Independent States of Eurasia: A Handbook of Former Soviet Republics*, by Stephen and Sandra Batalden (see ARBA 98, entry 125). [R: Choice, Nov 99, p. 520]—**Thomas A. Karel**

Former Yugoslavia

C
52. Matulic, Rusko. **Bibliography of Sources on the Region of Former Yugoslavia.** New York, Columbia University Press, 1998. 441p. index. $63.00. ISBN 0-88033-402-9.

Anyone who can profit from a comprehensive general bibliography of Yugoslavia will welcome the appearance of Matulic's work. This general, non-annotated bibliography covers 16 main subjects, primarily in Western languages, regarding the region of former Yugoslavia. Approximately one-sixth of all the entries deal with the dissolution of the country during 1991 and 1992. The entries are arranged according to main subjects, ranging from agriculture, archaeology, arts, history, languages, and literature to politics and government, religion, social sciences, and expatriates. There is further division into 64 specialized subheadings such as Macedonian, Serbo Croatian, Slovene, and minority languages. The entries are numbered consecutively in order to facilitate author and subject identification in the indexes. Most of the entries are not cross-referenced and appear only once under the most predominant category, which potentially slows down the search. The book and monograph entries are arranged alphabetically by the author's name, followed by the title of the book or the pertinent chapter, city and state or country of publication, year, number of pages, and related categories. If any entry consists of a chapter, then the pertinent publication source with its editor(s) is also noted. Periodicals are entered under their name, alphabetically arranged, and presented in chronological order under the particular heading or subheading. Preceding the main entries are explanatory notes that clarify conventions used throughout. Serbo-Croat-Slovene diacritic marks that are necessary for pronunciation are also provided. Following the main entries is a listing of unpublished sources covering microfilms and other documents deposited in U.S. and British archives. These comprise, among others, military and political events around and during World War II. The geographical essay shows black-and-white maps of tribal and ethnical boundary shifts from the time the Slavs came to the Balkan Peninsula (395 B.C.E.) until the present. Also presented is a sampling of video sources dealing with the scientific, literary, artistic, and other aspects of life in former Yugoslavia. These entries contain bracketed, explanatory notes and numbers indicating the subject category as used for printed entries. An index of authors and editors as well as an index of entries by headings and subheadings is provided.

Because this well-organized and comprehensive volume covers many aspects of the different regions of Yugoslavia, it can serve as a reference on many levels. This resource is a valuable tool for Slavic scholars and will be an important edition for university libraries.—**Magda Želinská-Ferl**

Great Britain

C

53.   **Britain 1999: The Official Yearbook of the United Kingdom.** 50th ed. By the Office for National Statistics. London, Stationery Office; distr., Lanham, Md., Bernan Associates, 1998. 564. illus. maps. index. $80.00. ISBN 0-11-621037-0.

Which women's magazine has the highest circulation in Great Britain? (*Take a Break*). Who won the Benson & Hedges Cup in Cricket in 1997-1998? (Essex). What is the largest British pharmaceutical company? (Glaxo Wellcome). This is the sort of handy information—and much, much more—that can be found in *Britain 1999*. In its 50th year of publication, this combination yearbook and encyclopedia provides a detailed overview of life and politics in Great Britain (see ARBA 95, entry 156, and ARBA 91, entry 112, for reviews of earlier editions).

As in recent editions, the book is organized into 5 main parts: Britain and its people, government and foreign affairs, social and cultural affairs, environment and transport, and economic affairs. Each part is further broken down into subsections (30 in all), though these have been reworked slightly and do not compare to the exact arrangement in previous volumes. The section on sustainable development has been reinstated in this volume and substantially expanded. Each of the subsections contains charts, diagrams, statistical tables, and short bibliographies (with Websites). Most of the content, however, is in the form of brief descriptive articles. All of the information has been updated, drawing from over 250 official government sources.

The text is interrupted by nine colorful photograph inserts (more than in earlier editions) that offer a selective look at aspects of British culture (e.g., postage stamps, gardens, museums, arts awards, and domes). Appended to the text are a directory of government departments and agencies, a discussion of recent legislation, brief obituaries, a list of abbreviations, and a list of public holidays. This continues to be a very useful reference source for current information on Great Britain and is most suitable for academic libraries.—**Thomas A. Karel**

P

54.   **The Encyclopedia of Britain.** Oxford, England, Helicon; distr., Farmington Hills, Mich., Gale, 1999. 1015p. illus. maps. $75.00. ISBN 1-85986-275-6.

There are few editorial tasks as daunting as assembling a single-volume encyclopedia on the culture and history of a country, much less a country as diverse and complex as Britain. In just over 1,000 pages, this book succeeds in presenting the United Kingdom in an "A-Z guide," accessible to the casual reader and useful to the professional researcher. This book should be in every library because of its comprehensiveness (more than 6,000 entries), efficient organization, and readability. It is also very up-to-date, with the latest entries from December 1998.

Encyclopedias often suffer from uneven editing, since numerous experts write entries in styles ranging from artistic to scientific to popular. This volume had a strong editorial hand that facilitates an even, unencumbered flow of information though the nearly infinite number of threads that can be followed by the extensive cross-referencing. There are hundreds of illustrations, including color and black-and-white photographs, maps, charts, and diagrams. Inset quotations related to nearby entries often tug the reader in unexpected directions, making this more than a simple reference book. An additional strength of this encyclopedia is its set of 45 special essays ("features") on both predictable topics ("The Vikings of Britain") and the unexpected ("British Food"). There are also dozens of chronologies to help plot the changing fortunes of the monarchy, the history of British higher education, the British publishing industry, British scientific advances, and much more. True to its contemporary form, the book even has a long list of relevant Websites in an appendix.

All collective volumes require choices as to which topics become entries and how much space each entry is given. The editors are quite specific about their criteria in the preface (when the Irish are included or not, how much of the former Empire is mentioned and under what circumstances, and so on). However, a book that combines popular culture with history, geography, and science will inevitably show some incongruities. The Austrian-invented postcard, for example, gets more space than the Falklands War. Nevertheless, most of the time the balance of emphasis is good, making the encyclopedia as much a pleasure to peruse as to use. [R: LJ, 1 Oct 99, p. 78]

—**Mark A. Wilson**

Greece

P

55.   Edwards, Adrian, comp. **Crete.** Santa Barbara, Calif., Clio Press/ABC-CLIO, 1998. 134p. maps. index. (World Bibliographical Series, v.215). $58.00. ISBN 1-85109-173-4.

The goal of books in the World Bibliographical Series is to provide annotated entries on works that deal with the history, geography, economy, politics, people, culture, customs, religion, and social organization of the countries of the world. This recent volume on Crete fulfills this goal, although it also has some weaknesses.

Edwards provides a serviceable history of Crete in his introduction. This is followed by a good chronology of major events in the history of Crete and a brief listing of the rulers of Crete. Most of the book is composed of the annotated entries themselves. Edwards has collected and annotated 386 entries, including books, journal articles, and Websites. Although a few sources in French, Italian, Greek, and German are included, the works are predominantly in English. Most sources are of recent publications, although major older works are also included.

The entries are organized into 27 thematic chapters; for example, geography, geology and paleontology, tourism and travel guides, archaeology, religion, health, coins and stamps, and food and drink, among others. Each entry gives the full bibliographic citation to the work as well as a brief annotation. Indexes for authors, titles, and subjects conclude the work.

The greatest weakness of the work is its exclusions. For example, although several standard works on coinage are included, others are absent, such as *The Coinage of Modern Greece, Crete, the Ionian Islands & Cyprus* by S. Gardiakos (Obol International, 1969) and *The Coinage of the Arab Amirs of Crete* by George Miles (American Numismatic, 1960). In addition, a quick search on the Historical Abstracts database, which indexes material dealing with 1450 and later, yielded more than 160 entries, many of which are missing from the bibliography.

With these weaknesses noted, Edwards has done a good job in bringing together material on an area of study that deserves greater attention. The work should be included in all libraries that strive to maintain collections on European history.—**Gregory A. Crawford**

Netherlands

C

56.   Huussen, Arend H., Jr. **Historical Dictionary of the Netherlands.** Lanham, Md., Scarecrow, 1998. 237p. (European Historical Dictionaries, no.32). $59.50. ISBN 0-8108-3514-2.

There are relatively few reference books dealing specifically with the Netherlands, so this historical dictionary is welcome. Huussen, from the University of Groningen, indicates in the preface that he intends to provide the English-reading public with "basic information on persons and topics from Dutch political, intellectual, and colonial history and culture." He includes the elements characteristic of this series: a detailed chronology, a summary of Dutch history, more than 500 dictionary entries, and a lengthy bibliography. The brief historical overview, which opens the volume, is readable and is reasonably successful in the difficult task of presenting enough historical details to inform without making the text unreadable. The dictionary entries are helpful and clear, but sometimes so brief that they lack interest and give short shrift to important topics. For example, Huussen devotes one short paragraph to the East India Company; in the *Lexicon Geschiedenis van Nederland & Belgie* (Kosmos, 1994), this topic rates a full page of small type. Because most English-speaking readers know so little about the Netherlands, more lengthy entries would have been helpful. In addition, the text of the entries is constantly interrupted by *see* references using the Latin abbreviation "q.v." traditional for this series instead of the more readable italics or bold typeface. These references appear frequently (nine in the paragraph on "Parliament"), and often refer the reader pointlessly to another entry. In the paragraph on William I (1772-1843), for example, the appearance of the word "government" is followed by a "q.v.," even though the article on government referred to describes the makeup of the Dutch cabinets after World War II. There are other English-language bibliographies on the Netherlands, including one in the World Bibliographical Series by Peter King and Michael Wintle (see ARBA 89, entry 120), but this dictionary fills a gap by providing detailed historical information in English. This work is recommended for academic and large public libraries.—**V. W. Hill**

Sicily

C, P

57.   Olivastri, Valentina, comp. **Sicily.** Santa Barbara, Calif., Clio Press/ABC-CLIO, 1998. 188p. maps. index. (World Bibliographical Series, v.213). $63.00. ISBN 1-85109-291-9.

This title, another in the voluminous ABC-CLIO World Bibliographical Series, treats Sicily, the largest island of the Mediterranean. After an introduction that sketches very briefly Sicily's history, a chronology dating back to 20,000 B.C.E. is provided. These sections are followed by an annotated bibliography with 155 pages and 456 entries. It is divided into 36 chapter headings with some further divided into subheadings. Among the major topics covered are geography; history; and social conditions, including organized crime, politics, religion, economy and industry, education, literature, the arts, sports and recreation, and agriculture. The annotations are concise yet quite descriptive in their summaries of the works. The compiler attempts to emphasize English-language material, but, out of necessity, must also include many Italian sources. Separate indexes of authors, titles, and subjects as well as a map of Sicily conclude the volume. This source is recommended to any academic or public library attempting to collect the entire series, or that has a special interest in Sicily, Italy, or the Mediterranean.

—**Lee Weston**

LATIN AMERICA
AND THE CARIBBEAN

C

58.   Crane, Janet, comp. **French Guiana.** Santa Barbara, Calif., Clio Press/ABC-CLIO, 1998. 160p. maps. index. (World Bibliographical Series, v.210). $59.00. ISBN 1-85109-241-2.

The World Bibliographical Series recently published volume on French Guiana is their first devoted to this area of South America, officially a department of France. The bibliography follows the usual format for the series: an introductory essay; approximately 400 annotated bibliographic entries organized into topical chapters; and separate indexes of authors, titles, and subject terms. The compiler also includes one map of the territory.

The introduction is longer than those usually found in this series and provides necessary background for this understudied region. Crane emphasizes the dearth of scholarly English-language publications on French Guiana, noting that fewer than 40 percent of the entries in this volume refer to such publications. She also comments upon the tendency of much research to focus on a limited number of themes in the department's history, such as its penal colony, failed attempts at European settlement, and adventurers' accounts. While including references to standard works that deal with major themes in French Guiana's history, Crane also attempts to document scholarship on lesser-studied topics and to point out gaps in the literature. The annotations are detailed and informative. Although the bibliography includes a sizeable number of entries, especially given the sparse amount of research that as been done on some topics, there seem to be some significant omissions. A subject search of the online version of the *Handbook of Latin American Studies* brings up several citations that are not included in this volume: for example, general histories of French Guiana published in the 1990s and older travel accounts. It would be helpful to know more about the compiler's parameters for inclusion of materials, given the necessary limits that must be set when preparing a bibliography. There also seem to be few materials listed that were published in French Guiana, and it would be interesting to see more background on this trend and its implications for scholarship.

Despite these omissions, this volume will be of much use to new and more advanced researchers. The lack of any other recently published bibliographies on French Guiana further increases its value. Crane has charted a needed course through the relatively inaccessible terrain of scholarship about this "complicated and therefore poorly understood place." [R: Choice, Dec 99, p. 700]—**Pamela M. Graham**

C, P

59.   **Social Panorama of Latin America.** 1997 ed. New York, United Nations, 1998. 231p. $25.00pa. ISBN 92-1-121224-3. ISSN 1020-5160. S/N E.98.II.G.3.

This annual publication of the Economic Commission for Latin America and the Caribbean (ECLAC) of the United Nations provides an "assessment of the most salient aspects of social development in Latin America, with particular emphasis on the question of equity. Among the issues it examines are poverty, education, the situation of children and young people, gender and social expenditure. It also presents on overview of how Governments are implementing their social agendas and reviews new policy directions in various social sectors" (p. 13). This 1997 edition gives particular attention to the situation with regard to children's rights, analyzes gender-based role differentiation early in life, and evaluates the frequency and implications of teenage pregnancies.

Information is presented by country in text, statistical tables, and charts; the statistical appendix summarizes data for Latin America as a whole. Just as the countries that are included in each table of the main text vary depending upon whether or not relevant data are available, the tables in the appendix are based on data varying from 9 to 15 countries. Sources for all statistics are identified. There is little information about the Caribbean islands, in spite of the fact that they are included in the area of ECLAC's coverage. Although some of the statistical data can be found in other annual sources, such as the *Statistical Abstract of Latin America* (University of California at Los Angeles) and the *Statistical Yearbook for Latin America and the Caribbean*, issued by ECLAC since the mid-1980s, the focus of this publication on the statistical facts impacting the contemporary social situation in the region and analysis of that data makes it a valuable source for any library whose users need information about current Latin America. It is even more valuable because social statistics and analysis of them are much harder to locate than detailed data about economic conditions.—**Ann Hartness**

P

60.   Williams, Raymond Leslie, and Kevin G. Guerrieri. **Culture and Customs of Colombia.** Westport, Conn., Greenwood Press, 1999. 148p. illus. maps. index. (Culture and Customs of Latin America and the Caribbean). $45.00. ISBN 0-313-30405-X.

This reference is part of a series on Latin American countries and provides a broad introduction to Colombian culture for the general reader. The authors concisely outline Colombian geography, history, religion, social customs, television, radio, newspapers, and arts (including literature, theater, music, cinema, photography, and architecture). The narrative demonstrates the authors' premise that Colombia is unique in Latin America with its extreme regionalism, its deeply founded traditionalism, an ingrained presence of the Catholic Church in daily life, and the country's political institutions, which surpass those of other South American nations. Features include an historical chronology, chapter notes, a glossary, a bibliography, and an index. The text is well written and effectively projects the authors' appreciation and affection for Colombia, its history, its literature, and its culture.
—**Adrienne Antink Bendel**

POLAR REGIONS

P

61.   Mills, William, and Peter Speak. **Keyguide to Information Sources on the Polar and Cold Regions.** London, Mansell/Cassell; distr., New York, Continuum Publishing, 1998. 330p. maps. index. $140.00. ISBN 0-7201-2176-0.

First published in Great Britain in 1997, this guide comes to the United States as the Shackleton exhibit is drawing record crowds as it tours the country and as more tourists opt for tours to polar regions. The compilers are specialists in polar and cold region information sources. Sources selected for inclusion in the guide include print publications, bibliographic databases, and Internet resources. Selected special and general, primarily English-language sources are included.

The book is organized into three sections, a survey of the polar and cold regions, key reference sources, and organizations engaged in polar research. The survey section covers the principal physical features of the regions and the development of scientific interest in them. The work of major international and national research groups is also covered. For those who dream of one day working in a polar region there is an informative section on education and career paths leading to such employment. The neophyte scholar will find a chapter on information searching, research strategies, relevant libraries, archives, and museums. Throughout this section *see also* references guide the user to related entries in the bibliography, and Internet addresses are given.

The bibliography is an introduction to key reference works. General and regional sources are covered. Subject resources are listed for a broad range of disciplines such as earth and life sciences, human and social sciences, arts and humanities, travel expeditions, and engineering and related subjects. Each subject area begins with an introductory essay. "Comfortable" is not an adjective usually applied to reference sources, but it describes perfectly the tone of these essays. The reader feels as though he or she is sitting with a favorite teacher discussing an approach to research.

The directory of selected organizations includes international and national research organizations. Complete addresses are given with Web and e-mail addresses provided. There is a list of libraries and archives that have significant holdings related to polar and cold region research. The SPRI Website also has this list, with collection size and focus given. Publishers located in polar regions or publishing monographs on the topic are listed, as are specialized rare and used book dealers.

This is an outstanding resource on a timely topic. Researchers, serious students, tourists, and even armchair travelers will find the guide a comprehensive source for research or the pursuit of a personal interest. Highly recommended.—**Marlene M. Kuhl**

4   Economics and Business

GENERAL WORKS

Biography

P

62.   **American Business Leaders.** [CD-ROM]. Santa Barbara, Calif., ABC-CLIO, 1998. Minimum system requirements: Pentium-compatible processor at 75MHZ or faster. Four-speed CD-ROM drive. Windows 95. 8MB RAM. 30MB hard disk space. SVGA monitor 640x480 (256 colors). 16-bit sound card with Windows drivers. $49.00 (standalone); $129.00 (lab pack); $249.00 (site license). ISBN 1-57607-020-4.

    This is a helpful electronic reference work that is structured around 413 biographies of significant business leaders over the course of American history. From the colonial era through the end of the twentieth century, this work outlines the lives and times of both famous and lesser-known men and women who have helped shape American business history. Individual entries provide a concise and straightforward summary of the events and achievements of particular business leaders and collectively create the sort of reference work that can be used to find not only specific information but can also be enjoyable to simply browse through. It provides specific and comparative information for these business leaders and can be used by a variety of users. Individual entries have a brief bibliography of practical works, but many of these bibliographies will probably be too brief for advanced users.

    ABC-CLIO has also published a 2-volume book that contains these same 413 biographies (ISBN 1-57607-002-6), but this electronic version may be easier to use for some since it allows for searches by text and other attributes. Indeed, the principal advantage to using a CD-ROM version of the reference work is that it provides easier cross-referencing and more detailed indexes. This reference work also provides 64 linked maps and a glossary of 198 defined terms. This reference work can be searched by name, subject, text, and a variety of attributes. These attributes include occupation, birth year, death year, gender, ethnicity, and even place of birth. Unfortunately, by searching through this work, users may find that some groups and categories are underrepresented. Despite the fact that since the colonial era white males have historically dominated the top rung of the American business ladder, this work lists only 24 women out of the 413 biographies. Likewise, there is an underrepresentation of race and ethnicity with biographies of only four African Americans, one Asian, and one Hispanic. Increasing the number of featured women and minorities would make this reference work more representative of American business history. Despite any shortcomings, this is still a useful and practical guide to the economic lives and times of a number of manufacturers, merchants, financiers, business executives, and developers.—**Timothy E. Sullivan**

P, S

63.   **Business Leaders for Students.** Sheila M. Dow, ed. Farmington Hills, Mich., Gale, 1999. 914p. illus. index. $95.00. ISBN 0-7876-2935-9. ISSN 1520-9296.

    The purpose of this new book in Gale's popular line of business products for students is "to provide readers with a comprehensive resource of business biographies, giving them easy access to information on past and resent business leaders." This goal is met with 248 alphabetically arranged, engaging entries of historical and popular business leaders. It is, of course, impossible to be comprehensive in one volume. The advisory board of five teachers and librarians of young adults from diverse geographic locations did an excellent job of selecting the leaders for inclusion. The first entry is illustrative of the selections—Scott Adams, creator of the *Dilbert* comic strip. Historical figures such as Alexander Graham Bell, Benjamin Franklin, and Samuel Morse balance modern business leaders like Bill Gates, Charles Schwab, and Ted Turner. Many different areas of business are included, from food processing (e.g., Colonel Sanders, Oscar Mayer, Will Kellogg) to cosmetics (e.g., Mary Kay, Estée Lauder) to entertainment (e.g., Jane Fonda, George Lucas, Michael Jordan). Minority leaders are well represented with businesspeople such as Wally Amos, Akio Morita, and Barbara Proctor.

The entries are 3 to 4 pages in length, usually with a black-and-white photograph. Each begins with a one-paragraph overview, including the leader's major contributions to business, industry, and society. Next comes a summary of their personal life, with family history, vital statistics, education, affiliations, and awards, among other items. The section on career details focuses on career highlights and often reports their management style, business philosophy, or development of a product. The final sections are titled "Social and Economic Impact," which contains more in-depth analysis, and "Sources of Information," which lists mailing addresses and Websites. A basic bibliography provides suggested readings in monographs, periodicals, and databases. The separately boxed chronology features an easy-to-read list of major dates in the leader's life.

A master index provides easy access to business leaders, companies, and industries. This book is fun to peruse and stop off at any stimulating name. Its value as a basic reference tool for students seeking quick data on business leaders is great. This one volume will be much easier to use than the traditional biographical research tools and it is suited for high school and undergraduate students as well as public library patrons. [R: BR, Sept/Oct 99, p. 65; SLJ, Aug 99, p. 182]—**Georgia Briscoe**

Dictionaries and Encyclopedias

P

64.   **Encyclopedia of African American Business History.** Juliet E. K. Walker, ed. Westport, Conn., Greenwood Press, 1999. 721p. index. $115.00. ISBN 0-313-29549-2.

Containing essays by more than 100 contributors, this encyclopedia covers a wide variety of topics from the seventeenth century through the 1990s on black business history, biographies of notable business people, and surveys of black participation in selected industries. Each entry includes a selected bibliography. An introductory chapter provides an overview of the topic followed by more than 200 alphabetically arranged entries, ranging from one to several pages. The work concludes with a chronology of black business history, a select bibliography, and an index. A fine ready-reference source, this work culls a vast amount of material covering an eclectic range of subjects, including insurance companies, black slave owners, sports enterprises and entrepreneurs, women business enterprises, and biographies of publisher John H. Johnson and black business scholar Joseph A. Pierce. The selected bibliography at the end of each entry provides invaluable citations for students and scholars looking to pursue further research.

This work, however, is not without its flaws. The entry on the "Nation of Islam Enterprises," for example, contains erroneous material and also omits significant information (i.e., the history of the sect—Farrakhan's death threats against Malcolm X are omitted as are the use of federal money to subsidize questionable housing project security and the unconscionable marketing of quack AIDS drugs at drastically inflated prices). Nevertheless, this unique work is generally an outstanding reference source on the various aspects of the history of African American business.—**Donald Altschiller**

C

65.   Foldvary, Fred E. **Dictionary of Free-Market Economics.** Northhampton, Mass., Edward Elgar, 1998. 307p. $85.00. ISBN 1-85898-432-7.

This is the first dictionary of free market terms. It includes entries on the theory of market economy, empirical studies of economic freedom, and informative biographies of free-market economists. The dictionary provides definitions of terms that other economic dictionaries omit, such as "intervention," "regulation," and "public goods." It also includes topic terms used in law, finance, and classical liberal philosophy as well as basic terms used in economics. Well-known economists' biographies, such as Keynes and Friedman as well as obscure ones such as Gerard Debren, a Nobel Prize winner for economics, are also included.

The dictionary is sorted alphabetically with extensive cross-referencing. A solid bibliography of source materials is also provided. This book is valuable to the student of economics and to the professor as well. Librarians will love it too for the short concise definitions. [R: Choice, June 99, p. 1764]—**Kay M. Stebbins**

C, P

66. **The New Palgrave Dictionary of Economics and the Law.** Peter Newman, ed. New York, Stockton Press, 1998. 3v. index. $550.00/set. ISBN 1-56159-215-3.

The field of law and economics, although rooted in the contributions of David Hume and Adam Smith and subsequently of Jeremy Bentham and Friedrich Hayek, experienced its main stimulus from the writings of Ronald Coase, and began with what the editor of these volumes regards as a "meteoric rise" in the 1970s and 1980s. The field has developed interconnections, one of which is demonstrated in the companion *New Palgrave Dictionary of Money and Finance* (see ARBA 93, entry 242), while several indicate the practical applications in the transforming post-Communist economies and in the less developed countries. The new field takes account of conventions, customs, and norms in the mix of formal and intellectual problems and solutions.

In the 3 volumes under review the "List of Entries" includes cross-references. A "Subject Classification," which is divided into 7 main categories of society, economy, policy, law in general, common law systems, regulation, and biographies, is subdivided into subheadings, and those are in turn (in a separate listing) helpfully divided into the subjects of the essays found in the 3 volumes under review. This reviewer missed the inclusion of "Subject Classification" in the "List of Entries," which might have helped a general user of the dictionary in finding areas of interest. Classifications are found at the end of each essay, together with cross-references and exhaustive bibliographies. Volume 3 also contains a list of relevant "Statutes, Treaties, and Directives" (many of them emanating from the European Community Council), and a 10-page, double-column list of "Cases." In addition to their usefulness as a focused reference source, these volumes could be used as a textbook, or as a source of individual readings in a course on law and economics, crafted according to the interests or needs of the instructor. About 300 contributors to these volumes hail from many countries, most from the United States, Canada, the United Kingdom, Italy, Germany, Holland, Greece, and international organizations. Their essays are uniformly excellent, informative, and helpful for deeper research. [R: BL, 1 Oct 98, pp. 364-365; LJ, Dec 98, pp. 92, 94; RUSQ, Spring 99, pp. 310-311]—**Bogdan Mieczkowski**

Handbooks and Yearbooks

C, P, S

67. **The Value of a Dollar 1860-1999: Prices and Incomes in the United States.** 2d ed. Scott Derks, ed. Lakeville, Conn., Grey House Publishing, 1999. 493p. illus. $90.00. ISBN 1-891482-49-1.

The purchasing history of the U.S. dollar for the last century and a half is interesting to most of us. We can see what the cost of food and clothing in our grandparents' and parents' childhood and young adult lives were, as well as our own lives. This 2d edition of *The Value of a Dollar* records the actual prices of thousands of items purchased from the Civil War to the present time, and provides information about investment options and income opportunities. It has been revised and updated to include chapters on the four-year periods of 1990 to 1994 and 1995 to 1999.

Each five-year chapter contains a chronology of key economic and historic events from each year, a report on per capita consumer prices of the day nationwide, and a selection of investment returns excerpted from Federal Reserve reports. Data in the chapters also include a selection of jobs listed in major newspapers' want ads and a list of national average wage paid for representative jobs traced annually and based on the Bureau of Economic Analysis. There is also a regional report of food prices compiled from the Bureau of Labor Statistics, a selection of prices chosen from the advertisements of the day, a selection of representative items tracked annually, and a selection of anecdotal prices and income reports from publications of the period.

There is an appendix that tracks the prices of the federal gasoline tax rate, the public debt of the federal government, the postal rate for first class mail, public elementary and secondary expenditure per pupil, federal hourly minimum wage, average cost of electricity, college tuition costs and expenditures, and other interesting historical prices.

This book is for high school and college students who are doing historical economic research. It is recommended for high school, college, and public libraries for their social history collections. [R: Choice, Oct 99, p. 316]—**Kay M. Stebbins**

Quotation Books

P

68.   **The Wiley Book of Business Quotations.** By Henry Ehrlich. New York, John Wiley, 1998. 430p. index. $30.00. ISBN 0-471-18207-9.

Could the proliferation of books of business quotations be related to the strong economy? Titles published in the past five years include *Bartlett's Book of Business Quotations* (Little, Brown, 1994), *The Ultimate Book of Business Quotations* (AMACOM, 1998), *Forbes Book of Business Quotations* (Black Dog & Leventhal, 1997), and *Quotable Business* (2d ed.; Random House, 1999).

Now comes another compilation of more than 5,000 quotes taken from the business press, books, television, and speeches. The focus is on themes that have developed over the past 20 years. Topics such as workplace diversity, the Information Superhighway, globalization, business education, e-commerce, deregulation, and the Asian market are included. The importance of the global economy is reflected in sections on Europe and Asia (subdivided by country), NAFTA, and the role of developing countries.

The quotes are organized under 45 main subjects with subcategories under most of them. For the most part, quotes are arranged chronologically. Sections begin with a few historical quotes to illustrate how things have changed. For example, the "glass ceiling" category opens with a turn-of-the-century quote by James Fargo, president of American Express, where he threatens to close the company rather than hire a female employee. The quote is followed by numerous 1990s quotes by women executives. The scope of the quotations is broad, from well-known names such as Bill Gates, Peter Drucker, Ross Perot, Ted Turner ("You're toast") and Bill Clinton to statements by eight-year-olds, college students, and cartoon characters (although *Dilbert* is not quoted).

Do not look here for the traditional epigrammatic one-liner. Ehrlich admittedly takes liberties with the term "quotation." He includes vignettes, paragraphs from articles and speeches that may contain an idea, lists, and statistics. The context for entries is given, and sometimes crucial, to the meaning of the quote. This is especially true of those quotes that are responses to questions (i.e., "Are you kidding? We reserve that right for the poor, the young, the black and the stupid"). These quotes would be meaningless without elaboration.

The author's approach makes for interesting and entertaining browsing. Speakers at the local Chamber of Commerce searching for an idea for a speech will find the collection useful. But researchers, speechwriters, and students looking for a specific quote or quotes on a topic will be better off using periodical, speech, and transcript databases or Websites that will give more complete bibliographic information. There are a name index of people quoted and a company index, but the table of contents is the only guide to topics. An alphabetical keyword index would have been useful. This is a fun collection but there is nothing here that cannot be found elsewhere.

—**Marlene M. Kuhl**

BUSINESS SERVICES
AND INVESTMENT GUIDES

P

69.   **The CRB Commodity Yearbook 1998.** By Bridge Information Systems America. New York, John Wiley, 1998. 316p. $99.95. ISBN 0-471-24705-7.

Researchers seeking commodities data generally must consult many sources to obtain a thorough overview. Sources such as Catherine Friedman's *Commodity Prices* (see ARBA 92, entry 159) and Karen Chapman's *Commodity Prices Locator* (see ARBA 90, entry 274) are excellent bibliographic guides, but do not provide data. Since 1939, the Commodity Research Bureau has been a leading source for commodities statistics and market overviews. Special topics are profiled in each edition (1998 featured El Niño). The bulk of this work is devoted to market surveys and data in both table and chart form for over 100 commodities and futures. While historical information is usually provided, frequency varies. Sources are always cited; this practice allows the researcher to go to the original source for more detailed information. Additional features, such as volume for international futures exchanges and a table of conversion factors, further aid the researcher. For those needing more frequent data, the yearbook is also available on compact or floppy disk with quarterly updates.—**Bobray Bordelon**

P

70.   Ryland, Philip. **Pocket Investor.** New York, John Wiley, 1998. 213p. (The Economist Books). $14.95pa. ISBN 0-471-29597-3.

As its name implies, *Pocket Investor* is a compact volume that is loaded with helpful information about the intricate and sometimes baffling subject of investments. It is one of a series of "pocket" books on management from *The Economist*, a long-standing and highly respected journal. The author is the deputy editor of *Investors Chronicle*. The purpose of *Pocket Investor* is to bring clarity to the complexities and jargon of the investment world. It achieves this purpose by providing a wealth of information in a convenient format that is easy to read. A unique aspect of *Pocket Investor* is that it reflects both U.S. and UK terminology.

Pocket Investor is divided into 3 parts. The 1st presents 4 essays on investing: the returns that can be expected from the market; whether excess returns are really possible; lessons from the most successful investors, such as Warren Buffet and Sir John Templeton; and the flaws in conventional stock market wisdom. These essays are concise, informative, and easy to read. A brief 5th essay describes differences in investment terminology between the United States and the United Kingdom. This is helpful because *Pocket Investor* includes information reflecting both countries' systems. The 2d part comprises the bulk of the volume and is a glossary of investment terms. Definitions are generous, sometimes providing a page or more of text. Figures and tables are included, although the content is primarily text. Interspersed throughout the glossary are quotes from famous people, from both within and outside of the financial world. Some of the terms included are quite advanced and reflect the world-wide investment arena, making *Pocket Investor* a unique and important reference source for patrons who need more than just the basics, although basic terms such as *asset* and *common stock* are also covered. Commonly used abbreviations are cross-referenced, as are country-specific terms. The 3d part is devoted to appendixes, with tables on stock and bond returns, market data, investing formulas, accounting terminology differences between the United States and the United Kingdom, and two pages of references of recommended readings. *Pocket Investor* is small enough for a briefcase, yet the typeset is clear and not too small.

In spite of a wealth of other choices, *Pocket Investor* would be a unique and appropriate addition to any public library's reference collection. Information included in *Pocket Investor* is succinct and easy to read, yet still comprehensive enough to reflect the complexity of the investment field. In addition, *Pocket Investor*'s inclusion of more global terms is useful in an investment environment that is no longer confined by geography. *Pocket Investor* would also be a good addition to collections supporting academic business programs and in libraries serving banking, investment, accounting, and consulting personnel.—**Sara Anne Hook**

CONSUMER GUIDES

C, P

71.   **The Catalog of Catalogs VI: The Complete Mail-Order Directory.** Edward L. Palder, ed. Bethesda, Md., Woodbine House, 1999. 567p. index. $25.95pa. ISBN 1-890627-08-9.

The 6th edition of this biennial and respected publication of American mail-order companies includes almost 15,000 entries. This is an increase of over 1,000 listings from the previous edition. The reader will find companies listed under 920 subject categories including 70 that are new to this edition, such as tandem bicycles, pasta sauces, totem poles, paintball, and yo-yos. Each listing includes the name of the company, address, a brief description of the product line, telephone number, and e-mail or Internet address. This title will see a lot of use in public library reference departments for those clients attempting to identify buyers for their product lines or suppliers for their stores. Shoppers will also find this a very tempting book to browse through.

This type of publication is never completely comprehensive or accurate since businesses come and go. The choice of subject categories can be debated, but with 920 subject categories, the editor has attempted to be specific in a way that would be useful to consumers.

Because we do hear about fraudulent mail-order operations and companies changing their names or moving, the compiler requests that users inform him of any problems so that they can be addressed in the next edition. The compiler also provides a few tips on how to shop online.—**Judith J. Field**

P

72.   **Consumer Sourcebook.** 12th ed. Sonya D. Hill, ed. Farmington Hills, Mich., Gale, 1999. 1165p. index. $265.00. ISBN 0-7876-3344-5. ISSN 0738-0518.

The first *Consumer Sourcebook* (CS) came out in 1974 just after the Consumer Protection Agency was formed by Congress. The organization, content, and entries have all been modified several times since then. However, the outstanding highlight of this edition is the inclusion of the Internet Database Subsection for each of the 17 fields with 360-plus online information sources. Therefore, today's edition of the CS is a very comprehensive guide to more than 17,500 free or low-cost programs, publications, multimedia sources, and services offered by a variety of public and private groups. For this update, some 7,000 of these groups were contacted.

Each chapter includes descriptive listings for live (media), electronic, and print resources; and within the chapter, listings are arranged in subsections by type of resource. The "User's Guide" is lengthy and thorough, giving users high-school age and above easy access to a variety of current, reliable information on consumerism. A unique feature of this guide is the inclusion of an issues list within the description of each chapter.

Another important section is the "Consumer Tips." Useful subsections here include "Getting the Most for Your Money and Avoiding Consumer Problems," "How to Write a Complaint Letter," "The Typical American Shopper," and more. Two appendixes, "Hotlines and Clearinghouses" and "Testing Laboratories," and a combined alphabetic and subject index complete the volume. Most libraries will want to provide this excellent resource for their clients.—**Susan C. Awe**

P

73.   Norrgard, Lee E., and Julia M. Norrgard. **Consumer Fraud: A Reference Handbook.** Santa Barbara, Calif., ABC-CLIO, 1998. 338p. index. (Contemporary World Issues). $45.00. ISBN 0-87436-991-6.

Part of ABC-CLIO's award-winning Contemporary World Issues series, this work reveals the spectrum of consumer fraud, from work-at-home and investment scams to credit issues and high tech merchandising. By learning what consumer fraud involves, how society is affected, and what tactics are used to combat it, readers may be able to understand their own vulnerability and avoid being taken. However, everyone pays for consumer fraud in the increased prices businesses must charge to recover their loses.

This vast, ubiquitous topic begins with a chronology starting from Hammurabi in 1800 B.C.E. and continues through telemarketing and car leasing on the brink of the twenty-first century. Brief biographical sketches of men and women, including three presidents, who either made consumer issues a career, or in the case of the presidents, played a critical role in governmental policy and legislation are included. Chapter 4 is titled "Documents, Laws, and Regulations"; "Directory of Agencies and Organizations," which is arranged alphabetically by state, is the 5th chapter. The final two chapters are annotated bibliographies of print and nonprint resources. Especially noteworthy are the 29 Websites listed.

A short glossary, a print advertisement that has the appearance of a news story or editorial, and a detailed index complete the volume. This unique, authoritative reference resource should be found in most public libraries and in business collections. Citizens, activists, students, and researchers will find a lot of information here. [R: Choice, June 99, p. 1765]—**Susan C. Awe**

FINANCE AND BANKING

P, S

74.   Allen, Larry. **Encyclopedia of Money.** Santa Barbara, Calif., ABC-CLIO, 1999. 328p. illus. index. $75.00. ISBN 1-57607-037-9.

Written for the general reader rather than for the scholar, this compilation of some 300 brief essays (500 to 1,000 words in length) presents a variety of historical information regarding important monetary experiences that have influenced the evolution of money and banking. Although the author indicates an intent not to dwell on proving or disproving any specific theories of monetary economics, it is evident that certain exceptions prove the rule. Likewise, theories are brought into discussion only when they result in bringing some order out of chaos. In essence, the guiding principle is identification of the common characteristics that are shared within and between various monetary systems.

The work opens with an alphabetic list of entries, followed by a brief preface and introduction. Some entries include illustrations and all include cross-references and a brief bibliography of resources. A full bibliography and index supplement the main text.

To trained economists, this work might prove too vague and unrewarding. However, to the general reader, armchair historian, and seeker of curious facts, the work should be quite fulfilling. High school, public, and college library users might benefit from the clarity of discussions. [R: BL, 15 Nov 99, pp. 649-652]

—**Edmund F. SantaVicca**

P

75.   Rider, A. J. **The International Dictionary of Personal Finance.** Harrogate, England, Take That; distr., North Pomfret, Vt., Trafalgar Square, 1999. 188p. $11.95pa. ISBN 1-873668-54-6.

The number of financial and business dictionaries published each year can be overwhelming. Since most libraries cannot buy them all, finding the ones that are best for specific clientele can be very challenging. Many focus on the United States or try to cover the international scene comprehensively. Rider's new paperback dictionary focuses on two major markets: the United States and the United Kingdom. However, common terms exclusive to other parts of the world are occasionally included. It is written for the consumer and focuses on annuities, banking, bonds, business, equity-based investments and mutual funds, insurance, pensions, taxation, and wills. If a term is used exclusively in one country, it makes this distinction. The definitions are concise and sometimes include usage, but can be overly simplistic. While a number of less familiar financial terms (contango, kangaroos, peppercorn rent) are covered, some that appear regularly in the business press (hedge funds, poison pill) are not. A peculiarity is using British spellings when referring to exclusively American terms. A more comprehensive, albeit more dated and expensive alternative is *Handbook of International Financial Terms* (see ARBA 98, entry 184). Recommended only for comprehensive investment research collections or libraries requiring an inexpensive international financial dictionary.—**Bobray Bordelon**

C, P, S

76.   Shook, R. J. **Wall Street Dictionary.** Franklin Lakes, N.J., Career Press, 1999. 506p. $11.99pa. ISBN 1-56414-402-X.

This is a necessary reference book in any library's collection. Shook has written a complete reference tool for those interested in the definitions of basic to advanced financial terms. Recommended for anyone in need of a reference tool on financial terms.

However, this book is not recommended for financial analysts or special libraries in businesses. This is not a good reference tool for patrons who need complete and detailed explanations of financial terms. Shook's description of terms is frequently short and sometimes inaccurate. Definitions of some terms are no more than a few words. For example, "interest" is defined as "the amount of money a lender loans a borrower to pay for using the borrower's principal." What the author means is that interest is the amount of money a borrower pays to use a lender's principal. It is also the amount of money a lender or bank patron receives for loaning money to a borrower or a bank. "Intangible cost" is defined as "a business cost that is tax deductible." In fact, intangible cost are costs that are difficult to define, such as employee productivity. Finally, many economists would disagree with Shook's definition of the Friedman Theory. Most economists would define the Friedman Theory as a theory of how the money supply influences long-term inflation rates and, while it may have short-term impacts on a country's economy, the money supply has little to do with a country's economic condition in the long term.

More than 5,000 terms are defined in this text. Overall it is a good text for beginning business students or the general population interested in business terms. However, some terms are not fully defined or are misrepresented. This is unfortunate for a reference text that patrons rely on to provide complete and accurate information. [R: LJ, 1 May 99, p. 70]—**Bruce Kingma**

INDUSTRY AND MANUFACTURING

Handbooks and Yearbooks

P

77.   **Dun and Bradstreet/Gale Industry Reference Handbooks: Hospitality.** Stacy A. McConnell and Linda D. Hall, eds. Farmington Hills, Mich., Gale, 1999. 722p. $99.00pa. ISBN 0-7876-3776-9.

This survey is one of nine planned to be published covering the most popular industries. Each will be updated annually. The information is a compilation of other Dun and Bradstreet and Gale reference books and as such represents material that is already owned in many libraries, but is collected here for convenience.

The opening chapter is an overview that describes the industry, its history, its key players, its workforce, and the relevance of the data collected. Particularly useful are the surveys of trends and future expectations of the industry. Next are the performance indicators and industry norms that compare a variety of data (employees, solvency ratios, profitability, and so on) by SIC code (Standard Industrial Classification). Data are from 1995 to 1997.

The largest section is an alphabetic company directory with address information, sales, employees, and private and public status. The data are similar to those of any Dun and Bradstreet directory. This is supplemented with ranking lists by sales (from 1st to 4,859th) and by employment. Next is a section chronicling merger and acquisition activity during 1997 and 1998, arranged by company, with a citation of the announcement from *Nation's Restaurant News*, *PR Newswire*, and other sources.

The associations list is selected from the Encyclopedia of Associations series and seems unnecessary here. The usual hotel and restaurant associations and unions are suitable, but the Bob Crane Memorial Fan Club seems to be a curious inclusion. The consultants and trade publications sections are adapted from more of Gale's commonly available reference books.

The indexes are essential for a collection like this, and the master index does cover each of the above sections. The geographic index is by state, not city and state, and there are very useful conversion lists of SIC to NAICS (North American Industrial Classification System, the successor to Standard Industrial Classification) and from NAICS to SIC.

This work is a useful compilation combining many features from two of the best-known reference publishers, and can be recommended for libraries that are willing to acquire it annually, either selectively or as an entire series. However, the majority of this information will already be available in a reasonably equipped reference collection, and each library will have to decide the ultimate cost of convenience.—**Gary R. Cocozzoli**

INTERNATIONAL BUSINESS

General Works

Dictionaries and Encyclopedias

P

78.   Hinkelman, Edward G. **Dictionary of International Trade: Handbook of the Global Trade Community.** 3d ed. San Rafael, Calif., World Trade Press, 1999. 412p. illus. $32.00pa. ISBN 1-885073-82-8.

Precise communication and understanding are essential to the conduct of international trade. To enable transactions to flow efficiently and rapidly, specialized terms and concepts have evolved. It is necessary to understand those terms and concepts in order to engage in foreign commerce or to evaluate international transactions. *Dictionary of International Trade* by Hinkelman, an international economist, author, and experienced importer/exporter, provides a concise, yet comprehensive, reference for locating appropriate terms for verifying one's understanding of concepts. More than simply a dictionary, the book contains useful appendixes that include data on acronyms, abbreviations, international dialing codes, maps, world currencies, types of business entities engaged in international trade, weights/measures, incoterms (i.e., terms of trade), letters of credit, and ocean/air freight containers. The author has included extensive lists of resources for those requiring more detailed information as well as lists of service providers. The dictionary represents a single source for obtaining much basic information on international trade. It should prove useful to importers, exporters, insurers, bankers, shippers, students, economists, and government officials, as well as readers who have a general interest in world commerce.

—**William C. Struning**

Handbooks and Yearbooks

C, P

79. **International Financial Statistics Yearbook 1998.** Washington, D.C., International Monetary Fund; distr., Lanham, Md., Bernan Associates, 1998. 961p. $65.00pa. ISBN 155775-749-6. ISSN 0250-7463.

This yearbook contains both worldwide and country-specific financial data for the years 1968 through 1997. The available data from 1948 through 1967 are maintained in the International Monetary Fund's Economic Information System. The yearbook is arranged in four sections, preceded by a detailed introduction that explains the arrangement and compilation of the tables. Section 1 consists of time-series charts on international reserves, interest rates, exchange rates, prices, unit values and commodity prices, and trade and national accounts. Section 2 presents world financial statistical tables on exchange rates, fund accounts, international reserves, measures of money, interest rates, real effective exchange rate indexes, prices, wages, production and employment, international trade, balance of payments, national accounts, and commodity prices. Section 3, the largest part of the volume, has individual country tables and section 4 contains country notes. The publisher indicates that additional country notes are contained in the monthly issues of *International Financial Statistics*.

This is an essential economics and business reference work for any library that serves a clientele interested in international affairs and world trade. Although the presentation of data is clear and readable, some novices may be put off by the seemingly arcane annotation system that the IMF uses throughout the volume. In addition, the country notes provide essential, useful information about the history of international liquidity, interest rates, government finance, monetary authorities, and banking institutions that gives context to the data presented.

—**Robert H. Burger**

C, P

80. **The Washington Almanac of International Trade and Business, 1998.** Gary P. Osifchin and William O. Scouton, eds. Washington, D.C., Almanac; distr., Lanham, Md., Bernan Associates, 1998. 840p. illus. $225.00pa. ISBN 1-886222-10-X.

The almanac, primarily a directory of information on international trade and foreign policy, is sponsored by the Greater Washington Board of Trade, and includes a brief introductory section describing that organization and extolling the virtues of the Washington, D.C., area as a place to do business. This is the 4th edition of a work originally published in 1994 as *The International Washington Almanac* (see ARBA 95, entry 760). It was issued for the first time under the current title in 1995 (see ARBA 97, entry 230).

It consists of 3 main parts: Foreign Diplomatic Corps in the United States, The U.S. Government: Who Does What?, and Other Entities Dealing with Foreign Trade. In addition there is an index and a five-page section on advertisements. The 1st part is divided into 4 sections: a directory of foreign ambassadors and staff arranged in alphabetic order by country, a directory of commercial contacts at foreign embassies in Washington, a list of foreign consular offices in the U.S., and a list of local holidays (i.e., the national holidays of other countries) alphabetically by country with a two-page world timetable, listing the time in each country when it is noon in Washington, D.C.

Part 2 is divided into 3 sections. The 1st section on general export information includes 4 nondirectory subsections: export services, export regulations, customs benefits and tax incentives, U.S. export and the economy, and also an export glossary. The 2d section covers the federal legislature, and it is essentially a series of directories of U.S. congressional contacts. The 3d section is a series of directories for the Executive Branch.

Part 3 has 13 sections, including directories of multinational banks, the International Monetary Fund, international interest groups, foreign agents, Washington's international press, world trade centers, international business learning opportunities in the Greater Washington area, and chambers of commerce.

In the foreword the editors say, "Somewhere in this book every user can find an idea, a name, a telephone or fax number that will be useful." This is undoubtedly true; the almanac contains an enormous amount of information, but it is presented in the complex organization described above. There is an index, but it lists only organizations, countries, and general topics. The index does not list states, cities, products, or people. This means it is relatively easy to find information for general topics. However, it requires intimate familiarity with the complex arrangement of the sections, parts, and subsections to find information related to a particular product or to find agencies, organizations, and contacts relevant to international business interests in any specialized area of complex situation.

This work consolidates information found in a wide variety of other sources. However, nothing contains all the information gathered here. The almanac should provide practically all the information needed by anyone interested in international business. An electronic version would be superb, but even in its current less-than-user-friendly print version, it is recommended to any library with an interest in international business.

—**Richard H. Swain**

P

81. **World Development Indicators, 1998.** Washington, D.C., World Bank; distr., Lanham, Md., Bernan Associates, 1998. 389p. index. $60.00pa. ISBN 0-8213-4124-3.

This is the 2d edition of the annual *World Development Indicators*. Most of the tables cover 148 countries with populations of more than 1 million. Generally, the indicators are given for a recent year (often 1996) and an earlier year. Time series of primary data can be found on the *World Development Indicators* CD-ROM, going back to 1960 when possible. The information is divided into 6 sections, each with an introductory essay of less than 10 pages that focuses on a few issues relevant to that section. The 1st section, "World View," reports on progress toward international development goals. A section follows on people, which includes population and labor force, income, education, and health data. The 3d section on environment has data primarily on water and air pollution, energy, land use, agriculture, and urbanization. "Economy," the 4th section, includes data on, but not limited to, the structure of output, exports, imports, and demand; government finance; monetary indicators and prices; and external debt. Next comes a section on states and markets. It has information on credit, the stock market, portfolio regulation and risk, tax policies, defense expenditures, state-owned enterprises, transport, and information among others. The final section, "Global Links," emphasizes merchandise trade, tariff barriers, global financial flows, and aid. The data come from a variety of sources. Every table has detailed information about the data—its source, collection, and definition of terms. This volume is a comprehensive source of data on most of the countries in the world. It is convenient and a valuable first (or only) resource to the desired information on a topic or country. It is likely to become a basic and much-used source.—**J. E. Weaver**

C, P

82. **World Investment Report 1999: Foreign Direct Investment and the Challenge of Development.** New York, United Nations, 1999. 541p. $45.00pa. ISBN 92-1-112440-9. S/N E.99.II.D.3.

This series from the United Nations Conference on Trade and Development (UNCTAD) provides an annual overview of foreign direct investment emphasizing the relationship between transnational corporations (TNCs) and economic development. The series will interest selectors for larger business or government document collections.

This 1999 report has a foreword from UN Secretary General Kofi Annan dated July 1999. He indicates this issue focuses on investment's impact on key aspects of development, including availability of capital, employment prospects, technical and skill levels, competitiveness, and environmental protection. It has 2 sections, each with multiple chapters. The 1st provides an overview of global and regional trends in investment; listings and statistics on the largest TNCs from the developed and developing countries and from the Central European transition economies; discussions of mergers, acquisitions, and strategic partnership trends; and policy changes, both international and national. The 2d presents background and analysis on the roles of TNCs in economic and social development processes and ways to maximize positive, and minimize the negative, impacts on host societies. Topics include discussions of environmental, technological, skills, competitiveness, and employment issues. The report combines extensive text with approximately 75 topical boxes of text, 76 figures, and 63 statistical tables. No index is provided, but there are detailed contents with lists of boxes, figures, and tables.

For suitable collections, this series and volume add valuable overviews of often ambiguous relationships between economic development, foreign investment, and TNCs in various regions of the world. This work belongs in larger economics research, academic, and general collections, as well as appropriate special ones, funding permitting.—**Nigel Tappin**

Latin America and
the Caribbean

C

83.   **Economic Survey of Latin America and the Caribbean 1997-1998.** 50th ed. By the Economic Commission for Latin America and the Caribbean. New York, United Nations, 1998. 368p. $75.00pa. (with disks). ISBN 92-1-121230-8. ISSN 0257-2184. S/N E.98.II.G.2.

This 50th edition (see ARBA 98, entry 210) provides an overview of the economy in 1997 and the first half of 1998, examines the economic performance of the region in 1997, analyzes some aspects of the economic situation during the first half of 1998, reports on 20 countries of Latin America and on the situation in the countries of the English-speaking Caribbean, and a final section reviews the 50 years of the *Economic Survey of Latin American and the Caribbean*. With the book is a set of two diskettes, which provide ready access to data for recent years and permits the preparation of spreadsheets covering a longer time period.

The regional economic survey reviews macroeconomic policy; economic performance; policy lessons from the Asian crisis; and structural reforms, including general trends, banking sector, capital markets, labor reforms, and trade reforms. Economic activity, inflation, investment and saving, employment and wages, and the external sector of the region are reviewed as well. Each country survey reviews general economic trends, economic policy, the main variables of economic activity, prices, wages and employment, and the external sector.

The study of the *Economic Survey* is an important and essential part of the text for academic libraries whose curriculums include Latin American studies. It is essential to a broad understanding of the regional and global economies.—**Gerald D. Moran**

LABOR

Career Guides

P, S

84.   **Career Exploration on the Internet: A Student's Guide to More Than 300 Web Sites!** Elizabeth H. Oakes, ed. Chicago, Ferguson, 1998. 208p. index. $15.95pa. ISBN 0-89434-240-1.

The Internet is transforming many facets of life. Its impact on the job search is dramatic for those in business, technical, and professional fields. This volume is a comprehensive narrative directory opening abundant information resources for anyone with access to the World Wide Web. Throughout the book, sites are listed and given helpful annotations that include scope, approach, and deficiencies where they exist.

Aimed primarily at the student or newly graduated job-seeker, these resources are most helpful for the job search, with chapters on how to find out about companies, nonprofit and public organizations, and international careers. Volunteer, internship, and summer job information and listings are covered also. Employment agencies, professional recruiting firms, and professional associations, as well as Websites of individual companies, are listed.

The opening chapters focus on sites for career exploration—sources of information on various fields and occupations. Some sites, frequently academic, offer self-assessment tools as well as occupational information. Clearinghouse sites are offered as "headquarters" for searching for career information. An individual's decision-making process may be made more difficult by such an abundance of information.

This guide assumes the reader is computer-proficient, particularly with the Internet. The style is lively and fast-paced, muck like where the listings lead. The only problem is that this means of job searching takes time and effort and diligence is clearly provided. This volume and others like it are essential tools for libraries and career centers. Anything in this venue will be outdated the minute after it is written, much less published, but the key resources and links will most likely linger even after newer and better sites come online. Thus, it provides an excellent base. [R: BR, Nov/Dec 98, p. 66]—**Barbara Conroy**

C, P

85.   **Career Opportunities in Television, Cable, Video, and Multimedia.** 4th ed. New York, Checkmark Books/Facts on File, 1999. 274p. illus. index. $35.00; $18.95pa. ISBN 0-8160-3940-2; 0-8160-3941-0pa.

This book offers coverage of a wide variety of career opportunities in the popular and expanding fields of broadcasting (radio aside), video technologies, and multimedia production of entertainment and information resources. It is an update of the 3d edition published nine years ago under the title *Career Opportunities in Television, Cable, and Video*. Nine years is a long time in these fields, and an update is welcome. The industry has expanded, and job responsibilities and titles reflect this. The whole new area of multimedia, including its Web aspects, has been added.

The introductory overview that precedes each section has been significantly updated to reflect changes in the field, new terminology, and to bring the numerous and varied statistics up-to-date.

Well organized and well laid out with better typography than the 3d edition, the material is basically divided into a television broadcasting and a cable, video, and media section. Within each of these two areas, the book is arranged by job function within a few broad areas of expertise. Each includes a job description, salary range, the education and skills required or expected, and information on unions. Within each of the two areas the book offers broad coverage of job opportunities. Nontechnical jobs as they relate to the electronic media industry are covered.

The television section is divided up by function within the areas of management, programming, production, engineering, performance, advertising, and news reporting. The functions are listed alphabetically within each area and are also included in the subject index at the back. In the 2d section, the functions or areas of competency are organized more under subject areas in which cable, video, and multimedia are used. Employment in private industry, government, the health field, the education field, commercial technical products, training, and producing (e.g., managing, engineering, programming, writing) are specified, and specific areas of competency are then arranged under each.

This guide is highly recommended for both public and academic libraries. Readers should find it comprehensive, readable, and a good place to start in seeking vocational information in electronic media production.

—**Florence W. Jones**

P, S

86.   **The Complete Guide to Environmental Careers in the 21st Century: The Environmental Careers Organization.** Kevin Doyle, ed. Washington, D.C., Island Press, 1999. 447p. illus. index. $39.95; $17.95pa. ISBN 1-55963-585-1; 1-55963-586-Xpa.

The Complete Guide to Environmental Careers in the 21st Century is a thoroughly updated, revised, and re-titled 3d edition of the *Complete Guide to Environmental Careers* (1993). This is an outstanding resource that is produced by the Environmental Careers Organization (ECO), an important nonprofit group dedicated to protecting and enhancing the environment through development of professionals, promotion of careers, and inspirational sharing. The book supports these goals very well. There is a 3-chapter overview of the environmental job field that is complete with statistics, major drivers behind trends, and useful advice. The remainder of the book provides detailed information in each chapter on where the jobs are, what is growing and what is not, earnings, education requirements, excellent resources in print and on the Web, case studies of active professionals, and profiles of people making a difference.

The "at-a-glance" section at the beginning of each detailed chapter is a valuable resource on its own. For example, in the chapter devoted to the planning segment of environmental professionals, the number of planners nationwide is given, along with the percentage of growth per year and predictions about future growth; a public, private, and nonprofit sectors breakdown; a list of 18 key job titles; a list of influential organizations; and a salary overview. Useful as an encyclopedia, dictionary, and bibliography, this is a resource highly recommended for all types of libraries.—**Barbara Delzell**

P

87. Cubbage, Sue, and Marcia Williams. **National Job Hotline Directory: The Job-Finder's Hot List.** River Forest, Ill., Planning/Communications, 1999. 376p. illus. $16.95pa. ISBN 1-884587-12-7.

Intended for job hunters and based on the authors' queries, this directory identifies 6,500 job hotlines operated by employers in the United States and Canada. An introduction discusses the search process, use of the telephone as part of a strategy, and its relationship to Internet and more traditional employment resources (e.g., newspapers).

Arranged alphabetically by state, chapters provide key state contacts and information. They are divided into as many as 10 topical categories, with alphabetic entries consisting of name (e.g., companies, agencies), city, and telephone number. Additional sections offer national and toll-free number hotlines, Canadian listings, free World Wide Web updates (http://www.jobfindersonline.com), and discount coupons. The separate resource lists refer job seekers only to other publications available from the publisher rather than important works available elsewhere.

This volume contains a lot of valuable information and deserves the attention of the serious job seeker. It has the makings of an excellent reference tool; however, several flaws should be noted. The lack of descriptive abstracts identifying types of jobs used by an employer and more specific topical divisions increases both time and monetary costs. An alphabetic list of all companies and agencies would improve access and assist those who have identified an employer but not a location. These limitations make it less useful for basic reference collections. [R: LJ, 15 Mar 99, pp. 66-68]—**Sandra E. Belanger**

P, S

88. Farr, J. Michael. **America's Top Jobs for College Graduates: Detailed Information on 112 Major Jobs Requiring Four-Year and Higher Degrees.** 3d ed. Indianapolis, Ind., JIST Works, 1999. 532p. index. $16.95pa. ISBN 1-56370-493-5.

This handy reference work is filled with information that anyone thinking of going to college or currently attending college will want to be familiar with. It lists and describes the top jobs for graduates with professional degrees, master's degrees, and bachelor's degrees, as well as those jobs that are often held by college graduates but do not necessarily require a degree.

The 1st section simply lists the top jobs in several different categories, including jobs with the fastest growth, those with the highest pay, and those with the largest number of openings. Section 2 lists the 112 top jobs for college graduates, describing working conditions, skills required, growth projections, training and education required, and typical salary, as well as other facts associated with each career choice. This is the largest part of the work and contains a great deal of information that readers will need. The 3d section provides advice from experts on writing résumés, getting interviews, and defining one's perfect job. The final 2 sections provide articles on the future of the job market and the outlook for college graduates up to the year 2006. The book concludes with a useful bibliography containing hundreds of career-related books, software, and Websites.

This book will be a valuable resource in any high school or university library. The information is both up-to-date and forward projecting, which adds to the books reference value. [R: Choice, Oct 99, pp. 312-314]
—**Shannon M. Graff**

P, S

89. Field, Shelly. **Career Opportunities in the Sports Industry.** 2d ed. New York, Facts on File, 1999. 280p. index. $18.95. ISBN 0-8160-3794-9.

Essential information on career opportunities in most aspects of sports is detailed for professional athletes, sports teams, and for individual sports such as boxing, wrestling, and horse racing. Positions in sports business and administration, coaching and education, officiating, sports journalism, recreation and fitness, sports medicine, and wholesaling and retailing are also described. Even though comprehensive, there are gaps, such as the position of team psychologist and the sport of auto racing.

Entries give a brief overview of the position and then expand that brief information into a longer narrative of two to three pages. Each entry describes the nature of the position together with its salary range and the employment and advancement prospects that can be anticipated. Strategic tips for entering the position are given. Entries also detail the characteristics, experience, and training required. Information about relevant unions and associations is included.

Helpful appendixes supplement the directory. One lists academic degree programs for sports administration and physical education. Sponsors of relevant workshops, seminars, and symposiums are cited in another. Leagues, associations, and unions offer contact points for information and a diligent job search. Listings of promoters and cable/network television sports departments will be helpful for the more specialized seeker.

This update of the 1991 edition evidences the rise in sports interest and participation. The field is, in many ways, informal and the diversity of titles and positions pronounced. This volume presents a useful framework for viewing scope and possibility. The approach is somewhat promotional, blending pragmatic information with enthusiasm for the field. The information has been gathered from interviews, questionnaires, and publications, so it is largely informal.—**Barbara Conroy**

P, S

90.   Field, Shelly. **Career Opportunities in Theater and the Performing Arts.** 2d ed. New York, Checkmark Books/Facts on File, 1999. 257p. index. $35.00; $18.95pa. ISBN 0-8160-3798-1; 0-8160-3799-Xpa.

Although this book was written for "the many thousands of people who aspire to work in theater and other performing arts," it is very basic and would probably not be useful beyond the high school level. It is divided into nine sections according to type of career, such as performing artist or educator. Within each section are descriptions of individual careers (e.g., actor, playwright), which include duties, salary, employment prospects, prerequisites/preparation, advancement, unions/associations, and tips for entry into the career. Position descriptions are generally adequate, but information on education, skills, training, and experience is often vague and frequently states the obvious (e.g., dancers "need to be flexible, agile, and coordinated").

There are several appendixes of varying usefulness. Useful are lists of educational opportunities in the performing arts and of theater and music companies that employ performing arts professionals. Less useful are a list of New York City–area theaters, a list of performing arts periodicals (not annotated), and a rather randomly selected bibliography. Although entries in the list give addresses and telephone numbers, it would have been helpful for the compiler to have included Website addresses, as many organizations and companies listed have excellent Websites that include e-mail addresses as well as information about auditions, educational programs, and job opportunities. In spite of its several flaws, this book covers an unusually wide range of careers, from secretarial to management, and may be appropriate for larger high school and public libraries or where there is particular interest in the performing arts.—**Gari-Anne Patzwald**

P, S

91.   **Job Hunter's Sourcebook: Where to Find Employment Leads and Other Job Search Resources.** 4th ed. Kathleen E. Maki Potts, ed. Farmington Hills, Mich., Gale, 1999. 1079p. index. $90.00. ISBN 0-7876-2645-7. ISSN 1053-1874.

This valuable, comprehensive presentation identifies employment leads and key resources for job-seekers, students, and career counselors. The resources address all levels of employment (executive, technical, professional, and support), enabling individuals to pinpoint essential sources for 193 broadly representative jobs. Organized by occupation, entries include publications, organizations, audiovisual and electronic resources, and other tools to use in designing an effective job-search strategy. These resources provide full citations for print sources, directories, job banks, clearinghouses, employment agencies, and executive search firms and organizations that lead to employment opportunities. Handbooks relevant to a particular occupational field are offered as guides to the job-hunting process particular to those fields. An extensive index offers broad access.

In addition, a 2d section (about 15 percent of the volume) gives citations and brief, informative descriptions of those resources focused on special job-hunting considerations for specific situations. For example, sections cover interviewing skills; government employment; international opportunities; résumés; relocation; and address special populations, such as the disabled, ex-offenders, independent contractors, and minorities.

All aspects of this guide have tapped useful, current, and reliable resources for the ever-challenging and competitive job search. Some of these will be available in local libraries and guidance centers; some might be feasible to purchase. As with any such compilation, it will be outdated quickly with more recent Internet and print resources, but it provides an excellent starting point for anyone exploring employment possibilities, motivating and guiding the pursuit of work.—**Barbara Conroy**

Dictionaries and Encyclopedias

C, S

92.   Murray, R. Emmett. **Lexicon of Labor: More Than 500 Key Terms, Biographical Sketches, and Historical Insights Concerning Labor in America.** New York, New Press, 1998. 207p. $13.95pa. ISBN 1-56584-456-4.

The *Lexicon of Labor* is basically a short, 1-volume encyclopedia of the American labor movement. It has more than 500 entries and provides concise definitions of commonly used labor terms, sketches of important labor figures, descriptions of labor organizations, and information about key events in labor history. Although not comprehensive, this volume's listings are representative and, taken together, they provide a reasonable intro-duction to American labor. Its value would appear, however, to be greatest to those with little knowledge or background in the subject. In this sense the book would seem to be most useful as a reference work for high school and college students, news reporters, and members of the general public, as opposed to scholars and pro-fessionals involved in labor-related work.—**Paul F. Clark**

Handbooks and Yearbooks

C, P, S

93.   **Handbook of U.S. Labor Statistics 1999: Employment, Earnings, Prices, Productivity, and Other Labor Data.** 3d ed. Eva E. Jacobs and Kendall J. Golladay, eds. Lanham, Md., Bernan Associates, 1999. 380p. index. $65.00pa. ISBN 0-89059-182-2. ISSN 1526-2553.

In its 3d edition, the *Handbook of U.S. Labor Statistics* provides a lot of information on population; em-ployment and unemployment by industry; hourly and weekly earnings; consumer and producer prices; export and import prices; consumer expenditures by household type; employment costs; productivity; employment benefits; and other labor data that will be useful to those in business, labor, health care, or the social sciences. Besides current data, the handbook contains both historical data (some back to 1913) on labor market trends and projections of future employment by industry and occupation to 2006. Among the new features in this edition are annual data on employment and unemployment in families, data on employee tenure with current employer, wages and employment by detailed occupation, and union affiliation by industry.

The introductory articles summarize the new Standard Occupational Classification and the revision of the standards for the classification of federal data by race and ethnicity. The tables are organized by subject matter, with each section preceded by descriptions of data sources, definitions, and methodology. The primary focus is on national data, but some of the statistics are by state and city. There are also some international comparisons. The scope and depth of information provided make this an indispensable volume for any library.—**Michele Russo**

C

94.   Lencsis, Peter M. **Workers Compensation: Reference and Guide.** Westport, Conn., Greenwood Press, 1998. 173p. index. $59.95. ISBN 1-56720-174-1.

Workers compensation in the United States is a simple concept in theory, but complex in practice. State, territorial, and federal laws are not uniform and questions frequently arise as to whether "payments are due from workers compensation as opposed to general liability insurance, health insurance, disability insurance, automo-bile no-fault, Social Security, Medicare, and other sources." In this guide to workers compensation, the author does a superb job of sorting out these distinctions. He writes in a simple, direct manner that is comprehensible to the layperson yet respectful of the legal principles and their ramifications.

Lencsis begins his work by tracing the history of workers compensation in Europe, England, and the United States and follows this with forerunner legislation on the federal level in the United States. From here he goes on to discuss current coverage in state and federal workers compensation laws as well as benefits and claims. He then covers related topics, such as the actual insurance policy, endorsements, rates, and experience and retrospective rating. Besides discussing rating and advisory organizations, he devotes a full chapter to special funds and residual markets. The final chapter covers current trends and issues.

Jack B. Hood, Benjamin A Hardy Jr., and Harold S. Lewis Jr. authored the 2d edition of *Workers Compensation and Employee Protection Laws in a Nutshell* in West Publishing's esteemed Nutshell series in 1989. Recent developments in the field suggest that many libraries need an updated source, and Lencsis's book fills this need very well. This work is highly recommended for all law libraries, large public libraries, academic libraries with business programs, mid-size and large business firms, and students and practitioners in the workers compensation field.—**Dene L. Clark**

MARKETING AND TRADE

C, P

95. **Direction of Trade Statistics Yearbook, 1998.** Washington, D.C., International Monetary Fund; distr., Lanham, Md., Bernan Associates, 1998. 477p. $32.00pa. ISBN 1-55775-748-8. ISSN 0252-3019.

This International Monetary Fund yearbook presents statistics on trade among countries and trading entities of the world on an annual basis for 1991 through 1997. Values of merchandise imports and exports are provided in tabular form for 182 states. Individual county information is broken down to show figures by major trading partners. Also included are aggregate figures for the world, major regions, and two other groupings. A quarterly version is also available. All figures are in U.S. dollars whether or not supplied in national currency by participating states and entities.

The brief introduction is repeated in English, French, and Spanish. It gives details on methodology, terminology, definitions, and other issues. There is a detailed table of contents. A table of country and area codes purports to give page references for the entries in the yearbook and the latest quarterly, but all the entries are listed as "X." The usefulness of the later is far from apparent.

The work is divided into 3 main table sets. The first covers world and regional data. The later divides into tables on industrial countries, developing countries, and those not covered elsewhere (effectively North Korea and Cuba). The developing countries section has aggregate figures and breakdowns for Africa, Asia, Europe, the Middle East, and the Western Hemisphere. Tables provide exports and imports for the world or region to or from the countries listed. The second part provides similar tables for the European Union, oil exporting countries, and non-oil developing countries. The longest section provides tables for the 182 countries or entities listed and is arranged alphabetically. Taiwan has no entry (under China, Republic of China, or Taiwan) nor is it included in the list of "not included elsewhere" entities in the introduction.

This useful source supplies detailed world, regional, national, and thematic trade statistics. It should be acquired by business or economics collections with the relevant client interests and budget.—**Nigel Tappin**

TAXATION

C, P

96. **The Encyclopedia of Taxation and Tax Policy.** Joseph J. Cordes, Robert D. Ebel, and Jane G. Gravelle, eds. Washington, D.C., Urban Institute, 1999. 452p. index. $75.00. ISBN 0-87766-682-2.

This is a compilation of the best essays on taxes and taxation policy published to date. The three editors gathered the best tax specialists and financial thinkers to write these taxation essays. This is the first publication of this kind and the editors plan to update it regularly and expand it internationally.

Each part of the book is in alphabetic order, from the table of contents to the entries and the index. Therefore, it can serve as a glossary of taxation terms. Each entry has an initial short definition of the term or phrase. The definition is followed by an essay and a bibliography for further research and cross-references. This is an essential addition for the taxation collection in academic, special, and public libraries. Every person interested in taxation will want to refer to this book.—**Kay M. Stebbins**

5 Education

GENERAL WORKS

Dictionaries and Encyclopedias

C, P, S

97. **Historical Dictionary of American Education.** Richard J. Altenbaugh, ed. Westport, Conn., Greenwood Press, 1999. 499p. index. $95.00. ISBN 0-313-28590-X.

This historical dictionary provides factual information about important persons and significant topics related to the development of American public, private, and parochial schools. Both elementary and secondary school levels are covered. In addition to major state and regional leaders and reformers, the volume includes biographies of significant national educators, philosophers, psychologists, and writers. The broad array of subjects includes core ideas, events, institutions, agencies, and pedagogical trends that have shaped American policies and perceptions regarding education. The more than 350 entries are arranged alphabetically and written by expert contributors. Each entry closes with a brief bibliography, and the volume ends with a list of works for further reading.

This volume is one of the best historical dictionaries that this reviewer has found on the subject. The entries are relevant, clearly written, and include key bibliographic references for further reading. The index is a model of completeness and facilitates access to the man individuals, concepts, and other information points contained in the individual entries. The *Historical Dictionary of American Education* is recommended for all libraries supporting a curriculum in K-12 education and the history of education.—**Arthur P. Young**

P, S

98. Mitchell, Bruce M., and Robert E. Salsbury. **Encyclopedia of Multicultural Education.** Westport, Conn., Greenwood Press, 1999. 304p. index. $65.00. ISBN 0-313-30029-1.

Multicultural education, sometimes termed multiethnic or multiracial education, refers to educational efforts that attempt to inculcate more positive values toward human diversity. Its goals are to reduce bias by teaching respect for the rights of others to be culturally different, to ensure equity, and to develop school and social structures that help students and teachers to cross racial and ethnic boundaries. This 1-volume encyclopedia contains some 400 alphabetically arranged entries related to multicultural education. They include key terms, events, concepts, notable persons, and court cases, each followed by references used for that article. The items in the references are usually not found in the general bibliography at the end of the volume. Except for certain classics in the field, such as Alex Haley's *Roots*, most of the works cited are from the 1990s.

The entries, selected by the two authors and an advisory group representing various areas of multicultural education, were chosen for their relationship to the content and method of education and not just for their importance in general. Thus, Will Rogers, well-known movie actor and humorist, was included because he was a Cherokee and one of the first Native Americans to gain fame in the entertainment field. The article points out that he provides an excellent example for teachers to use for contributions of Native Americans. Many of the articles contain statements of how the material can be used in helping students acquire a positive attitude toward diversity.

In addition to the bibliography at the end of the volume, there is a general index. As might be expected, it shows the incongruity of some of our politically correct terminology. The article on African Americans, for example, is properly found under that term, but most of the related articles are found under "Black"—black education, black colleges, etc. Likewise, with Native Americans, one must look under "Indian" for some of the related material. Because there are very few *see also* references in either the articles or the index, it is important to be aware of this fact.

The work as a whole is an excellent source of information and teaching suggestions on this increasingly important topic. The format, arrangement, and straightforward, well-written text and references make it a worthwhile addition to any academic library, particularly on the secondary school level. [R: Choice, Dec 99, p. 703]

—**Lucille Whalen**

Directories

P, S

99.   **Guide to American Educational Directories: A Guide to the Major Educational Directories of the United States.** 8th ed. Barry Klein, ed. West Nyack, N.Y., Todd Publications, 1999. 286p. index. $75.00pa. ISBN 0-915344-9-6.

Metabooks, or books that describe other books and information resources, have always enjoyed a secure position on the library reference shelf. This particular directory of directories offers a gold mine of information. Approximately 5,000 U.S. and major foreign directories are categorized under more than 100 educational headings, which cover the gamut of subjects from accounting to electronics, optometry to zoology. Each record contains the directory's title and a concise description of its contents. Publisher and distributor information, including telephone and fax numbers, is provided along with a current price. Alphabetic subject and title indexes append the guide.

This interesting and easy-to-use resource is aimed at educational organizations, educators, and researchers, but could be useful to anyone. It is particularly useful to librarians, who may find its greatest value lies in putting users in touch with unique resources they never knew existed, and which their particular library may not own. Where else might one find out about such resources as the *Pattern Designers Directory* or the *Registry of Drama Therapists*? Of course such entries share the pages with the many well-known, classic directories one would expect to locate in any respectable research library.

This 8th edition has been weeded of 500 directories no longer published, and includes more than 1,000 new entries. In this reviewer's opinion, the nature of the data included in this guide makes it an ideal candidate for distribution via CD-ROM, or better yet, on the World Wide Web. The ability to perform keyword searching online would enhance access to this information and permit continual updating.—**Judith A. Matthews**

S

100.   **The Princeton Review Guide to Performing Arts Programs: Profiles of over 600 Colleges, High Schools, and Summer Programs.** By Muriel Topaz and Carole Everett. New York, Princeton Review/Random House, 1998. 638p. index. $24.95pa. ISBN 0-375-75095-9.

This guide is directed to prospective secondary school graduates interested in pursuing careers in the performing arts—dance, acting, and music. It is basically comprised of 2 sections. The 1st section deals with preliminary considerations: career considerations, application processes, financial aid, and 3 chapters that cover special advice for each of the unique features of the 3 performing arts areas. This covers approximately 60 pages and contains some valuable information, especially for students without proper guidance counseling. The 2d section contains profiles of more than 600 colleges, high schools, and summer programs and comprises the majority of the guide. Arranged by state and identified with appropriate icons, each program description contains pertinent data, including address, telephone and fax numbers, contact person, type of institution, enrollment, curriculum, students and faculty, renowned alumni, facilities, and audition and performance information. The data presented here tend to be somewhat general. The programs list is not comprehensive and includes only institutions that are members of the National Association of Schools of Music and of Dance and others that responded to a questionnaire. Some international programs are also profiled. There is an index followed by appendixes that list books, periodicals, organizations, and sample résumés. Although somewhat awkwardly organized and vague in data, this would be useful for high school students, especially before their graduating year, aspiring to careers in the performing arts. [R: BL, 15 Feb 99, p. 1092]—**Jackson Kesler**

Handbooks and Yearbooks

P, S

101.   **Education Statistics on the United States 1999.** Mark S. Littman and Deirdre A. Gaquin, eds. Lanham, Md., Bernan Associates, 1999. 643p. index. (U.S. Databooks Series). $65.00pa. ISBN 0-89059-066-4. ISSN 1524-394X.

This volume, from the Bernan's award-winning U.S. DataBooks Series, pulls together education-related data from numerous sources, including the U.S. Bureau of the Census (Census) and the National Center from Education Statistics (NCES). The book is divided into 4 parts. The data exhibited in part A (school enrollment) and part B (educational attainment) are no longer available in print from the Bureau of the Census. The data tabulations in part D (school enrollment and financial data by county) have been arranged for the first time from computer files of the NCES.

Part A of this book provides the most recent national school enrollment data from the U.S. Census Bureau, October 1996. Historical tables on school enrollment are provided covering the period from 1947 to 1996, when obtainable. Part B of this volume includes national-level data on educational attainment measured by the highest grade completed and degrees received based on the March 1997 Current Population Survey.

Part C of this book includes an assortment of state-level tables that can be compared with other parts of the book. Tables were collected mostly from the National Center of Education Statistics' Digest of Education Statistics 1997. When more recent information has become available, the tables have been updated to reflect the changes. For example, the private school enrollment figures are more recent than the 1997 Digest. Part D of this publication includes education data tabulated for each county or its equivalent in the United States collected by the National Center for Education Statistics for those users who are interested in education statistics at the county level. Of the 14,700 regular public elementary and secondary school districts in the United States, there is a substantial difference in the number and size among states.

An educator looking for information about total enrollment, minority enrollment, number of schools by level, number of teachers, number of dropouts, students eligible for free lunch, and indicators of school revenue and expenditures will find this book a valuable resource. Geographic codes are appended to these data, such as the Federal Information Processing Standards and the Beale codes, to allow readers to relate the statistics to their own local information. Immediately following each group of tables are notes and definitions important to each group.

Because this book contains many statistics and detailed tables created by the Bureau of the Census that are not readily available elsewhere in print, this book is a valuable resource for obtaining data on educational attainment by age, race, employment status, and occupation, as well as income and earnings. The school district data taken from the National Center for Education Statistics and developed into county- and state-level totals on enrollment, expenditures, class salaries, and more, should serve as a useful tool for district-level administrators and state education officials to use as they plan for future educational programs. This volume is recommended. [R: BL, Aug 99, p. 2104; Choice, Nov 99, p. 516]—**Betty J. Morris**

ALTERNATIVE EDUCATION

P, S

102.   **Barron's Guide to Distance Learning: Degrees, Certificates, Courses.** By Pat Criscito. Hauppauge, N.Y., Barron's Educational Series, 1999. 537p. index. $18.95pa. ISBN 0-7641-0725-9.

The Internet has breathed new life into the concept of "distance learning" during a time when many adults are demanding high-quality college courses for career advancement and personal enrichment. Traditional modes of delivery, such as correspondence courses and educational television, have been supplemented or even replaced by content delivered through Websites, e-mail, and real-time chat groups. Distance learning has grown to meet the needs of today's world and is being offered by established colleges and universities as well as new entities like the University of Phoenix. With so many choices available, potential students need an accurate and comprehensive source of information. This is the niche that *Barron's Guide to Distance Learning* is trying to fill. It covers nearly 800 colleges and universities in the United States and Canada that offer some form of distance learning, either degrees, certificates, or individual courses.

Barron's Guide to Distance Learning begins with an overview of distance learning, with chapters covering accreditation and accrediting agencies, transferring credits, financial aid, and Internet resources. There is a very good chapter on the history, status, and future potential of distance learning. Chapter 7, the bulk of the volume, is devoted to the profiles of institutions offering distance learning. The profiles are arranged in alphabetic order and include such specialized organizations as the Hypnosis Motivation Institute and the International Aviation and Travel Academy, along with highly respected universities from around the country. Seminaries and community colleges are particularly well represented among the profiles. Each profile contains directory information, including Website and e-mail addresses, lists of degree and certificate programs, lists of class titles, teaching methods, how credits are granted, admission requirements, on-campus requirements, tuition and fees, financial aid, accreditation, and a narrative description. Several indexes are provided: state and province, on-campus requirements, undergraduate degree programs, graduate degree programs, doctoral degree programs, certificate and diploma programs, and individual classes.

Barron's Guide to Distance Learning is one of several possible sources that a public, school, or academic library might include in its reference collection. Similar publications are offered, including *The Oryx Guide to Distance Learning* (see ARBA 98, entry 280), *The McGraw-Hill Handbook of Distance Learning* (1999), *The Best Distance Learning Graduate Schools* (see ARBA 99, entry 304), along with several others that are not from big-name publishers. One problem with all of these volumes is the tendency for information to be quickly outdated, because most institutions are only beginning to fashion permanent programs and courses through distance learning.—**Sara Anne Hook**

C, P

103.   Krebs, Arlene. **The Distance Learning Funding Sourcebook: A Guide to Foundation, Corporate, and Government Support for Telecommunications and the New Media.** 4th ed. Dubuque, Iowa, Kendall/Hunt Publishing, 1999. 419p. index. $48.00pa. ISBN 0-7872-4980-7.

Distance learning is an offspring of information technology. It is an integral part of the digital education development of the millennium. In order to provide programs for distance learners, educators seek funding to implement their proposed projects. According to the author, "this funding sourcebook offers the latest research on grants for telecommunications, multimedia, curricula development, and teacher training for private and public schools, higher education, museums, libraries, arts and culture organizations, health and social service agencies, and grassroots community organizations." The printing of the 4th edition signifies its popularity. Both Sony and Ameritech support the research of this unique resource.

The introduction of this book includes a list of foundations grouped by subject, such as business and management, curriculum development, education policy, and funding trends. The foundation chapter lists 38 foundations. Each foundation has full postal address, contact name, e-mail address, Website address, history, strengths, philosophy, supports, limitations, application, and previous recipients. The chapter on corporate giving programs lists 18 corporations that would provide distance learning funding. The descriptive format is similar to the foundation chapter. The third chapter is titled "Regional Bell, Local and Long Distance Telecommunications Companies." A total of 12 foundations are listed in this chapter. The fourth chapter is on the cable television industry. A chapter on federal government agencies that fund distance learning follows. The rest of the chapters are on intellectual property and distance learning, grant writing for success, Internet and multimedia resources, and print references. The grant writing chapter gives pointers on how to put a grant together. The appendixes on equipment donations and Internet resources for funding and grant information and the "Goal 2000: Education America Act" are worth noting. There is a Website at http://www.technogrants.com/ for those who wish to find out more about this book.—**Polin P. Lei**

COMPUTER RESOURCES

P, S

104.   Andriot, Laurie, comp. **Uncle Sam's K-12 Web: Government Internet Resources for Educators, Students, and Parents.** Medford, N.J., CyberAge Books/Information Today, 1999. 244p. illus. $24.95pa. ISBN 0-910965-32-3.

This useful guide to more than 400 online government Websites is divided into sections for students, parents, and teachers. The section for students is the longest, with 11 chapters on such topics as the natural world; work; money; the mail; and math, science, and space. Each chapter lists a number of Web pages or sites appropriate for the stated audience, giving the title, URL, suggested grade level, and a paragraph describing the content. A long chapter on research resources gives sites that, although not designed specifically for students, will prove useful for background information. It is divided into broad subject areas (e.g., African American history and culture, military history, statistics) that are not listed in the table of contents or at the beginning of the chapter, making this section a bit frustrating to use. Examples of sites from all sections include NASA's "How Things Fly," the "CIA Kids Page," the EPA's "Student Center," "ArtsEdge," "Renewable Energy for Teachers," and "Marijuana: Facts Parents Need to Know." The nonevaluative descriptions note the agency or site's purpose and the topics or presentations found online. These can be a bit difficult to read when 10 or more topics are run together in paragraph format; an item list would have made it easier to read and pick out something of interest. Fortunately, users can use the detailed index to look up most of the topics found within site descriptions. For example, "earthquakes" in the index leads to the "American Memories" entry for "Great Earthquake and Fire: San Francisco." The appendix for finding government information online offers advice on using Boolean strategies and Web and government (general and agency-specific) search engines. The Website at http://www.fedworld.com gives updated links for all entries in the book. This will make a convenient bookmark for teachers since URLs do change frequently, and its also easy to make a mistake when typing in long URLs. A couple of major resources of value to educators are omitted from the book such as http://www.usgovsearch.northernlight.com, the Northern Light database that is free to school and public libraries. This commercial site that indexes government Web pages should probably be part of the appendix on finding government information. Another is the National Library of Education's "Gateway to Educational Materials," (http://www.thegateway.org), a government consortium project that indexes more than 7,000 lesson plans and teacher guides on the Internet. It is comparable to, but more extensive than, the "AskERIC Lesson Plans" site listed in the section for teachers. Librarians who serve children, parents, and teachers will want to consider adding this unique and inexpensive guide to government Internet resources to their collection.—**Deborah V. Rollins**

C, P, S

105.   Miller, Elizabeth B. **The Internet Resource Directory for K-12 Teachers and Librarians.** 1999/2000 ed. Englewood, Colo., Libraries Unlimited, 1999. 438p. index. $27.50pa. ISBN 1-56308-812-6.

This is the 6th edition of this well-written, very popular, and extremely useful directory. This edition includes 55 more Websites than the previous edition, to bring the number of entries included up to 1,497, of which 400 are new (see ARBA 99, entry 307). There is still a free publisher's update Website, which is updated every month in order to maintain currency and accuracy of Website information and location. Entries remain selective and evaluative based upon several criteria, among which are their contribution to the K-12 curriculum, free or minimal expense, and designed with the educator in mind. Entries are arranged alphabetically by the name of the Website under the broad subject or curriculum area, and are assigned an entry number. Following the Website name are the URL and an annotation describing the Website's features and content. An introduction is also provided for each subject or curriculum area section.

This source continues to be used by librarians, teachers, and students as an aid in supplementing curriculums with up-to-date online information resources. Several changes are included in this edition. There is an addition of national and state standards for each curriculum area. The foreign languages chapter has been expanded and completely updated. Early childhood and special education have been added to the education chapter, and mathematics and computer sciences have been split into separate chapters. The social studies chapter has added more resources on immigration and twentieth-century U.S. history. The school library chapter has included more pages created by media specialists. There are two indexes, a Website index, and a subject index that refer to the entry number. This resource is highly recommended for school media centers, academic libraries (especially those with a teacher education program), and public libraries.—**Jan S. Squire**

ELEMENTARY AND SECONDARY EDUCATION

P, S

106. **Funding Sources for K-12 Education 1999.** 2d ed. Phoenix, Ariz., Oryx Press, 1999. 710p. index. $34.50pa. ISBN 1-57356-198-3.

The introduction to this hefty volume states that it covers "more than 1,500 funding opportunities available in the United States and Canada, the directory includes all of the information necessary to help individuals and organizations secure funding by submitting grant proposals to the right people at the right time." This is a grand statement, but for both the novice and experienced grants writer, the directory delivers on its claim. The previous volume (see ARBA 99, entry 290) was named the Best New Directory by the Simba Awards for Excellence in Directory Publishing; the excellence has continued.

For those who are new to or perhaps heretofore unsuccessful in securing funding for their programs or projects, there are carefully executed directions for effective and efficient use, a user-friendly and convenient format, realistic examples, extensive entries, invaluable indexes, and time-saving Websites. A sample proposal and the "Guide to Proposal Planning and Writing" provide sound and practical guidance. Further, the introduction, written by a seasoned "resource developer," is insightful, dispelling grants writing as some kind of magic. Her advice is based upon real experience.

Anyone who is attempting to find the "right people" for their particular needs will appreciate the numerous indexes that make navigating this extensive resource exceptionally manageable. Included are a subject index, sponsoring organizations index, grants by program type index, and geographic index. Honestly, it is difficult to imagine what else the prospective "resource developer" might need other than perhaps successful experience.

Oryx's electronic GRANTS Database is suggested as an additional resource that is updated daily, and several other electronic resources are also indicated. Again, for those novice or experienced grants writers who are determined to seek and obtain funding for their school programs, this is an excellent resource.—**Karen D. Harvey**

HIGHER EDUCATION

Directories

P, S

107. **Barron's Profiles of American Colleges.** 1999 ed. [CD-ROM]. Hauppauge, N.Y., Barron's Educational Series, 1998. Minimum system requirements (Windows): IBM or compatible 486. Double-speed CD-ROM drive. Windows 95. 16MB RAM. 640 x 480 display (with 256 colors). Soundblaster compatible sound card. Minimum system requirements (Macintosh): 68040 (Power PC recommended). Double-speed CD-ROM drive. System 7.1 or higher. 16MB RAM. 640 x 480 display (with 256 colors). $34.95. ISBN 0-7641-7273-5.

For the high school or continuing student, this product provides a quick and easy method of searching for institutions of higher education that meet personal requirements and expectations. A link to general information provides the user with an explanation of how to use the CD-ROM, frequently asked questions, and a list of abbreviations. This is followed by brief essays concerning finding the right college, how to score high and get into the college of choice, finding necessary financial aid, and surviving the freshman year. A separate essay details aspects of the degree of competition for entrance into colleges.

The user can also create a search profile, choosing location, major, cost, competitiveness, and enrollment size as limiting factors. Results retrieved match search parameters. Profiles for individual colleges are quite extensive, providing enrollment statistics, calendars, application deadlines, quality of life, housing, activities, sports, services for disabled students, campus safety and security, programs of study, admission requirements, financial aid packages, computing facilities, and various other categories of interest to prospective students. Locator maps provide the user with college location, and photographs and brief videos are provided for some 300 campuses. Affordable and easy to use, this handy guide should be in almost all reference collections, especially in high school and public libraries.—**Edmund F. SantaVicca**

C, P

108. **The Best Graduate Programs: Engineering.** 2d ed. By the Staff of the Princeton Review. New York, Princeton Review/Random House, 1998. 439p. index. $21.00pa. ISBN 0-375-75205-6.

This book, the only one bearing the seal of approval from the American Society for Engineering Education (ASEE), presents a detailed yet easy-to-read guide to graduate programs in engineering. The Princeton Review starts off with basic information on the status of engineering and engineering education, how to choose an engineering program, applying and getting in, and paying for school. Readers can learn about the hot engineering degrees and jobs of today, tips on getting through the application process, and how to negotiate financial aid.

The rest of the work is devoted to profiles of engineering programs found in the United States. Each profile includes standard data on the number of Ph.D. students, addresses of departments, application deadlines, and so on. However, unlike most program guides, this one does something unique by including what students currently enrolled in the programs really think of their studies, school, and area in which they live. This is where the reader can find out just how rural a school is; about crime, housing availability; and information on happiness and satisfaction of students with their programs. The combination of general information and student insight makes this book a welcome addition to any science and engineering library or career center.—**Kelly M. Jordan**

P, S

109. **Christian Colleges & Universities 1999.** Princeton, N.J., Peterson's Guides, 1998. 189p. illus. index. $14.95pa. ISBN 0-7689-0050-6. ISSN 1521-9070.

This edition continues the "official guide to campuses in the Coalition for Christian Colleges [and] Universities," first published in 1982 under the title *A Guide to Christian Colleges*. Later editions have been published by Peterson's Guides with variant titles (see ARBA 89, entry 285; ARBA 94, entry 334; ARBA 96, entry 1474). Schools that meet eight criteria for membership as enumerated in the "How to Use This Book" section are included (see also http://www.gospelcom.net/cccu). Short essays about the benefits of Christian higher education and ways of financing a college education introduce the book. For each of the 93 schools, including 3 Canadian, there is a 1-page profile alphabetic by name with data supplied by the institution. The profile includes information on enrollment, academic offerings, costs, athletic programs, admission procedures, international admissions, and financial aid. Lists serving as indexes include by state, by religious affiliation, majors by school, schools by major, athletics by sport, and graduate majors. Another list indicates by country the schools that offer study-abroad opportunities. The guide also gives brief descriptions of other special programs sponsored by the coalition, such as Chinese and Russian studies. This guide cannot be considered a comprehensive directory to denominationally affiliated schools. Depending on a library's clientele, this nominally priced guide may be appropriate for the college directory collection.—**Margo B. Mead**

C, P

110. **College Blue Book.** 27th ed. New York, Macmillan Library Reference; distr., Farmington Hills, Mich., Gale, 1999. 5v. maps. index. $215.00/set. ISBN 0-02-865300-9. ISSN 1082-7064.

The *College Blue Book* has been a standard professional reference on higher education since it was first published in 1923. The work is now also available in a CD-ROM format. It provides comprehensive, up-to-date information on more than 18,000 colleges, universities, trade, technical and proprietary schools, state departments of education, and other sources throughout the United States and Canada. The 1999 edition includes descriptions and data from more than 3,000 4-year institutions, more than 2,000 sources of financial aid, a guide to some 7,500 institutions providing occupational education, and more than 4,500 subject areas in which degrees are offered. Each entry contains the name of the institution, address, essential telephone numbers and fax numbers, e-mail and Web addresses, a description of the institution, entrance requirements, tuition and fee costs, a description of the collegiate environment, and a description of the community environment. In addition, there are state and province maps showing the locations of the institutions. Separate indexes of U.S. and Canadian institutions are provided.

The *College Blue Book* is a well-established reference source for information on institutions of higher education. The information is obtained from responses to more than 18,000 questionnaires sent to the institutions. The editors point out in the introduction that "the information, especially in the areas of tuition, room and board, enrollments, and library holdings, is constantly changing [and because of this] it is difficult to maintain up-to-date figures in these areas, especially since our data is gathered early in the year of publication" (p. ix).

Even with this caveat the *College Blue Book* is probably the most reliable reference source in this area. It is highly recommended for all academic libraries and for larger public libraries. It is a logical purchase for academic advising offices and other areas where counseling of students occurs as well.—**Robert L. Wick**

P, S

111. **Colleges that Encourage Character Development: A Resource for Parents, Students, and Educators.** Radnor, Pa., Templeton Foundation Press, 1999. 408p. illus. index. (The Templeton Guide Series). $16.95pa. ISBN 1-890151-28-9.

Individuals and institutions identified in this work were chosen by the John Templeton Foundation based on replies to a nomination packet sent to all 4-year accredited colleges and universities in the United States and to higher-education associations and centers that promote character development. In addition, the Institute on College Student Values at Florida State University conducted a search to identify strong programs for which the information packets were not returned. More than 1,000 institutions and 2,500 programs were reviewed.

The resulting guidebook is divided into 3 major sections: 405 exemplary programs listed in 10 categories, 50 presidents, and 100 colleges and universities that inspire students to lead ethical and civic-minded lives. The categories of exemplary programs are first-year programs, academic honesty programs, faculty and curriculum programs, volunteer service programs, substance-abuse prevention programs, student leadership programs, spiritual growth programs, civic education programs, character and sexuality programs, and senior year programs. The 50 men and women presidents profiled illustrate what a leader can do to establish priorities and programs to help prepare students to accept personal and civic responsibility. The 100 public and private profiled schools are listed alphabetically by category and by state. The book also contains a glossary and a resource directory of higher-education organizations.

Most, not all, states are represented by the 555 profiles of exemplary programs, presidents, and institutions. There are, doubtless, those who would disagree with the selections made, but deserving institutions not included in this edition could be included in a future edition. The Foundation encourages suggestions and input. Enough information is provided in this guidebook to assist parents, counselors, and students interested in character building with the process of selecting an appropriate institution of higher education.—**Lois Gilmer**

P, S

112. Custard, Edward T., Christine Chung, Tom Meltzer, and Eric Owens. **The Best 331 Colleges.** 2000 ed. New York, Princeton Review/Random House, 1999. 746p. index. $20.00pa. (with disc). ISBN 0-375-75411-3. ISSN 1093-9679.

The Princeton Review gives profiles of 331 colleges and universities in print format and also contains a CD-ROM with an additional 1,500 colleges and universities. Profiles include information provided by the institutions and by students who go there. The data are fresh and original, aiming to "provide a (relatively) uncensored view of life at the particular college, and acknowledge that even the best of the best of America's 3,600 or so colleges have their drawbacks." The Princeton Review prides itself on its approach: qualitative and anecdotal rather than quantitative and scientific. But they do allow colleges and universities to respond to their entries before they are printed. Each entry has a double-page spread with similar components: addresses; statistics; campus life; academics; admissions; financial facts; student voices; and interesting bits of information such as colleges they also applied to, popular majors, and pointed comments on life on campus. The front and back matter also offers interesting reading, including quotes from individual students and a rationale for the survey. This review is timely, lively, easy to read, and informative. High school counselors as well as parents and students will want to look at this when considering colleges and universities.—**Anne F. Roberts**

C

113. **Graduate Study in Psychology 1998-1999.** 32d ed. Washington, D.C., American Psychological Association, 1998. 545p. index. $21.95pa. ISBN 1-55798-589-8. ISSN 0742-7220.

Anyone planning graduate study in psychology will want to check out this essential directory. Covering 500 departments and schools in the United States offering programs in psychology, this directory lists admission requirements, tuition, financial assistance, goals, enrollment, and degrees awarded. Programs can also include interesting features that might be attractive to candidates, such as objectives of the department, women-oriented courses, special facilities, internships, and even physical disabilities information. In many cases, e-mail and

Website addresses are given. Another nice feature is the subject directory where programs are categorized by fields, such as child development, aging, behavior therapy, and so on. The directory is made up-to-date with a 1999 addendum. This is a sensible purchase for any library seeking graduate school information.—**Carol D. Henry**

C, P, S
114.   **Higher Education Directory, 1999.** Mary Pat Rodenhouse and Constance Healy Torregrosa, eds. Falls Church, Va., Higher Education, 1998. 660p. index. $53.00pa. ISBN 0-914927-28-0. ISSN 0736-0797.

This directory lists postsecondary, degree-granting institutions in the U.S. and its outlying areas that are accredited by bodies recognized by the U.S. Secretary of Education and the now dissolved Council of Postsecondary Education (COPA)/Commission on Recognition of Postsecondary Accreditation (CORPA). The Council for Higher Education (CHEA) accreditation recognition policies and procedures will be used for future editions when they are fully developed.

Addresses and other methods for contacting the institutions, some institutional history, enrollment, Carnegie class, accreditation, and other information are provided through short, uniform descriptions of large and small, public and proprietary institutions arranged in alphabetic order by state. Included also are names of key administrative officers. A detailed index provides the sections of the pages, the page numbers, and the telephone numbers for key administrators. Another index, arranged alphabetically by acronym of accrediting bodies, lists institutions accredited by regional, national, professional, and specialized agencies. A third index lists institutions by name. Although this commercially published work claims to have served as the "official" directory of higher education institutions since 1982, when the U.S. Department of Education ceased publishing their directory, there are other, similar directories available.—**Lois Gilmer**

Financial Aid

C, P
115.   Bauer, David G. **The Teacher's Guide to Winning Grants.** San Francisco, Calif., Jossey-Bass, 1999. 150p. $24.95pa. ISBN 0-7879-4493-9.

Although written for educators, *The Teacher's Guide to Winning Grants* lays out an excellent game plan for anyone seeking grant money. Bauer is a former teacher who turned his successful gift for writing grants into a 20-year career as a consultant and public speaker. He demystifies the grant process, taking the reader through the process step–by–step. Chapters cover writing an effective needs statement, researching the potential founders, making the first contacts, developing objectives, and writing government or corporate proposals. Submitting a federal grant application and dealing with the final outcome are also included. Sample letters and worksheets illustrate his ideas and provide models for beginners. Keywords and terminology are suggested to help in the writing of the grant. *The Teacher's Guide to Winning Grants* will help grant seekers with the steps they must follow for successful grant writing. This will be a good purchase for any school or library looking for grant advice.
—**Carol D. Henry**

P, S
116.   Schlachter, Gail Ann. **How to Find Out About Financial Aid and Funding: A Guide to Print, Electronic, and Internet Resources Listing Scholarships, Fellowships.** San Carlos, Calif., Reference Service Press, 1999. 439p. index. $37.50. ISBN 0-918276-75-6.

This volume is a new and improved edition of a 1987 Reference Service Press guide to financial aid resources. In the dozen years since the original guide was published, there have been numerous changes in the areas of financial aid and funding. Today, for instance, there are more publicly funded loans and fewer publicly funded scholarships, more grant-making institutions, and more opportunities for funded internships. This bibliographic guide provides a listing, assessment, and ordering information for some 750 financial aid publications. Each of the reviewed publications directs readers to the sources that award some $100 billion in scholarships, fellowships, loans, grants, and internships every year.

In 1987 few of the publications about financial aid resources were available in digital format. In this volume, however, about 40 percent of the listed sources are available in electronic form or on the Internet. Internet addresses are provided for these items. The titles described in the present volume include those publications that have been issued or updated between 1994 and February 1999. Recognizing the rapid changes in these source materials, Reference Service Press plans to update this volume with a new edition every two years.

The publications listed in this bibliographic guide are presented in six chapters: "Scholarships," "Fellowships & Loans," "Grants for Individuals," "Grants for Organizations," "Awards and Prizes," "Internships," and "Federal Government Bookmarks." The items within each chapter are conveniently arranged by discipline (i.e., social sciences, humanities), geographical region, and intended audience (i.e., ethnic groups, women). Also included are five indexes that offer access to the entries by title, author, and publisher as well as geographical coverage and subject focus. Reference librarians, financial officers, career counselors, researchers, and parents of college students will find this informative volume to be well worth its moderate price.—**Terry D. Bilhartz**

P, S

117.   Schlachter, Gail Ann, and R. David Weber. **College Student's Guide to Merit and Other No-Need Funding 1998-2000.** San Carlos, Calif., Reference Service Press, 1998. 470p. index. $32.00. ISBN 0-918276-62-4.

This is a directory that will be an excellent resource for both prospective college students and those who will most likely be paying for this college education, their parents. Listed are nearly 1,600 sources for college financial aid. The types of sources in the volume include scholarships, forgivable loans, and research grants. According to the introduction, numerous examples are given on how the authors have conducted a thorough revision from the previous edition.

The vast majority of the entries reflect the types of sources described in the book's title—financial aid that does not require repayment. These entries are arranged alphabetically within general areas—humanities, sciences, and social sciences. Within each entry is a surprising amount of information for the user. Each entry can include the following information in addition to the name of the awarding organization and the organization's address: purpose of the financial aid, eligibility requirements, duration of an award, special features (variables unique to the award), limitations, the number awarded, and the application deadline. The authors present this large amount of information in succinctly worded and clearly formatted entries.

Additionally, there is a short section titled "State Sources of Information on Educational Benefits" that lists state financial aid programs, including guaranteed student loan programs. Following the "State Sources" section is an annotated bibliography titled the "Financial Aid Library," which lists additional directories of financial aid. One addition is the inclusion of Websites, making this a directory providing both paper and electronic sources. Finally, there are numerous indexes to access the book. Besides the usual subject and program title indexes, there are indexes listing those awards requiring fulfillment of residency and tenability stipulations. Also, a most unique, but perhaps helpful index is that which is called a calendar index, which lists the months when each letter of application must be submitted.—**Phillip P. Powell**

P

118.   Schlachter, Gail Ann, and R. David Weber. **Financial Aid for Research and Creative Activities Abroad, 1999-2001.** San Carlos, Calif., Reference Service Press, 1999. 484p. index. $45.00. ISBN 0-918276-63-2. ISSN 1072-530X.

Intended for Americans seeking financing for travel, study, or research abroad, this source lists more than 1,300 entries, arranged by level of study (e.g., high school/undergraduate, graduate, postdoctorate, professionals and other individuals). Many of the entries are duplicated because they are listed repeatedly in more than one level. Each annotated entry includes the following information: title, contact information (with e-mail, Web address, and fax if available), purpose, eligibility, financial data, duration, special features, limitations, number of awards available, and deadlines. Because some of the awards listed are very specific, such as the James A. Swan fund intended for research of the Batwa peoples of Africa, the subject index is essential. A future enhancement could be an electronic file (CD-ROM or diskette) to facilitate searching. A selective annotated bibliography lists some 50 entries leading users to other potential resources. With its international focus, this resource is unique enough to warrant purchase by libraries that are in need of this type of information. It is worth updating if you have an earlier edition as well. *The Annual Register of Grant Support* (32d ed.; R. R. Bowker, 1998) and *Grants Register* (see entry 128) provide more costly but better coverage of U.S. and international nonrepayable financial support.
—**Christine Drew**

C, P

119.   Schlachter, Gail Ann, and R. David Weber. **Financial Aid for Study and Training Abroad 1999-2001.** San Carlos, Calif., Reference Service Press, 1999. 372p. index. $39.50. ISBN 0-918276-64-0.

This directory is a response to the National Security Act of 1991 and other programs that emphasize the importance of foreign language study and undergraduate scholarships for study abroad. Included in the information provided for both structured and independent study are eligibility requirements, financial data, duration of the funding, special features and limitations, number of awards given, and application date. While other financial aid directories exist, this one is recommended for current and comprehensive coverage of more than 1,000 programs.

A currency conversion table identifies currency used in key countries covered by this directory and is to be used as a guide to the approximate value of the support offered. Additional assistance is provided by an annotated bibliography of general financial aids such as scholarships, fellowships, loans, grants, internships, awards and prizes, and financial assistance to special population groups.

Programs are identified and listed in 5 separate indexes: program titles, sponsoring organizations, geographic, subject, and calendar (deadline dates). The calendar index is divided into 4 major sections (the 4 categories addressed by this work), high school and undergraduate students, graduate students, postdoctorates, and professionals and other individuals. Other sections also indicate level of study covered.—**Lois Gilmer**

C, P

120.   Schlachter, Gail Ann, and R. David Weber. **Financial Aid for Veterans, Military Personnel, and Their Dependents 1998-2000.** San Carlos, Calif., Reference Service Press, 1998. 332p. index. $40.00. ISBN 0-918276-66-7. ISSN 0896-7792.

According to the information presented in the introduction to this book, more than one-third of the U.S. population today has either direct or indirect ties with the armed services and billions of dollars a year have now been set aside for financial aid to these veterans, military personnel, and their dependents. Obviously there is a need for a comprehensive and user-friendly resource to enable those qualified for these funds to locate and access them. This directory is designed to meet that need and does so in a way that is indeed both convenient and sufficient for most users. It provides the right information, complete and accurate (to the degree that is possible in such a rapidly changing environment). To meet the challenge of escalating change, an online source is listed for updates and new information.

A clear explanation of how to use the directory and a sample entry are given. The directory is divided into 4 major sections: financial aid programs for veterans, military personnel, and their dependents (scholarships, fellowships/grants, loans, grants-in-aid, and awards); state sources of information on benefits; annotated bibliography of financial aid directories; and indexes. The indexes are worth noting. They are intuitive and greatly increase the convenience of the directory. Included are a program title index, a sponsoring organization index, a residency index, a tenability index, a subject index, and a calendar index.

It seems as though this particular resource would be exceptionally useful for high school counselors and college advisors in schools where there is a high proportion of students searching for financial aid. It provides information on sources that are not as widely known as others and, of course, if it does not provide desired information, the directory provides an annotated bibliography of financial aid directories.—**Karen D. Harvey**

C

121.   Schlachter, Gail Ann, and R. David Weber. **Money for Graduate Students in the Humanities 1998-2000.** 2d ed. San Carlos, Calif., Reference Service Press, 1998. 332p. index. $40.00. ISBN 0-918276-68-3.

Graduate study can be an expensive proposition, forcing many prospective students to seek funding to pay for or defray costs. This directory aids that effort by identifying scholarships, grants, loans, and awards for graduate study, training, research, or creative activities in the humanities, including such disciplines as art, architecture, music, filmmaking, journalism, dance, creative writing, religion, and philosophy. More than 900 funding sources are described, with the only requirements for inclusion being that they must target humanities graduate students and have a minimum funding level of $750.

The funding source descriptions are arranged alphabetically in 2 major sections: study and training (619 entries), and research and creative activities (305 entries). For each source there are an address, telephone number, and e-mail and Website addresses (if available), as well as descriptive categories for the purpose, eligibility, financial data, duration, limitations, number awarded, special features, and deadline. Limitations on the funding may include such factors as the applicant's group affiliation, the residency of the applicant, the field of study, and a geographic limit on where the funds may be spent. Some of these variables, as well as the subject, sponsoring organization, and program title, comprise the six indexes provided to aid in locating the most appropriate funding sources. Also included are lists of state financial aid offices and student loan programs as well as an annotated list of useful financial aid reference books.

This book's strengths are its extensive number of entries, its detailed descriptions of the grants and loans, and its thorough indexing. The fact that it is updated biennially ensures that it will remain reasonably current. It compares more than favorably with similar directories, and also has a companion volume for the social sciences (see entry 122). This should be invaluable for college and university libraries.—**Stephen H. Aby**

C

122.   Schlachter, Gail Ann, and R. David Weber. **Money for Graduate Students in the Social Sciences 1998-2000.** 2d ed. San Carlos, Calif., Reference Service Press, 1998. 364p. index. $42.50. ISBN 0-918276-70-5.

Schlachter and Weber report that 70 percent of the programs included in this book had substantive changes since the 1st edition. Additionally, some 200 new entries have been provided for a total of 1,032 entries. The 1st edition was well received in published reviews, and the 2d edition with the upgrades continues to be a highly useful tool. Students will find information on fellowships, grants, awards, loans, and forgivable loans. Areas covered include graduate study, training, and research as well as creative activities. Only "portable programs" are included (those that can be used at "any number of schools," with institution-based funding options specifically excluded). Programs for use in the United States are considered, with opportunities for noncitizens and nonresidents left uncovered.

No secondary sources were used to gather the data. Up to four letters and three follow-up calls were placed, with nonrespondents not presented in the compilation. There are four sections to the volume: funding opportunities, state sources, bibliographic resources, and indexes. The funding portion is divided into two categories, namely "Study and Teaching" and "Research and Creative Activities." Within each entry the following information is included: name, address, telephone and fax numbers, e-mail address, purpose, eligibility, financial data, duration, limitations, number awarded, and deadline. These categories seem to be the ones of immediate need to prospective applicants. The text is simply presented with just enough information to clarify a particular funding option without providing unnecessary detail.

The "State Sources" section lists the state financial aids and student loan programs for each state. Some 400 directories for financial aid and funding programs have been published in the past 10 years. The authors selected 40 for inclusion in their "Financial Aid Bookshelf." Indexing for the volume is available for the following categories: program title, sponsoring organization, residency, tenability, subject, and calendar.

This title provides a simple, easy-to-use format giving the prospective graduate student in the social sciences many options to pursue. Without the financial means to study, many a career would be halted. Schlachter and Weber have performed a valuable service and generated a product that will be well placed in academic as well as public libraries. This resource is highly recommended.—**Graham R. Walden**

Handbooks and Yearbooks

P, S

123.   **The College Board College Costs & Financial Aid Handbook 2000.** 20th ed. College Board, New York; distr., New York, Henry Holt, 1999. 709p. index. $21.95pa. ISBN 0-87447-628-3.

Next to buying a home, the money paid toward college costs may well be the largest investment people ever make in their lifetime. Anyone who has ever financed a college education, or is hoping to do so, recognizes this challenge with trepidation. Not only is the cost of higher education daunting, but the search for financial assistance is difficult and confusing. This reference is designed to organize and make readily available the information that is needed to make informed decisions about this major investment.

This volume is organized into three major sections: using the book effectively and detailed information about financial aid, college descriptions, and college indexes. Because the information is complicated, it is critical that the first part is reader-friendly and comprehensive. As the authors point out, to improve chances of getting help, readers must know what they have to do, when they have to do it, and how to do it right—the first time. The handbook helps readers understand what constitutes the cost of attending college (much more than just tuition), the language and acronyms, the complexity of standard forms, the variety of funding opportunities, and the unique features of various federal programs and individual colleges. The tables and worksheets, a glossary, and an explanation of the information included in the college descriptions are most helpful.

The comprehensive college descriptions (community, state, private, and proprietary) are listed by state and include detailed cost facts—tuition and fees, out-of-district/state tuition, room and board figures (as well as costs for dependent students living at home), books and supplies, and estimates of personal expenses.

These two sections are well-researched by the College Board, as realistic and accurate as possible, and, so importantly, written in a way that makes complex and often confusing information quite understandable. As a reference for high school and college counselors, it is invaluable. Further, the cost is reasonable for determined individuals and their families. Finally, the indexes include listings for academic scholarships, art scholarships, music/drama scholarships, ROTC scholarships, and athletic scholarships, as well as an alphabetic list of all colleges profiled.—**Karen D. Harvey**

P, S

124.   **The College Board College Handbook 2000.** 37th ed. New York, Henry Holt, 1999. 1882p. index. $25.95pa. (with disc). ISBN 0-87447-625-9.

The current edition of this college guide provides detailed information for more than 3,200 institutions of higher learning. Four-year and two-year colleges are grouped in separate sections alphabetically by state. Background information is provided about each school, along with facts about variables such as basis for sections, high school preparation, 1999–2000 annual costs, financial aid, application procedures, academics, majors (including most popular majors), computing on campus, student life, athletics, and student services. Contact information is often provided in the form of the address of a specific campus administrator, phone and fax numbers, and e-mail addresses. The book's consistency in format facilitates access to information and makes for easy comparative analyses of institutions.

A variety of indexes—college types, colleges with special characteristics, undergraduate enrollment size, admission selectivity, admission and placement policies, student life, NCAA sports, and ROTC—make the book user-friendly. There is useful generic information provided in "Guidance at a Glance" tabs. This includes a guide to using the *College Explorer* CD-ROM enclosed with this book that contains video clips and links to college Websites and College Board Online. This is a thoroughly documented and well-organized guide that would surely help college-bound individuals or those trying to assist them.—**G. Douglas Meyers**

P, S

125.   **The College Board Scholarship Handbook 2000.** 3d ed. New York, Henry Holt, 1999. 590p. index. $24.95pa. (with disc). ISBN 0-87447-627-5.

The College Board Scholarship Handbook has information for more than 2,000 undergraduate scholarships, internships, and loan programs. It is designed to direct users toward specific award programs that match the user's personal and academic qualifications. The introductory pages include useful information on the components of the cost of attending college and some ground rules for college planning. Awards are listed in the eligibility indexes according to corporate and employer sponsors, disabilities, fields of study, gender, military participation, national and ethnic background, organization and civic affiliation, religious affiliation, returning adult, state of residence, and study abroad. Additionally, there are indexes that list award programs by internships, loans, sponsor name, and program name. Not included are local awards programs or programs offered by colleges themselves. A personal characteristics checklist is included to aid the user in determining eligibility in various categories. Accompanying the volume is a CD-ROM that quickly matches awards based on the user's eligibility.

The main part of the volume contains the program descriptions in alphabetic order. Included in each entry is the type of award (public or private scholarship, internship, or loan), eligibility requirements, application requirements, amount of award, number of awards given, deadline, and contact information including a URL. Although there is no mention of how the information for this title is gathered or how often it is updated, students and parents will nonetheless find it valuable as they seek funding to pay for college.—**Michele Russo**

C

126.   Gilbert, Nedda. **The Best 80 Business Schools.** 2000 ed. New York, Princeton Review/Random House, 1999. 318p. index. $20.00pa. (with disc). ISBN 0-375-75463-6. ISSN 1067-2141.

Readers do not expect a reference book about business schools to be extraordinarily informative and relevant but also interesting, engaging, and even a little humorous now and then. The organization of the book, topics addressed, information presented, and style of writing answer the real-world needs of adults who are hoping to make a sound personal and career decision. For those who recognize the importance of the decision they are making, it is undoubtedly frustrating to find sound advice. As graduate students, these are people who are without high school guidance counselors and probably without unbiased and comprehensive advice.

This reference is based upon data collected from 18,500 students, hundreds of admissions officers, dozens of recruiters, and business school graduates. While reporting many critical statistics such as demographic information on students and faculty, other more subjective opinions that are important in the selection process are provided; for example, the opinions of students on topics such as academics, pressure, social life and fellow students, facilities, and placement and recruiting.

For those determined to seek admission to one of these top 80 business schools, there is a wealth of useful information. Common essay questions; case examples of admissions officers from Dartmouth, Harvard, Stanford, and other prestigious institutions who critique winning essays; and 15 surefire ways to torpedo your application are included.

This type of reference usually provides correct information, if you are willing to dig for it, but it is often data without the richness that allows individuals to examine their own lifestyles, needs, and professional goals to make sound, informed, personal and educational decisions. Surely it is important to know faculty-to-student ratios and average starting salary of graduates, but readers might also like to know pertinent information on student life. For those who want guidance and support for selecting and being admitted to a recognized business school, this book is likely to be fascinating and helpful reading. Once the decision has been made (or as part of the decision process), there is also a CD-ROM that contains 59 MBA and 63 LAW program applications.—**Karen D. Harvey**

C

127.   **Graduate School: The Best Resources To Help You Choose, Get In, & Pay.** Jane Finkle, ed. Issaquah, Wash., Resource Pathways, 1998. 271p. index. (Higher Education & Careers Series). $24.95pa. ISBN 0-9653424-7-6.

This Resource Pathways guidebook is written like a bibliographic essay, focusing on the challenges of pursuing an advanced degree. It contains reviews of more than 170 resources chosen to help prospective students understand the factors involved in pursuing an advanced degree and learn how to evaluate programs as well as identify opportunities unique to minority and handicapped individuals. Practical advice is also presented on how to obtain financial aid and how to create winning applications. Recommendations are based on all available resources—books, CD-ROMs, and Websites.

This paperback book, part of the Higher Education & Careers Series, is reasonably priced. It is divided into 7 sections. The introduction seeks to explain why such a guidebook is needed and why and how Resource Pathways chose to publish it. Most helpful is an explanation regarding the organization of the book. Sections 2 through 4 contain short reviews of resources on the following topics: "Graduate School: The Best Resources To Help You Choose, Get In, and Pay"; "The Single Best Resource for Selected Graduate and Professional School Topics"; and "Resources of Interest to Specific Groups."

Section 5, longer than all of the other sections combined, is the heart of the book. It contains full-page reviews of all resources recommended for the publication. The reviews are arranged by subjects and within subjects. Most are ranked from 1 to 4. Recommended resources, from a great range of publishers, cover the following topics: obtaining a Master's degree or Ph.D.; choosing, applying to, and excelling in such different schools as business, medicine, and law; financing graduate or professional school; scholarship directories and search services; and resources of general interest.

The book concludes with five indexes and two appendixes. Access points in the indexes are title, author, publisher, media, and subject. The subject index is in rank order. The appendixes contain additional information about Resource Pathways and about the editor of this particular guidebook.

The guidebook should be helpful to anyone contemplating graduate school. The unvarnished truth about what is involved in advanced study could discourage some, but at the same time, others may have their fears of the unknown alleviated by this work and by the resources it reviews.—**Lois Gilmer**

C, P

128.   **The Grants Register 2000.** 18th ed. Sara Hackwood, ed. New York, St. Martin's Press, 1999. 982p. index. $125.00. ISBN 0-312-22520-2. ISSN 0072-5471.

Higher education, even at state-supported institutions, is expensive, and the deferred income and costs involved in pursuing postgraduate study are even more daunting. The reality in today's higher-education market is that students' ability to pay educational expenses may limit their opportunities to pursue advanced study. Students' options are either to go into massive, long-term debt, to continue working and delay completion of their education, or to seek grants and fellowships. Fortunately, many sources of funding exist, and directories like this one help students identify the most appropriate sources. This volume lists over 3,500 awards for postgraduate funding in most disciplines and in over 80 countries. Covered are such activities as graduate study, postdoctoral work, professional development, and research.

The directory's arrangement is straightforward. The largest section is the grants register, an alphabetic listing of granting organizations, accompanied by addresses, phone numbers, fax numbers, contact names, e-mail addresses, and Web addresses. For each organization there is descriptive information on each of its grants arranged alphabetically by title. This information includes the broad subject of the grant, eligibility requirements, level of study supported, type of grant, number of awards offered, frequency of the awards, value of the awards, country of study, application procedure, closing dates, and additional information. Further access to these entries is provided by a subject index that lists grants hierarchically according to their subject, country of study, and name of grant (with page reference). There is also an index of discontinued awards, as well as an alphabetic list of granting organizations.

This directory's strengths are its straightforward arrangement, multidisciplinary coverage, and regular publication schedule. However, libraries should also carry grant and scholarship directories for students of other levels and group affiliation (e.g., women, minorities). That said, this should be considered part of a core collection of grant directories.—**Stephen H. Aby**

P, S

129.   **The Princeton Review African American Student's Guide to College.** 1999 ed. By Marisa Parham, with Manie Barron. New York, Princeton Review/Random House, 1998. 250p. index. $17.95pa. ISBN 0-679-77878-0.

This specialized source is divided into four parts emphasizing African American students' approach to college: getting in, staying in, resource guide, and college profiles. The getting-in part offers advice from choosing a school based on personal factors, to the admissions process, to the cost involved, along with suggestions for acquiring financial aid. A two-year plan, describing what should be done when, is outlined in considerable detail. In addition, marginal notes are provided as reminders throughout the chapters. Worksheets complete the chapters.

Almost as much attention is devoted to staying in as to getting in. The makeup of the chapters is the same as for the 1st section. The staying-in section contains such topics as learning to live with roommates, choosing classes, and working with advisors. Staying on top of academics and staying healthy are emphasized. The resource guide by its nature deviates from the format of the two previous sections. It contains sample letters to be used in applying for admissions and scholarships, contact information in relation to the ACT and SAT and College Board offices, and suggested readings. By far the largest part of the guide is the college profiles section. It is an alphabetic listing of 150 predominantly black institutions and other U.S. institutions that offer programs in African studies. All states are not represented, while some are represented many times. Each college or university profile consists of one page. In addition to contact information, admissions procedures, and financial aid advice, there are statistical descriptions of the student body, faculty-to-student ratio, admissions ratings, most popular majors, and financial information relating to tuition and room and board.

Any college-bound student could benefit from the sound, practical advice provided in this guide. For the African American student interested in African studies or environments that enhance the African American experience, however, the guide is indispensable.—**Lois Gilmer**

P, S

130.   **The Princeton Review Student Athlete's Guide to College.** By Hilary S. Abramson. New York, Princeton Review/Random House, 1999. 227p. illus. $12.00pa. ISBN 0-375-75426-1.

If one is good enough at sports to play at the intercollegiate level and one's grades are acceptable, then it is possible to win a scholarship or other grant-in-aid worth many thousands of dollars. Drawing upon the author's own experience as a student-athlete and having worked for a company that prepares students for college-admission tests, Abramson offers students help with writing letters of application and résumés (including sample letters), gives information on the complicated eligibility rules enforced by regulatory bodies, and demonstrates techniques for scoring well on entrance tests such as the SAT. In addition to this essential information, Abramson gives useful advice on how to attract attention from college coaches, how to evaluate institutions and athletic programs, and the like. The book also provides some vignettes of college coaches and a number of drawings.

Abramson's writing is straightforward and effective in conveying its points. The arrangement of material makes it easy to work through it; thus the lack of an index is no great loss. And, commendably, the coverage in this book is thoroughly nonsexist, being directed as much to women as to men.

There are a few deficiencies. Some of the text, which is printed on a dark background intended for color contrast, is so dim as to make for uncomfortable reading. The author does not shrink from touting the publications of her former employer (The Princeton Review). And one suspects that coaches and college officials may get weary of receiving many identical copies of those form letters. Otherwise this book serves its purposes very well.—**Samuel Rothstein**

INTERNATIONAL EXCHANGE PROGRAMS AND OPPORTUNITIES

C, P

131.   **International Exchange Locator: A Resource Directory for Educational and Cultural Exchange.** 1998 ed. New York, Institute of International Education, 1998. 249p. index. $11.95pa. ISBN 0-87206-244-9.

The Alliance for International Education and Cultural Exchange is a nonprofit association of organizations comprising the international exchange community in the United States. Its mission is to formulate and promote public policy that supports the growth and well-being of international exchange between the people of the United States and other nations and to provide information on such exchanges. The locator provides a comprehensive and accessible inventory of government agents and private organizations involved in international education and cultural exchange. This book provides the most extensive collection of information on international exchange programs available. The book lists the Alliance member organizations and an extensive index dividing organizations into those involved in international exchange, industry-specific exchanges, research/support organizations, foreign affair agency and exchange programs, other federal government exchanges, and key congressional committees and members of Congress involved in international activities.

The paperback book is printed on average paper, sufficient in size, and has an average binding. The work should be useful to anyone interested in obtaining information about exchanges on a global, national, or individual basis and also to those interested in international relationships between various areas of the world. The book should be in all public and university libraries where students are looking for exchange opportunities.—**Herbert W. Ockerman**

P, S

132.   **Peterson's Summer Study Abroad 1999: The Complete Guide to More Than 1,400 Summer Academic and Language Programs.** Princeton, N.J., Peterson's Guides, 1999. 614p. illus. index. $29.95pa. ISBN 0-7689-0152-9.

Basic information on more than 1,400 summer academic and language programs is given in this comprehensive guide to study programs held in countries around the world, from Argentina to Zimbabwe. Entries for each program are arranged under country, then by the city they are located in or where they mainly take place. Finally, they are alphabetically listed under the program or the sponsor's name. Each program description describes the academic focus; student profile; living arrangements or accommodations; and gives information on eligibility requirements, onsite student support, and costs. Other information includes the program's founding date, background and history, credits given, class sizes, and methods of instruction. Addresses and Websites where further information can be obtained are provided. A separate chapter describes multicountry programs. Direct access to each program's entry is provided by four indexes: fields of study, program sponsors, host institutions, and internship programs. Helpful, well-written introductory chapters give realistic and common sense information and recommendations on the essentials of travel abroad, getting around on a budget, choosing the right country and program for personal satisfaction, and health and safety precautions. Other chapters are devoted to volunteering abroad and options in international exchange for people with disabilities. This extremely thorough and carefully prepared guide will be a necessary addition to any collection that serves persons who are interested in summer study abroad.—**Shirley L. Hopkinson**

6 Ethnic Studies and Anthropology

ANTHROPOLOGY AND ETHNOLOGY

C

133. **Anthropological Resources: A Guide to Archival, Library, and Museum Collections.** Library-Anthropology Resource Group, comp. Lee S. Dutton, ed. New York, Garland, 1999. 517p. index. (Garland Reference Library of Social Science, v.864). $135.00. ISBN 0-8153-1188-5.

This uniquely valuable reference volume (the latest work coordinated by the Chicago-based Library-Anthology Research Group) fills a major gap in the research literature of anthropology by addressing a long-standing need for in-depth data on primary artifactual and documentary materials in all formats held in museums, archives, and libraries. Geographic coverage emphasizes Canadian and American holdings, but also profiles major collections in 15 other nations from western Europe, Central and South America, east and southeast Asia, Australia, and New Zealand. The 246 entries present full contact information on each institution (including Internet access when available), areas of specialization, collection contents (ranging from archival and manuscript holdings—both agency records and personal papers—to classes of objects, audio, and visual recordings), and related articles, books and guides. Of particular value are the histories of the inception and development of individual collections, often written by their curators. Indexing is by personal name and selected ethnic group names. Useful for undergraduate reference collections in college and university libraries (particularly those supporting baccalaureate and master's programs in anthropology), museums and historical societies, special collections in the social sciences, and all public library reference collections.—**Robert B. Marks Ridinger**

C, P

134. **Encyclopedia of Canada's Peoples.** Paul Robert Magocsi, ed. Toronto, University of Toronto Press, 1999. 1334p. $200.00. ISBN 0-8020-2938-8.

Like many countries today, Canada's peoples are represented by a variety of nationalities that constitute a wide range of cultural traditions. This encyclopedia explores the many different ethnic backgrounds of Canadian history and describe how they interrelate to shape Canadian society. As opposed to other immigrant countries, including the United States, this is the first comprehensive encyclopedia devoted to the ethnic make up of Canada. This great undertaking includes the expertise of 182 advisors who assisted on the editorial board, and 132 authors who compiled information and wrote the entries. The entries are arranged in encyclopedic format with 119 ethnic groups represented; the aboriginal peoples are further broken down into 13 groups (e.g., Siouan, Algonquians/Eastern Woodlands, Iroquoians). Every possible group is discussed here, from Acadians to Welsh, from Arabs to Spaniards. The topics discussed within each entry include the peoples origins, migration, arrival and settlement, economic life, community life, family, culture, education, religion, politics, intergroup relationships, and ethnic commitment. A bibliography is provided for each ethnic group discussed.

Nearly a decade in the making, this work is a truly scholarly contribution to the literature on Canada and especially Canadian peoples. It will be a worthwhile contribution to all academic libraries and many public libraries.

—**Shannon M. Graff**

ETHNIC STUDIES

General Works

C, P, S

135.   **Junior Worldmark Encyclopedia of World Cultures.** Jane Hoehner, ed. Farmington Hills, Mich., Gale, 1999. 9v. illus. maps. index. $225.00/set. ISBN 0-7876-1756-X.

This new encyclopedia is modeled after *Junior Worldmark Encyclopedia of the Nations* (see ARBA 97, entry 79). Although the information contained in its predecessor is general in scope, this work focuses on the culture of 295 ethnic groups outside of the United States. It is designed for use by upper elementary students; however, it is suitable for readers of all ages because it contains much information that may not be readily available elsewhere.

The format is attractive. The type is easy to read and there are black-and-white illustrations, including location maps. There are a reader's guide and a cumulative table of contents at the beginning of each volume, a glossary, and a cumulative index at the end of each. The arrangement is alphabetic by country and is continuous in the nine volumes. Within each chapter, cultural groups are treated individually. Information about each group follows the same pattern in 20 subheadings, which include language, religion, holidays, living conditions, and a bibliography. An interesting feature is the inclusion of ethnic recipes.

Political problems and ethnic conflicts are addressed only briefly under social problems. A critical omission, in the light of current events, is the lack of inclusion of Yugoslavia and its ethnic groups. However, Bosnia-Herzegovina and Croatia are included. It is hoped that the former omission will be rectified in subsequent editions.

This set is recommended as a worthwhile addition to a children's library collection or a supplement to social studies classes. If budgetary restrictions necessitate a choice between this set and its predecessor, one would probably choose the earlier work, although each deserves consideration. [R: BL, June 99, pp. 1881-1882; SLJ, Feb 99, p. 136; RUSQ, Fall 99, p. 95]—**Patricia A. Eskoz**

P, S

136.   **Peoples of the Americas.** Tarrytown, N.Y., Marshall Cavendish, 1999. 11v. illus. maps. index. $329.95/set. ISBN 0-7614-7050-6.

Dense with facts, this compact multivolume geography and demography of the Americas is a meditation on survival. The nature of our land and its resources, who came first, what has been our social history, and where are we now are all told in scholarly paragraphs at the junior high school reading level. Topics include ethnic foods and folk celebrations, traditional patterns, education, and urban industrialization. But the authors neglect to discuss our debt to European intellectual civilization, which influenced American modernism with arts and sciences made public in museums, concert halls, theaters, libraries, engineering, government, and the law. Most pages have old prints of scenes of former generations or modern-day candid photographs. The indexes are effective and the glossaries are rudimentary. The maps, sidebars, and timelines are essential. Further study is facilitated by the bibliographies and text. Besides helping junior high school students, this work could be informative and interesting for American history and sociology enthusiasts.—**Elizabeth L. Anderson**

Arab Americans

S

137.   Hall, Loretta, and Bridget K. Hall. **Arab American Biography.** Farmington Hills, Mich., U*X*L/Gale, 1999. 2v. illus. index. $63.00/set. ISBN 0-7876-2953-7.

Defining an Arab American as an individual who traces his or her ancestry to 1 or more nations belonging to the League of Arab States, this 2-volume set profiles 75 persons who have made noteworthy achievements in a variety of fields, including politics, business, entertainment, science, and religion. Each entry includes date and place of birth (most of the individuals are currently alive), a narrative biographical description, often a black-and-white photograph, and a bibliography. Frequent sidebars provide interesting facts related to the individual.

Each of the two volumes includes a table of contents, indexes by occupation and country of ancestry, and a cumulative alphabetic index for names and subjects.

Like some other ethnic reference publications, the criterion for inclusion is the individual's ancestry, not necessarily a professed commitment or involvement in the culture of his or her heritage. While many essays in this volume do describe individuals with strong Lebanese or other Arab background, some entries (such as race car driver Bobby Rahall, football star Doug Flutie, or high school teacher-turned-astronaut Christa McAuliffe) reveal little information pertinent to a student consulting a specialized reference work on Arab Americans. A future revised edition would be better as a 1-volume work, limited to individuals who were genuinely shaped by their ethnic background. The elementary level of the glossary and timeline demonstrate that this work is aimed—like other volumes in the U*X*L imprint of the Gale Group—at students in grades 5 and up. [R: BR, Nov/Dec 99, p. 71; RUSQ, Fall 99, p. 86]—**Donald Altschiller**

Asian Americans

P, S

138.   **Asian-American Experience on File.** Carter Smith III and David Lindroth, eds. New York, Facts on File, 1999. 1v. (various paging). illus. maps. index. $125.00 looseleaf w/binder. ISBN 0-8160-3696-9.

This major new reference work from one of America's most respected publishers deserves special attention and recognition. Part of Facts on File's Ethnic Minorities in America set, it joins other titles on African and Hispanic Americans. It appears in a sturdy looseleaf, three-ring binder so that users may remove individual pages for copying, reference, or overheads. The publisher freely grants permission for copying of individual pages for educational purposes. The volume is self-contained and there are no evident provisions to add additional pages.

The arrangement is chronological. The introduction gives an overview of Asian American immigration and compares it with immigration from other regions. Chapter 1, "Background," examines political and cultural factors that have influenced Asian American immigration from 1820 to the present. The next four chapters are arranged into historical areas: pre-1900, 1990 to 1945, 1946 to 1974, and 1975 to the present. Chapter 6 contains valuable and fascinating information on Asian American cultural contributions (e.g., Chinese medicine, Asian-Indian cooking).

The book is strong on accessibility and visual resources, including maps, charts, black-and-white photographs, and diagrams on every page. It is printed on heavy paper and its quality is outstanding throughout. It includes valuable data on Asian Indians and Southeast Asian refugees in addition to the well-known Chinese, Japanese, Korean, and Filipino immigrants. Sources for each chapter and an unannotated bibliography list books, journal articles, and online references. The index is complete and well constructed.

This is an incredibly rich resource for anyone interested in the Asian American experience. It is especially valuable for students and teachers at all levels.—**Marshall E. Nunn**

S

139.   **Distinguished Asian Americans: A Biographical Dictionary.** Hyung-Chan Kim and others, eds. Westport, Conn., Greenwood Press, 1999. 430p. illus. index. $65.00. ISBN 0-313-28902-6.

Distinguished Asian Americans presents the lives and achievements of 166 well-known Asian Americans who have contributed to American society. Although not all of the persons discussed were born in the United States (some have immigrated to America), each has made their mark here. By using the term "Asian Americans" the authors of this work are referring to descendants of China, India, Japan, Korea, Pakistan, the Philippines, Cambodia, Laos, and Vietnam. The people featured include businesspeople, journalists, artists, community leaders, political leaders, authors, and celebrity personalities (e.g., Connie Chung, Kristi Yamaguchi), among others. Each entry averages one to two pages and provides birth and death dates (if applicable), a brief life story, major contributions to their field, and a bibliography. Many of the entries provide a black-and-white photograph. The two appendixes at the end of the work list the individuals featured by professional field and by ethnic subgroups. A name/subject index completes the volume.

This work is intended for middle to high school age children doing research on significant Asian American figures. It will be a good purchase for school libraries or larger public libraries.—**Shannon M. Graff**

P, S

140.   Ng, Franklin. **The Taiwanese Americans.** Westport, Conn., Greenwood Press, 1998. 163p. illus. maps. index. (The New Americans). $39.95. ISBN 0-313-29762-2.

Chinese Americans are the largest Asian American group, only slightly outnumbering Filipino Americans. Taiwanese Americans are the second largest subgroup of Chinese Americans, following in size immigrants from mainland China and outpacing those from Hong Kong and Singapore. These figures add more importance to this book because it is the first one published on Taiwanese Americans. It is another title in The New Americans series, which is "designed for high school and general readers" (p. x). It focuses on community organization, information networks, religion, culture, and the nature of the second generation. Even though it does provide helpful historical background information, its main emphasis is on the cultural and sociological aspects of Taiwanese American life.

The author covers his subject in 4 parts. The introduction gives basic background information on Taiwan's land, people, language, religion, and history. "Coming to America" discusses early Chinese and Taiwanese immigration, composition of the new immigrants, and family and youth patterns. "Living in America" is concerned with associations, newspapers and the media, religion, and festivals. The last part, "An Evolving Taiwanese American Identity," gives valuable information on conflicts with mainlanders, politics in Taiwan, the second generation, intergroup relations, and Taiwanese Americans' "complex and evolving identity" (p. 126). Black-and-white photographs illustrate scenes from contemporary cultural life and activities. Two appendixes profile biographies of six successful Taiwanese Americans and provide eleven statistical immigration tables. There is also an unannotated bibliography that includes Internet Websites.

Ng is a professor of anthropology at California State University, Fresno, and has authored and edited several notable books on Asian American studies, including *The Asian American Encyclopedia* (see ARBA 96, entry 394) and *Chinese American Struggle for Equality* (Rourke, 1992). He writes with clarity and authority, and this book, although not strictly a reference work, belongs in all libraries. [R: SLJ, Nov 98, p. 141]—**Marshall E. Nunn**

P, S

141.   Posadas, Barbara M. **The Filipino Americans.** Westport, Conn., Greenwood Press, 1999. 190p. illus. maps. index. (The New Americans). $39.95. ISBN 0-313-29742-8.

Historically, Filipino Americans have been known as an invisible minority, and there has been a real need for a comprehensive, up-to-date, reliable guide to their immigrant experience. Posadas' book admirably fills this need. Even though the books in the New Americans series are designed for high school and general readers, they are quite valuable for college students and teachers as well.

The book is tightly and logically organized into two parts and nine chapters. Its emphasis is on immigration, particularly after 1965; social and cultural issues, including values, customs, and economic and political power; identity in a multicultural society; contemporary issues for adults and elders; and the future of Filipino immigration.

A map, 5 statistical tables detailing Filipino immigration from 1920 to the present, and 18 black-and-white photographs effectively supplement the text. There are two appendixes: "Filipinos in the U.S. Census, 1910-2000" and "Notable Filipino Americans" (with eight short biographies). A glossary of cultural and immigration-related terms; a bibliography of films, videos, and distributors; and an unannotated bibliography of books and articles are also included. This is a survey but more information on certain aspects or the subject, especially on Filipinos in Alaska and Hawaii, would be helpful.

With this book, Posadas has established herself as the leading authority on Filipino Americans. She is eminently qualified as a professor of history at Northern Illinois University, as a member of the editorial boards of *Amerasia* and the *Journal of American Ethnic History*, and as the director of the Filipino National Historical Society.—**Marshall E. Nunn**

Blacks

Atlases

P
142.   Asante, Molefi K., and Mark T. Mattson. **The African-American Atlas: Black History and Culture—An Illustrated Reference.** New York, Macmillan General Reference/Simon & Schuster Macmillan, 1998. 251p. illus. maps. $34.95. ISBN 0-02-864984-2.

From ancient African origins to present-day status, this reference, an update of the 1991 *Historical and Cultural Atlas of African Americans* (see ARBA 92, entry 343), examines African American history and culture with maps, photographs, statistics, and narratives. Arranged chronologically, chapters are given thematic titles based on spirituals that represent various aspects of African American history and life.

Although it is called an atlas, this work is much more. There are clear, detailed maps that provide graphic representation of events and information. The text integrates the history and culture of African Americans. There are also graphs, statistical charts, photographs, and drawings. One of the strengths of this work is the biographical information of leading African Americans, enhanced by clear, captioned photographs. Other appealing features include discussions of famous court cases significant to African Americans and insets that provide interesting tidbits, such as the Reconstruction Amendments, selected African American inventors, traditional African American colleges and universities, and African American servicemen awarded the Medal of Honor. Appendixes offer dates to remember, a reference list, and a comprehensive index. The oversized format allows for wide margins, generous type size, and easy-to-read maps and graphs. Bold chapter headings on every page allow easy access.

This reference should be a welcome addition to most libraries in that it provides a concise, chronological history of African Americans. The maps and other graphic materials serve to enhance the text and to provide statistical data, including that on the current status of African Americans. [R: Choice, Oct 99, p. 311]—**Dana McDougald**

Bibliographies

C, P
143.   **Strong Souls Singing: African American Books for Our Daughters and Our Sisters.** Archie Givens, ed. New York, W. W. Norton, 1998. 145p. illus. index. $22.00; $11.00pa. ISBN 0-393-02745-7; 0-393-31780-3pa.

A companion to *Spirited Minds: African American Books for Our Sons and Our Brothers* (W. W. Norton, 1997), also edited by Archie Givens, this annotated bibliography provides descriptions of more than 100 titles recommended for young readers. The volume is divided into 5 sections—History, Drama, Novels and Short Stories, Autobiographies and Biographies, and Poetry—with Novels and Short Stories being the lengthiest. One title is listed on each page and includes publication year, author, names of other contributors and awards received (if applicable), and number of pages. The descriptions are a paragraph in length and are followed by a suggested reading level. The typeface and layout are appealing and woodcut illustrations add to the appeal. The book includes title, author, and reading level indexes. Although a number of books have been published recently to offer reading lists to African American children, such as Pamela Toussaint's *Great Books for African American Children* and Donna Rand's *Black Books Galore!*, this title is designed particularly for female readers and incorporates the broadest spectrum of reading levels and interests. [R: BR, Nov/Dec 98, p. 84; SLJ, April 99, p. 45]
—**Susanna Van Sant**

Biographies

S
144.   **African American Biography, Volume 5.** By Judson Knight. Lawrence W. Baker, ed. Farmington Hills, Mich., U*X*L/Gale, 1999. 255p. illus. index. $39.00. ISBN 0-7876-3562-6. ISSN 1522-2934.

The 5th volume of the *African American Biography* continues as an excellent source for middle school and junior high school students. This new volume includes 40 biographies; 22 are new and 18 are updates from earlier profiles. The new biographies include historical figures such as Cinque and the Delaney sisters; sports heroes such as Tiger Woods, Dominique Dawes, and Venus Williams; entertainers; political leaders; and authors. Each biography includes a picture of photo, a readable narrative that also includes controversial aspects of the person's life, a quotation summarizing their philosophy, and a short bibliography. The bibliographies consist of Web pages, books, and popular magazines. Special features include extensive cross-references and a timeline of significant African American events from 1731 through 1998. Some of the terms in the glossary are curious (e.g., Halley's Comet, Soviet Union, and Yoga). There is a comprehensive list of all entries indicating volume and page number. Also included is a general bibliography of books and magazines. This series is not as comprehensive as other Gale publications, such as *Reference Library of Black America* (94th ed., 1994), *Notable Black American Women* (see ARBA 97, entry 34; see ARBA 93, entry 52), and *Who's Who Among African Americans* (1998/99 ed.; see ARBA 99, entry 379). This volume is highly recommended for school and public libraries.—**Karen Y. Stabler**

P, S

145.   Haskins, Jim. **African American Military Heroes.** New York, John Wiley, 1998. 182p. illus. index. (Black Stars Series). $19.95. ISBN 0-471-14577-7.

Haskins, a prolific writer of African American young adult books, highlights the careers of 30 black military figures, both male and female, from Private Peter Salem's service at the Battle of Lexington in 1775 through the contributions of General Colin Powell and Commander Robert O. Goodman Jr. Few of these names will be familiar even to older students, and although the volume is aimed toward a young adult audience, readers of all ages will find something new here. The well-written essays are brief, sometimes no more than 300 words long, but all include a photograph or artist's rendering of the subject. Sidebars throughout further explicate the milieu of the individuals (e.g., buffalo soldiers). The author also makes it a point to highlight the subjects' educational backgrounds, which parents and teachers will appreciate. Unfortunately, although Haskins includes a brief bibliography at the end of this work, there are no references for further reading tied to specific essays.

This work is the only up-to-date work on this subject with a younger audience in mind. Students seeking more detailed information should refer to Michael Lee Lanning's *The African-American Soldier* (Birch Lane, 1997) and Gerald Astor's *The Right to Fight* (Presidio, 1998), in addition to the numerous recent works on specific military branches and units. This work is highly recommended for all young adult and undergraduate collections. [R: SLJ, Nov 98, p. 136]—**Anthony J. Adam**

C, P, S

146.   Kranz, Rachel, and Philip J. Koslow. **The Biographical Dictionary of African Americans.** New York, Facts on File, 1999. 310p. index. $35.00; $18.95pa. ISBN 0-8160-3903-8; 0-8160-3904-6pa.

This is a revised and expanded edition of Kranz's work of the same title issued in 1992. The book is intended for young adults, but would be useful to any age group. Entries are well-written and substantial (most entries being about 1,000 words in length), and there are cross-references and suggestions for further reading. Entries are initialed to indicate authorship. The selection of people for inclusion was intended to be representative and not all-encompassing. It includes as many black "firsts" as possible. A sampling of key figures in the development of Black American history and those involved in its major movements from the eighteenth century into the 1990s. The authors tried to include persons that many readers will know, or will find inspiring. The initial entry is for Henry Louis (Hank) Aaron, the all-time home run king. The final entry is for Charles Young, an army officer, who was the third black person to graduate from West Point. Between these 2 names are an additional 235 entries with numerous portraits, some full-page. Entries include civil rights activists and leaders, actors, artists, athletes, educators, musicians, soldiers, and writers. Judge Thomas has an entry, but not Anita Hill. O. J. Simpson is included, but not Johnnie Cochran. Naomi Campbell, Della Reese, Redd Foxx, Dennis Rodman, Al Sharpton, and Mike Tyson did not make the book. Back matter includes a 4-page bibliography of source books on African American studies, most published in the 1980s and 1990s. Also, appendixes include entries by area of activity, entries by year of birth, and a chronology. The index not only includes the biographies, but also book titles and references to other persons and events. Rachel Kranz is an award-winning radio and video journalist who has written numerous books for young people. Philip Koslow has taught modern history and political science at the university level, and written and edited many books for young people. [R: SLJ, Aug 99, p. 184]—**Frank J. Anderson**

C, P

147.   **Notable Black American Men.** Jessie Carney Smith, ed. Farmington Hills, Mich., Gale, 1999. 1365p. illus. index. $90.00. ISBN 0-7876-07633.

Ever since the publication of Smith's excellent *Notable Black American Women* (see ARBA 93, entry 52), patrons have demanded a similar volume covering men. *Notable Black American Men* (NBAM) in every way measures up to the quality of that work, offering 500, 1- to 5-page biographies of African American men, both living and dead, from poet Jupiter Hammon to golfer Tiger Woods. Nominees for inclusion represent all fields of endeavor and meet at least one or more strict criteria, such as a leading businessman, noted orator, government official, or leader for social justice. Each signed essay includes essential biographical information and a brief secondary bibliography; most feature black-and-white portraits, current addresses, and collection locations. Separate geographical, occupational, and subject indexes conclude the volume, although each of these could have used more work.

With so many different essayists, quality varies widely, but Smith's editorial team achieves an overall uniformity of tone and scope. However, controversial matters tend to be glossed over. Additionally, the difficult task of choosing only 500 representative men forces many well-known names off the list. Duke Ellington and Michael Jackson are included, but Count Basie and Marvin Gaye are not. General Frank Peterson made the cut, but not General Calvin Waller. The lesser-known and forgotten individuals who are included (e.g., Rex Ingram, William DeHart Hubbard, Robert Purvis) make NBAM a major biographical reference for all libraries. [R: BL, 15 Feb 99, p. 1085; Choice, July/Aug 99, p. 1915]—**Anthony J. Adam**

Dictionaries and Encyclopedias

C, P

148.   **Africana: The Encyclopedia of the African and African American Experience.** Kwame Anthony Appiah and Henry Louis Gates Jr., eds. Reading, Mass., Basic Civitas Books Perseus Books, 1999. 2095p. illus. maps. $100.00. ISBN 0-465-00071-1.

At long last, W. E. B. Du Bois's dream of an *Encyclopedia Africana* has come to fruition, thanks to the efforts of editors Appiah and Gates, along with an international team of 220 scholars. More than 3,500 signed articles cover the full scope of Africa and the Diaspora, with approximately two-fifths of the text devoted to Africa and the rest primarily covering North and South America. The editors also chose to focus on the entire continent of Africa rather than just "Black Africa," giving a broader perspective on the various cultures and peoples. The articles in this rather heavy volume range from a brief paragraph to five tri-column pages and aim to provide both fact and interpretation whenever warranted, particularly on socioeconomic topics (e.g., "Islam and Fundamentalism"). Each country study receives a general article and a ready-reference follow-up with almanac-type data. *See also* references abound, although some of the subject headings are awkward and some topics (e.g., education) are given short shrift. However, the numerous stunning black-and-white and color charts, maps, and photos alone are worth the purchase price. Geared toward a mainstream audience, this encyclopedia is extremely well written, although some Afrocentrist scholars deplore its Eurocentric basis.

Africana has also been expanded in a CD-ROM format as *Microsoft Encarta Africana 2000* to include a library of Black America, a music timeline, and other special features. Even with its arguably philosophical flaws, *Africana* is a must purchase for all academic and public libraries. [R: LJ, 15 Nov 99, p. 58]—**Anthony J. Adam**

Handbooks and Yearbooks

C, P, S

149.   **The New York Public Library African American Desk Reference.** New York, Songstone Press/John Wiley, 1999. 606p. illus. index. $34.95. ISBN 0-471-23924-0.

This new addition to the New York Public Library's series of desktop references derives from the extensive collections of the Schomburg Center for Research in Black Culture, one of the largest and best sources for African-American studies. As with earlier almanacs in this series, the *African American Desk Reference* includes brief information, lists, contact information, and special terms (e.g., recipes) on all aspects of African-American life, from the transatlantic slave trade to the present. Given the potential scope of this work, it is not surprising that the 17 chapters range over history, law, the performing arts, sports, media, health, science and technology, education, religion, and business. However, as is the nature of almanacs, the information is rarely in-depth, although the editors wisely included numerous bibliographies and Websites for further research.

Although most of the information here will have a relatively long shelf life, some of it, particularly addresses and lists, will date rapidly. The editors have attempted to feature the latest available data (e.g., *Black Enterprises*'s top companies for 1999), and updates should be included in future editions, along with corrections of minor errors (e.g., Prairie View A&M University was founded in 1876, not 1878 as listed). More illustrations, especially charts and graphs, would help future editions also. However, this well-edited inexpensive volume is one of the best in the series and is highly recommended for all public, academic, and school libraries. [R: LJ, 15 Sept 99, pp. 70-71]—**Anthony J. Adam**

P, S

150.   Patrick, Diane. **The New York Public Library Amazing African American History: A Book of Answers for Kids.** New York, John Wiley, 1998. 170p. illus. index. (New York Public Library Answer Books for Kids Series). $12.95pa. ISBN 0-471-19217-1.

This latest New York Public Library (NYPL) adolescent reference work tells the story of African Americans from the beginning of the slave trade through the mid-1990s in a refreshing, balanced manner. Every aspect of African American history is covered, from politics to arts and business, with attention paid to significant personalities and events in each era. Patrick does not aim for comprehensiveness, but it is impressive to see just how much she includes without bogging down. Although the subtitle proclaims this book is written for kids, the audience is closer to at least junior high level and above. The language and writing style throughout are simple and direct, but never condescending.

Patrick's Socratic approach offers one brief definition or explanation to a question (e.g., "What is the Ku Klux Klan?") that automatically leads to another ("What other white hate groups existed?"). It is easy to get caught up in the flow of expositions and the reader will undoubtedly accidentally learn new facts along the way. However, as a dictionary, the format does not hold together well. The numerous photographs, reproductions, and insets with quick information only add to the quality of this volume. Public and high school libraries will be well served by this text, but academics will find it too juvenile.—**Anthony J. Adam**

C, P

151.   Torres-Saillant, Silvio, and Ramona Hernández. **The Dominican Americans.** Westport, Conn., Greenwood Press, 1998. 184p. illus. index. (The New Americans). $39.95. ISBN 0-313-29839-4.

During the 1930 to 1961 dictatorship of Trujillo, the Dominican Republic's population increased from 900,000 to 3,000,000. During recent decades, the United States has supported Western-leaning but unpopular dictators of this island by allowing entry visas to revolutionaries. These dictators have taken international loans and accepted global corporations but neither have increased the incomes of the poorer class—the majority of the population. Since the 1970s as many as 20,000 uneducated people migrate each year, usually to New York City. Because the United States has changed economically from industrial to service oriented, low-level jobs are not common and when found are low paying. The 1990s cutoff of welfare money is parallel to youth being attracted to the drug culture. Some Dominicans write and create music and art but Latin American professional organizations have been slow to acknowledge this. This story is clearly and coherent told by two Dominican Americans, emphasizing gender, race, and class issues. Although religion, health, and family perspectives might be the genesis of a solution, they are not developed; instead social determinism has precedence. Education, work, and political muscle are believed to be the paths to rectitude of dire circumstances. The prevalence of poverty around the world and the problem of how to curtail it, say nothing of escape it, make this book valuable. Self-respect and validation from neighbors and communities are well supported by these writers and their data. The bibliography, created by a separate scholar, is a treasure in itself.—**Elizabeth L. Anderson**

Indians of North America

Dictionaries and Encyclopedias

C

152.   **The Encyclopedia of Native American Economic History.** Bruce E. Johansen, ed. Westport, Conn., Greenwood Press, 1999. 301p. index. $85.00. ISBN 0-313-30623-0.

Any student or scholar of Native American history understands that economic interests were and are the driving force in the relationship between Native Americans and the white race. These interests are not always clearly articulated in Native American studies, but they underlie almost all interactions. This volume provides a sound single source for an overview of many of the economic issues. Johansen suggests, in the introduction, there is no active body of scholarship addressing economic issues; however, his 18-page selected bibliography suggests there is a rather large literature by Linda Barrington titled *The Other Side of the Frontier: Economic Explorations into Native American History* (Westview Press, 1999). Topics range in scope from place names to broad areas, such as contemporary economic development; from precontact economic activities to modern mining operations. Coverage also includes people (Popé) and national organizations (National Center for American Indian Enterprise Development). The majority of entries end with a reference or two to other resources on the topic. There is no claim that the work is comprehensive. The index is useful but does not provide any insight as to why some topics are or are not included. One can find reasonably concise summaries of many but not all tribal economics; the problem is which ones. For example, for the southwestern United States there are entries for the Apaches, Navajos, and Pueblos but none for the Pima or any of the Pai–speaking groups. There is a long entry for the Yamasee but nothing for the Yakima. Some of the information can be found in other general encyclopedias dealing with Native Americans. However, this reviewer is unaware of any other single source covering such a wide range of Native American economic issues. This work will be most useful in an undergraduate reference collection. [R: BL, 1 May 99, p. 1616; Choice, Oct 99, p. 312]—**G. Edward Evans**

C, P, S

153.   Green, Rayna, with Melanie Fernandez. **The British Museum Encyclopedia of Native North America.** Bloomington, Ind., Indiana University Press, 1999. 213p. illus. $39.95; $27.95pa. ISBN 0-253-33597-3; 0-253-21339-8pa.

This is not your grandfather's encyclopedia. Instead, in an unusual format, it is an exciting reference on American Indian history and cultures from a Native perspective. Extraordinarily readable, it extends beyond the common purpose of an encyclopedia to a different kind of reference. Difficult to explain in many ways, it addresses many widely divergent topics important to Indian people such as Africans, African Americans and Indians, diplomacy, dams, coyotes, clans, land, pipes, population, Pocahontas, the Bureau of Indian Affairs, self-determination, self-government, squash, and stomp dance. Abundantly illustrated with historical and contemporary photographs, art, and historical documents, it is fascinating reading. Many of the entries are explained through essays; historical and current quotations from poetry, literature, and newspapers; and even some "Indian" jokes.

Readers should caution that because the book was first published in Britain, British spellings and grammatical structure prevail. Teachers might wish that the maps were more clear and abundant. But this could be remedied easily in the classroom.

In addition to providing a new and compelling perspective on Native America, the book is well organized and convenient, with words in bold typeface to note where there are entries on that particular subject. There is a comprehensive general index and an index of individuals. Also for those who want to know more, there are sections that provide the sources of information, picture credits, and the sources of all quotations. The list of errata is longer than one would like, but it is a small issue in a book that meets a great need.

The authors state that this encyclopedia "offer[s] some introduction to the people's issues and ideas (past and present) that make up Native North American history and culture." As such, and because of its urgently needed Native perspective, it should be in every high school, college, and public school library. [R: LJ, Aug 99, pp. 76-78]—**Karen D. Harvey**

C, P

154.   Johnson, Michael. **Macmillan Encyclopedia of Native American Tribes.** 2d ed. New York, Macmillan Library Reference USA, 1999. 288p. illus. maps. index. $80.00. ISBN 0-02-865409-9.

Much of North American society has been influenced by Native American culture. This beautifully illustrated encyclopedia presents an overview of 400 separately identifiable tribes. The presentation has been largely improved in this new edition. The previous edition was printed in black-and-white with a short, central section of Robert Hook's color illustrations. The editors have now integrated these illustrations into the text along with the captions that were missing from the 1st edition. The text itself, aside from a few corrections, remains mostly the same. The glossary has been expanded and the appendixes now include a list of pow-wows, another of Native American museum exhibits, and tables of Native American populations in North American (based on the 1990 census). Also new to this edition is a useful almanac of Native American holidays and festivals and a list of Websites relating to the study of Native Americans. Johnson has researched the material, culture, demography, and linguistic relationships of Native Americans for more than 30 years, and has led numerous field studies with the cooperation of many present-day Native American communities. He is also a former associate editor of *American Indian Crafts and Culture* as well as *Pow-wow Trails.* This encyclopedia is recommended for all Native American collections.—**Cari Ringelheim**

C

155.   Lyon, William S. **Encyclopedia of Native American Shamanism: Sacred Ceremonies of North America.** Santa Barbara, Calif., ABC-CLIO, 1998. 468p. illus. maps. index. $64.00. ISBN 0-87436-933-9.

Over the past six years there has been a surprising interest in publishing reference works dealing with various aspects of Native American spirituality and religion. Undoubtedly, some of that interest comes from the market potential for "New Age" publications and some from a true interest in understanding Native American spiritual/religious beliefs and practices. Lyon has compiled an interesting, if narrowly focused, book that draws on anthropological data on Shamanism. According to the preface, it is also a continuation of the *Encyclopedia of Native American Healing* (see ARBA 97, entry 340). Entries range in length from fewer than 50 words to 2 or 3 pages. Most of the entries contain several quotations and references to ethnographic monographs. Full bibliographic information for the material cited in entries is provided in an appendix. Approximately two-thirds of the entries relate to specific aspects of Shamanism and other Native American terms. Thus, this volume will be of greatest value to a person who has some prior knowledge of the topic rather than a person seeking general information. One useful aspect of the index is it brings together information about Shamanism by group (Fox, Hopi) and broad topics such as dreams, ghosts, and hunting medicine. There is very little overlap between this title and *The Encyclopedia of Native American Religions* (see ARBA 93, entry 432) or the *Dictionary of Native American Mythology* (see ARBA 94, entry 418). Given that this is a continuation of the author's previous book on healing, there is little overlap between the two titles. A 7-page ethnobotanical bibliography and 27-page index round out the volume. Coverage also includes Canadian and Inuit material (some listed under Eskimo). This will be a useful volume for collections supporting anthropology course work. [R: LJ, 1 Mar 99, p. 74; BL, 15 April 99, p. 1353; Choice, Oct 99, p. 314; RUSQ, Fall 99, p. 89]—**G. Edward Evans**

C, P

156.   **U*X*L Encyclopedia of Native American Tribes.** Sharon Malinowski, Anna Sheets, and Linda Schmittroth, eds. Farmington Hills, Mich., U*X*L/Gale, 1999. 4v. illus. maps. $99.00/set. ISBN 0-7876-2838-7.

This encyclopedia, written at a 5th grade reading level, contains entries on 80 Native American tribes, confederacies, or groups. The entries are divided into 10 sections in 4 volumes: The Northeast and Southeast; The Great Basin and Southwest; The Arctic, Subarctic, Great Plains, and Plateau; and California and the Pacific Northwest. Each section begins with an essay that introduces the area's history and shared cultural experiences. The entries for individual groups follow. Each begins with basic information, such as name, location, population, language family, and group affiliations. This is followed by specific topics, such as history, language, religion, government, and arts. Suggestions for further reading conclude each entry.

One problem with this title is that there are simply not enough tribal entries. For example, the Southeast includes six tribal entries: Caddo, Cherokee, Chickasaw, Choctaw, Creek, and Seminole. On the map entitled "Historic Locations of U.S. Native Groups," there are 10 tribes in Georgia alone. Six is not representative of the region as a whole.

"Moundbuilders" is an extremely curious entry considering it combines 4 distinctively different cultures, dating from 1500 to 1751 B.C.E., into 1 group. The Creeks and Cherokees had much more in common than these four groups but they certainly merit separate entries. The Mississippian Culture also extended further west than Arkansas. Some of the finest examples of Mississippian shell engravings come from the Spiro Mound Group in Eastern Oklahoma. Readers interested in the moundbuilders would be better served by *Archaeology of Prehistoric Native America: An Encyclopedia* (see ARBA 99, entry 443).

Sections entitled "Words to Know" and "Timeline" are included, along with many maps and pictures that supplement the text nicely. Each volume also contains a complete bibliography of books, periodicals, Websites, and CD-ROMs. The volumes uses continuous pagination and each contains the index for the entire set.

Future editions of this work are planned to expand on the number of Native American groups profiled. Rather than wait and buy each subsequent edition, interested individuals should just purchase *The Gale Encyclopedia of Native American Tribes* (see ARBA 99, entry 389). It shares both general format and two editors with this volume. It also contains nearly 400 tribal entries in much more detail. [R: BR, Nov/Dec 99, pp. 79-80]

—**John R. Burch Jr.**

C, P

157.   Waldman, Carl. **Encyclopedia of Native American Tribes.** rev. ed. Illustrated by Molly Braun. New York, Facts on File, 1999. 312p. illus. maps. index. $65.00. ISBN 0-8160-3963-1.

Carl Waldman has prepared several reference books about Native Americans for Facts on File—*Who Was Who in Native American History* (see ARBA 91, entry 402) and *Word Dance: Language of Native American Cultures* (see ARBA 95, entry 437). In addition to the preceding titles, he has compiled two other titles in collaboration with illustrator Molly Braun—*Atlas of the North American Indian* (see ARBA 86, entry 380) and *Encyclopedia of Native American Tribes* (see ARBA 89, entry 364). This is a revised edition of the latter title and is 20 pages longer. Entries and illustrations that appeared in the 1st edition appear to be only slightly changed. This is based on checking eight entries selected at random. Most of the changes are in the form of rewording the same information and in one case a new sentence about current economic conditions. Some of the increase in length is due to an extra 10 pages of front matter, additional entries in the glossary, as well as an updated and expanded bibliography. The question for libraries with the 1st edition is, is there enough new information to make this a worthwhile purchase? For libraries with only limited customer interest in Native Americans the answer is probably no. Where there is a strong interest in Native American studies and the library holds the 1988 edition, it would be best to get an examination copy before making a final decision. For libraries that did not buy the 1st edition the answer is clearly this is a worthwhile addition to a general reference collection.—**G. Edward Evans**

Handbooks and Yearbooks

C, P

158.   Carrasco, Davíd, with Scott Sessions. **Daily Life of the Aztecs: People of the Sun and Earth.** Westport, Conn., Greenwood Press, 1998. 282p. illus. maps. index. (The Greenwood Press "Daily Life Through History" Series). $45.00. ISBN 0-313-29558-1.

Carrasco, director of the Moses Mesoamerican Archive and professor of history of religions at Princeton University, and Sessions, doctoral candidate in the department of religion at Princeton University, have combined their talents to present this overview of pre-Columbian Aztec culture that reflects the latest scholarship while remaining accessible to lay readers. It provides a glimpse of Aztec life that is often overlooked in texts that tend to dwell on subjects such as ritualistic human sacrifice and cannibalism. These subjects are also included in this book but are examined in context with their role in society as a whole.

The first two chapters are designed as an introduction to the geography and cosmology of the Aztec world. Chapter 3 focuses on life in the community in general. Three chapters focusing on education, societal dynamics, and aesthetics supplement it. Chapter 7 is extremely informative and focuses on human sacrifice and its role in Aztec religion. The authors carefully explain the role of priests and the function of sacrifice in an effort to dispel the stereotypical view of bloodthirsty priests that has dominated the literature on the subject. The 10th chapter focuses on the clash of cultures between the Aztecs and Spaniards that proved to be the end of the Aztec Empire. The 11th chapter serves as an epilogue, which examines the impact of the Aztecs on Mexican culture today. All of the chapters are greatly enhanced by the large number of pictures and photographs scattered throughout the text. The book also includes both an index and a selected bibliography. Especially noteworthy is a glossary, which includes a pronunciation guide for Nahuatl terms. This excellent book is recommended for public and academic libraries.—**John R. Burch Jr.**

C, P, S

159.   Pritzker, Barry M. **Native America Today: A Guide to Community Politics and Culture.** Santa Barbara, Calif., ABC-CLIO, 1999. 453p. illus. maps. index. $75.00. ISBN 1-57607-077-8.

Although it is common to find reference sources on how Native Americans lived hundreds of years ago, it is more difficult to find up-to-date information on the current situations of Native tribes today. This work from ABC-CLIO examines education, health, and tribal identity issues. After a brief introduction the book is arranged into 3 sections: "Contemporary Issues"; Contemporary Profiles of Tribes and Groups"; and "Documents: Acts of Congress, Executive Orders, Court Decisions, Laws, and Resolutions." Each section has entries that are arranged alphabetically. "Contemporary Issues" explains in detail the current situations of Native tribes concerning things like arts and crafts, education, land acquisition or reacquisition, economic development, sacred sites, and control of natural resources. "Contemporary Profiles of Tribes and Groups" examines the current status of 32 tribes within the United States today. Each tribe is described within two to three pages and topics of most concern to that particular tribe are noted. The 3d section provides reproductions of political documents, including Congressional acts, executive orders, court decisions, laws, and resolutions. The three-page bibliography that follows will be useful for researchers. The four appendixes at the end of the volume provide names of federally recognized tribes, Indian groups who have petitioned for federal recognition, first nations in Canada, and maps of federal Indian lands.

This work will serve as a basic tool for those researching the current status of Native American affairs. It will be useful in school, undergraduate, and public libraries.—**Shannon M. Graff**

Jews

P

160.   **American Jewish Desk Reference.** By the American Jewish Historical Society. New York, Random House, 1999. 642p. illus. index. $39.95. ISBN 0-375-40243-8.

This compilation of information, principally biographical, focuses on the Jewish experience in America from the sixteenth century to the present day. It is a comprehensive guide to the history, religious observances, culture, and achievements of the Jewish people in the United States. The publication is sponsored by the American Jewish Historical Society, which since 1893 has been publishing works documenting and recording the Jewish experience in America. The 12 contributors include well-known scholars and academics. However, the authors of the nearly 900 entries are not identified, which is a limitation of the book. The book includes a short guide to its use, which is helpful.

The entries are arranged in 13 thematic parts, each dealing with 1 aspect of American Jewish life and culture. The book begins with history—a useful brief chronology of the history of Jews in America from 1585 to 1999. Other parts include "Judaism and Community in America"; "Rituals, Celebrations, Holidays and Family Life"; "Law, Government and Politics"; "American Zionism and United States Relations with Israel"; "Business, Labor and Finance"; "Education and Intellectual Life"; "Sports and Games"; "Art, Architecture and Photography"; "Music, Dance and Theater"; "Radio, Television and Film"; "Books, Newspapers and Magazines"; "Language and Literature"; and "Science, Medicine and Social Science." Each part begins with a brief overview, and includes background descriptive information, biographies of key figures in the subject area, and a bibliography. The biographical information predominates. The biographies include dates, a brief identification of the person, and his or her major contributions. The structure and organization of each part are not clearly evident, which is sometimes puzzling.

It is useful that the table of contents lists all the main entries. Each part also lists the entries included in that section of the book. This improves access to information included in the text. There is also a detailed, comprehensive index that provides easy access to specific entries. Entries in the text are printed in bold typeface. The numerous interesting black-and-white photographs are another strong feature of the book.

The 2 appendixes, "Finding Out About Jews Around the World" and "Organizations and Resources," are useful guides for further study and research. They include recommended titles and brief descriptions of books as well as names and addresses of selected organizations, research institutes, museums, libraries, local historical societies, and newspapers and magazines.

Even though the scope of the book is broad, its coverage is uneven. The section on music, dance, and theater has the greatest number of entries, followed by radio, television, and film. The science, medicine, and social science section is the weakest, with many notable omissions, including Jewish Nobel Prize-winners such as Stephen Weinberg, Josh Lederberg, and Salvador Luria. The section on Judaism and community in American fails to include mention of the Jewish Renewal Movement, and does not include biographies of important contributors to Jewish Renewal, such as Rabbi Zalman Schacter Shalomi and Rabbi Arthur Waskow.

The book is aimed more toward a popular rather than scholarly audience. It is an interesting, convenient compilation, balancing its strong and weak points, and a useful addition to public, school, temple, and synagogue libraries.—**Susan J. Freiband**

P, S

161.   Burstein, Chaya M. **A Kid's Catalog of Israel.** rev. ed. Philadelphia, Jewish Publication Society, 1998. 279p. illus. maps. index. $16.95pa. ISBN 0-8276-0651-6.

First published in 1988, the revised edition of *A Kid's Catalog of Israel* provides an overview of the land and its cultures and peoples. Israel is a young country with an ancient history and a diverse population. The 17 chapters of this book are a trip through time and the land. They point out historical sites, geographic features, and wildlife. Interviews with Arab and Jewish adults and children provide a personal connection between readers and their Israeli peers. Maps, quizzes, games, songs, stories, recipes, and craft projects offer opportunities for hands-on activities that increase understanding of the country and its rich heritage. Although this is a children's book, adults will enjoy it. The reading level is appropriate for ages 10 and up. It is an excellent source of projects for classes, youth groups, and families. *A Kid's Catalog of Israel* is recommended for school, synagogue, and public libraries. Families with young children will want it for their homes as well.—**Barbara M. Bibel**

P

162.   Orleck, Annelise. **The Soviet Jewish Americans.** Westport, Conn., Greenwood Press, 1999. 216p. illus. index. (The New Americans). $39.95. ISBN 0-313-30074-7.

One of a series of books that study recent groups of immigrants to the United States, this lively, moving narrative provides the first comprehensive account of the immigration of nearly 500,000 Soviet Jews to the United States between 1967 and 1997. By weaving immigrant voices and numerous photographs together with historical, journalistic, social service, and psychological studies, this book offers a highly readable introduction to the history, politics, and culture of this important new American population. Following a format similar to other books in the series (see ARBA 99, entry 374, for a review of *The Korean Americans*), topics covered include the varied reasons for the exodus of Soviet Jews from the Soviet Union, their experiences in the United States, the communities they have created, and the cultural problems they have encountered. Readers will find fascinating details on religion, politics, foods, festivals, gender roles, employment trends, and general community life. The author, an expert on this group, dispels stereotypical notions about Soviet Jewish immigrants by exploring their tremendous social, political, and cultural diversity, and also shows the impact this ethnic group has had on their adopted country. An appendix profiles some noted Soviet Jewish Americans and is followed by an extensive bibliography and an index. The book is targeted toward the high–school–age and general reader; this might seem overambitious, but due to the scarcity of books dealing with this subject and to its engaging style, it achieves its goal admirably.—**Larry Lobel**

P, S

163.   **The Shengold Jewish Encyclopedia.** Mordecai Schreiber, ed. Rockville, Md., Shengold Books/Schreiber Publishing, 1998. 301p. illus. $36.00. ISBN 1-887563-43-1.

First published as the *Junior Jewish Encyclopedia* (14th rev. ed.; Shengold Books/Schreiber Publishing, 1997), this source has been revised and rewritten as a tool for all age groups. It is a ready-reference source with brief entries on a wide variety of Judaica-related subjects. Users are encouraged to consult other sources for more comprehensive, in-depth information.

The layout is attractive with double columns and ample margins. The alphabetic entries range in length from a few sentences to four pages. They cover people (Abraham, Martin Buber, Jeremiah), places (Iowa, Poland, Uruguay), religious concepts (heaven and hell, Kabbalah, Teshuvah), holidays (Passover, Sukkot), historical events (Holocaust, Yom Kippur War), and arts and letters (music, Hebrew literature, stage and screen). There are also articles on diverse subjects such as stamps, sports, and education. Maps, charts, and illustrations augment the text. Cross-references appear in bold typeface within the entries. *See* references direct users to the proper entry when necessary. As in any general work, there are some inconsistencies. Well-known musicians Isaac Stern, Andre Previn, and Jan Peerce are in the article on Jews in music, while Artur Rubinstein, Itzhak Perlman, and Pinchas Zuckerman have their own entries. Reconstructionism has an article, but the Orthodox, Conservative, and Reform denominations are covered under Judaism. There is no entry for the term *kosher*, but if one looks up *kashrut*, there is a *see* reference to dietary laws.

Although less comprehensive than *The New Standard Jewish Encyclopedia* (7th ed.; see ARBA 93, entry 448) or *The Encyclopedia of Judaism* (see ARBA 91, entry 1449), this is an excellent, inexpensive ready-reference source. With articles on exotic groups such as the Karaites and the Khazers as well as the mythical golem, it is a good choice for school, synagogue, and small public libraries as well as home collections. [R: BL, 15 Nov 98, pp. 613-614; Choice, May 99, p. 1594]—**Barbara M. Bibel**

Latin Americans

P, S

164.   Fernández-Shaw, Carlos M. Alfonso Bertodano Stourton, and others. **The Hispanic Presence in North America from 1492 to Today.** updated ed. New York, Facts on File, 1999. 396p. illus. maps. index. $45.00. ISBN 0-8160-4010-9.

This book traces the Spanish presence in the United States from the sixteenth-century explorers and explorations. It is organized geographically by state with separate chapters for those states with a significant Hispanic community: Florida, Arizona, Colorado, California, New Mexico, Texas, Louisiana, and Missouri. The first part presents a general history of Spain's influence in the United States, including the missionaries, colonization, present Hispanic population, outstanding Americans of Spanish origin, Hispanic culture, and contributions to the economy and the law. The second part focuses on the Atlantic Coast states with a historical overview and a section on Spanish place-names for each state. Part 3 covers the states on the east bank of the Mississippi River; part 4 the states on the west bank; part 5 states of the Southwest; part 6 the Rocky Mountain states; and part 7 Pacific Coast states.

The book includes several appendixes: a chronology, a listing of Spanish governors, Spanish missions, Spanish forts and presidios, historical societies, national parks, monuments and other sites of historic interest, North American universities and colleges with chapters of the National Collegiate Hispanic Honor Society, state chapters of the American Association of Teachers of Spanish and Portuguese, Hispanic associations, holidays and festivals, periodicals published in Spanish that highlight Hispanic history and culture, and radio and television stations that broadcast in Spanish. In addition, there is a list of selected readings and an index. The illustrations include black-and-white photographs and maps.

The author is a Spaniard, historian, lawyer, writer, and diplomat. The work was originally written in Spanish (in 1987) and translated in 1991. This edition includes updated appendixes prepared by Dr. Gerardo Piña Rosales, a professor of Spanish language and literature at City University of New York. The handbook is a useful reference tool for high school, community college, and public library collections, particularly in institutions and communities with notable Hispanic populations.—**Susan J. Freiband**

P, S

165.   Ochoa, George. **The New York Public Library Amazing Hispanic American History: A Book of Answers for Kids.** New York, John Wiley, 1998. 192p. illus. maps. index. (New York Public Library Answer Books for Kids Series). $12.95pa. ISBN 0-471-19204-X.

Amazing Hispanic American History is an easy-to-read book of questions and answers for young adults, covering historical and cultural topics. The glossary, recommended reading list, and index are all clear and helpful.

Several ruled boxes contain short paragraphs of additional information. Shorter factual notes of one or two sentences enhance the broad margins of the page, providing trivia related to the topic being discussed.

Ochoa provides chapters with broad overviews, such as "Who are Hispanic Americans?" and "Hispanic American Life." He also looks at specific immigrant groups from Mexico, Puerto Rico, Cuba, Dominican Republic, Central America, South America, and Spain in seven separate "Coming From" chapters. He focuses on historical topics in "Before the United States" and "The Lost Land."

The book is for the most part successful in presenting balanced answers to difficult questions, such as "Are Hispanics a race?" and "Why are so many Hispanic Americans poor?" However, there are a few occasions where trends have been missed, or somewhat under-discussed. For example, in answering a question about the rise of Spanish-language church services, Ochoa mentions that there is a growing minority of Protestant Latinos. Yet in answering a question about how Hispanic Americans get along with each other, he writes that while there are many differences, Hispanic Americans share many things, including a "wide-spread Catholic faith."

This book is an important resource for self-understanding and acceptance of others. It is also a good reference book for quick historical facts and social trivia. [R: SLJ, Nov 98, p. 141]—**Sandra E. Fuentes**

C, P, S
166.   Smith, Carter, III, and David Lindroth. **Hispanic-American Experience on File.** New York, Facts on File, 1999. 1v. (various paging). illus. maps. index. $125.00. ISBN 0-8160-3695-0.

This compilation, part of a 3-volume series titled Ethnic Minorities in America, presents clear, concise information from graphic sources on the history of Hispanics in the United States. The binder consists of 7 major sections: a background, Spanish and Mexican Settlement in North America (1565-1835), Manifest Destiny and Hispanic American (1836-1900), the Early Twentieth Century (1901-1945), La Raza Unida (1945-1974), Hispanic America Today (1975-present), and Hispanic American Cultural Contributions. The information, taken from many different sources, is presented in a series of black-and-white maps, graphs, diagrams, drawings, photographs, and timelines, along with accompanying brief text.

The scope is broad, providing an overview of Hispanic American history rather than an in-depth coverage of any topic. Although there is a list of sources used for each, the complete bibliographic information for every source is not included. The binder also contains a bibliography (with many Websites) and an index. Access to specific information is facilitated by the detailed table of contents, which lists the subdivisions in each section. Tabs are included to separate and mark each of the sections. There is a brief introduction that describes each section.

Because the format of the work is a looseleaf binder, each page can easily be removed for photocopying. The type, although small in some of the graphics, is clear and easy to read. This reference tool, like others in the Facts on File series, is aimed at students and teachers in need of visual resources for reports, papers, handouts, or oral presentations. It is a convenient, useful resource for reference collections in public, school, and academic libraries.
—**Susan J. Freiband**

7 Genealogy and Heraldry

GENEALOGY

Dictionaries and Encyclopedias

C, P

167. Schaefer, Christina K. **Genealogical Encyclopedia of the Colonial Americas: A Complete Digest of the Records of All the Countries of the Western Hemisphere.** Baltimore, Md., Genealogical Publishing, 1998. 814p. illus. maps. index. $49.95. ISBN 0-8063-1576-8.

This ambitious project covers Colonial history from European colonization to the American Revolution and presents many interesting records. Some of the work is divided into "Colonies Founded by Spain" and "Colonies Founded by England, France, Netherlands, and Portugal." The original 13 colonies of America, plus Maine and Vermont, are each given extensive coverage in their respective chapters, with some important sources listed for each town or county of the state; frequently including the Family History Library (Salt Lake City) microfilm numbers. More confusing is the section titled "Other U.S. States with Settlements Prior to the Revolution." The 18 states listed did have genuine settlements in pre-Revolutionary times, and in some cases there are fascinating diaries and journals that survived. A few sources, such as "Ohio Vital Records, 1750-1880s," are misleading with a starting date of 1750, which may be a birth date taken from some of the cemetery records included, rather than genuine vital records as named.

Other helpful information appears in a section titled "Colonial Sources in Great Britain." There are also similar sections for France, Germany, Spain, and so on, along with some beneficial maps. There is an intriguing chapter on foreign records at the Library of Congress, including many in microform; for example, "Reformed Protestant Sources, German and Dutch, 1600s and 1700s." This extensive compilation will suggest numerous original and printed sources, leading the serious researcher to new and exciting works. [R: BL, 15 Dec 98, p. 764]—**Carol Willsey Bell**

Directories

P

168. Arends, Marthe. **Genealogy on CD-ROM.** Baltimore, Md., Genealogical Publishing, 1999. 258p. index. $29.95pa. ISBN 0-8063-1623-3.

The explosion of materials available on CD-ROM has led to the creation of this guide to assist users. Included in this publication are topics such as biographies and historical references, journals, newspapers and periodicals, as well as special-interest items. Following these topics the reader will find an alphabetic state listing and lists for territories, U.S. possessions, and foreign countries. Each entry typically gives the title, publisher and price, system requirements, and a description. Nearly all of the descriptions are taken directly from publishers' lists. A few selected items were examined by the author and are highlighted by a "closer look."

The introductory material includes a section on pros and cons of genealogical CD-ROMs that discusses accuracy, completeness, and sources. Some comments on specific discs would have been helpful, such as "Ohio 1800 Census Index, Selected Countries," which includes Lake Co. (created 1840), Mahoning Co. (created 1846), and Summit Co. (created 1840). One wonders where data were found for the 1810 census index of Ohio, since it was destroyed in the War of 1812 fire. An index to the 1860 census of Pennsylvania claims to be "for the entire state," when in actuality at least six counties are missing.

Nevertheless, this guide is very useful, containing a detailed index and a list of addresses for publishers and vendors of CD-ROM products. Numerous illustrations show visual examples of data on screen.

—**Carol Willsey Bell**

P

169.   Arends, Marthe. **Genealogy Software Guide.** Baltimore, Md., Genealogical Publishing, 1998. 269p. index. $24.95pa. ISBN 0-8064-1581-4.

An impressive compendium of software resources and related information, this work opens with a discussion of the basic issues regarding hardware and software, followed by an overview of what genealogy software can and cannot do. A brief chapter on locating software leads into sequential chapters focused on evaluation of 27 individual genealogy database programs, as well as 43 genealogy utilities and research tools. A separate chapter discusses 12 Macintosh databases and utility programs, as well as older products. Screen snapshots enhance the explanations and evaluations throughout the work.

Several appendixes provide a database comparison chart; a list of genealogy software vendors; guides to older and superseded files; Internet software resources; a list of programs not reviewed; an explanation of Genealogy Data Communication (GEDCOM), a genealogy product created by the Church of Jesus Christ of Latter-day Saints; and a bibliography of computer genealogy publications. A glossary and index supplement the main text. Both the novice and the seasoned researcher should find this work immensely valuable just for the sheer variety of options it provides. [R: LJ, 1 Feb 99, p. 76]—**Edmund F. SantaVicca**

P

170.   Bentley, Elizabeth Petty. **The Genealogist's Address Book.** 4th ed. Baltimore, Md., Genealogical Publishing, 1998. 832p. index. $39.95pa. ISBN 0-8063-1580-6.

Earlier editions of the *Genealogist's Address Book* have been very popular with genealogists and genealogical librarians. The 4th edition has 182 more pages than the 1995, 3d edition (see ARBA 96, entry 428). The introduction states that the work "is based largely upon data received in response to direct-mail questionnaires, supplemented by information from printed and Internet sources." "Still, a few organizations, especially religious archives, cited the inability of their limited staff to cope with the mounting demands of genealogists—hobbyists, in their view, rather than serious scholars" (p. v). Coping with and not being "serious scholars" is understandable, because some genealogists are not scholars. However, labeling genealogists as "hobbyists" is a mischaracterization and discriminatory.

Because of the above-admitted prejudices of some organizations, users of Bentley's book should also check other appropriate directories such as the *American Library Directory* (49th ed.; see ARBA 98, entry 572); the *Directory of Historical Societies and Agencies in the United States and Canada* (see ARBA 79, entry 413); the *Directory of Archives and Manuscript Repositories in the United States* (see ARBA 89, entry 424); and the *Hereditary Society Blue Book* (Historic Trust, 1994).

The major portion of the book is arranged by state, then subdivided into topics, such as archives and libraries, historical societies, and genealogical societies. These are arranged alphabetically by the name of the institution, agency, or society, with some inconsistencies in its alphabetizing. Because most genealogists research geographically, many of the topical sections of this work would serve their users better if they were sub-arranged geographically by city. For example, if a genealogist were looking for libraries in the communities where his ancestors resided, the *American Library Directory* would be the better of the two sources to consult, because it is arranged by city. In Bentley's work, libraries that use the name of their city or county are easy to find; but the Monterey Park, California, public library is listed under its memorial name, Bruggemeyer Memorial Library.

The first index is for periodical titles; the second, for the names of the institutions, agencies, and societies. One Website that should be added to the section of antiquarian book dealers is http://www.bibliofind.com. There are also a few bookstores that should be added to the booksellers section. [R: Choice, July/Aug 99, p. 1915]—**J. Carlyle Parker**

P

171.   **The County Locator: The Guide to Locating Places and Finding the Right County for Public Record Searching.** Michael L. Sankey and Carl R. Ernst, eds. Tempe, Ariz., BRB, 1998. 473p. index. $19.50pa. ISBN 1-879792-39-7.

Whether one is searching for genealogical or business records, it is important to first find where the records for the transaction are kept. This is sometimes difficult to answer. This publication will help.

The work is divided into 3 sections. Section 1 is zip code to county cross-reference, section 2 is the place-name index, and section 3 is a county index. Section 1 includes all the zip codes assigned as of January 1998 as well as zip codes in existence as of May 1992. Each of the possible 99,999 zip codes is listed in this section so the searcher can determine if a zip code is valid or not. The low and high zip codes are listed at the bottom of each page, and the state for those zip codes is listed at the top of the page. Some zip codes are not geographic, and this is indicated by the codes.

Section 2 contains more than 100,000 place-name/zip Code combinations. It is ordered alphabetically first by place-name and then by state in order to help distinguish between the same place-names in different states, giving the zip codes for each place. Section 3 lists counties by state alphabetically, along with some basic information about the state and the counties, such as the zip code range for the state, the 1997 population estimate, and capital of the state. The entries for the county include the 1997 estimated county population and the county seat.

There is a detailed introductory section telling how to use this work along with the exceptions to the ways public records are handled. This will be a tremendous resource for locating records.—**Robert L. Turner Jr.**

P

172.   Howells, Cyndi. **Cyndi's List: A Comprehensive List of 40,000 Genealogy Sites on the Internet.** Baltimore, Md., Genealogical Publishing, 1999. 858p. $49.95pa. ISBN 0-8063-1556-3.

This very extensive guide to at least 40,000 sites on the Internet is organized by major topics, as listed in the table of contents. Among some of the intriguing topics are "Citing Sources," "Calendars and Dates," "Obituaries," "Queries & Message Boards," "Societies & Groups," and "Supplies, Charts & Forms." The "Forms to Print" section gives the URL addresses for census forms, checklists, ancestor charts and family group sheets, and more.

Given the size of this work, creating an index would have been a formidable task. Using the contents' list of topics seems to work well. Once the topic has been selected, a category index appears listing each subtopic covered in that section. It may take a little while to navigate through all of the choices, but it certainly would have taken as much time, or more, to peruse the same material on the computer.

The choice of places to explore is almost overwhelming. For the busy librarian who may not have quick and easy access to the Internet, *Cyndi's List* is an excellent place to look for answers for the genealogical patron. This is an excellent reference tool for electronic media. [R: LJ, 1 Sept 99, pp. 178-180; BL, 15 Nov 99, p. 644]
—**Carol Willsey Bell**

P

173.   Schaefer, Christina K. **Instant Information on the Internet! A Genealogist's No-Frills Guide to the 50 States & the District of Columbia.** Baltimore, Md., Genealogical Publishing, 1999. 86p. $9.95pa. ISBN 0-8063-1608-X.

This is a compilation of URLs of the author's choice of genealogy resources on the Internet. The preface states that the book was designed for speed and convenience, and it is indeed a compact paperback that would fit in a researcher's briefcase. The book is organized alphabetically by state. Grouped together under each state's listing are URLs for the state department of vital records; the state archive, library, and historical society; any National Archives Branch located in the state; and other important library and archival resources. Separate headings follow for local information sites; indexes, searchable databases, and digitized documents; and comprehensive Websites with multiple links to relevant resources. There are no annotations.

Designed for individual genealogists and family historians who want to harness the Internet for their research, this guide will be a good addition to a library's circulating collection. However, librarians serving genealogists will be better advised to acquire Thomas Jay Kemp's *Virtual Roots: A Guide to Genealogy and Local History on the World Wide Web* (see ARBA 98, entry 366). A more comprehensive resource, this work is international in scope and also includes sites maintained by family associations. Unlike the book under review, Kemp lists sub-addresses for sites, provides postal addresses and telephone numbers to facilitate reference contact, and flags some sites as "outstanding" or "extraordinary." [R: LJ, 1 Sept 99, pp. 178-180]—**Ruth A. Carr**

Handbooks and Yearbooks

P

174.   Szucs, Loretto Dennis. **They Became Americans: Finding Naturalization Records and Ethnic Origins.** Orem, Utah, Ancestry, 1998. 294p. illus. maps. index. $19.95pa. ISBN 0-916489-71-X.

This well-written guidebook to naturalization records and ethnic origin leads the user through a multitude of varying records created in differing time spans. It is imperative for the researcher to understand the naturalization process and to learn where to find surviving records. It is noted that "perhaps only about one-quarter of the foreign-born were naturalized," creating a problem in trying to find alternative records. This work explores the other types of documents to be found, and presents visual examples of them.

The author carefully and methodically leads the reader through early time periods into the twentieth century with samplings of the wide range of various sources. Each new discussion provides creative ideas and possibilities of places to search for additional data. Information about the many different ports of entry is given, plus facts on Castle Garden, the predecessor to the more recent Ellis Island in New York Harbor. Szucs' excellent and well-written research guide should quickly become the epitome of the subject in the field of genealogy.

—**Carol Willsey Bell**

P

175.   Woodtor, Dee Parmer. **Finding a Place Called Home: A Guide to African-American Genealogy and Historical Identity.** New York, Random House, 1999. 499p. illus. index. $25.00; $18.00pa. ISBN 0-375-40595-X; 0-375-70843-Xpa.

This nicely done research guide is arranged into logical chapters, and provides an excellent pattern for the novice genealogist to follow. Among some of the topics presented are "Searching for Your Ancestors During Reconstruction," " The Genealogy of Your Slave Ancestors," "The Records of Slavery," and "African American Institutional Records."

The author directs the new researcher through the various mazes common to anyone starting work on family history, with helpful suggestions for ways to proceed. Special instructions are given for using sources that are unique to African American genealogy, as well as how to efficiently use other records common to everyone. There are many illustrations showing good examples of special records.

In addition, information is provided on African American genealogical societies and Internet sites. There is a good index and a lengthy bibliography included. This reviewer would have preferred more importance placed on documenting and citing sources. This is an excellent book and is highly recommended. [R: LJ, 15 Mar 99, p. 73]—**Carol Willsey Bell**

HERALDRY

P, S

176.   **Flags.** New York, DK Publishing, 1998. 240p. illus. maps. index. (Eyewitness Handbooks). $18.95 flexibinding. ISBN 0-7894-4224-8.

This handbook for the study of flags throughout the world is delightfully illustrated in color and enhanced with the use of world maps as endpapers. The introduction gives thumbnail sketches about historical usage of flags for identification, and later for political reasons. Today, many private and professional organizations are adopting flags.

Typical entries inform the reader of the date the current flag was adopted, a description of the colors used and why, a complete explanation of the coats of arms if used, and other distinguishing facts. Regional flags, if used by a country, are also described. In the case of the United Kingdom, there are subnational flags for England, Scotland, Isle of Man, Jersey, Wales, and Guernsey. The U.S. section shows some of the historical flags, as well as all of the state flags with brief descriptions. Some international flags are presented, such as the North Atlantic Treaty Organization (NATO), Olympic Movement, United Nations (UN), and Red Cross. Signal flags for each alphabet letter and numbers are included. This is a nicely done handbook on the subject, and will surely help to answer many questions in a quick and concise manner.—**Carol Willsey Bell**

PERSONAL NAMES

P

177.   Reaney, P. H., and R.M. Wilson. **Dictionary of English Surnames.** 3d ed. New York, Oxford University Press, 1997. 520p. maps. $15.95pa. ISBN 0-19-860092-5.

A close examination of the present volume reveals it to be a reprint of the 3d edition published in 1995. The prefaces, introduction, and A–to–Z name entries appear to be identical, the sole apparent changes being the cover illustration and a new 10-page appendix essay by David Hey titled "Locating the Home of a Family Name."

A favorable review for the 3d edition will be found in ARBA 96 (entry 427). This reprint is not recommended for libraries that already possess it. It is, however, recommended for other libraries with an interest in English genealogy.—**Donald E. Collins**

8   Geography

GEOGRAPHY

General Works

Atlases

P, S

178.   **Collins Essential Atlas of the World.** London, HarperCollins; distr., North Pomfret, Vt., Trafalgar Square, 1998. 159p. maps. $22.95pa. ISBN 0-00-448611-0.

HarperCollins has published an inexpensive atlas on quality paper using maps by Bartholomew Ltd. The atlas is visually pleasing, from the clarity of the maps to the presentation of the information associated with the maps. The table of contents not only gives the name of the map and page location, but also the scale and a visual depiction of the maps on an outline map of the continent or region. The reference section is arranged by continent and gives the name of each country followed by area, population, capital city, languages, religions, and currency. This is followed by information on world economic groups, international organizations, time zones, physical features, vegetation, climate, population patterns, world health, travel and tourism, global telecommunications, and political changes through the world during the twentieth century. The vegetation section not only uses maps to show the locations of the various types of vegetation in the world but also gives a definition and a picture of the type of vegetation. The six pages of "Century of Change" will be useful to students studying the influence of wars and revolutions on political boundaries. A segment on how to use the atlas precedes the main body of maps. Both relief and political maps are included, with major cities, roadways, railways, and physical features noted. Boundaries are marked according to their location at press time with disputed and cease-fire lines also marked. Maps of oceans are included. The volume concludes with a glossary, list of abbreviations, and extensive index. This is a user-friendly, affordable atlas for home, schools, and libraries. [R: Choice, Sept 99, p. 103]—**Elaine Ezell**

P

179.   Cumming, William P., Louis De Vorsey Jr. **The Southeast in Early Maps.** 3d ed. Chapel Hill, N.C., University of North Carolina Press, 1998. 362p. maps. index. $90.00. ISBN 0-8078-2371-6.

A classic book on cartography has come back to life. First published in 1958, *The Southeast in Early Maps* is a tribute to its originator, deceased cartographer and collector William Cumming. A 2d edition appeared in 1962 but the 3d edition is more complete with 95 maps, 24 color plates, and a new essay by the editor on mapping by Native Americans. The majority of the volume is a descriptive bibliography of 449 maps of the colonial southeastern United States. Entries include map topic, size, an extensive description, where reproductions were published, and location of the original. Indication is made if the map is reproduced in the volume. Cumming's original introductory essay on early maps is reprinted. There are brief listings—a chronological list and a short-title list—as well as an index to the two essays. The volume is handsome and the reproduction quality of the maps is excellent. Maps of early settlement and civilization are a key research element for the historian, sociologist, and cartographer, and a new edition of this volume is welcome. Earlier editions are out of print and quite expensive on the open market. Reviews of the 1st edition praised the work and, although expensive, this new edition of *The Southeast in Early Maps* is a must for research libraries and collections focusing on colonial history. [R: LJ, 1 Oct 98, p. 76]—**Boyd Childress**

89

C, P

180. **National Geographic Atlas of the World.** 7th ed. Washington, D.C., National Geographic Society, 1999. 134p. maps. index. $125.00. ISBN 0-7922-7528-4.

This 7th edition of National Geographic's *Atlas of the World* is completely updated and will continue to serve as a standard source for all types of libraries—college, public, special, and school. Extending National Geographic's cartographic expertise to the Web, National Geographic has teamed up with the Environmental Systems Research Institute (ESRI) to develop a highly innovative Website to access maps and geographic data online. The comprehensive index offers some 140,000 entries and there are new maps of major cities of the world. This atlas is highly recommended.—**Bohdan S. Wynar**

S

181. **National Geographic Beginner's World Atlas.** Washington, D.C., National Geographic Society, 1999. 64p. illus. maps. index. $17.95. ISBN 0-7922-7502-0.

S

182. **National Geographic United States Atlas for Young Explorers.** Washington, D.C., National Geographic Society, 1999. 176p. illus. maps. index. $24.95. ISBN 0-7922-7115-7.

Both the *National Geographic Beginner's World Atlas* (for children ages 5 to 8) and the *National Geographic United States Atlas for Young Explorers* (for children ages 8 to 12) are excellent atlases designed specifically for use by young people and families. The atlases are the most recent addition to a children's series begun by the National Geographic Society in 1998 with *National Geographic World Atlas for Young Explorers*.

The *Beginner's World Atlas* focuses on the seven continents. There is an introductory chapter called "Understanding Your World," which provides age-appropriate explanations about maps and mapmaking as well as vivid illustrations portraying the physical world map, physical world map symbols, and the political world map. Completing the introduction are two pages describing "what this atlas will teach you." The seven sections that follow describe each of the seven continents. A young child introduces each continent and a scenic vista portrays a beautiful part of the landscape. The section called "The Land" describes major land regions, waterways, climate, plants, and animals in brief, fact-filled text. Another division, "The People," tells about various countries, cities, native peoples, languages, and products for each continent.

Accompanying the large-format, easy-to-read maps are more than 100 color photographs with great appeal to young children. A page of world facts, a glossary, and an index complete the atlas. The *United States Atlas for Young Explorers* combines beautiful photographs, two-dimensional maps, and information presented in colorful, fact-filled pages. Two introductory pages explain how to use the atlas and show that the United States has been divided into five regions. The following two sections contain in-depth information about the physical and political U.S. areas. These pages have excellent maps, beautiful photographs, and clear and brief explanations—all with the younger student in mind. Another brief section has a map and information about our nation's capital. The main portion of the atlas is devoted to each of the five regions of the United States. A panoramic photograph with a list of the states in the margin introduces each region. A physical map of the area is followed by clear and concise descriptions and photographs of the region. To complete the regional coverage, each state is portrayed with a map, fact capsules, and a brief summary. Completing the atlas are several pages covering the U.S. territories, facts and figures, a glossary of terms, abbreviations and Websites, and a comprehensive index.

National Geographic's high standards are evident throughout both volumes. Their world-renowned quality and accuracy are further validated by a collaboration of education consultants and geographers. Both atlases should be on every shelf at home as well as school and public libraries.—**Mary L. Trenerry**

P, S

183. **New Millennium World Atlas Deluxe.** [CD-ROM]. Skokie, Ill., Rand McNally, 1998. Minimum system requirements: IBM or compatible Pentium processor with 100MHz. Eight-speed CD-ROM drive. Windows 95 or Windows NT 4.0. 16MB RAM. 40MB hard disk space. Video adapter card. Monitor. Internet service. $44.95.

User-friendly and highly interactive, this flexible atlas provides a variety of features that will likely be appreciated by many high school and college students. More than 1.6 million place-names are included as part of a sophisticated three-dimensional model that provides impressive shaded relief. In addition, interactive city center street maps are provided for 65 major cities of the world. Pan and zoom navigational tools allow the user to roam about the street; to search for key sites; and to connect with texts that describe a country's geography, people, economy, history, and politics.

Other features include thematic maps that highlight significant social, economic, and environmental themes; "exploration" maps that cover such topics as the oceans, glaciation, volcanoes, and historic empires; comparison tools that allow the user to compile statistics for up to four countries; dynamic links between map and nonmap content; hyperlinks and cross-references; drawing tools and map markers; and online connectivity to pertinent Internet links. The user is also able to use any of these capabilities to create personal notebooks.

Although data are current only through 1997, this product is a strong value for its price. This CD-ROM is recommended for school and public library reference collections. [R: LJ, 15 Mar 98, pp.103-104; SLJ, Mar 99, p. 134]—**Edmund F. SantaVicca**

Biography

C, P, S

184.   **Explorers: From Ancient Times to the Space Age.** John Logan Allen, E. Julius Dasch, and Barry M. Gough, eds. New York, Macmillan Library Reference/Simon & Schuster Macmillan, 1999. 3v. illus. maps. $275.00/set. ISBN 0-02-864893-5.

Younger readers are always enthusiastic about the adventure and drama of exploration. They are inspired by the men and women who ventured into unknown territory on land, sea, and into space. Explorers from ancient times to the space age are the kind of reference material designed for students at middle school level or above. This 3-volume set contains profiles of 333 early adventurers, such as geographers, merchants, navigators, botanists, archaeologists, and treasure hunters. Readers will also find people who made essential contributions to the progress of discovery by working in their own countries as cartographers, inventors, and historians.

A group of experts in history, geography, and space science selected the subjects of these profiles. They are arranged alphabetically by the explorer's last name. Each profile begins with a note that lists the explorer's nationality, dates of birth and death, and main activities. The text of the profile summarizes the explorer's accomplishments and the cause and the effect of the exploration. A list of suggested readings is placed at the end of each profile. There are 3 introductory essays at the beginning of volume 1—"The Technology of Exploration," "Causes and Effects of Exploration," and "The History of Exploration." These articles "provide technical and historical background and help students to understand how each explorer's efforts were a part of the long and complex process of discovery." A glossary, list of explorers by nationality, list of explorers by area of exploration, bibliography, and index are at the end of the profiles to help readers search from different aspects. The editors have included many pictures and maps with the purpose of trying to help readers gain a better understanding. Like other new students' encyclopedias from Macmillan Library Reference, this well-designed reference source is curriculum focused and written at an appropriate reading level. It is an essential for school libraries, public libraries, and academic libraries. [R: BL, 15 April 99, pp. 1354-1356; Choice, July/Aug 99, pp. 1926-1928]—**Xiao (Shelley) Yan Zhang**

S

185.   Pear, Nancy, and Daniel B. Baker. **Explorers & Discoverers, Volume 7: From Alexander the Great to Sally Ride.** Edited by Jane Hoehner. Farmington Hills, Mich., U*X*L/Gale, 1999. 295p. illus. maps. index. $39.00. ISBN 0-7876-3681-9. ISSN 1522-9947.

The latest supplement to this set, volume 7, adds 30 biographies of men, women, and machines that have expanded our horizons. The 20 men, 8 women, 1 museum, and 1 ship newly inducted into the set include Thor Heyerdahl, Nearchus, Mel Fisher, John Bryon, Helen Thayer, and the National Air and Space Museum. Although they represent a time range from ancient to modern, they are mainly European or American. Arranged alphabetically, the entries focus on the motivation driving these explorers and discoverers and the journeys themselves. There is little information about family or early life. Sources are included for each entry. Entries do include items such as illustrations, maps, geographic details of journeys, and similar information. The volume begins with a section of 16 black-and-white maps of major world regions. The end sheets provide a general world map. The section on chronology and exploration covers all seven volumes by area explored. The index is cumulative. This is a nice supplement to upper elementary and middle school history classes. It brings to the forefront some figures who might otherwise be forgotten and will provide additional information for research. [R: BR, Nov/Dec 99, p. 72]—**Esther R. Sinofsky**

Dictionaries and Encyclopedias

C, P, S

186. **Merriam-Webster's Geographical Dictionary.** 3d ed. Springfield, Mass., Merriam-Webster, 1998. 1361p. maps. $29.95. ISBN 0-87779-546-0.

Librarians will welcome this new edition of a standard reference source, one that is relatively inexpensive for the amount of information provided. More than 48,000 entries are arranged in alphabetic order and include countries, cities, towns, villages, mountains, oceans, islands, rivers, lakes, deserts, valleys, major buildings, large constructions, and other significant human additions to the landscape. As for the United States, nearly all incorporated places with a population of 2,500 or more have been included, as well as all county seats regardless of population size. Information in entries includes variant spellings, pronunciations, size, population, and location. Entries for significant topics (larger cities, countries, significant landforms) provide additional information such as description and history. There are more than 252 maps and hundreds of tables throughout the book. Introductory material includes explanatory notes, abbreviations and symbols, map projections and symbols, a list of maps, a world map, and pronunciation symbols. There are two appendixes—a glossary and a list of geographical terms in other languages.

Other aids that make this a user-friendly reference are guide words at the top of each page, bold letters for entry words and references, a pronunciation guide key at the bottom of each odd-numbered text page, references to other entries, and map legends. This is a highly recommended reference source for those needing quick, easy access to basic geographical information.—**Dana McDougald**

P, S

187. Skinner, Malcolm, David Redfern, and Geoff Farmer. **Dictionary of Geography.** Chicago, Fitzroy Dearborn, 1999. 311p. illus. $40.00. ISBN 1-57958-154-4.

Geography is a rather large topic to be the subject of a dictionary. With no limitations on the subject, fairly large definitions, and a modest number of pages, it is any wonder that there are gaps in this work.

No particular audience is given for this dictionary, so it is difficult to say whether it meets the target expectations. The book is relatively small, so one assumes that the work is not necessarily for professionals, and yet it is not the sort of thing to buy for Christmas presents either. Definitions are clear enough for the intelligent, novice reader, although an understanding of the entries does require some application. The range of coverage is broad but not deep—even though geography is not this reviewer's subject, some entries prompted me to look for others, and I was surprised at the number of listings not found.

Some of the terms are a bit surprising, although a moment's thought can explain the inclusion of terms for topological mathematics and other fields. Further contemplation suggests that because this is a geographical dictionary rather than a geological one, political and economic concepts do have a place. The reason that these latter terms seem odd becomes clear after a more thorough perusal. Right–wing political and social views seem to have a definite preponderance. This is a business-oriented geographical glossary.

It is not clear who this dictionary is aimed at, and it is difficult to think of an appropriate group. It may do for a high school reference, but some work may have to go into plugging the holes. [R: LJ, 15 Nov 99, p. 62]

—**Robert M. Slade**

Handbooks and Yearbooks

C, P

188. **The Columbia Gazetteer of the World.** Saul B. Cohen, ed. New York, Columbia University Press, 1998. 3v. $750.00/set. ISBN 0-231-11040-5.

For many years *The Columbia-Lippincott Gazetteer of the World* (1952) was the standard reference source for geographic names and data. For many years to come, the standard source will be *The Columbia Gazetteer of the World*. Indeed, the new gazetteer should rank among the most important reference books currently in print.

Under the editorship of Saul B. Cohen, one of the world's most recognized geographers, a staff of more than 150 geographers, editors, and advisors compiled a list of some 165,000 entries that reflect the massive changes in the geopolitical landscape since the early 1950s. Since publication of the previous gazetteer, widespread colonialism ended resulting in the recognition of scores of new countries, towns, and cities; Eastern Europe was freed from Soviet domination; and the United Nations grew threefold. Renewed nationalism inspired thousands of name changes and spelling changes. Of the 165,000 entries in *The Columbia Gazetteer of the World*, 30,000 are new.

Entries reflect the geopolitical world (countries, provinces, states, regions, and cities), the physical world (continents, regions, lakes, islands, valleys, and peninsulas), and so-called special places (national parks, airports, harbors, dams, and shopping malls). Where appropriate, physical, economic, political, historical, and cultural descriptions are included as are population, latitude, longitude, and elevation. Pronunciations and changed and variant spellings are also included. A monumental work of great authority and utility, *The Columbia Gazetteer of the World* should be in the core reference collections of virtually every library. [R: Choice, Oct 98, pp. 283-284; C&RL, Sept 98, p. 613; BL, 15 Oct 98, pp. 437-438; RUSQ, Spring 99, p. 316]—**Edward Kurdyla**

P, S
189.   **The National Geographic Desk Reference.** Washington, D.C., National Geographic Society, 1999. 699p. illus. maps. index. $40.00. ISBN 0-7922-7082-7.

The National Geographic Society may be most widely known for its maps, monthly magazine, and television specials, but it is also an organization responsible for serious scientific research. For those among us who feel that "geographic expertise" may be demonstrated by reciting the names of 25 African nations and their capitals, this book may be overwhelming; for the rest of us it is a comprehensive reference to what geography is all about. If a working definition of geography is the interaction of a population and its environment, then a single-volume guide to geography must be a combination of almanac, atlas, and textbook about earth science, history, politics, and economics. This is a book about how humans are influenced by the Earth and how, in turn, our activities affect the Earth and each other.

It is divided into 4 parts (each with multiple chapters); the 1st and last can almost be considered appendixes to the middle 2. Part 1, "What Is Geography?" is an introduction to the interactions of people and the Earth, a history of geography, and a survey of the differences among maps and globes and how they are made. Part 2, "Physical Geography," is essentially a 200-page earth science textbook describing the physical nature of the Earth that forms the stage upon which the human drama occurs. It includes an overview of the Earth, weather, climate, geology (materials and processes, landforms and landscapes, and soils and bio-regions). Part 3, "Human Geography," is a 200-page description of that drama. It includes sections about population; migrations; cultural, economic, urban, and political geography; and the environment and society. Part 4, "Places," provides a list of independent countries and dependencies by region, almanac-type information on all the world's 191 countries (as counted by the Society), and a mini-atlas for quick reference. The end matter includes a glossary and an index.

Each chapter is well illustrated with color photographs, maps, diagrams, and charts and contains highlighted text sections of special interest, such as how the meter was originally defined as a fraction of the Earth's circumference, the development of the Pentecostal movement, and how the zebra mussel is affecting water supplies. Terms in bold typeface are included in the glossary. Each chapter is followed by a summary and a list of sources of further information (there is no bibliography).

The publishers consider this a "prodigious volume" that defines "the world and all that's in it." As immodest as that claim may sound, this book comes arguably close to meeting it. It is an affordable and useful volume for the home, office, or school library and can be enjoyed as both a readable text and a desktop reference.

—**Craig A. Munsart**

9   History

ARCHAEOLOGY

C, P

190.   **A Dictionary of Archaeology.** Ian Shaw and Robert Jameson, eds. Malden, Mass., Blackwell, 1999. 624p. illus. maps. $99.95. ISBN 0-631-17423-0.

Shaw and Jameson's volume is the latest in a line of works in archaeological reference publishing that began with the appearance of *Adeline's Art Dictionary* in 1883, and has seen increased emphasis on regional archaeology (mainly biblical and Egyptian) since 1950. An editorial approach reflecting the definition of archaeology as both a process and a discipline in constant change has been adopted in the crafting of the articles. Content selection, while emphasizing traditional topics (such as terminology, theoretical concepts, field techniques, and summaries of important sites worldwide), also incorporates practical applications of theory and method as well as terms from the fields of art history, sociology, human biology, and philosophy. A significant difference from similar volumes, such as the *Collins Dictionary of Archaeology* (ABC-CLIO, 1993), is the lengthy overview essays on individual continents, which provide expanded coverage of the archaeology of areas less thoroughly covered in previous Western dictionaries such as Oceania, China, and Japan. Each entry is followed by a short chronological bibliography of significant primary and secondary publications, including major subdiscipline periodicals such as *Azania*. Illustrations are limited to high-quality maps, charts, and line drawings reproducing artifact designs. This volume is most applicable to university library reference collections supporting undergraduate and graduate degree programs in archaeology. However, given its scope and accessible writing style, large public libraries should consider it for acquisition as well. [R: Choice, July/Aug 99, p. 1926]
—**Robert B. Marks Ridinger**

C, P

191.   **Encyclopedia of Archaeology: The Great Archaeologists.** Tim Murray, ed. Santa Barbara, Calif., ABC-CLIO, 1999. 2v. illus. index. $150.00/set. ISBN 1-57607-199-5.

This superb 2-volume set (part of an envisioned 5-volume *Encyclopedia of Archaeology* conceived in 1992) significantly augments the pool of scientific biography extant within anthropology. It presents highly readable accounts of 58 men and women active in the study of the past as antiquarians, prehistorians, or archaeologists from the sixteenth and the twentieth centuries. Written by practicing archaeologists from Australia, the United States, France, England, New Zealand, Wales, India, and Mexico, these essays (chronologically arranged by birth year) interweave personal biography with the gradual development of distinctive professional geographic, temporal, and theoretical interests. Of special value are their bibliographies, divided into primary writings by the individual, followed by a sampling of commentary and criticism regarding their significance. The editor provides a historical overview of evolving approaches to writing an effective autobiography in his epilogue, "The Art of Archaeological Biography," that users should read despite its awkward placement at the end of the 2d volume. A short glossary and detailed author, title, and subject index are included. Seventeen of these individuals are also reviewed in shorter pieces in the 1991 *International Dictionary of Anthropologists* produced by the Library-Anthropology Resources Group (LARG). Useful for social science reference collections in public and undergraduate libraries of all sizes.—**Robert B. Marks Ridinger**

AMERICAN HISTORY

Almanacs

C, P, S

192.   Burg, David F., and L. Edward Purcell. **Almanac of World War I.** Lexington, Ky., University Press of Kentucky, 1998. 320p. illus. maps. index. $22.00. ISBN 0-8131-2072-1.

World War I continues to fascinate the public and the media, just as its sequel a short two decades later has recently rekindled the imagination of novelists and filmmakers. Given the enormous number of publications on the Great War, it is difficult to conceive that another new book might offer something not covered in previous studies. However, the *Almanac of World War I* does precisely that in a surprising but extremely effective way.

The book consists of a series of entries arranged chronologically from the start of the war in 1914 to its tragic, exhausting finish in 1918. Each entry compresses the battle or campaign of the day in a succinct and readable fashion. In addition, the last 50 or so pages offer brief biographies of the major political and military leaders as well as a selected bibliography. The index is well organized and easy to use.

Another welcome feature in this volume is the large number of maps, illustrations, and photographs (many from the Library of Congress), which add interest and prevent the almost diary-like narrative from becoming too tedious. The reproduction of the maps is not as clear as readers would like, but the photographs are sharp and detailed. Moreover, authors Burg and Purcell, who previously produced *The World Almanac of the American Revolution* (World Almanac Books, 1992), include a host of intriguing sidebars on such diverse topics as World War I technology, tactics, weaponry, and cultural life (including the machine gun, tanks, poison gas, and patriotic songs). Finally, it should be noted that William Manchester's introduction is an eloquent piece of writing about World War I. It captures the pathos and absurdity of the conflict in a way that few others have. [R: BL, 1 Feb 99, p. 990]—**John B. Romeiser**

Atlases

C, P

193.   **Atlas of the Official Records of the Civil War.** [CD-ROM]. Carmel, Ind., Guild Press, 1999. Minimum system requirements: IBM or compatible 386. Four-speed CD-ROM. Windows 3.1, Windows 95, or Windows 98. 16MB RAM. $59.95. ISBN 1-57860-028-6.

This work was originally published to accompany the monumental *The Civil War CD-ROM: The War of the Rebellion* (see ARBA 97, entry 401). Although it is primarily an atlas devoted to military aspects of the Civil War, its uses extend beyond that. The detail of these maps enable users to identify creeks, towns, and other geographical features that have since changed names or ceased to exist. Family historians will appreciate the fact that the names of landowners are shown on many maps. And, although there is no text beyond the one-page preface, the atlas is interspersed with numerous illustrations of Civil War military scenes and equipment. Color charts show Union and Confederate uniforms, ranks, and buttons. Numerous charts illustrate types of bridge construction; weapons; medical equipment; plans of forts; defensive structures; means of transportation; and federal, southern national, and military flags. Multicolor maps show the entire theater of the war, military divisions and departments, military operations in the field, campaigns, battles, and skirmishes.

Access to the contents is good via the subject search window to the CD-ROM itself as well as the several indexes within the original volume. An authority index guides users to maps according to the person or persons responsible for creating them. A geographic and topical index provides locations of various topical and pictorial materials as well as to maps by geographic location or military action. Of particular value is a separate index to maps contained not on this CD-ROM. Such items might be overlooked if one relies solely on the atlas as a source. Maps are reproduced in the same size and colors as the original, making them easily read. Because of the sizes of the various maps, however, scroll bars must be used to view an entire map. Because these maps are solely for military purposes, users should not expect to find every geographic name indexed. Nevertheless, when the general area is known from another source, scanning will produce good results. Many users will also appreciate the ability to bookmark, annotate, and store maps for future use. This title is highly recommended and should be considered by libraries and individuals with an interest in the American Civil War, or that already possess the print or CD-ROM versions of the Army or Navy editions.—**Donald E. Collins**

Chronology

P, S

194.   **The American Scene: Events.** Danbury, Conn., Grolier, 1999. 9v. illus. maps. index. $265.00/set. ISBN 0-7172-9448-X.

This 9-volume set is designed for young readers (grades 4 and up) and highlights many of the important events and people who have helped shape U.S. history. With a total of more than 1,000 pages, an important subject is portrayed on each page. Ranging from the Watson Brake Mounds in Louisiana that were built 3,500 years ago by Native Americans to the Clinton scandal, the books are packed with key information about the United States that will educate students and teachers alike.

The well-designed pages start with a colorful photograph or image of the subject at the top, a location map, and a handy U.S. history timeline along the right margin. Written descriptions vary in length from 200 to 300 words and adequately cover the significance of the event. The page concludes with highly interesting facts in bold typeface under the heading "Did you know . . ."

Including *all* of the important events of U.S. history in a series of this scope is impossible, and selection must be somewhat subjective. For the most part the coverage is thorough, but some glaring omissions are Sitting Bull, Crazy Horse, and the Reconstruction era. Blank space is left at the bottom of each page that would have been a perfect spot for further reading citations or an extra 100 words of text, either of which would have enriched the entries. Occasional oddities also crop up; for example, volume 4, "The Civil War and Its Aftermath," begins in 1863 (the 1861–1862 war years are covered in "Growth and Conflicts"—it would have been more logical to have all the Civil War in one volume). The image for "The Battle of Wounded Knee" actually has nothing to do with the battle—there are far better historical events to choose from that better illustrate this tragedy. These inconsistencies aside, the set serves as an adequate introduction to U.S. history for the young reader. [R: BL, 1 Sept 99, p. 178; BR, Nov/Dec 99, pp. 76-77]—**Mark J. Crawford**

P, S

195.   **Events That Shaped the Century.** Alexandria, Va., Time-Life Books, 1998. 192p. illus. index. $19.95. ISBN 0-7835-5502-4.

This volume cites all of the events one would expect to find in a work with this title and by this publisher. Besides the predictable catastrophic, momentous, or triumphant events, there are the less obvious trends, inventions, and personalities that have likewise impacted our everyday lives at the end of this century. As usual for a Time-Life series, it is the striking, poignant, or intentionally repugnant photographs (some famous and familiar) that tell much of the story and make the book a visual archival summary of the past 100 years in the United States.

The treatment is more superficial than Peter Jennings and Todd Brewster's *The Century* (Doubleday, 1998) or Harold Evans' *The American Century* (Knopf, 1998) by necessity of its size. Although the text lacks the eyewitness accounts of ordinary persons' reactions found in other books, the sources of information reflect both contemporary and historical interpretations.

Of the 125 events included, the majority deal with political affairs, although the economy, society, science, education, medicine, fine arts, and sports are also covered. Notable by its absence is any significant comment on religion, considering it is a right as sacred to Americans as the other freedoms in the Bill of Rights. Many of the happenings emphasize controversial, debatable issues that serve to illustrate or test the tenets of the Constitution as the nation has progressed through the twentieth century. This work, along with many others appearing on the market that deal with important people and events in the 1900s, is sure to be of interest, and provides a concise look at the United States' direction as the new century approaches. [R: BR, Nov/Dec 98, p. 72]—**Janet J. Kosky**

Dictionaries and Encyclopedias

C, P

196. **American History.** Mark C. Carnes, ed. New York, Macmillan Library Reference/Simon & Schuster Macmillan, 1998. 1198p. illus. index. (Macmillan Compendium). $125.00. ISBN 0-02-864978-8.

Covering the American experience in one volume has always been an exciting challenge. The standard work in this field, the *Dictionary of American History*, consists of eight volumes and a 2-volume supplement (see ARBA 77, entry 384). *American History* is an attempt at producing a 1-volume version of the *Dictionary of American History* for ready-reference use.

This work, although published in 1998, contains no bibliographical material after 1994. Some articles, such as the one on the hydrogen bomb, contain only older references, the latest being Henry Kissinger's 1957 work, *Nuclear Weapons and Foreign Policy*. The hydrogen bomb article, alas, ends with the following virtually worthless piece of information, probably from the 1950s: "The ultimate threat of such weapons to national security is matched only by the potential benefits of thermonuclear reaction as a source of controlled energy for peaceful purposes."

Other articles, such as the one on the antinomian controversy, are summaries by well-known historians, this one being done by Perry Miller. The Civil War article, for further example, is written by J. G. Randall. If this 1-volume source to American history is not brief enough, the editors have in some cases reduced the topics to one sentence. For instance, Andersonville Prison is mentioned as follows: "To the Union Prisoners at Andersonville and their northern friends it appeared that the Confederates were deliberately murdering the captives through deprivation." Similarly, the 19th Amendment is reduced to: "The Nineteenth Amendment, which gives women the vote, grew out of pressures for equal rights set in motion at the 1848 Seneca Falls Convention organized by Elizabeth Cady Stanton."

There are no entries for individuals, but instead topics such as "Burr Conspiracy," "Burr-Hamilton Duel," and "Burr Trial" are given. Individuals must be researched through the indexed entries under their names. For example, there are extensive entries under "Washington, George" in the index, but only one article, "Washington's Farewell Address," is alphabetically in this compendium. There are a few minor not very well-selected illustrations accompanying the text. A table of contents provides an alphabetic listing of the entries. This is supplemented, as mentioned by the index, at the conclusion of the volume. This work is hardbound, but it is doubtful the binding will stand up to extensive use. Most libraries will want to order this as a 1-volume companion to the *Dictionary of American History*. [R: SLJ, Aug 99, p. 181]—**Ralph Lee Scott**

C, P, S

197. Crawford, Mark. **Encyclopedia of the Mexican-American War.** Santa Barbara, Calif., ABC-CLIO, 1999. 350p. illus. maps. index. $75.00. ISBN 1-57607-059-X.

Recently, in celebration of the 150th anniversary of the Treaty of Guadalupe Hidalgo ending the Mexican-American War, 1846 to 1848, several reference books have been published. This reasonably priced encyclopedia provides an informative presentation of key persons, battles, treaties, health issues, cities and states, and groups (e.g., abolitionists, the Texas Rangers). There are 459 entries of which 275 are biographical—mostly of U.S. persons. Special features include a selected bibliography, an annotated chronology from 1830 to 1848, portraits and pictures of battles from collections at the Library of Congress, and an introduction outlining the author's 11 causes of the war. There are only six maps; more would have improved the work. The encyclopedia entitled *The United States and Mexico at War: Nineteenth Century Expansionism and Conflict* (1998) has nearly 600 entries and includes more pictures, maps, and bibliographic citations; however, it is more expensive ($175). The *Historical Dictionary of the United States–Mexican War* (see ARBA 99, entry 462) includes 840 entries, of which 567 are biographical. All three of these works are biased toward the United States. This work is recommended for high school, public, and academic libraries. [R: BL, 15 Nov 99, p. 649]—**Karen Y. Stabler**

S

198. **Scholastic Encyclopedia of the Civil War.** By Catherine Clinton. New York, Scholastic, 1999. 112p. illus. maps. index. $18.95. ISBN 0-590-37227-0.

The title, *Scholastic Encyclopedia of the Civil War*, is somewhat misleading if one accepts the traditional definition of an encyclopedia as alphabetically arranged information. Written for juveniles, this slender volume skims the surface, yet contains a great deal of information, much of which is not the kind usually seen in such texts.

The table of contents lists six chapters, which are arranged chronologically. The first, "Before the War," is followed by others for each year, 1861 to 1864. The final chapter, "1865 and After," places much emphasis on the Reconstruction period and the Civil Rights Movement of the 1960s. The volume also includes an alphabetic index. The inside covers provide a clear, color-keyed map showing Union and Confederate capital cities, state capitals, major cities, other locales, places where major battles occurred, and the route of Sherman's March to the Sea.

The text is illustrated with an abundance of period art and photographs, including political cartoons and sketches made by soldiers on the scene. Sidebars with labels like "Eyewitness" (diary excerpts), "Battle-at-a-Glance" (number of troops and casualties on each side and the winner), and "Did You Know" (facts and anecdotes) can be found on nearly every page.

The vocabulary is often above juvenile level, and some might question the author's dwelling on the extended post-war period in a work ostensibly about the war itself. However, the *Scholastic Encyclopedia of the Civil War* provides a lively introduction to a complex subject at a reasonable cost.—**Kay O. Cornelius**

C, P

199.   Sifakis, Carl. **The Mafia Encyclopedia.** 2d ed. New York, Facts on File, 1999. 414p. illus. index. $40.00; $19.95pa. ISBN 0-8160-3856-2; 0-8160-3857-0pa.

This volume, an expanded and updated version of the 1987 1st edition (see ARBA 88, entry 589), is part of a continuing series of popular criminology reference works on aspects of organized crime by former wire service reporter Sifakis. It is written for a nonspecialist audience, its principal focus remaining the provision of biographical data on major figures belonging to or associated with the Mafia in the United States. Other categories covered include the Mafia's public history and mythology, slang terms and their meanings, and types of businesses run by members of various crime families. Contents are arranged alphabetically, with indexing by proper name and subject. The addition of index headings for specific court proceedings and the wide range of colorful nicknames used by mob figures would have improved the work considerably. This volume will be most useful for large public libraries wishing to augment their biography holdings and university collections supporting degree programs in criminology. [R: LJ, 1 Apr 99, pp. 88-89; BR, Nov/Dec 99, p. 85]—**Robert B. Marks Ridinger**

Handbooks and Yearbooks

P, S

200.   **American Immigration.** Danbury, Conn., Grolier, 1999. 10v. illus. index. $325.00/set. ISBN 0-7172-9283-5.

American Immigration is a 10-volume encyclopedia dealing with the topic of immigration from the earliest Asian settlers of 30,000 years ago to modern-day immigrants such as the Kurds, Haitians, and Bosnians. Volume 1 provides an overview of the subject, discussing immigration in a historical context—immigration laws, patterns, and issues. Volume 2 is dedicated to Ellis Island. The remaining volumes contain topical entries, covering individual ethnic groups, terms associated with immigration, and social issues. Each volume is the same length and each contains a bibliography as an index to the entire work.

The coverage of the individual groups will prove valuable. The history of the group in its native land is provided as well as the issues prompting the exodus. Problems encountered by the group are discussed, the names of famous members are given, and, in the case of recent immigrants, some idea of their progress and future is projected. Numerous photographs add interest, and sidebars and inserts giving highlights and little-known facts will get readers' attention.

No one is given total editorial credit for the work, although names of a project coordinator, writers and editors, and researchers are listed. Also included here are the names of several individuals associated with Ellis Island. No credentials are given for any of the participants.

American Immigration is a fascinating and useful overview of a basic thread in U.S. history. Although not scholarly in nature (data are not footnoted and interviews have been "lightly edited for readability"), the work will prove to be a helpful tool for middle and high school students. [R: BL, 1 Mar 99, p. 1234]—**Michele Tyrrell**

P, S

201.   **Campaigns of the Civil War and the Navy in the Civil War.** [CD-ROM]. Carmel, Ind., Guild Press, 1999. Minimum system requirements: IBM or compatible 386. Four-speed CD-ROM drive. Windows 3.1, Windows 95, or Windows 98. 16MB RAM. $39.95. ISBN 1-57860-030-8.

   This CD-ROM presents the military history of the Civil War as witnessed and written about by Union Army and Navy participants and contemporaries. Written in the decades immediately following the war, these 19 volumes describe the land and water campaigns and battles of that conflict from a decidedly Northern viewpoint. Authors include such noted individuals as famed Naval historian and Union Admiral Alfred T. Mahan, General Abner Doubleday of baseball fame, and John G. Nicolay (private secretary to Abraham Lincoln), as well as lesser-known Naval and Army officers and civilians. The final volume is devoted to statistical data on the war. Most of these works include maps and appendixes, and some contain bibliographies of other Civil War era books. Although most of these writers attempted to present an unbiased treatment of the war, some do not attempt to hide their hostility towards the Southern Confederacy. This is particularly true in the intemperate writing of Lincoln's private secretary. Despite the bias, these works provide valuable information about the military history of the war. Purchasers may, however, wish to provide some balance to these titles by also considering the acquisition of the same publisher's CD-ROM *Confederate Military History* (1997), in which Southern authors of Confederate sentiment describe the war from the opposite point of view.

   This CD-ROM is easy to install and use. The onscreen manual, available via the help menu, provides clear instructions on its various features and search methods. Information retrieval is excellent through the use of Boolean operators as well as field searching of documents by signer, addressee, greeting, and date. Searching may also be constrained to a single document or the entire database. Highlighting enables fast and easy retrieval of specific information within often lengthy documents. These and other features enable users to read entire books or to find very precise information with ease. The availability of bookmarking and file folders facilitate organization and storage, as well as retrieval, by topic. This CD-ROM offers a significant number of books not normally available in most libraries, and is highly recommended for any library, person, or institution with an interest in the Civil War.—**Donald E. Collins**

C, P

202.   **Civil War CD-ROM II: Official Records of the Union and Confederate Navies in the War of the Rebellion.** [CD-ROM]. Carmel, Ind., Guild Press, 1999. Minimum system requirements: IBM or compatible 386. Four-speed CD-ROM drive. Windows 3.1, Windows 95, or Windows 98. 16MB RAM. $69.95. ISBN 1-57860-027-8.

   This title contains the official records of the Union and Confederate Navies during the American Civil War as reported by the officers and government officials involved in the naval actions and activities of that war. Although these are frequently regarded as less historically important than land warfare in the popular mind, this is nevertheless an extremely important work. The Union Navy was responsible for blockading Southern ports while the Navies of both sides were used to aid their respective armies in actions that took place along the rivers and sounds of the Confederacy. As a rule, the army that was supported by Naval craft on either side was able to dominate that action.

   This is a companion piece to Guild Press's *The Civil War CD-ROM: The War of the Rebellion* (see ARBA 97, entry 401), which included the official records of the Union and Confederate armies. While the original compilers failed to include all the written reports of the war, and the documents are subject to the biases of the Union and Confederate officials who wrote them, the two titles taken together contain the best available collection of primary source, official records relating to the Civil War. As such, they are essential to any serious research on the war.

   This is a well-done product. Search methods and procedures are clearly explained onscreen via the help function that guides users through all aspects and features of this title. Information is easily found and printed. Both simple and complex searching enables users to perform precise searches via the Boolean operators of "and," "or," and "not." Proximity searches may be set for as little as two or as many as 32,000 words. Field searching allows users to retrieve documents by signer, addressee, date sent, or by range of dates. Highlighting of search topics make them easy to retrieve within often lengthy documents. File folders enable the grouping of topics and searches, while the availability of highlighting makes the location of specific search terms simple within often lengthy documents. This is an extremely important work and is highly recommended for all libraries, groups, and individuals with an interest in the American Civil War.—**Donald E. Collins**

C, P

203.   Genovese, Michael A. **The Watergate Crisis.** Westport, Conn., Greenwood Press, 1999. 197p. illus. index. (Greenwood Press Guides to Historic Events of the Twentieth Century). $39.95. ISBN 0-313-29878-5.

As an addition to the Greenwood Press Guides to Historic Events of the Twentieth Century, this highly readable and interpretive study takes its place alongside entries on matters such as civil rights, Islamic fundamentalism, German unification, and the Cold War. The series makes no attempt to impose some unifying theme on, or to discover some comprehensive meaning of, the twentieth century, but rather strives more modestly to identify and analyze developments of ongoing influences. Genovese, an established authority on the era of President Richard Nixon, easily meets expectations with this effort. He skillfully unfolds not only the story of Watergate, that umbrella term which encompasses all the varied misdeeds of the Nixon presidency, but also attributes to Watergate much of the contemporary cynicism toward government and politics, an increasingly adversarial relationship between the press and political leaders, a decline in civility in public discourse, and the constant scrutiny of public officials by special prosecutors. So, to understand modern politics in this country, Genovese correctly asserts, one should begin with Watergate.

As with all studies in the series, this one adheres to a prescribed format. A detailed chronology is followed by a historical narrative and interpretive essays, brief biographies of key players, a sampling of documents, a glossary of terms, an annotated bibliography, and an index. Rather than finding something startlingly new here, one will be reminded of the connection between Vietnam and Watergate, Nixon's paranoia and the frightening extent to which he was prepared to go to get his "enemies," and the president's knowledge of and involvement in the cover-up. Reference librarians should add this one to their collections, for students and interested laypersons will find it an excellent guide to this nation's most serious political scandal.—**John W. Storey**

C

204.   **The Southern Historical Society Papers.** [CD-ROM]. Carmel, Ind., Guild Press, 1998. Minimum system requirements (Windows version): IBM or compatible 386. Four-speed CD-ROM drive. Windows 3.1 or Windows 95 with Pentium 100. 16MB RAM. Minimum system requirements (Macintosh version): System 7.0 or higher. 8MB RAM. $69.95. ISBN 1-57860-058-8.

As a source of published primary material on the Civil War, these papers are perhaps secondary only to the monumental *The War of the Rebellion: A Compilation of Official Records of the Union and Confederate Armies* and that work's corresponding volumes of Naval records. From 1876 until its conclusion in 1959, the Southern Historical Society collected and published records of the Confederate side of the Civil War in 52 annual volumes. Among the most significant of its contents are the multivolume proceedings of the Confederate Congress and the roster of the 26,300 soldiers who surrendered at Appomattox with Robert E. Lee. The contents tell the stories of leaders and common people of the Confederacy in the form of lengthy monographs, essays, biographies, diaries, rosters, correspondence, speeches, statistics, and even poetry. The topics treated include large and small battles, treatment of war prisoners, the life of the average soldier, justification for secession, and various controversies coming out of the war. All of these materials were collected through the efforts of members of the Southern Historical Society, which included some of the biggest names in the Confederate government and military as well as such imminent historians as Douglas Southall Freeman. Because of the miscellaneous nature of the contents, not all aspects and battles of the war are included. However, the material that is found here is first rate and should be consulted alongside the titles mentioned above.

As a rule, search features and strategies are standard on CD-ROM products from this publisher. Typical users will find them easy to understand and follow. As in its other Civil War CD-ROMs, searchers are guided through every step by onscreen help instructions. Searching is precise and easy via Boolean operators and such field searching features as proximity, dates, and addressees and signers of documents. This is highly recommended for any collection where the Civil War is a significant interest.—**Donald E. Collins**

AFRICAN HISTORY

P

205.   Eades, Lindsay Michie. **The End of Apartheid in South Africa.** Westport, Conn., Greenwood Press, 1999. 209p. illus. index. (Greenwood Press Guides to Historic Events of the Twentieth Century). $39.95. ISBN 0-313-29938-2.

For decades the world had feared that the black majority of South Africa would rise up violently against the oppressive white-run government, leading to a massive bloodbath and possible foreign military intervention. What a pleasant surprise it was when Prime Minister F. W. deKlerk willingly gave up his office in a relatively peaceful change of power in the middle of 1994 after the electoral defeat by the African National Congress (ANC), led by Nelson Mandela. This was one of the great political events of the 1990s, right up there with the fall of Communism. This guide contains a variety of information that readers can use for quick answers to questions before they do more in-depth research. Five chapters explain how the end of the apartheid came about. The historical background of apartheid, the structure of racial separation, the parties and the process of painful transition, and internal and external pressures on the parties are all examined. The last chapter on the challenges facing the new country can be complemented by *Security and State in Southern Africa*, written by Agostinho Zacarias (Tauris Academic Studies, 1999). There are reference notes at the end of each chapter. Following this are biographical essays for 16 key players in these momentous events; unfortunately, there are no suggested reading notes for these essays. Then come reprints of 13 important documents of the ending of the apartheid that can be hard to find. The chronology goes from 1652 to 1997, but there is not enough detail for the entries. Interested readers should examine Jacqueline A. Kalley's *South Africa Political History: A Chronology of Key Political Events from Independence to Mid-1997* (Greenwood, 1999). The work is supplemented with a glossary, an index, and a five-page annotated bibliography of resources. There are also two outline maps of the old and new South Africa on one page; matters would have been improved had these maps each had a separate page, with more detail. The author previously published *A Case Study of an Appeaser: Robert Hadow in the Foreign Office, 1931-1939* (Praeger, 1996). The title under review is suitable for the reference and circulating collections of academic and public libraries.—**Daniel K. Blewett**

C, P

206.   Vernus, Pascal. **The Gods of Ancient Egypt.** Jane Marie Todd, trans. New York, George Braziller, 1998. 202p. illus. maps. $75.00. ISBN 0-8076-1435-1.

This lavishly illustrated volume consists of a very readable text surrounded by pages of photographs, each of which is completely described. Beginning by elaborating the deities' functions, the author continues by discussing various general ideas such as cult organization, the different ways that deities manifested themselves, and the coherence among the deities, followed by a presentation on the practice of syncretism, by which Egyptian deities combined to share traits or foreground specific traits. Next, one learns about the creation of the world, including the creation of humanity as well as its end, with brief discussions of the different narratives, cosmogonies, and the various deities involved, finishing with a brief description of Akhenaten, the heretic king who proscribed gods other than the Aten.

The final two chapters present the intersection of the human and divine worlds. The first of these examines beliefs and practices relating to the afterlife, such as tombs, mummification, and the different mortuary texts designed to assist the individual to the afterworld at his or her death. The final chapter describes how the ancient Egyptians approached the world of the divine, including a considerable discussion of personal piety and dialogues with the gods.

This volume provides a clear, comprehensible, and accurate presentation of ancient Egyptian deities. The excellent and up-to-date annotated bibliography, the clear texts and generally smooth translation, the fine glossary combined with an index of the deities, and the superb photographs of objects not commonly seen in books on ancient Egypt make it deserving of a place in public, private, art, and academic libraries.

—**Susan Tower Hollis**

ASIAN HISTORY

China

C, P

207.   Chang, Tony H., comp. **China During the Cultural Revolution, 1966-1976: A Selected Bibliography of English Language Works.** Westport, Conn., Greenwood Press, 1999. 199p. index. (Bibliographies and Indexes in Asian Studies, no.3). $65.00. ISBN 0-313-30905-1.

The Chinese Cultural Revolution was one of the most tumultuous periods in modern Chinese history. It affected virtually all aspects of Chinese life, including economic planning, art, music, drama, education, and even the daily life of many Chinese people. This bibliography includes more than 1,000 titles of monographs, dissertations, theses, and audiovisual materials. The arrangement consists of 8 divisions, including "Documents and Reference Works"; "General Works"; "Special Periods"; "Cultural Revolution in Provinces and Municipalities"; "Special Subjects"; "Biographies, Memoirs, and Firsthand Observations"; "Travelers' Reports"; and "Audio-Visual and Microform Materials." Each entry contains a full bibliographic description of the author, title, edition, imprint, and pagination. Also included are brief annotations for most entries along with special notes where appropriate. Entries are numbered consecutively. There are title, subject, and author indexes.

Several bibliographies on the Cultural Revolution in China have been published. Robert Goehlert published *The Chinese Cultural Revolution: A Selected Bibliography*, which was only 10 pages, but included the major works to that time (Vance Bibliographies, 1988); even earlier, Stewart E. Fraser published *Chinese Education and Society, a Bibliographic Guide: The Cultural Revolution and Its Aftermath*, which included major books, articles, and other items to about 1970 (International Arts and Sciences Press, 1972); and finally, James Wang published *The Cultural Revolution in China: An Annotated Bibliography* (see ARBA 97, entry 320), which was the most inclusive treatment to date. Wang's bibliography included more than 300 items and was the major list for a number of years. The present work is a much-needed addition to the bibliographic coverage of the Cultural Revolution begun by these other works. Also, the scope of this present work makes it a valuable addition to Cultural Revolution research.

This book is highly recommended for all larger public and academic libraries with Chinese history and culture collections. It would also be a valuable addition to smaller academic libraries that wish to maintain a Chinese research collection. Because of the cost it would probably not be a logical addition to personal collections. [R: Choice, Sept 99, p. 117]—**Robert L. Wick**

C

208.   Wortzel, Larry M. **Dictionary of Contemporary Chinese Military History.** Westport, Conn., Greenwood Press, 1999. 334p. maps. index. $95.00. ISBN 0-313-29337-6.

Despite its title, this dictionary is more of a concise encyclopedia in its treatment of each entry. Although the word "contemporary" is not strictly defined, the author initially intended to limit treatment to the twentieth century and does focus on communist forces in earlier periods and on the People's Republic of China. However, the dictionary includes earlier historical information on China and the Chinese military as background information. This is especially evident in the introduction, where there is a brief history of dynastic succession and sections such as "the philosophical basis of Chinese society develops," and "China is unified for the first time." The author, a colonel in the U.S. Army and a military intelligence officer specializing in China and East Asia, has a Ph.D. in political science and has served twice at senior levels in the Army Attaché Office in the American Embassy in Beijing. Three other identified contributors are equally qualified in education and experience. The length of entries varies according to the subject, with some running several pages and others a single paragraph. In addition to bibliographic references at the end of each entry, an extensive selected bibliography concludes the volume. This dictionary on the recent military history of China is a useful reference tool for the study of contemporary China.

—**Hwa-Wei Lee**

Japanese

P

209.   **The Columbia Guide to Modern Japanese History.** By Gary D. Allison. New York, Columbia University Press, 1999. 259p. maps. index. (The Columbia Guides to Asian History). $45.00. ISBN 0-231-11144-4.

Even during its current recession, Japan somehow manages to capture the curiosity and interest of scholars and the general public. In 125 pages, University of Virginia professor of East Asian Studies Gary D. Allison has boiled down the essence of Japan's transformations since the Meiji Revolution and the opening of its ports to the West. In addition to this abbreviated historical narrative, Allison has created 13 topical brief essays (ranging from 1 to 13 pages), introducing key players and themes in Japanese modern literature, politics, and business. A resource guide to published studies in English, brief lists of Japanese films, and a sprinkling of electronic resources follow. As a reference guide, the appendix is valuable for its inclusion of translated full-texts and extracts of several key documents in Japanese history. The chronology is also helpful. Public, high school, and undergraduate libraries are encouraged to purchase this book—but not for their reference collection. The bibliography is uneven and the remainder of the work is not helpful as a reference source—unlike *The Kodansha Encyclopedia of Japan* (see ARBA 84, entry 305) or *Japan: An Illustrated Encyclopedia* (see ARBA 94, entry 115). However, a casual reader could certainly peruse the guide in about as much time as the actual flight to Japan and would arrive at Narita with a basic understanding of modern Japanese history.—**Andrew B. Wertheimer**

Pakistan

C

210.   Long, Roger D. **The Founding of Pakistan: An Annotated Bibliography.** Pasadena, Calif., Salem Press and Lanham, Md., Scarecrow, 1998. 327p. index. (Magill Bibliographies). $45.00. ISBN 0-8108-3557-6.

Although titled the "founding" of Pakistan, this bibliography contains material relevant to the founding of Pakistan in the widest sense and will be useful for those interested in the nationalist movement(s) that led to the independence of India and Bangladesh as well as Pakistan. The works referenced include imperial histories, subaltern interpretations, biographies, and novels, some dating from the 1930s, but with most material from the 1960s to the present. The first part contains general reference materials, many useful for further searches. Here, readers find dissertations, guides to government archives in the subcontinent and the U.S., gazetteers, and guides to special collections (like the Hartley Library, which contains the Mountbatten papers). A selection on "Political Studies" contains books, articles, and some dissertations and reference works. A third section contains books, articles, bibliographies, microform catalogs, and government white papers dealing with the provinces of pre-independence India. The fourth section is devoted to works on Mohammad Ali Jinnah, including collections of his speeches, letters, newspaper reports, and papers as well as other bibliographies and books. The last section contains references to biographies of other players, both Indian and English, in the subcontinent's independence movement. There is material here on the Aga Khan, Stafford Cripps, Gandhi, the Nizam of Hyderabad, and many others who were connected with the independence movement. Each entry in the book is annotated, placing the work within its historical and historiographical framework, making the bibliography useful for both nonspecialists and specialists. Given the works contained in the bibliography, the annotations, and the useful author and subject indexes, this should be the one bibliography consulted by anyone investigating the processes of Pakistan's independence from Britain in 1947. [R: Choice, Feb 99, p. 1045]—**David L. White**

CANADIAN HISTORY

C

211.   Gough, Barry M. **Historical Dictionary of Canada.** Lanham, Md., Scarecrow, 1999. 271p. maps. $55.00. ISBN 0-8108-3541-X.

This dictionary provides a historical and cultural context to understand Canada and its contributions to the world. The majority of the entries center on the people, places, and events of the twentieth century, from Nobel

Prize winner Sir Frederick Grant Banting, who discovered insulin, to Agnes Campbell Macphail, first female member of Parliament.

The introductory essay discusses four continuities of Canadian history: the imperial connections to both Britain and France, the interrelationship and conflicts of the French and English as the founding European influences, provincial relations and Canada's success as a federation, and the undeniably profound effect of the United States as Canada's neighbor. Other features include a chronology, maps, acronym definitions, a bibliography, and lists of past governors general and prime ministers. This reference gives the serious scholar as well as the casual visitor to Canada a better appreciation for the uniqueness of this interesting country.

—**Adrienne Antink Bendel**

CUBAN HISTORY

C, P

212.   Leonard, Thomas M. **Castro and the Cuban Revolution.** Westport, Conn., Greenwood Press, 1999. 188p. illus. index. (Greenwood Press Guides to Historic Events of the Twentieth Century). $39.95. ISBN 0-313-29979-X.

Historian Thomas M. Leonard has compiled and written a useful overview of Cuba during the second half of the twentieth century. He examines many elements of the history of Cuba, including Cuba as a Spanish colony and a slave society; post-slavery plantocracy; after the Cuban War for independence and the Spanish-American War; and Cuba as a U.S.-dominated, sugar- and tourism-dependent country. He also discusses Cuba's society as highly stratified with a small economic and mostly lighter-skinned elite and masses of impoverished and mostly darker-skinned workers—the independent Cuban nation. This "independent" Cuba was run for the elite by the dictator Fulgencio Batista.

In the fight against Batista, the plantocracy, and U.S. economic domination, Fidel Castro emerged as a leader. Leonard is evenhanded in his description of the events that led up to the revolution and the revolution itself. He also describes Castro's adoption of communism and his consolidation of power in post-Batista Cuba, Cuba's fractious relations with the United States and supportive relationship with the Soviet Union, the experiences and impact of the Cuban exile community, and the relative successes and failures of the Castro regime.

In addition to nearly 90 pages of historical description, this volume includes a chronology (1492-1998) and 23 biographies of key players in twentieth-century Cuban affairs. The text also includes 15 primary documents related to the revolution, Castro's Cuba, and U.S. perceptions of it (from José Martí to Che Guevara, Bill Clinton, and Pope John Paul II). A glossary and a classified and briefly annotated bibliography conclude the work. Black-and-white photographs and an index also enhance this historical study.

This book is a well-written introduction to Castro's Cuba. It will be extremely useful for undergraduate research, though it would have benefited from the inclusion of more illustrations.—**Fred J. Hay**

EUROPEAN HISTORY

General Works

C, P

213.   **The Hutchinson Encyclopedia of the Renaissance.** David Rundle, ed. Boulder, Colo., Westview Press, 1999. 434p. illus. maps. index. $65.00. ISBN 0-8133-3670-8.

This volume has more than 1,500 entries on all aspects of the Italian and Northern Renaissances of the fourteenth through sixteenth centuries. Its well illustrated, $7\frac{1}{2}$-by-10-inch page makes a welcome addition to European history and humanities reference works available for library collections. The encyclopedia is the U.S. edition of a 1999 imprint first published in Britain. The editor is an Oxford academic and the other contributors are drawn principally from Oxbridge colleges and London University.

Entries range in length from a long paragraph to a double-columned page or more for important figures such as Michelangelo, Raphael, or Erasmus families like the Medici and concepts like exploration or reform and Reformation. The arrangement is alphabetic. In addition to the main articles, there are 20 "Feature Entries" boxed and set apart from the main text, although roughly in the right alphabetic position. These longer entries are perhaps one to two pages long. The extensive cross-references appear thorough. Topics range from antiquarianism and azulejos to botany, climate change, art history, and homosexuality. There are 17 gloss pages with full-color plates of major art and architectural works accompanied by 4 pages of explanatory text. There are eight maps and nine pages of schematic dynastic charts. The latter deal mainly with key Italian families, plus Burgundy, the Habsburgs, the Anjous, and the Tudors. Many black-and-white illustrations and portraits accompany the text. The thematic index is somewhat confusingly laid out with main headings and subheadings without apparent alphabetic or other organization. The contents and lists of maps and genealogies are useful. The general editor provides a useful but brief introductory essay.

The work is admirable. Where budgets permit, it deserves strong consideration as an addition to collections needing reinforcement in its perennially popular topic. [R: Choice, Dec 99, pp. 702-703]—**Nigel Tappin**

P

214.   Singman, Jeffrey L. **Daily Life in Medieval Europe.** Westport, Conn., Greenwood Press, 1999. 268p. illus. index. (The Greenwood Press "Daily Life Through History" Series). $45.00. ISBN 0-313-30273-1.

The subtitle of this work might well read "Northwestern Europe in the High Middle Ages, 1100-1300," for such is its scope. Because the so-called Middle Ages extended over such a long time, Singman concentrates on the period when feudal and manorial systems predominated. He selects specific examples of medieval institutions, each of which embodies the character of the period: Cuxham, a small English village; Dover Castle in England; the monastery of Cluny in France; and Paris as an exemplar of the town. The result is an intriguing view of life and thought in medieval society and the world of that time. This social history approach delves into practical aspects of everyday life; for example, the structure of medieval society; the life cycle; and material culture with practical discussions on food, sanitation and personal hygiene, and sleeping accommodations, among others. Although Singman's research incorporates important sources, the text of this introductory study is both lively and enlightening and not weighed down with footnotes. This is not a scholarly work, but one that will hold the fascination of the ordinary reader interested in the living history of another time and place. A selected bibliography of English-language materials is appended, along with a brief glossary and appendixes on games, recipes, and music. This book and others in the series are recommended for public, high school, and college libraries.

—**Bernice Bergup**

Austrian

C

215.   Fichtner, Paula Sutter. **Historical Dictionary of Austria.** Lanham, Md., Scarecrow, 1999. 301p. (European Historical Dictionary Series, no.36). $65.00. ISBN 0-8108-3639-4.

Fichtner, an eminent scholar in the field of Austrian and Central European studies, has produced an outstanding general dictionary of the history of Austria from the earliest times to the present. Fichtner has served on the executive committee of the Society for the Study of Austrian and Habsburg History. She has also been a member of the editorial board of the Austrian History Yearbook, and has taught in the department of history at Brooklyn College for three decades.

The structure of this work includes a chronology, covering the period 5000 B.C.E. to 1998. This is followed by a thorough and superbly written introduction, stressing Austria's land and people, the economy, Austrian prehistory and antiquity, the Austrian medieval period, the Habsburg lands from 1273 to 1490, the Turkish period, the Reformation and Counterreformation, the Revolutionary era (1789 to 1848), Neoabsolutism to the Ausgleich of 1867, Austria from 1867 to 1918, the First Austrian Republic (1918 to 1938), World War II to 1955, and Austria from 1955 to the present. There are four general maps depicting Austria from 1848 to the late twentieth century.

The dictionary section contains entries on the major themes of Austrian history. It covers the country's Habsburg and pre-Habsburg legacy, its political and culture elite, its component provinces, and leading cities. Each entry, meticulously researched and well organized, contains numerous references to other entries in bold typeface; additionally, there are *see also* references at the end of most entries. For example, the entry "Habsburg, House of," describes the origins of the Habsburg dynasty and their early history. The entry continues the historical narrative with the Central European Habsburg period, providing bold typeface references to the Holy Roman

Empire, the Babenberg dynasty, Maximilian I, Ferdinand I, Emperor Friedrich III, Protestantism, World War I, and Archduke Franz Ferdinand. The work also contains an appendix section on Austrian heads of state from the Babenberg era to the Second Austrian Republic, providing dates for monarchs, presidents, and chancellors from 976 to the present.

Perhaps the most useful section of the volume other than the dictionary entries is the concise bibliography. Designed with the English reader in mind, Fichtner has provided a bibliographic essay, including various Austrian Websites, and a list of the most significant works on Austria by historical period from antiquity to the present.

This reviewer, an Austrian history buff who studied at the University of Vienna, would like to emphatically state that Fichtner's *Historical Dictionary of Austria* is one of the best general reference works on the subject available. It is a mandatory selection for undergraduate collections, and would be welcome in graduate and research collections as well.—**Mark Padnos**

Belgium

C

216. Stallaerts, Robert. **Historical Dictionary of Belgium.** Lanham, Md., Scarecrow, 1999. 303p. (European Historical Dictionaries, no.35). $59.50. ISBN 0-8108-3603-3.

The number of English-language reference books on Belgium is small, so this is a welcome and much-needed addition to that collection. People, places, groups, events, themes and organizations of Belgian history, and current events are all covered in approximately 450 entries. Users should read the introduction for a short historical narrative of the country. French and Dutch words are provided where necessary, and helpful cross-references are plentiful. The 6 appendixes list the kings and governments of the country, along with some economic statistical information. Those interested in more recent data should look at the latest edition of the *Europa World Year Book* (39th ed.; see ARBA 99, entry 66) or a Belgian government Website. No index is provided, and there are no suggestions for further reading at the end of the entries. There are many bibliographic citations to foreign-language materials in the 117-page bibliography, which comes with its own introduction. There is also a table of contents of the index's many topic subdivisions, 4 pages of acronyms and abbreviations, and a 14-page chronology that stretches from 58 B.C. to 1998 B.C.E. The author is a native of Belgium, and previously wrote (with Jeannine Laurens) the dictionary in this series on the Republic of Croatia (see ARBA 96, entry 549). This book is the companion to similar works in this series on the Netherlands and Luxembourg (see ARBA 97, entry 119). This work is recommended for the reference shelves of academic and larger public libraries.

—**Daniel K. Blewett**

Dutch

C, P

217. Hooker, Mark T. **The History of Holland.** Westport, Conn., Greenwood Press, 1999. 236p. index. (The Greenwood Histories of the Modern Nations). $35.00. ISBN 0-313-30658-3.

In keeping with the policy of the Greenwood Histories of the Modern Nations editors, this work was designed to provide students and interested laypersons with concise, up-to-date information on the history of Holland, officially known as "The Kingdom of the Netherlands," and its people. While it summarizes the country's entire history, particular emphasis is placed on events of the last 30 years that have helped to shape contemporary social issues with worldwide impact. An introductory section gives brief coverage to Holland's geography, natural resources, transportation and communications, major cities, the 12 provinces, the economy, political systems, society, and culture. Holland's history is traced from the Ice Age through the Golden Age of exploration and colonization, the war crisis and recovery, the rise and fall of the welfare state, and the post-Cold War era. The text is especially well-written for its intended audience—it is readable, interesting, and informative. The indexing is thorough. Supplementary sections provide additional reference information. A timeline lists important events from 57 B.C.E., when Julius Caesar began the conquest of the Belgian tribes, to the projected 65th birthday of Queen Beatrix in 2003. A biographical dictionary gives brief sketches of the lives of 33 notable men and women from all periods of Dutch history. A bibliographic essay comments on selected works in the English language and leads the reader to sources of chronologies, documents, narrative histories, and works on the Dutch government, educational system, geography, and literature. A list of abbreviations gives full-name identification for the many acronyms used in the text. Also included are a bibliography of English-language translations of works by twentieth-century Dutch authors and a list of Dutch print media companies.—**Shirley L. Hopkinson**

French

C

218.   Evleth, Donna, comp. **The Authorized Press in Vichy & German-Occupied France, 1940-1944: A Bibliography.** Westport, Conn., Greenwood Press, 1999. 234p. index. (Bibliographies and Indexes in World History, no.48). $69.50. ISBN 0-313-30784-9.

France was the only major European country during World War II with the dubious distinction of being both occupied by the Nazis and, to a large extent, a willing participant of its own occupation. During the past two decades, French, British, and U.S. scholars have looked closely at archival material that tends to validate the view that collaboration was a fact of daily life in both the occupied and unoccupied zones among all classes of people. Evleth's useful bibliography provides further evidence of this sordid chapter of modern French history.

Evleth examines 2,500 periodicals that were published on a daily, weekly, or monthly basis throughout the period of France's occupation. The bibliography is organized alphabetically for the departments or regions of the country and by subject heading for Paris. Each entry indicates the name of the publication, where it was published, its frequency, and, if available, its political or religious orientation. In addition, the bibliography provides each periodical's approximate beginning and ending dates, the library or archive where it is held, and any books or articles that have been written about it. There is truly a wealth of information here for the scholar or student interested in delving into the convoluted politics of collaboration during "les années noires" (the dark years) in France.

What is particularly striking in this reference work is the enormous number of newspapers and magazines that ceased publication after France was liberated by the Allies in August 1944. Either the periodical disappeared altogether or it was replaced by a new publication with a different title and management. It is equally intriguing to note the large number of ephemeral publications, especially in Paris, that came to life after the Nazis marched in (June 1940) and that survived for only 4 years. For the most part, these publications tended to be rabidly right-wing, fascist newspapers that welcomed the German occupiers with open arms and assisted them in their efforts to integrate France into the Third Reich.

The Authorized Press in Vichy & German-Occupied France, 1940-1944 is more than just a niche work about wartime France. It will prove to be a vital resource for researchers who seek to explore the tribulations of a great democratic country engulfed by totalitarianism.—**John B. Romeiser**

C, P

219.   Nicholls, David. **Napoleon: A Biographical Companion.** Santa Barbara, Calif., ABC-CLIO, 1999. 318p. illus. index. (ABC-CLIO Biographical Companion). $55.00. ISBN 0-87436-957-6.

This encyclopedia outlines the personalities, places, battles, institutions, and events in Napoleon's life as a soldier, ruler, administrator, and legend. Each notation indicates related entries and suggestions for further reading. The editor gives a well-rounded view of Napoleon by including not only major historical figures, such as Charles Talleyrand-Périgord, but also lesser-known influences like François Joseph Talma, an acclaimed French actor who coached Napoleon in oratory. Useful features include an introductory biographical essay on Napoleon, a bibliography, a chronology, an index, and a selection of documents written by Napoleon and others that give a flavor of the subject and his times. The selections provide insight into different facets of the Napoleonic myth and are a helpful companion to narrative biographies and other readings of this period. [R: LJ, 1 Nov 99, p. 74]—**Adrienne Antink Bendel**

German

P

220.   Leiby, Richard A. **The Unification of Germany, 1989-1990.** Westport, Conn., Greenwood Press, 1999. 197p. illus. index. (Greenwood Press Guides to Historic Events of the Twentieth Century). $39.95. ISBN 0-313-29969-2.

The titles in this series all conform to a standard format and this work follows the norm in relation to its subject. It offers a chronology of the events from 1946 to 1995 that bear on German reunification. There is a narrative of these events that provides an overview of the history of postwar and modern Germany and its unification. In following chapters, five related topics are investigated: emigration and escape, the influence of the clergy, the influence of the major powers, the effects of unification on the former West and East Germanys, and the settling of accounts. A final essay attempts to put the whole in perspective. This work also includes a biographical section, a selection of primary documents, a short glossary of terms, and a selective bibliography of English-language sources and studies.

The work succeeds because the topic is not too broad for the space allotted and the writing is good. All of the primary sources are in English and most are translations of German documents and speeches and thus accessible to American students. Strictly speaking, this is not a reference but a subject monograph. Academic and public libraries will probably wish to include this title in their circulating collection because it is one to be read through. It is appropriate for readers from upper-class high school students to adults.—**Eric R. Nitschke**

P

221.   Turk, Eleanor L. **The History of Germany.** Westport, Conn., Greenwood Press, 1999. 231p. maps. index. (The Greenwood Histories of the Modern Nations). $35.00. ISBN 0-313-30274-X.

Germany's reunification in 1989-1990 is one of the most important events of the late twentieth century. The recently completed relocation of Germany's capital from Bonn to its traditional location in Berlin provides further demonstration of Germany's renewed importance in Europe. This compendium provides a succinct overview of German historical development from antiquity to the present for readers desirous of a quick and painless introduction to German history.

The History of Germany opens with a historical event timeline and introduction to contemporary Germany's geography, government, economy, and culture. It proceeds to cover prominent events in Germany's historical development through chapters on historical periods, such as the growth of Prussia, the Weimar Republic, Hitler and World War II, postwar occupation, the development of East and West Germany, and events after reunification.

Entries on key individuals and events are highlighted in black within these chapters. Examples of such emphasis include feudalism, Charlemagne, Thirty Years War, Joseph II of Austria, Congress of Vienna (1814-1815), Frankfurt Parliament, Bismarck's Domestic Politics, Triple Entente, Weimar Constitution, Nuremburg Laws, Sudeten Germans, Russian Front, Marshall Plan, Ludwig Erhard, Walter Ulbricht, and the European Union. The work concludes with a list of notable personalities in German history and an annotated bibliography.

Succinct works of this nature will undoubtedly contain omissions that will displease German history specialists. Works of this nature, however, are not intended to be comprehensive scholarly monographs or appraisals. Instead, they serve as concise introductions to events on important developments in the topic being covered. Recognizing this fact and the scope of this work, one can recommend it as a useful introduction to the historical personalities and events that have formed and continue to influence Germany at the close of the twentieth century.—**Bert Chapman**

Greek

C, P

222.   Ashley, James R. **The Macedonian Empire: The Era of Warfare Under Philip II and Alexander the Great, 359-323 B.C.** Jefferson, N.C., McFarland, 1998. 486p. index. $55.00. ISBN 0-7864-0407-8.

Historians, the author of this massive study argues, have stressed political and cultural aspects of the Macedonian era, but have relegated the military ones to secondary importance. The intent of the author is to right this deficiency. To the degree historians have written about Macedonian military affairs, the author thinks, have been derivative borrowings from secondary sources. The book consists of 3 parts: ancient warfare, the reign of Philip II and III, and campaigns of Alexander the Great. Further, the subject is subordinated into 12 chapters. The author studies Macedonian armies, siege operations, logistics, and naval operations. It is a well-argued study and the author sets a standard for all future studies of Macedonian warfare to be measured by. The work is thoroughly footnoted and contains nine appendixes, a lengthy glossary, and a bibliography and index.

—**Andrew Ezergailis**

Italian

C, P

223.   Gilbert, Mark F., and K. Robert Nilsson. **Historical Dictionary of Modern Italy.** Lanham, Md., Scarecrow, 1999. 463p. (European Historical Dictionaries, no.34). $65.00. ISBN 0-8108-3584-3.

Continuing Scarecrow's series of historical dictionaries, Italian studies scholars Gilbert, of the University of Bath, England, and Nilsson, Professor Emeritus of Dickinson College, offer this contribution to the history reference shelf. Containing more than 350 cross-referenced entries, Gilbert and Nilsson's dictionary furnishes information regarding the historical odyssey of modern Italy from the mid-nineteenth century to the present. It spans the liberation and political unification of the Risorgimento, through the dark years of fascism, to the present-day Italy born of the "Italian miracle"—a country that is one of the largest industrial nations in the world. The authors transport the reader through the labyrinth of modern Italian history. Unlike Frank J. Coppa's *Dictionary of Modern Italian History* (Greenwood Press, 1985), which provides coverage of Italian history from the eighteenth century to the modern period, this work focuses more upon the twentieth century. While addressing political and economic matters, the authors pay particular attention to notable individuals, intellectual movements, and events relating to modern Italian cultural and social experience that are not addressed by the Coppa work. For example, in terms of cultural/artistic figures, entries are provided for the authors, directors, and painters.

A detailed bibliography in English and Italian, as well as 18 tables of appendixes, complements this excellent work of Italian studies scholarship. This work is highly recommended for academic and public libraries.

—**Glenn S. McGuigan**

Polish

P

224.   Wróbel, Piotr. **Historical Dictionary of Poland, 1945-1996.** Westport, Conn., Greenwood Press, 1998. 423p. maps. index. $85.00. ISBN 0-313-29772-X.

Poland, as the eighth largest country of Europe, is of increasing strategic, economic, and political importance. This historical dictionary, covering the period 1945 to 1996, is a sequel to a similar dictionary, issued by the same publisher in 1996. Personalities, events, and concepts are arranged alphabetically. An indication is given if terms appearing in the texts of entries are themselves accorded a separate listing. Each entry provides basic information about the term or personality in question and also includes bibliographic references to items in both English and Polish that contain a more complete exposition of the topic. The reference work also includes several useful maps, a chronology of important events, a selected bibliography of books in English on Poland, and an index to the contents of the entries themselves. Wróbel has compiled an extremely useful volume that will serve as a handy desk reference for anyone studying contemporary Polish politics, economics, and current affairs in general.—**Robert H. Burger**

Russian

C, P

225.   Rappaport, Helen. **Joseph Stalin: A Biographical Companion.** Santa Barbara, Calif., ABC-CLIO, 1999. 372p. illus. maps. index. (ABC-CLIO Biographical Companions). $55.00. ISBN 1-57607-084-0.

Soviet dictator Joseph Stalin was one of the twentieth century's most important political leaders. His shadow still remains over Russian and international politics nearly five decades after his death. This compendium provides detailed yet succinct portraits of Stalin and the individuals, events, and policies contributing to his career and historical legacy.

Following an introductory preface, this work consists of entries arranged alphabetically by subject that describe and analyze the personalities and forces that were part of Stalin's life and career. Topics covered in these individual entries include Stalin's daughter Svetlana Allilueva, art and architecture, Lavrenty Beria, Nikolai Bukharin, Finland, Georgia, the Great Terror, historiography, the Korean War, nomemklatura, religion, science, the Shakhty Trial, the United Nations, and the White Sea-Baltic Canal. Entries range from one to six pages in length and include cross-references to related entries as well as bibliographic references.

Concluding sections provide a chronology of Stalin's life and important Stalin-related events after his death; a glossary of Stalinist political institutions; and a selected bibliography featuring Stalin's writings, writings about Stalin and his career (broken down into historical and political works), and assessments of his cultural and literary policies.

Joseph Stalin: A Biographical Companion is a helpful addition to those interested in learning more about Stalin's career. The entries are well written and informative, with the historiography entry being a particularly noteworthy example in this regard. Although this volume is not intended for Stalinist historians (as the preface indicates), it represents a substantive and scholarly contribution to further our understanding of a political leader whose policies and personality had and continue to have a strong influence on Russian and international political development. [R: LJ, 15 Nov 99, p. 62]—**Bert Chapman**

Slovakia

C

226.   Kirschbaum, Stanislav J. **Historical Dictionary of Slovakia.** Lanham, Md., Scarecrow, 1999. 213p. maps. (European Historical Dictionaries, no.31). $55.00. ISBN 0-8108-3506-1.

Kirschbaum, who was born in Bratislava, Slovakia, has written an excellent dictionary that focuses on the territory that now comprises the country of Slovakia. The politics and history of this region from 1790 to 1997 are the center of the volume, even though there are entries for notable social and cultural topics. Special attention is paid to both the first Slovak Republic, which existed briefly from 1939 to 1945, and the second Slovak Republic, which came into existence January 1, 1993.

There are five maps provided, which are reproduced from a previous work by Kirschbaum entitled *A History of Slovakia: The Struggle for Survival* (St. Martin's Press, 1995). The maps are titled "The Great Moravian Empire," "Slovak Counties in Hungary," "The First Czecho-Slovak Republic1918-1938," "The Slovak Republic of 1939," and "The Slovak Republic of 1993." The inclusion of additional maps showing the region in all its incarnations would have been extremely useful. A 31-page "Chronology of Slovak History" follows the maps. The chronology is supplemented by an introduction that puts the various events into context for the user. The dictionary portion of the text comprises 188 pages and makes limited use of cross-references. The appendix, entitled "Ruler, King, or Head of State on Slovak Territory," begins with Samo (623 to 658 C.E.) and ends with Vladimir Meciar. The volume concludes with a 17-page bibliography that begins with a short bibliographic essay. The author's work fulfills its mission admirably and is recommended for large public and academic libraries. [R: Choice, June 99, p. 1765]—**John R. Burch Jr.**

Spanish

P

227.   Pierson, Peter. **The History of Spain.** Westport, Conn., Greenwood Press, 1999. 223p. maps. index. (The Greenwood Histories of the Modern Nations). $35.00. ISBN 0-313-30272-3.

Good, relatively concise histories of Spain covering the whole range of its history are difficult to find, so this work is welcome. Pierson, a history professor at Santa Clara University and noted scholar on early modern Spain, is well qualified to write such a work. He begins by giving an overview of Spain today, including geography, languages, government, religion, and culture, and then proceeds with a succinct chronological account of the major influences and events on Spanish history from the peninsula's first inhabitants. Spain provides a particular problem for the historian because for so much of its history it was divided into a large number of separate political and cultural entities. For this reason, and the concise format of the book, Pierson at times seems to be reciting a list of kings and political events; the whole reign of Philip II is covered in a mere six pages. But he does bring out the major influences on Spanish history and culture, including Iberian, Celtic, Roman, Visigothic, and particularly Moorish contributions, as well as the influence of the Catholic Church and Spain's European and American empires. The second half of the book, covering the last two centuries, is considerably more detailed on economic, social and cultural, and political issues. The book lacks notes but provides a bibliographic essay, timeline of historical events, directory of important historical characters, and index. Pierson's writing style is clear and concise. The book is recommended for all types of libraries as a good, brief introduction to all of Spain's history.

—**Marit S. MacArthur**

United Kingdom

C, P

228.   **The Blackwell Encyclopaedia of Anglo-Saxon England.** Michael Lapidge, John Blair, Simon Keynes, and Donald Scragg, eds. Malden, Mass., Blackwell, 1999. 537p. illus. maps. $99.95. ISBN 0-631-15565-1.

The Blackwell Encyclopaedia of Anglo-Saxon England is a comprehensive reference work covering every aspect of its subject: art, literature, archaeology, history, and linguistics. There are 150 contributors, including some of the most prominent scholars in the field, who have joined to create this valuable resource. Anglo-Saxon studies is a huge and active area of study, producing some 1,000 publications every year, and this volume is a useful addition, especially for nonspecialists in need of a brief but reliable treatment of a particular subject. Readers will find that the editors have served them well in the breadth of the book. Articles are brief (that on King Alfred is about a page; Northumbria is spread over two columns) but coverage is wide and includes standards such as Bede, Beowulf, and Sutton Hoo as well as an article on dragons and a host of lesser-known kings, princes, and saints. Each article is signed and accompanied by an up-to-date bibliography; some articles are illustrated.

This work sets a high standard for its genre. Articles are informative and well written; browsing through its pages is a real pleasure. Although the single-volume format limits the depth of information presented, those needing more detail can follow the bibliographic citations provided. Blackwell's encyclopaedia is a volume well worth having. [R: Choice, June 99, pp. 1761-1762]—**Victor L. Stater**

C, P

229.   **The Hutchinson Illustrated Encyclopedia of British History.** Chicago, Fitzroy Dearborn, 1998. 384p. illus. maps. $75.00. ISBN 1-57958-107-2.

This book is a model historical encyclopedia. It is easy to use, attractively illustrated, accurate, politically-balanced, and has a good bibliography. Too many such volumes fail by either being so comprehensive they are unwieldy, or so light in content they are unusable. An encyclopedia should hold readers with each reference, tempting them to read all the related entries, and then to pursue the topic in other resources. This book does it. Any library with history collections will do its readers a service by carrying this title.

British history is a complex and tangled narrative including the ancient Celts and Romans in Britain; the origins of England, Wales, Scotland, and Ireland; colonization of the world; maintenance of the empire; and the development of the Commonwealth. A short book like this can only touch on this rich heritage, but it can provide effective introductions to the many stories. This encyclopedia succeeds by keeping its individual entries relatively short and tying them together with almost two dozen historical essays by noted experts and detailed chronologies. The Civil War, for example, is covered by a half-page entry; at least a dozen specific entries on battles, documents, and personalities; a full-page chronology of events; and a thoughtful essay that provides connecting concepts. The many maps in the book are clearly drawn and well planned. No summary of British history is complete without some explanations of the tortuous relationships among the royal houses, and this book meets the task with numerous genealogies, the earliest stretching back to distant and mysterious Scots. Adding to the interest of the book, the editors have included pertinent quotations from various characters in the otherwise unused page margins.

Encyclopedias are by definition eclectic, and the best will provoke readers to learn more about topics they did not know existed. This encyclopedia will draw people to the drama of British history, and to history in general, by making it fascinating. [R: Choice, Nov 99, p. 518]—**Mark A. Wilson**

C, P

230.   **Medieval England: An Encyclopedia.** Paul F. Szarmach, M. Teresa Tavormina, and Joel T. Rosenthal, eds. New York, Garland, 1998. 882p. illus. maps. index. (Garland Reference Library of the Humanities, v.907; Garland Encyclopedias of the Middle Ages, v.3). $135.00. ISBN 0-8240-5786-4.

Medieval England forms an important subject area within many disciplines—art, music, literature, and history. That circumstance creates a demand for ready-reference information, which this new title in the successful series Garland Encyclopedias of the Middle Ages fills. *Medieval England: An Encyclopedia* contains 708 alphabetically arranged entries written by an international group of more than 300 expert contributors. The entries cover various topics of importance from the years 500 to 1500 B.C.E. concerning England, Anglo-Saxon and English language, and Continental influences on English culture and history. Political, religious, social, and economic history dealt with, as are music, art, and literature. Many entries are biographical and range from Abbo of Fleury to Andrew Wyntoun, with Roger Bacon, Julian of Norwich, and William Marshall along with many others featured in between. Individual entries are signed and range from about 200 words to several thousand. The entries are uniformly well written and researched. A bibliography concludes each entry and, where appropriate, is divided into primary and secondary sources. Lists of kings, popes, and archbishops of Canterbury and York; a glossary of musical and liturgical terms; diagrams of castles and churches; and maps supplement the volume. *Medieval England* is especially strong in its coverage of cultural topics. Traditional historical topics do not fare as well. The statutes of Provisors and the Praemunire are not even listed in the index, let alone treated in their own entries. It is debatable as to whether the decision to cover both pre- and post-Conquest England in one volume was wise. Although the encyclopedia deals with Continental influences on England, it gives only minimal mention to connections with Wales, Scotland, and Ireland. What is the justification for having entries on Aquitaine and Normandy but not Wales? The amount of space devoted to individual topics is sometimes problematic. Margery Kempe's entry is longer than Archbishop Thomas Becket's, and Archbishop Thomas Arundel has no entry at all. Compared to the overall usefulness of this volume, these criticisms, although not isolated instances, become venial sins. *Medieval England* is a highly useful and well-done work that students and professors working in the area will want to consult frequently. [R: BL, 1 May 99, pp. 1634-1636; Choice, Sept 99, p. 120; RUSQ, Fall 99, pp. 97-98]—**Ronald H. Fritze**

Yugoslavia

C, P

231.   **Conflict in the Former Yugoslavia: An Encyclopedia.** John B. Allcock, Marko Milivojevic, and John J. Horton, eds. Santa Barbara, Calif., ABC-CLIO, 1998. 410p. illus. maps. index. (Roots of Modern Conflict). $55.00. ISBN 0-87436-935-5.

The articles for this encyclopedia are all by recognized authorities on Yugoslavia. The purpose of the encyclopedia is to bring together a wide range of information about the conflict in Yugoslavia in order to understand the basis for the tragedy that occurred there. This information includes articles on people; geographic terms (important towns, rivers, and so on); political terms such as citizenship and democratization; Dayton Agreements; and names of plans, actions, and economic terms. In short, almost every conceivable aspect of the Yugoslav conflict, including an article on the Cyrillic alphabet, is included. The editors note that in spite of the large number of contributors, there are themes that recur again and again throughout the articles. One of these themes is the unbalanced press treatment that saw on one hand the conflict as an inevitable outcome of the region's ethnic diversity and on the other as the result of actions and intentions of powerful individuals.

As the editors indicate, however, "there is no simple explanation of the roots of the Yugoslav conflict, only a complex braid of explanatory factors, the nature, interdependence, and significance of which still have to be fully evaluated" (p. xv). The articles are brief; very few extend beyond one page. Terms and names used in the articles that are themselves entries are presented in bold typeface. Appendixes include a chronology covering events from the 1941 Axis invasion of Yugoslavia to November 26, 1995, when Commissioner Westendorp announced that a UN presence would be necessary in Bosnia-Herzegovina for two to three more years, and a copy of the Dayton Agreements. This encyclopedia is an extremely useful reference source for providing brief summary information on almost any aspect of this tragic conflict. [R: LJ, 1 Mar 99, p. 72; BL, 15 April 99, p. 1543; Choice, July/Aug 99, p. 1925]—**Robert H. Burger**

MIDDLE EASTERN HISTORY

C, P

232.   Brier, Bob, and Hoyt Hobbs. **Daily Life of the Ancient Egyptians.** Westport, Conn., Greenwood Press, 1999. 253p. illus. maps. index. (The Greenwood Press "Daily Life Through History" Series). $45.00. ISBN 0-313-30313-4.

This book attempts to describe ancient Egyptians—a paradoxical society of startling modern accomplishments with incredibly ancient thought processes, people who looked both forward and back. Ancient Egyptians were stunningly advanced in architecture, food, clothing, and medicine, but their view of the world was closer to that of a prehistoric caveman. Egyptians were among the first people to develop writing, and these writings, along with their accurate tomb paintings, enable archaeologists and historians to study Egyptian life. Egyptians made lists of what they owned, recorded court cases, described battles, preserved recipes, wrote books on medicine and religion, and told stories. Tomb paintings illustrated the clothing, the conduct of professions, and the leisure activities of actual people. Thanks to the recovered objects, inscriptions, paintings, and surviving temples and tombs, today's society knows a great deal about how these ancient people lived and what they thought. The book provides a chronology followed by 10 chapters on various subjects: history, religion, government and society, work and play, food, clothes and other adornments, architecture, arts and crafts, warfare, and medicine and mathematics. An annotated bibliography and an index conclude the work. This is a good introductory reference for archaeology and ancient history students to better understand the Egyptian culture.—**Cari Ringelheim**

WORLD HISTORY

Biography

C, P

233.   **Dictionary of World Biography: The 20th Century.** Frank N. Magill, ed. Chicago, Fitzroy Dearborn and Hackensack, N.J., Salem Press, 1999. 3v. illus. index. $295.00/set. ISBN 0-89356-320-X.

The latest contribution to the mass of biographical reference tools available for twentieth-century individuals, the 3 volumes of *Dictionary of World Biography: The 20th Century* are only part of a larger projected 10-volume set. Although 921 of the 1,054 essays originally appeared in Salem Press's Great Lives from History series, this new project (covering 1901-2000) adds 133 personalities and updates older entries, with expanded annotated bibliographies and illustrations. Each entry begins with birth and death dates, area of specialization, and a brief statement of the contribution made to the era. A section on early life outlines the environment within which the person was born and educated, followed by a detailed discussion of his or her life's work and a summary placing their complete life experience within the century's context. Indexes by area of achievement, geographical region, and surname are provided at the end of the 3d volume. School, public, and academic libraries possessing the earlier sets may wish to add this collection to their biographical holdings but should consider that much of the data are duplicated and that there is no indication of which names have been added.—**Robert B. Marks Ridinger**

C, P
234.   **Dictionary of World Biography, Volume 3: The Renaissance.** Frank N. Magill, ed. Chicago, Fitzroy Dearborn and Englewood Cliffs, N.J., Salem Press, 1999. 813p. illus. index. $125.00. ISBN 0-89356-315-3.

This work follows the same format as the previously published first two volumes (see ARBA 99, entries 519 and 520). It contains 211 essays, 185 of which were drawn from Salem Press's 30-volume Great Lives from History series and 26 new ones. The cutoff point between this volume and the *Dictionary of World Biography, Volume 2: Middle Ages* is 1400 C.E., with 1600 C.E. being the point of demarcation with the next volume in the series. Like the previously published volumes, this one includes three indexes: "Area of Achievement," "Geographical Location," and "Name Index." This is an excellent dictionary for those libraries that do not own the Great Lives from History series, but those that do need to be aware that the essays that have been reprinted have not been updated, with the exception of their bibliographies. [R: Choice, Oct 99, p. 301]—**John R. Burch Jr.**

C, P
235.   **Dictionary of World Biography, Volume 4: The 17th and 18th Centuries.** Frank N. Magill, ed. Chicago, Fitzroy Dearborn and Englewood Cliffs, N.J., Salem Press, 1999. 1515p. illus. index. $125.00. ISBN 0-89356-316-1.

Part of a projected 10-volume set, volume 4 of the *Dictionary of World Biography* includes 377 essays covering important figures from 1601 to 1800. Most of the essays were originally published in the Great Lives from History series (see ARBA 96, entry 942), but 40 are new, as is the arrangement.

The scope of selections is diverse and broad. Major world leaders, religious figures, artists, authors, scholars, scientists, and explorers are included if they were important in shaping civilization in the seventeenth and eighteenth centuries. Examples are Catherine the Great, James Madison, Abas the Great, Betsy Ross, George Fox, Pocahontas, K'ang-His, and Leeuwenhoek. Neither Shakespeare (1564-1616) nor Malthus (1766-1834) is included because their major accomplishments came in different centuries.

The format of the alphabetic entries (consisting of 2,000-3,000 words) includes an initial "ready-reference" paragraph with birth and death dates, areas of achievement, and statement of major contributions. The main body of the entry is an essay divided into three parts: Early Life, Life's Work, and a Summary or "overview of the individual's place in history." More than 200 scholars contributed the entries and they are listed with their academic affiliations. The entries vary in quality but most are engaging and easy to read.

Each biography concludes with a briefly annotated bibliography of 8 to 10 citations. Most entries also have a quarter- to full-page black-and-white portrait; 95 percent of these are from the Library of Congress. Indexes include an area of achievement (with handy cross-references), geographical locations (24 countries), and a name index.

This set is one of the last editorial works of the late Frank Magill, who was a respected and experienced editor of scores of useful reference titles. His chronological arrangement of this set allows individual purchase as well as quicker and easier access to specific historical time periods. This is not possible with the similar *Encyclopedia of World Biography* (see ARBA 99, entry 23). [R: LJ, 15 Nov 99, p. 58]—**Georgia Briscoe**

C, P
236.   **Dictionary of World Biography, Volumes 5 and 6: The 19th Century.** Frank N. Magill, ed. Chicago, Fitzroy Dearborn and Englewood Cliffs, N.J., Salem Press, 1999. 2v. illus. index. $195.00/set. ISBN 0-89356-317-X.

Volume 5 and 6 of *The Dictionary of World Biography* are part of a 10-volume series. The series covers the lives of important personages from the ancient world through the twentieth century. These two volumes cover some of the important people in the nineteenth century. In addition to the 544 essays from the *Great Lives from History* series, there are 69 new biographies. A total of 613 essays cover biographical information on the important figures who flourished in the nineteenth century. Each essay begins with a summary of facts, such as the birth and death dates and place and areas of achievement and contribution. The body of the articles is divided into 3 parts: early life, life's work, then a concluding overview of the individual's place in history. Articles are supplemented by annotated bibliographies that can be useful for those interested in conducting further research on the individuals.

This new series is a reformatted version of Salem Press's 30-volume *Great Lives from History* series. The contents from the earlier series have been rearranged from a geographical perspective into a chronological one. Regretfully, the world as defined is limited to the European countries; therefore the scope of the dictionary heavily emphasizes those in the Western Hemisphere. Very few important people in Asian and African countries are included. However, the editors of the *Dictionary of World Biography* are successful in including people who are distinguished in one of the broad areas of achievement. People such as political and religious leaders, scholars, philosophers, scientists, explorers, and artists were selected because they have shaped the history and civilization in their own time.

The uniform format of the essays offers users quick and easy access to the information needed. For convenience of reference, these volumes are indexed by areas of achievement, geographical areas, as well as by names. This dictionary is definitely a useful reference tool for those who are interested in finding quick information about the nineteenth century and the important figures who shaped history during that time. Recommended for both academic and public libraries. [R: LJ, 15 Nov 99, p. 58]—**Eveline L. Yang**

S

237.   **Kings and Queens.** New York, Macmillan Library Reference/Simon & Schuster Macmillan, 1999. 500p. illus. index. (Macmillan Profiles). $75.00. ISBN 0-02-865375-0.

Written for high school students, this title in the Macmillan Profiles series provides short biographies of some 170 monarchs in world history, including those ruling at the end of the twentieth century. Choices were made based on curricular relevance and historical importance, and a broad range of cultures is represented. Alphabetically ordered, the biographical essays run two to three pages, and are attractively enhanced by such marginalia as quotations, important historical facts, definitions of political terms, and biographical timelines. Black-and-white photographs and special topic boxes add further appeal. A list of suggested reading, a 15-page glossary, and a thorough index finish the book. *Kings and Queens* is a well-designed reference and should find a much-deserved place in high school and public libraries.—**Lori D. Kranz**

P

238.   **Who's Who in Political Revolutions: Seventy-Three Men and Women Who Changed the World.** Jack A. Goldstone, ed. Washington, D.C., Congressional Quarterly, 1999. 164p. illus. index. $29.95pa. ISBN 1-56802-461-4.

The importance of revolutionary leaders and visionaries in shaping world events over the past 200 years is the focus of this authoritative and extremely accessible biographical dictionary. The editor is an acknowledged expert in the field of international politics and government. An international cadre of scholars contributed the signed essays, which are drawn from Congressional Quarterly's acclaimed *Encyclopedia of Political Revolutions* (see entry 242).

Introductory material includes an essay on the nature of revolutionary leaders and a useful timeline by region of events and leaders. Each essay contains a picture and a short bibliography. From the well-known to lesser-known leaders such as Rigoberta Menchú Tum or Hong Xiuquan, the descriptions are lively and thorough. This volume is a valuable addition for most libraries wanting a smaller cumulation of biographies of political revolutionary leaders for students and general patrons. [R: BR, Sept/Oct 99, p. 65]—**Ingrid Schierling Burnett**

Chronology

P, S

239.   Rodriguez, Junius P. **Chronology of World Slavery.** Santa Barbara, Calif., ABC-CLIO, 1999. 580p. illus. index. $99.00. ISBN 0-57607-155-3.

Despite its preachiness, which quickly becomes wearisome, this is a useful reference. It illustrates the universality of slavery. The institution is as old as humanity, has existed in some form in every part of the world, has involved all major racial groups, and continues to this day in some areas of the world. Of course, the nature of slavery has varied considerably from place to place over time. For Muslims, it served primarily household, administrative, and military objectives. For certain premodern peoples, such as the Carthaginians, some Africans, and the Aztecs of Mexico, its purpose was largely ritualistic. The Aztecs, for example, regularly "adopted" captives, thereby enabling them to sacrifice "beloved family members" to the gods. And in the West, particularly Latin America and the southern United States, slavery became a major economic institution, ultimately affecting all aspects of society.

Sensibly organized, the study begins with the ancient world (the first entry dates from 6800 B.C.E.), then moves in successive chapters through Europe, Asia, Africa, Latin America, and the United States. A concluding chapter treats contemporary developments, beginning with an 1880 entry on slavery in China and ending with a 1998 note on the end of slavery in Mauritania. Adding to the volume's overall appeal are numerous maps, sketches, and photographs, a substantial bibliography, and an extensive section of documents (almost 20 percent of the text). An exhaustive index facilitates access to this material. Given the ongoing interest in this subject, this work should be added to the reference collections of high school and college libraries. [R: LJ, 1 Oct 99, p. 82; BR, Nov/Dec 99, p. 87]—**John W. Storey**

P, S

240.   **The Wilson Calendar of World History.** John Paxton and Edward W. Knappman, eds. Bronx, N.Y., H. W. Wilson, 1999. 460p. illus. index. (Wilson Chronology Series). $70.00. ISBN 0-8242-0937-0.

This chronology begins at 3500 B.C.E. and continues to 1998. A massive undertaking, more than 25,000 historical landmarks are listed under 6 categories—4 geographic regions, science and technology, and culture and the arts. Entries cover people, places, concepts, inventions, discoveries, and titles of specific artworks and literary pieces. This timeline provides balanced representation for Europe, Asia, the Americas, and Africa including the Middle East. The notations are formatted to allow readers to scan down a vertical column to follow related items or across to track the same date around the world.

The authors provide a detailed index allowing ready access to a specific subject. For example, when readers look up "printing," they will learn that the 1st printed newsletter circulated in China in 748 C.E. Later developments ending with Guttenberg in 1457 C.E. are also noted. This reference is a helpful research tool and complements narrative histories by showing the interrelationship of ideas and events occurring simultaneously.

—**Adrienne Antink Bendel**

Dictionaries and Encyclopedias

P, S

241.   **Encyclopedia of North American History.** John C. Super, ed. Tarrytown, N.Y., Marshall Cavendish, 1999. 11v. illus. maps. index. $459.95/set. ISBN 0-7614-7084-0.

This multivolume encyclopedia will be accessible to at least the well educated among the seventh graders who are its target audience, although many entries are sophisticated enough to be useful to high school students and general readers. The work contains 493 alphabetically arranged entries by a broad array of scholars. Not surprisingly, it is heavily weighted toward U.S. history. Entries range from one to seven pages, all include "causes and effects" sidebars, and the longer ones feature summaries; bibliographies; and six types of sidebars dealing with turning points, daily life, laws and cases, profiles of individuals, temper of the times, and viewpoints. Each volume is indexed, but there is a comprehensive index in volume 11, which also includes biographical, geographical, and various subject indexes; a rather brief bibliography; a glossary; and a timeline. The illustrations are excellent, although it would be nice to have more maps. The selection of topics for entries at times reveals the lack of a sense of proportion (e.g., "Branch Davidian Complex Burns" and "Million Man March" are included, but the presidencies of John Adams and James Madison are not); in fact, a number of U.S. presidents fail to rate individual entries. The choice of battles and treaties is also a bit idiosyncratic. The same is true of religious topics. Although religion is dealt with under several general headings (e.g., Great Awakening, Great Puritan Migration, Separation of Church and State), there are no separate entries on major denominations. All this notwithstanding, there is much useful information in this user-friendly set, and it should help make middle school students more interested in and informed about North American history. [R: BL, 1 Sept 99, p. 179]—**William B. Robison**

C, P

242.   **The Encyclopedia of Political Revolutions.** By Jack A. Goldstone. Washington, D.C., Congressional Quarterly, 1998. 580p. illus. maps. index. $125.00. ISBN 1-56802-206-9.

This is a well-done, one-volume encyclopedia that supplies information on today's revolutionary world. While the coverage is broad, 1500 to the present, it nevertheless provides articles on revolutions, civil wars, and similar uprisings worldwide—large and small, bloody and bloodless, cultural and political. The quality of entries varies. Most of the articles are generally excellent.

The title does not do justice to the topic. The term "revolution" is treated broadly to include civil wars, cultural revolutions, guerrilla movements, and popular uprisings. The alphabetically arranged articles cover not only the events, but also include biographical entries on prominent revolutionary leaders. Concept articles are included to help readers understand how class, race, politics, and other factors relate to such movements. Specific events include the American Revolution and Civil War, the Palestinian Intifada, the Shining Path Revolt in Peru, the Chinese Cultural Revolution and the Tiananmen Square uprising, numerous Irish rebellions, the recent wars in Yugoslavia, and the sixteenth-century Aztec and Inca revolts against the Spanish. Biographical entries include such recent and past revolutionary leaders as Ho Chi Minh, Ernesto "Che" Guevara, Lech Walesa, Thomas Jefferson, Martin Luther, Martin Luther King, Jose Marti, Patrice Lumumba, and Oliver Cromwell. More than 50 articles discuss revolutionary movement concepts such as gender, class, colonialism, capitalism, elitism, fundamentalism, race, student protest, tyranny, and terrorism. Each entry was written by an expert in the field, and is accompanied by a bibliography for further reading.

From an organizational standpoint, this encyclopedia is all one could ask for. Separate alphabetic lists identify contributors and articles, while a third lists entries in biographical, event, and concept categories. The introduction provides readers with a general history of revolutions. A geographical timeline gives overviews of the revolutions described in the main body of the work. The text is further enhanced by a good selection of maps and pictures. Overall access to the contents is excellent via an extensive subject index, while the articles themselves are more easily scanned through the use of interior subheadings.

This is a first-rate work on a topic that will always be of current interest as long as unrest continues in the world. Highly recommended for public, college, university, and any other library with an interest in this topic. [R: BL, 1 May 99, pp. 1622-1624; Choice, Oct 99, p. 312]—**Donald E. Collins**

P

243.   Kohn, George Childs. **Dictionary of Wars.** rev. ed. New York, Facts on File, 1999. 614p. index. $50.00. ISBN 0-8160-3928-3.

This ambitious volume provides concise information on more than 1,800 global conflicts, civil wars, mutinies, punitive expeditions, undeclared wars, rebellions, and revolutions as well as religious, sectarian, ethnic, and racial conflicts from all parts of the world. The book spans 4,000 years of history from 2000 B.C.E. to the present, including "The Kosovo Uprising of 1998," in a revision that includes more than 70 new entries. Arranged alphabetically, each entry gives the conflict's name(s), dates it spanned, how it began, the opposing sides involved in the conflict, a summary or description of events, and the outcome or significance. Each entry also discusses the political, social, economic, and cultural influences on the military actions. Entries are cross-referenced to related conflicts. When known by more than one name, all names are included and cross-referenced to the most familiar name. A geographic index gives a chronological listing of all the wars for each country. The book also includes an alphabetic index.

The scope of this volume is impressive, especially with the addition of conflicts that have occurred since its first publication more than 12 years ago. The narrative style of each entry makes for easy reading while providing a lot of information in a concise format. No bibliography is included, however, so the reader has no suggestions of where to go for further information. Although the inclusion would have increased the length of the volume considerably, its lack makes the book less valuable as a research tool. As a starting place or for general information, this work should prove quite useful. [R: LJ, 15 June 99, p. 72; BL, 15 Nov 99, pp. 644-646]

—**Janet Hilbun**

P, S

244.   **Oxford Encyclopedia of World History.** Market House Books, comp. New York, Oxford University Press, 1998. 775p. illus. maps. $30.00. ISBN 0-19-860223-5.

The more than 4,000 entries in this work cover the major events and figures of world history. The world's nation-states are also included, with tables of geographic and demographic data. A reference book of this size and scope would necessarily be very general, but abundant cross-references set off typographically within the text expand its utility. Each entry introduces a topic and touches upon causes and effects related to the subject for a succinct presentation. Two-color, shaded maps and black-and-white illustrations enhance some entries.

Written in British English, this encyclopedia focuses more on the Western than the Eastern world, but politically it is fairly neutral (e.g., the entry on Richard Nixon is devoted mostly to his foreign policy, with only brief mention of Watergate—although Watergate has its own entry). The 26-page chronology at the end of the book lists events in Europe and the Mediterranean region with corresponding information on history and culture in other parts of the world. Up to date through 1996, this reference would be most useful to high school students or general readers in need of background material. It would also serve as a handy desk reference. [R: BL, 1 May 99, p. 1636]—**Lori D. Kranz**

P

245.   Schechter, Michael G. **Historical Dictionary of International Organizations.** Lanham, Md., Scarecrow, 1998. 247p. (Historical Dictionaries of International Organizations, no.16). $60.00. ISBN 0-8108-3479-0.

This volume is the 16th of the historical dictionaries of international organizations. Schechter has clarified the often confusing world of international organizations by providing a brief overall history of their origins and functions. There are a list of acronyms, a selected chronology of the founding of international organizations, an introduction, the dictionary itself, and an extensive bibliography. International organizations grew out of conferences of sovereign states that met to discuss and resolve certain issues of peace or war or to standardize weights and measures in a discordant and distant world.

International travel and communications have altered the meaning and purpose of international organizations. There is a vast array of organizations with an equally vast array of motivations and agendas. The only real clear notion for the future of these organizations is change. There is no longer a cold war to polarize international organizations into east, west, or nonaligned. International organizations deal with a wide variety of economic, environmental, humanitarian, social, diplomatic, and military issues. Schechter's work helps sort these issues and organizations and provides an understanding of the changing international scene. This small informative volume is a valuable addition to any public, college, university, or government reference collection. [R: Choice, June 99, p. 1767]—**Norman L. Kincaide**

C, P

246.   Wagner, John A. **Historical Dictionary of the Elizabethan World: Britain, Ireland, Europe, and America.** Phoenix, Ariz., Oryx Press, 1999. 392p. illus. maps. index. $59.95. ISBN 1-57356-200-9.

Audiences of the recent films *Elizabeth* and *Shakespeare in Love* who want to know more about the era of the Virgin Queen will profit from this volume. In a comparatively brief space for a work of this breadth, Wagner provides useful entries under such general aspects of Elizabeth's England as government, religion, education, women, and science, to name a few. To each entry is appended a brief bibliographic supplement of several current secondary titles for further reading. Inevitably, some "major minor" figures have been omitted; for example, the entry on music cites longer entries on Peter Carew, William Byrd, and Thomas Tallis, but there is no reference to John Bull or John Dowland. Literary entries tend to be more historically factual than critically summative; Ben Jonson's hallmark neoclassicism is not mentioned. For broader biographical coverage of this period one should supplement this volume with R. H. Fritze's biographical dictionaries of the Tudor and Stuart periods (1991, 1996).

But these shortcomings are minor in a book intended "primarily for students and other non-specialists." Such readers will be impressed by the book's overall design and layout, and its wealth of ancillary tables, charts, maps, bibliography, and seven appendixes, one of which includes the two quite recent movies cited above. Others tabulate genealogies, archbishops, popes, monarchs, plus selected historical fiction and sound recordings. Frequent black-and-white illustrations enhance the text. Those coming to this historical era for the first time will be enticed to further study by the book's attractive format and user-friendly organization. More experienced students of the period will also appreciate the appendix on selected Elizabethan and Tudor Websites. This is an appropriate acquisition for all libraries from the secondary level on up. [R: BL, 1 Dec 99, pp. 722-724]—**Christopher Baker**

Handbooks and Yearbooks

P

247.   Brogan, Patrick. **World Conflicts.** Lanham, Md., Scarecrow, 1998. 682p. index. $49.50. ISBN 0-8108-3551-7.

It is refreshing to come across a reference work that is well-organized, meaningful, and well written. Patrick Brogan has provided a lively, informative, and entertaining narrative style for this work on world strife and conflict since 1945. The world did not remain at peace after World War II, and perhaps there have been as many casualties of war, rebellion, and revolution in the second half of the century as there were in the first half. Five sections deal with world conflict regionally: Africa, Asia, Middle East, Europe, and Latin America. The last section deals with terrorism and provides a timeline of wars, coups and revolutions, and assassinations since 1945. This thick but manageable volume has a lively historical narrative style, making it a joy to read. Anecdotal material and lively quotes make the topic come alive and carry the reader from topic to topic as easily as one flips through the pages. Patrick Brogan is to be commended on this fine work. It is highly recommended for private, public, college, university, and government reference collections. [R: Choice, Dec 99, p. 699]—**Norman L. Kincaide**

P

248.   George, Linda S. **The Golden Age of Islam.** Tarrytown, N.Y., Marshall Cavendish, 1998. 80p. illus. maps. index. (Cultures of the Past). $19.95. ISBN 0-7614-0273-X.

P

249.   Hinds, Kathryn. **The Incas.** Tarrytown, N.Y., Marshall Cavendish, 1998. 80p. illus. maps. index. (Cultures of the Past). $19.95. ISBN 0-7614-0270-5.

P

250.   Hinds, Kathryn. **The Vikings.** Tarrytown, N.Y., Marshall Cavendish, 1998. 80p. illus. index. (Cultures of the Past). $19.95. ISBN 0-7614-0271-3.

P

251.   Service, Pamela F. **The Ancient African Kingdom of Kush.** Tarrytown, N.Y., Marshall Cavendish, 1998. 80p. illus. index. (Cultures of the Past). $19.95. ISBN 0-7614-0272-1.

These 4 books of an attractive 14-volume series, designed for older elementary through high school readers, bring key vanished cultures to life as they were at the height of their development. The authors, who are either authorities or persons with a special interest in the culture, use narrative, sidebars, descriptive captions, photographs of places, works of art, and sometimes persons, all currently in existence, to discuss these cultures. The daily lives of the people, including their religions, are brought into focus, as are the culture's legends and political history. The authors note the lives of women and the place of slavery. A chronology, glossary, and two bibliographies—one aimed at the younger student and one for use by the teacher or older student—assist readers in each volume. The titles can be purchased singly as can other titles in the series, including *The Ancient Egyptians*, *The Ancient Greeks*, *The Ancient Maya*, *The Ancient Romans*, *The Aztec Empire*, *The Celts of Northern Europe*, *China's Tang Dynasty*, *India's Gupta Dynasty*, *The Kingdom of Benin in West Africa*, and *The Persian Empire*.

—Edna M. Boardman

P

252.   **The Holocaust: Memories, Research, Reference.** Robert Hauptman and Susan Hubbs Motin, eds. Binghamton, N.Y., Haworth Press, 1998. 320p. index. $49.95. ISBN 0-7890-0379-1.

The Holocaust: Memories, Research, Reference is a collection of essays exploring this historical tragedy from three different directions. The first part, "Memories," emphasizes the memories of those who witnessed the Holocaust and the importance of documenting and recalling those memories in order to preserve an accurate record of historical facts. For example, Arnost Lustig writes a powerful essay recalling his own experiences at Auschwitz-Birkenau. Part 2 concentrates on research and methods of studying and investigating the Holocaust. This section also discusses different methods of integrating Holocaust study into high school and college curriculum. The final part contains essays discussing different sources for reference in the study of the Holocaust. This section provides

direction for researchers both in the library and on the Internet. An index is also provided to guide users in their research. This work is a significant reference tool in itself as well as a guide to further research. This is a must-have for all libraries, especially those with patrons interested in Holocaust documentation and research.
—**Cari Ringelheim**

P, S

253.   Kaufman, Burton I. **The Korean Conflict.** Westport, Conn., Greenwood Press, 1999. 193p. illus. index. (Greenwood Press Guides to Historic Events of the Twentieth Century). $39.95. ISBN 0-313-29909-9.

Unlike the Vietnam War, the Korean conflict, as the author and the editor of the series have aptly pointed out, has been a "neglected war in the history of the United States." However, interest in the Korean War has resurfaced recently, perhaps because of the end of the Cold War, which has enabled scholars to examine the exact nature of the roles of Russia and China—the enduring questions of more than 30 years—in this conflict with the opening of their archives to the public.

The Korean Conflict, like other volumes in the series of Greenwood Press Guides to Historic Events of the Twentieth Century, includes a chronology of events, six topical essays, biographical entries on important or key individuals in the conflict, primary documents of the conflict, and a topical annotated bibliography. In the reviewer's mind, the most valuable features of the work are the 6 topical and 15 primary documents. The essays examine the causes, events, and implications of the war; they are brief but thorough, balanced, up-to-date, and readable. The inclusion of the primary documents, however, has further illuminated the views presented in the text. What is missing from the biographical section is the exclusion of Zho En-lai, a major figure in the conflict.

This work should prove to be a useful tool for high school students, especially students taking advanced high school American and Asian history courses, and beginning undergraduates. School, public, and academic libraries should purchase this work.—**Binh P. Le**

Quotation Books

P

254.   Langer, Howard J., comp. **World War II: An Encyclopedia of Quotations.** Westport, Conn., Greenwood Press, 1999. 449p. illus. index. $75.00. ISBN 0-313-30018-6.

This reference provides more than 1,000 quotes from more than 300 individuals about World War II. The selections come from heads of state, military officers, diplomats, government officials, chaplains, intelligence officers, scientists, journalists, historians, civilians, and soldiers and sailors speaking from the heat of battle. Both the Allied and the Axis sides of the conflict are represented. Entries come from public addresses, military orders, secret documents released after the war, press reports, private diaries and letters, published histories, memoirs, and many other sources. These excerpts take the reader back in time and impart a visceral understanding of what the war meant to those who lived through it. The most chilling and telling comments are those from ordinary citizens—again from both sides of the war.

Very short coverage is given to the Holocaust in this volume. The editor has done a companion piece dedicated to this tragic dimension of the war. An extensive bibliography is provided as well as two indexes in which pieces are listed by category and by subject and name. Additional features are an inventory of movies made about World War II during the war and a guide to slang, code names, and other terms used during the period. This work brings alive the tenor of the war years and portrays an inspiring time in our history. [R: LJ, 1 Mar 99, p. 76; BL, June 99, p. 1884]—**Adrienne Antink Bendel**

10 Law

GENERAL WORKS

Dictionaries and Encyclopedias

C

255. **Dictionary of Law.** 2d ed. P. H. Collin, ed. Chicago, Fitzroy Dearborn, 1999. 258p. $55.00. ISBN 1-57958-155-2.

Although this book purports to cover both British and U.S. law, its emphasis seems to be on the former; indeed the 1st edition was titled *English Law Dictionary*. It is a handy volume containing 6,000 main words and phrases that cover criminal, civil, commercial, and international law. According to the 1st edition's preface (reprinted in this edition), the level of vocabulary ranges from the very formal to prison slang. In addition to their definitions, examples are given of words and phrases used in context. Words with particular grammatical challenges have short grammar notes and explanations of differences between British and U.S. use. Particularly useful are the comments on certain words that explain particular points of law.

The 1st edition's preface curiously refers to a supplement not found in the 2d edition. The 2d edition's preface explains that the text has been completely updated with an emphasis on adding legislative process materials.

Although the book is extremely interesting, it is unclear what audience would appreciate comparing the British and U.S. systems of law in a dictionary format. Other titles must surely cover British legal terms at a less expensive price.—**Bev Cummings Agnew**

Directories

C, P

256. Eis, Arlene L., comp. **Directory of Law-Related CD-ROMs 1999.** Teaneck, N.J., Infosources, 1999. 328p. index. $75.00pa. ISBN 0-939486-5309. ISSN 1065-0334.

Directory of Law-Related CD-ROMs 1999 is published by one of the foremost compilers of legal reference products, Infosources Publishing. Eis, MLS and former law librarian, began publishing annual titles for this niche market as early as 1981 with *Legal Looseleafs in Print* (see ARBA 84, entry 484). The CD-ROM directory has been issued annually since 1993. Paper quality and the inclusion of advertisements in this work suggest that currency of information is valued above a formal presentation style, which is appropriate for such a rapidly changing subject area.

This one-of-a-kind directory is a collection of almost everything law librarians and lawyers need to know about the purchase of domestic and international law-related CD-ROMs. Compiled and edited by Eis, this directory provides multiple access points through several detailed indexes. Entries for each of the CD-ROMs (more than 1,500) contains up to 19 information fields and are uniformly formatted for easy comparison.

The *Directory of Law-Related CD-ROMS* is really part of a suite of products. A newsletter/update service released three times a year may be purchased separately and a Web site, partly accessible only to this directory's subscribers, is also available. The *Internet Guide for the Legal Researcher* (2d ed.; Infosources), by Don MacLeod, may be used as a companion reference.

Although CD-ROM technology usage appears to be waning, it is still being used in conjunction with legal online subscription sources, such as LEXIS-NEXIS and "free" Internet sites such as findlaw.com. When Website subscriptions decrease in price and can guarantee more privacy, stability, and ease of access, CD-ROMs may go the way of many paper subscriptions. For the time being, legal research seems best conducted using a combination of formats: print, CD-ROM, and Internet. Internet addresses of most CD-ROM vendors are provided, an indication that publishers themselves are trying to balance the cost effectiveness, stability, and comprehensiveness of CD-ROMs against the timeliness and sophisticated retrieval features of commercial Web products.

The *Directory of Law-Related CD-ROMs* should be considered an indispensable tool for law offices and law libraries that continue to subscribe to CD-ROM products. As the only reference work of its kind, it is well worth the price.—**Linda D. Tietjen**

Handbooks and Yearbooks

P

257.   **American Law Yearbook 1998.** Kris E. Palmer and others, eds. Farmington Hills, Mich., Gale, 1999. 337p. illus. index. $140.00. ISBN 0-7876-3783-1. ISSN 1521-0901.

The *American Law Yearbook 1998*, a supplement to West Publishing's *Encyclopedia of American Law* (1997), updates the contents of the encyclopedia with material through May 1998 and adds additional subjects, largely biographies. An appendix gives descriptions of lobbying organizations. Articles include definitions and discussions of legal terms and concepts; descriptions of events and legal cases; and biographies of people who are significant in American law, politics, and government. The articles are well written, and variations in type size and subheadings make the work easy to use. Special "In Focus" pieces highlight issues of particular interest, importance, or controversy (e.g., campaign financing reform). Black-and-white photographs, a table of cases cited, an excellent index, and cross-references to articles in the encyclopedia are included.

This is an excellent resource for the layperson who wants information on issues (e.g., school prayer) and events (e.g., Whitewater) from a legal perspective that is often lacking in the media, or for the reader, layperson, or professional who is interested in an overview of American legal developments in the period covered by the yearbook. This is a necessary purchase for libraries that own the encyclopedia, where it would be most useful, and it would find users in other libraries with substantial budgets where there is a strong interest in current events and American politics and government.—**Gari-Anne Patzwald**

P

258.   Eisaguirre, Lynne. **Affirmative Action: A Reference Handbook.** Santa Barbara, Calif., ABC-CLIO, 1999. 222p. index. (Contemporary World Issues). $45.00. ISBN 0-87436-854-5.

This is another introductory overview and guide in the Contemporary World Issues series designed to address critical issues current in public policy debate. Similar publications in this series include topics such as hate crimes, feminism, and sexual harassment, the latter guide written by Eisaguirre as well. The series provides people beginning research on a contemporary social issue an objective and clear overview and guide to the issue's history, development, and current status. The series succeeds admirably. High school and college students should begin their research on these issues with the relevant text from the series.

Affirmative Action is divided into 7 chapters. The introductory chapter introduces the reader to a clear and concise overview of the historical development of the affirmative action debate. The chapter moves from the roots of affirmative action, including a definition, through the developments and realities of the 1980s and 1990s. The chapter concludes with a short but useful list of references. Chapter 2 provides a brief but equally useful chronology of important historical events. Chapter 3 presents brief biographical sketches of some of the key players in the debate. Students new to the debate will profit immensely from these sketches. Chapter 4, the longest and arguably the most important chapter, consists of sundry facts and statistics that help focus the debate. This chapter concludes with a helpful list of references. Chapter 5 lists numerous organizations that address the issue. Chapter 6 offers an annotated list of select print resources. Chapter 7 lists select nonprint resources, including several Internet addresses. Any but the most advanced researcher will profit from the clarity and brevity of presentation. A glossary and an index complete this excellent overview and guide to this highly contentious public debate. This volume is highly recommended for all libraries.—**Michael A. Foley**

C, P

259. Jost, Kenneth. **The Supreme Court Yearbook 1997-1998.** Washington, D.C., Congressional Quarterly, 1999. 325p. illus. index. $38.95; $30.95pa. ISBN 1-56802-411-8; 1-56802-411-Xpa. ISSN 1054-2701.

The Supreme Court Yearbook 1995-1996 was reviewed in ARBA 97 (see entry 603), and the format and style of this source has not changed since then. Jost has been the author since the 1992-1993 edition. Highlighted cases in the overview chapter include several that concerned sexual harassment, one that considered the rights of people with HIV under the Americans with Disabilities Act, and the nullification of the Line Item Veto Act. The chapter that provides case summaries of all the Court's decisions in this term is divided into 13 broad subject areas, such as environmental law, First Amendment, and torts. The text is supplemented by several tables and graphs as well as a few photographs (including one of performance artist Karen Finley with her body partly covered in chocolate to dramatize the sexual oppression of women). Jost writes in a clear and incisive style that is consistent with that of other Congressional Quarterly reporters and researchers. Although there are evaluative and analytic statements made, these are nonpartisan in tone and are generally supported by factual evidence or quotations from sources. Although all public and academic libraries will find it useful, this yearbook should be particularly helpful for smaller libraries where the complete texts of Supreme Court decisions are not available.—**Jack Ray**

P

260. Olson, Kent C. **Legal Information: How to Find It, How to Use It.** Phoenix, Ariz., Oryx Press, 1999. 333p. index. $59.00; $39.95pa. ISBN 0-89774-961-8; 0-89774-963-4pa.

Modeled on Michael R. Lavin's *Business Information* (Oryx, 1992), "this volume aims to explain where legal information is located, whether in general libraries, in law libraries, or electronically, and to provide the background knowledge necessary to make effective use of that information" (p. vii). It emphasizes materials available in general libraries and on the Internet. Part 1 provides an overview of the U.S. legal system, dictionaries and guides to legal language, legal citations and abbreviations, and research guides. Part 2 covers general reference sources, law books, journals and periodicals, and finding lawyers and institutions. Part 3 turns to federal law, including the U.S. Constitution and the Supreme Court, federal legislation, federal courts, and federal administrative law. Part 4 focuses on state law, including state legislation, administrative law, and state courts. In each part, specific resources are analyzed for their good and bad points. For example *Black's Law Dictionary* (West Publishing, 1990) is one of the most extensive legal dictionaries, but contains many obsolete terms and needs modernization. Illustrations from various resources complement the text. The 8½-by-11-inch page size, two-column-per-page, clean layout is easy to read. Olson nicely weaves discussion of the materials' points into an easily understood narrative. Budding lawyers and laypersons seeking insights into legal research will find this volume helpful. It may also be used for specialized library school reference courses. [R: Choice, July/Aug 99, p. 1929]—**Esther R. Sinofsky**

P

261. Palmer, Louis J., Jr. **The Death Penalty: An American Citizen's Guide to Understanding Federal and State Laws.** Jefferson, N.C., McFarland, 1998. 285p. index. $39.95. ISBN 0-7864-0444-2.

Palmer's book provides a clear and coherent guide to the death penalty in the United States. To paraphrase Supreme Court Justice Thurgood Marshall's opinion in the 1972 Supreme Court capital punishment case *Furman v. Georgia*, the American public does not understand the reality of the death penalty. Palmer's book will help anyone come to understand the legal complexities that surround the capital punishment debate in today's society. There is no attempt to proselytize here. The material presents information relevant to the legal realities of the death penalty. The book is divided into four parts. Part 1 provides a brief background on the common-law influences on the death penalty, the position of the Eighth Amendment on the death penalty, and death-eligible offenses. Part 2 examines prosecutorial issues, such as the role of the prosecutor in criminal justice cases, the discretionary power prosecutors have in bringing a penalty case to trial, the indictment, and prosecuting a "nontriggerman." Part 3 offers information relating to the court proceedings, including the capital penalty phase of a capital trial, aggravating and mitigating circumstances relevant to a determination of sentence, and the appellate review of a death sentence. Part 4 explains barriers to execution, witnessing an execution, and execution methods. There are tables and boxes throughout the book that make points and issues dramatically clear. For example, there is a murder time clock, a table of murder weapons used from 1990 to 1994, a table of aggravating circumstances of murder from 1990 to 1995, and age and gender of murderers in 1994. The book contains an appendix of eight tables of selected death penalty provisions, an appendix of federal death penalty laws, and concludes with a glossary, chapter notes, a bibliography (including death penalty sentencing statutes, books, articles, and cases), and an index. This work is highly recommended. [R: BR, Sept/Oct 98, p. 76]—**Michael A. Foley**

P

262.   Sitarz, Daniel. **Laws of the United States: Corporations.** Carbondale, Ill., Nova Publishing, 1999. 223p. (Quick Reference Law). $16.95pa. ISBN 0-935755-67-5.

This is a useful reference book that contains not the laws relevant to corporations, but where to find those laws in every state and the District of Columbia. This title is part of the Quick Reference Law series, whose purpose is to provide concise, comprehensive, and authoritative guides to the laws of the states in specific legal areas. Certainly this title has fulfilled the purpose of the series.

Four or five pages for each state include the following helpful information: the address (but not the telephone number) for the appropriate corporation department, such as the Secretary of State's office; a citation to that state's statute; the title of the corporate filing document; and the fees. Listed are the requirements for the corporate name, the corporate purpose, the director, paid-in capital, publication, assumed name, shareholder, and records. Also included are the corporation's duration, the stock share regulations, corporate powers, amendments, and bylaws. The information from the statutes "has been abridged for clarity and succinctness."

A caveat suggests checking for the most current information. Although the publishing date of 1999 is some guidance, it would have been useful to include in the introduction the date upon which the compiled information was current.

A 1998 Investor Responsibility Research Center publication by Grant A. Gartman and Jack D. Isaacs entitled "Corporate Governance State by State: A Guide to Selected Statutes," will be more useful for legal patrons. It does not, however, contain the information on the corporation's office for each state. More sophisticated patrons may want Websites and e-mail addresses for the appropriate offices; neither are found here. Nevertheless, this handy and inexpensive compilation will be useful in any public library.—**Bev Cummings Agnew**

P

263.   Sitarz, Daniel. **Laws of the United States: Divorce.** Carbondale, Ill., Nova Publishing, 1999. 191p. (Quick Reference Law Series). $16.95pa. ISBN 0-935755-68-3.

The purpose of this book is to provide concise, comprehensive, and authoritative guides to the law of all states regarding divorce. The publication is alphabetic by state and gives residency requirements and where to file, legal grounds for divorce, name of court in which to file for divorce, legal separation, simplified or special divorce procedures, meditation or counseling requirements, alimony or maintenance spousal agreements, spouse name change, child custody, child support; and premarital agreements. The major drawback of legal publications is that laws can and do change, so one must always check to see if laws have changed since the material was published. The language of the publication is more geared to the layperson than is the *Martindale-Hubbell Law Digest: United States*, whose language is much more legalistic. The subject covered here is more complete than in the above-mentioned publication. This is an inexpensive book that all public libraries ought to purchase for their collection.—**Theresa Maggio**

CRIMINOLOGY AND CRIMINAL JUSTICE

Biography

P, S

264.   Bijlefeld, Marjolijn. **People for and Against Gun Control: A Biographical Reference.** Westport, Conn., Greenwood Press, 1999. 324p. illus. index. (The Greenwood Press "People Making a Difference" Series). $49.95. ISBN 0-313-30690-7.

As both accidental and deliberate shootings occur more frequently in upscale neighborhoods and young people are increasingly the targets, gun control becomes a more intense controversy. It is often a topic for student papers and debates. This volume, part of a series titled "People Making a Difference," is intended to help high school and college students involved in such projects to explore the complex issue of gun control through the lives of 50 people who are very much involved in the debate. They include doctors, elected officials, lobbyists for various organizations, and victims. The one trait they all have in common is their dedication to making a safer society.

Preceding the biographies is an excellent introduction by the author that covers the main elements of the gun control debate; the roles of law enforcement, gun manufacturers, health professionals, and others; statistics; and public opinion. The profiles contain such information as where and when the person was born, family background, education, and present position. More important, however, is the story of how each of these persons became involved in the gun control debate, the contributions they have made to the movement, and the obstacles they have faced from the opposition. Readings by or about the person are appended to each profile and photos frequently accompany the text. Material appended to the main section is helpful in itself, but also to a certain extent in evaluating the evenhandedness of the author. Included are summaries of state and federal gun control laws and state constitutional clauses relating to the right to bear arms; lists of the biographies by pro- and anti-gun control legislation, by profession, and by states represented; a general bibliography; and an index.

All of the profiles were written by the author, a freelance writer and former director of the Educational Fund to End Gun Violence. She also worked with the Coalition to End Gun Violence—activities that obviously put her in the pro-gun control category and would most likely raise questions about her objectivity in presenting both sides of the issue fairly. The text itself, however, gives no indication of bias. Neither is any bias shown in the selection of those profiled—25 for gun control and 25 against it—nor was any detected in the types of persons or geographical locations, as both showed a wide variation. The value of this work is that it presents gun control issues from a different perspective than what students usually find available. The profiles are well written and compelling; they enable the student to consider a reasoned presentation of an opposing viewpoint. It would be particularly helpful for students taking a pro or con side in the gun control debate. Although recommended for school and college libraries, it would also be useful for public libraries where interest in the subject is high.

—**Lucille Whalen**

Handbooks and Yearbooks

P

265.   Altschiller, Donald. **Hate Crimes: A Reference Handbook.** Santa Barbara, Calif., ABC-CLIO, 1999. 204p. index. (Contemporary World Issues). $45.00. ISBN 0-87436-937-1.

ABC-CLIO's Contemporary World Issues series offers authoritative and clear guides to some of the most critical social issues. For example, the series includes guides to affirmative action, censorship, feminism, victims' rights, and welfare reform, to name a few. These guides are useful at all levels of research, including high school. In general, the guides share the same basic format and organization. *Hate Crimes* begins with some general background information on a few major targeted groups (e.g., African Americans, gay men and lesbians, Asian Americans). This brief but useful chapter ends with a history of hate crimes legislation (both federal and state), U.S. Supreme Court decisions, and a brief overview of the opponents of hate crime legislation. Chapter 2 provides an excellent chronology of hate crimes from 1955 to 1999. Chapter 3 lists biographical sketches of some prominent individuals engaged in confronting and challenging racism and bigotry in our society. One of the more interesting sketches is that of Floyd Cochran, an avowed racist who came to recognize the destructiveness of hate and now speaks out against hate groups. Chapter 4 offers vital statistics and documents on hate crimes. This section is extremely useful and informative. Chapter 5 is a directory of organizations that monitor hate crimes and extremist groups. Chapters 6 and 7, covering some 50 pages, list print and nonprint resources on hate crimes. These two chapters are vital to people beginning research on this issue. The book concludes with a good index. This resource is highly recommended for al libraries and anyone seeking information about hate crimes.

—**Michael A. Foley**

P

266.   **Capital Punishment in the United States: A Documentary History.** Bryan Vila and Cynthia Morris, eds. Westport, Conn., Greenwood Press, 1997. 337p. index. (Primary Documents in American History and Contemporary Issues). $49.95. ISBN 0-313-29942-0.

This excellent volume features over 100 documents relating to various aspects of the capital punishment debate in the U.S. The book is arranged in six chronological sections, starting with the colonial era and the biblical arguments on which colonial capital punishment laws were based. The book includes a brief but informative introduction and each chronological section begins with a discussion of the trends in capital punishment in the period. Each document is preceded by a statement that places the document in context and identifies the author where appropriate. The documents are well chosen and include scholarly articles, book excerpts, position statements, legislation, court documents such as Supreme Court rulings, items relating to high-profile cases (e.g., the Rosenbergs, Gary Gilmore), and newspaper articles. There is a glossary of legal terms, a list of federal and state capital offenses, a table of numbers of executions from 1600 to 1995, a directory of relevant organizations, and a select bibliography.

The compilers have met their goal to provide a variety of perspectives on the major issues relating to capital punishment (e.g., religious and moral arguments, deterrence, irrevocability) and users will find a wide range of materials. The volume provides an excellent overview of the debate on capital punishment and may well meet the documents needs of the general public and high school and college students, while providing a good starting place for more advanced researchers. This book is highly recommended for public, academic, and special libraries.

—**Gari-Anne Patzwald**

P

267.   **Crime State Rankings 1999: Crime in the 50 United States.** 6th ed. Kathleen O'Leary Morgan and Scott Morgan, eds. Lawrence, Kans., Morgan Quitno Press, 1999. 508p. index. $49.95pa. ISBN 1-56692-334-4. ISSN 1077-4408.

At century's end the overall drop in the rate of conventional crime, including violent crime, has been quite remarkable. Various possible reasons for this drop have been offered, but it remains to be seen whether this trend will continue in the new century. Nevertheless, concern with crime endures. This reference work, now in its 6th edition, seeks to provide users with a wealth of statistical data pertaining to crime and criminal justice, and is formatted to facilitate interstate comparisons. Single state volumes are also available from this publisher, and a companion volume, now in its 5th edition, compares crime data for major American cities. Altogether, the present volume includes 508 tables. The data for most of these tables are current through 1997, although in some cases only through earlier years (1993 to 1996).

This volume includes seven major sections: arrests, corrections, drug and alcohol, finance, juveniles, law enforcement, and offenses. Additional sections make comparisons between urban and rural crime, and provide data comparing crime rates in 1993 and 1997—highlighting changes. An appendix includes several tables on population data. The section on arrest rates for conventional crimes (and some nonpredatory crimes, such as prostitution) includes tables on ranks between the states for each offense, absolute numbers, and the state's percentage of all such arrests nationally. The corrections section documents the enormous, current size of the correctional populations, with breakdowns on such variables as race and gender, correctional facility and status, and the death penalty. With 82 tables, this is the largest section. A 3d section on drugs and alcohol provides data on attributes of patients in treatment programs (i.e., by gender and race), and on expenditures for such programs. The finance section documents the substantial governmental expenditures on justice-related activities (with per capita expenditures highlighted). The tables in this section specifically compare state and local government expenditures. A section on juveniles, which was not part of the original volume published in 1994, consists mainly of juvenile arrest rates for conventional offenses, with some tables on treatment admissions and rates of reported abuse of children. The section on law enforcement agencies provides breakdowns on such matters as number of different categories of law enforcement officers, percentages of full and part-time workers, and criminal case filings. The final major section, on a range of conventional offenses, includes information on percent changes between 1996 and 1997, and on the use of different weapons. In light of the debate on gun control some of this data should be of particular interest.

This volume opens with a ranking of the 50 states, from most dangerous (Nevada) to least dangerous (North Dakota). This ranking is based upon data for six major conventional crimes, and weights assigned to these different crimes. Altogether, the 508 tables published here are laid out in an easy-to-read format, and a variety of information finding tools are provided. State rankings are a uniform feature of the tables.

The major limitation of this volume is the absence of any interpretive discussion of the limitations of all such statistical, comparative data on crime and criminal justice. Accordingly, those who consult these tables may be prone to unsophisticated and distorted readings of the data contained therein. With that caveat in mind *Crime State Rankings 1999* can certainly be said to contain a wealth of useful information about crime and criminal justice in the United States at the end of the twentieth century.—**David O. Friedrichs**

P
268.   Rafter, Nicole Hahn, and Debra L. Stanley. **Prisons in America: A Reference Handbook.** Santa Barbara, Calif., ABC-CLIO, 1999. 226p. index. (Contemporary World Issues). $45.00. ISBN 1-57607-102-2.

A few startling facts: the United States spends an estimated $30 billion a year to house in excess of 1 million men and women in more than 1,000 state and federal penal institutions. With 450 people for each 100,000 in the general population behind bars, the United States has the highest rate of incarceration in the world. In this volume in ABC-CLIO's well-regarded Contemporary World Issues series, Rafter, chair of the Crime, Law, and Deviance section of the American Sociological Association, and Stanley, an assistant professor of criminology and criminal justice at Central Connecticut State University, present a concise and useful starting point for research on this timely topic. Following a brief historical overview of the prison system since colonial times, including various attempts at penal reform, the authors examine the ongoing debate over rehabilitation versus punishment. Of particular interest is a chapter on issues and controversies that identify and address conflicting positions in penology. These include the purposes of incarceration, sentencing options, prisoners' rights, health care in prisons, and the trend toward private prisons run by corporations. Short biographies are presented for 23 individuals (philosophers, jurists, prisoners, reformers, administrators, researchers) who have contributed to the development of American prisons. Other sections include documents and statistics (with heavy emphasis on prisoners' rights cases), prison data (sentencing, prisoner characteristics), an annotated list with contact information for 52 agencies and organizations, annotated bibliographies for print and nonprint resources, Internet addresses, and a short glossary. Rafter and Stanley have done a creditable job packaging a mountain of information into a clear, well-written introduction to the topic geared toward the high school and undergraduate researcher. [R: LJ, 15 Nov 99, pp. 61-62]
—**David K. Frasier**

ENVIRONMENTAL LAW

P
269.   Goldsteen, Joel B. **ABCs of Environmental Regulation.** Rockville, Md., Government Institutes, 1999. 294p. illus. index. $49.00pa. ISBN 0-86587-629-0.

There are few books written to make sense of the multitude of environmental laws and regulations of the United States. This book, however, does a commendable job of providing the basics of the bewildering set of government programs and laws that have multiplied over the years. Goldsteen, a professor of urban affairs at the University of Texas, wrote the book to provide his students with a comprehensive structure of the regulations and their controlling agencies. To do this, he uses clear and succinct explanations, brevity, large print, and frequent bold section headings. Photographs and sidebars enhance the ease of usage, as do endnotes, a glossary, an appendix, and an index.

The book is organized into seven sections. Section 1 gives the governmental programmatic framework and outlines the major environmental laws in 2 to 4 pages, such as the "National Environmental Policy Act." The remaining six sections have laws on the subjects of air, water, waste and tanks, safety, responding to contaminant releases, and nature and natural resources. For example, section 2 on air has a chapter on the Clean Air Act, the Noise Control Act, and the Airport Noise Abatement Act. Each chapter is further organized for easy understanding, with an overview at the start of the chapter and a chronology of the laws with full citations at the end.

Although the book presents only elemental information, it does so with enough references that a researcher could easily move into more detail with other sources such as the *Environmental Law Handbook* (15th ed.; see ARBA 2000, entry 543), or a similarly titled book published by the Bureau of National Affairs. This book will be useful in many types of libraries, which need to provide the "big picture" of the U.S. environmental scene.
—**Georgia Briscoe**

HUMAN RIGHTS

C, P

270. Langley, Winston E. **Encyclopedia of Human Rights Issues Since 1945.** Westport, Conn., Greenwood Press, 1999. 392p. index. $65.00. ISBN 0-313-30163-8.

Anyone in need of a succinct account of the chief provisions of the United Nations Declaration on the Rights of Mentally Retarded Persons, the Nuremberg war crimes trials, or the mission of Amnesty International is likely to find what they need in this reference tool. Specific entries answering any of these needs typify the range of topics covered in Langley's concise encyclopedia. Important documents, events, organizations, agencies, concepts, individual countries, persons, and issues are all presented here. The articles are well written and authoritative, although sometimes a little too deferential to current United Nations positions. They are also on the brief side—on average, a bit less than 1 page or 300 to 400 words. Except for very basic information or ready-reference needs, they will usually serve only as starting points for inquiry. It is fortunate, therefore, that each concludes with at least one to five references for further reading. Appendixes include the full texts of four declarations and covenants comprising the International Bill of Human Rights, plus the Convention on the Rights of the Child.

Most libraries apt to consider acquiring this work will already have alternative sources for much of the information gathered here. Still, the convenience of a single source may be compelling—where it is affordable and not redundant to an unjustifiable degree. Edward Lawson's far bulkier and pricier *Encyclopedia of Human Rights* (2d ed.; see ARBA 97, entry 517) covers much the same ground in greater depth, especially by including full texts of many more documents. Nonetheless, this work has a fair number of entries not offered by Lawson (the reverse is also true). R. Gorman and E. Mihalkanin's *Historical Dictionary of Human Rights and Humanitarian Organizations* (see ARBA 98, entry 564) also has considerable overlap in coverage, but takes in a broader sweep of history and is less in-depth on the post–World War II period.—**Hans E. Bynagle**

C, P

271. Redman, Nina, and Lucille Whalen. **Human Rights: A Reference Handbook.** 2d ed. Santa Barbara, Calif., ABC-CLIO, 1998. 301p. index. (Contemporary World Issues). $45.00. ISBN 1-57607-041-7.

Human Rights: A Reference Handbook is a well-written and timely monograph dealing with the many aspects and issues that concern human rights. A fairly comprehensive introductory chapter attempts to define human rights and to include historical, religious, legal, political, and philosophical foundations and development. A summary of the development of international human rights is included along with discussions of the United Nations, the United States, nongovernmental organizations, and human rights. International law and human rights and current human rights issues complete the introductory section.

Chapters include a chronology of the major human rights documents and events with brief descriptions that begin with 1941, and another has concise biographical sketches of individuals who have made significant contributions to human rights advancement. The majority of the book is devoted to chapter 4, which includes complete text for many selected human rights documents. The remaining chapters are bibliographies of organizations, print resources, and nonprint resources (including computer networks and databases). An index is included to aid the researcher. Redman and Whalen have produced an excellent resource for researchers or anyone needing information on a variety of human rights issues.—**Mary L. Trenerry**

P, S

272. Stein, Laura W. **Sexual Harassment in America: A Documentary History.** Westport, Conn., Greenwood Press, 1999. 297p. index. (Primary Documents in American History and Contemporary Issues). $49.95. ISBN 0-313-30184-0.

This collection of documents relating to the history of sexual harassment policy and litigation features 96 documents arranged in sections, including a general overview and definitions, employment, the military, education, housing, and 1998 U.S. Supreme Court cases. The emphasis is on federal law and policy, and major high-profile events are included (e.g., the Clarence Thomas hearing, Tailhook) as well as lesser-known but often equally important cases. Among the documents are laws, court decisions, government reports, congressional hearings, and newspaper and periodical articles. Each series of related documents begins with a brief introductory statement that places the documents in context. Each section concludes with a brief but potentially useful bibliography. The documents are carefully selected and well edited. This work provides an excellent introduction to resources for the study of a complex and evolving area in which there is wide interest. *Sexual Harassment in America* is highly recommended for libraries serving the general public and high school and college students. [R: BR, Sept/Oct 99, p. 82]—**Gari-Anne Patzwald**

11 Library and Information Science and Publishing and Bookselling

LIBRARY AND INFORMATION SCIENCE

Reference Works

Bibliographies

C, P

273.   ***Choice*'s Outstanding Academic Books 1992-1997: Reviews of Scholarly Titles that Every Library Should Own.** Rebecca Ann Bartlett, ed. Chicago, American Library Association, Association of College and Research Libraries, 1998. 618p. index. $85.00. ISBN 0-8389-7929-7.

This compilation of 3,112 highly recommended books for undergraduate libraries was selected from titles previously reviewed in *Choice* magazine. According to the editor, the books were chosen from more than 22,000 scholarly and trade books examined annually, hence the present compilation consists of roughly 2½ percent of all titles reviewed in the 6-year period. The selections cover most but not all academic subject areas. For example, there were no outstanding books listed for that period directly in either information science or librarianship.

The major criteria for selection are excellence of presentation, scholarship, overall significance, uniqueness, and importance to undergraduate library collection. However, because the process of applying these criteria was not fully described, it is not clear how the "outstanding" titles were distinguished from other important but perhaps less prominent publications. The reprinted, unabridged reviews are grouped in 5 categories: Reference, General, Humanities, Science and Technology, and Social and Behavioral Sciences, with discipline-specific subject subdivisions. Within each category the entries are arranged alphabetically by author. The indexes consist of book, author, title, and topical listings. Names of the reviewers, although printed, are not indexed. The individual sections are not limited by a predetermined number of reviews. Social and Behavioral Sciences is by far the largest category. The most numerous are the books in "Women's Studies," followed by "African and African American Studies."

This is an important compilation for undergraduate collections but not necessarily for every library, as its subtitle suggests. It will be particularly useful for any acquisition librarians who did not previously subscribe to the 1992 to 1997 editions of *Choice* magazine.—**Joseph Z. Nitecki**

P, S

274.   Safford, Barbara Ripp, comp. **Guide to Reference Materials for School Library Media Centers.** 5th ed. Englewood, Colo., Libraries Unlimited, 1998. 353p. index. $45.00. ISBN 1-56308-545-3.

This is a useful, if limited, guide to reference books suitable for elementary and secondary school library media centers in the United States. There has been a concentrated effort to include materials in a variety of formats. The author states that she previously thought that books would be eclipsed by CD-ROMs and the Web, but, as she announces in the introduction, identifying new titles available in book form, finding one new book source after the other, was like surfing the reference shelves. The limitation therefore is not in the format of the reference materials, but in the necessary paring down of items to fit into 350 pages. All resources are currently available (as of the time of publication) and most were published between 1992 and 1997. As this is the 5th edition of the title, it will probably be a familiar resource to most school library personnel. Safford discusses the changes from the former volumes that have occurred in organization in the introduction. As before, however, all included items are recommended, although some titles have been highlighted for their excellence. All entries include full bibliographic citations, grade level codes, annotations, and citations to reviews.

The book itself is divided into 5 major parts: collection management tools, general reference, social sciences (subdivided further into 25 varied subject headings), humanities (13 subdivisions), and science and technology (15 subdivisions). Author/title and subject indexes round out the volume. Each descriptive annotation is an adequate length to give the reader a basic understanding of the resource being discussed. The volume is attractively put together and is organized for easy access.—**Gail de Vos**

Handbooks and Yearbooks

P, S
275.   Hull, Mary E. **Censorship in America: A Reference Handbook.** Santa Barbara, Calif., ABC-CLIO, 1999. 233p. index. (Contemporary World Issues). $45.00. ISBN 1-57607-057-3.

Hull has written a well-balanced and up-to-date summary of censorship. A history of censorship is presented, but only as a brief chronology. This work is written to emphasize modern problems and cases. The first chapter deals with current controversies. Censorship in the arts, music (rap), news (Sudan slavery atrocities), textbooks, and the Internet (pornography, filters, v-chip) are all discussed. These essays are well balanced and the rest of the book excels in areas where others do not.

The biographies of major current players in this arena are presented. Some are in the current political area, such as Gary Bauer and Tipper Gore. The short biographies, about a page in length, are well balanced and objective. The next section presents summaries of the major court cases in this area, such as Janet Reno's CDA suit of 1996. The author follows with a full-text section of opinion documents from the various organizations involved. The last document is surprisingly mild and has much to say about the purposes of media in the effects of entertainment on the human mind and soul. The book concludes with about 50 pages of the author's selected reference books, magazines, videos, and Websites. A list of all the major organizations involved in this issue and their Websites concludes the work.

This book is a modern and well-done examination of censorship. As a part of the Contemporary World Issues series from ABC-CLIO, it is a solid choice for any library from high school on up.—**Gary L. Parsons**

P, S
276.   Karolides, Nicholas J., Margaret Bald, and Dawn Sova. **100 Banned Books: Censorship Histories of World Literature.** New York, Facts on File, 1999. 420p. index. $18.95pa. ISBN 0-8160-4059-1.

This volume is an abridged version of the 4-volume Banned Books Series published by Facts on File in 1998 (see ARBA 99, entries 603, 604, 605, and 606). The 4 sections of the book each have 25 entries covering works banned on political, religious, sexual, or social grounds. Each entry has a summary of the book's contents followed by a censorship history. The books include novels, histories, biographies, children's books, polemics, and religious and philosophical works from all over the world. The Bible, Talmud, Koran, *All Quiet on the Western Front, Candide, The Autobiography of Benjamin Franklin,* and *The Diary of Anne Frank* are among the banned works included. They accompany the censored works of Henry Miller, James Joyce, D. H. Lawrence, William S. Burroughs, and Judy Blume, which have been involved in highly publicized court cases.

Because censorship is a major concern in schools and libraries, this book is very timely. It demonstrates the wide variety of works that have been condemned. A look at the table of contents will serve as proof that the efforts of censors are futile and ineffective. All of these books are still readily available and many are classics. *100 Banned Books* is an excellent choice for school and public libraries that do not own the 4-volume set. [R: LJ, July 99, p. 83]—**Barbara M. Bibel**

PUBLISHING AND BOOKSELLING

Directories

P

277.   **Directory of Small Press/Magazine Editors and Publishers 1999-2000.** 30th ed. Len Fulton, ed. Paradise, Calif., Dustbooks, 1999. 328p. $23.95pa. ISBN 0-916685-75-6.

There are thousands of publishers in the world but it is difficult to find the information about all of them, especially small publishers, in one place. Dustbooks, the leader in the small press information field, certainly has done a great service to the profession by publishing *Directory of Small Press/Magazine Editors and Publishers*. The 30th edition of the book lists more than 6,000 names of editors and publishers in alphabetic order. This comprehensive list includes name of editor or publisher, complete address of the company, telephone and fax numbers, and e-mail addresses. Even Web page addresses have been included, if available. Another excellent feature of the directory that will be helpful to users is the cross-references for many entries. Although the emphasis in this well-prepared directory is on the United States, many entries from foreign countries have also been included. It is certainly an excellent source for finding the information on those editors and publishers who are employed by small presses. It is recommended for reference collections of all types of libraries.—**Ravindra Nath Sharma**

P

278.   **The International Directory of Little Magazines & Small Presses 1998-99.** 34th ed. Len Fulton, ed. Paradise, Calif., Dustbooks, 1998. 946p. index. $55.00; $34.95pa. ISBN 0-916685-66-7; 0-916685-70-5pa.

Although not stated in the text, this is obviously a reference work aimed at freelance writers who want to find out where to submit material. It lists publishers of both books and periodicals. Each list has contact information, plus an indication of the market to which the publisher sells, the type of printing done, and some pricing information.

Two indexes support the main entries. A regional index is set forth by states within the United States, and by country for non-American listings. (The vast majority of the houses are in the United States; there are almost twice as many records for California alone as for all non-U.S. countries combined.) There is also a subject index, but no indication as to how topical divisions were decided upon. There is, for example, a section for "Dada," but computers are lumped in with calculators, technology has exactly six entries, and there is no entry at all for telecommunications or any related subject.

The information is based on self–report. There is a slight allusion to this in the key to directory listings, and slightly stronger evidence in the fact that many descriptions of the operation, scope, and interests of the house are enclosed in quotation marks. Only one of the small presses and little magazines of which this reviewer has personal knowledge was listed, and many were not. The question of what constitutes a small press is going to be subjective, but at least one fairly major player was included.—**Robert M. Slade**

12 Military Studies

GENERAL WORKS

Atlases

P, S
279. **The Hutchinson Atlas of Battle Plans: Before and After.** John Pimlott, ed. Chicago, Fitzroy Dearborn, 1998. 237p. maps. index. $55.00. ISBN 1-57958-203-6.

Although this small, attractive volume is called an atlas, it is more correctly a case study of battle plans, before and after. It was not intended to be a comprehensive work on battle plans. Instead, this book looks at types of military action and how plans were implemented and what was the result. There are six headings: classic ploys, surprise, misunderstanding, mission impossible, underestimating the enemy, and narrow margins. Battles from ancient times to World War II are covered. Included among them are Cannae, Crecy, Balaklava, Battle of the Bulge, Austerlitz, and Gettysburg.

Most of the contributors are lecturers at the Royal Military Academy at Sandhurst. The main thrust of the work delves into the variables that come into play during battle, not the least of which is the human variable. Battle is a dynamic activity with two sides acting and responding to each other's moves. This small volume is an excellent introduction to analyzing battle plans and the battles themselves and is highly recommended for private, public, high school, and college and university library reference collections.—**Norman L. Kincaide**

Biography

C, P, S
280. Fredriksen, John C. **American Military Leaders: From Colonial Times to the Present.** Santa Barbara, Calif., ABC-CLIO, 1999. 2v. illus. index. $150.00/set. ISBN 1-57607-001-8.

Few subjects attract more readers than military history and, when combined with a biography, the result is more often than not a successful book. In *American Military Leaders*, Fredriksen offers 422 sketches of the men and women who make up the leadership of the U.S. military experience. Included are 2– to 3–page biographies spanning time from the colonial period to Norman Schwarzkopf and Colin Powell. The 2-volume set also includes names such as Native Americans Sitting Bull and Geronimo. Military leadership, not military heroism, is the primary criterion for inclusion, thus names like Abraham Lincoln, William Gorgas (who found a cure for yellow fever during the building of the Panama Canal), and Russian-born aeronautical engineer Alexander De Seversky are included. Women include aviator Jackie Cochran and Civil War nurse Dorothea Dix. Some may argue against the inclusion of Benedict Arnold and Jefferson Davis, yet both excelled at leadership. Notes for further reading are added after each biography. A 15-page index provides ample access to individuals, battles, and events throughout the text of all the sketches. Fredriksen's work surpasses the *Dictionary of Military Biography* (see ARBA 86, entry 620) and should be an asset to military history in all libraries. [R: LJ, 15 Sept 99, pp. 68-70]
—**Boyd Childress**

Dictionaries and Encyclopedias

C, P

281.   **Ame.ica at War.** New York, Macmillan Library Reference/Simon & Schuster Macmillan, 1998. 846p. illus. maps. index. (Macmillan Compendium). $125.00. ISBN 0-02-865061-1.

This is a 1-volume military history of the United States, dating from the earliest days of colonization to the Gulf War of 1991. It is not a new work, as it is made up entirely from selections taken from an earlier 3-volume set titled *The Encyclopedia of the American Military* published in 1994 and edited by John E. Jessup of the American Military University (see ARBA 95, entry 688).

Despite the abridgement, this is a good work, one that smaller libraries will appreciate for its size, affordability, and usefulness. The book begins with an overview of American history provided in a 3-column chronological chart that lists leading persons, general history, and military history. The remainder of the volume is divided into 3 parts. The 1st part, covering more than half the contents, provides a clear, generally well-written military history of this country. Each chapter is written by a historian, with the writing ranging from average to excellent depending on the author. There are some errors, and some may disagree with the fullness or interpretation of certain events. However, in a work of this magnitude, this is a minor consideration. A particularly valuable characteristic of this book is its coverage of military aspects of the periods between wars.

The 2d part provides brief histories of each of the armed forces, while the 3d part gives brief biographies of 39 military leaders, including 2 Native Americans, Crazy Horse and Sitting Bull. One might question the inclusion, however, of Davy Crockett in such a short list of great military personages of the United States. Three appendixes provide lists of Medal of Honor recipients arranged according to the war it was received in, a selection of wartime speeches and documents, and the texts of 11 peace treaties, although 3 are included in excerpts only. Access to the contents is solely through a 20-page general index that, despite its length, could be improved upon.

This is a reference book that anyone with an interest in history will enjoy. It is recommended for all libraries with an interest in American history, and to those history-minded persons in the general public as well. [R: SLJ, Aug 99, p. 181]—**Donald E. Collins**

C, P, S

282.   Beckett, Ian F. W. **Encyclopedia of Guerrilla Warfare.** Santa Barbara, Calif., ABC-CLIO, 1999. 303p. illus. index. $75.00. ISBN 0-87436-929-0.

This is a timely book given the increasing rise in guerrilla warfare during the twentieth century. Readers are introduced to the topic through a well-written bibliographic and explanatory essay that provides a good understanding of the topic and the major literature related to it. Users are provided information on a variety of terms and persons related to guerrilla movements over the past two centuries, with emphasis on the present and recent past.

The book is well organized for ease of use. Access to information is excellent through a detailed subject index and an alphabetic list of subject entries. A list of acronyms helps users identify specific guerrilla and related organizations when only their letter designations are known. A chronology of events from 1755 to 1998 is also useful, while a substantial bibliography leads to further reading on the topic. The main body of the book consists of brief to moderate-length essays that are generally well written and that are followed by *see also* references and suggested books for further reading.

There are criticisms, however. The articles vary in quality. Biographical entries are particularly well done, whereas many others lack sufficient depth and are too sketchy. This reviewer wonders why such persons as General George A. Custer, a regular army officer, are included, while well-known guerrilla leaders like William C. Quantrill and John Singleton Mosby are relegated to a few lines in a survey article. There are also a number of factual errors. For example, Andrew Jackson's Indian removal policy was not limited, as stated, to the "five civilized tribes of the southeast" (p. 214), nor did the Wounded Knee massacre take place at Big Foot's "village," but at a temporary stopping place forced upon the tribe by the U.S. cavalry (p. 11). Also, the First Seminole War (1816-1818) was not connected to an Indian removal policy (p. 11). With the noted exceptions, however, this is a good and useful reference work and is recommended for school, college, university, and public libraries with an interest in history and current events. [R: BL, Aug 99, pp. 2106-2107; Choice, Oct 99, p. 311; BR, Nov/Dec 99, p. 86]

—**Donald E. Collins**

AIR FORCE

C, P

283.   Terry, Michael Robert. **Historical Dictionary of the United States Air Force and Its Antecedents.** Lanham, Md., Scarecrow, 1999. 460p. maps. (Historical Dictionaries of War, Revolution, and Civil Unrest, no.11). $89.50. ISBN 0-8108-3631-9.

This compact volume gives an excellent overview of Air Force history through its comprehensive chronology and introduction and list of well-selected and encyclopedic definitions. The chronology begins with the 1903 flight 97 years ago by Orville Wright at Kitty Hawk, North Carolina, and ends with the show of force over the Adriatic in 1998 in response to the Serbian shelling of Kosovo. The 22-page introduction outlines the growth of the Air Force from its inception in 1914 as the Aviation Section, U.S. Army Signal Corps, to the U.S. Army Service (1918-1926), to the U.S. Army Air Corps (1926-1941), to the U.S. Army Air Forces (1941-1947), to the present U.S. Air Force.

The major part of the volume is the alphabetically arranged dictionary. The terms range from the well known, such as *ace, air power, B-17 Flying Fortress, Eighth Air Force,* and *Generals Doolittle, LeMay, Spatz,* and *Arnold* to the less familiar, including *Operations Bolo* and *Barrel Roll.* Virtually every aircraft used in combat operations and every officer who played a major role in any of the air wars is listed. Each entry includes cross-references. Thus in the entry for "Persian Gulf War (1990-1991)" one will find *Desert Shield, Berlin Airlift, AIM-7,* and *ordnance.* The volume concludes with an extensive bibliography and 10 appendixes, 5 of which identify aces of air wars. Reference departments with even a modest military history collection will likely want to purchase this outstanding, yet expensive, dictionary.—**Charles R. Andrews**

13   Political Science

GENERAL WORKS

Directories

C, P

284.   Hernon, Peter, John A. Shuler, and Robert E. Dugan. **U.S. Government on the Web: Getting the Information You Need.** Englewood, Colo., Libraries Unlimited, 1999. 349p. illus. index. $39.50pa. ISBN 1-56308-757-X.

The occasional user needs more than a general search engine to find the vast scope of material available from the U.S. government online. Currently there is no single access point for finding the specific data desired. This guide provides a construct for understanding how to find federal sources on the World Wide Web.

The key is understanding how the three branches of government are structured. The major agencies within each arm are detailed, with descriptions of the information found on each site with Web identifiers and appropriate links. Independent commissions and quasi-government agencies are also listed. Within the text, Web addresses are highlighted boldly in blue. Each chapter ends with easily spotted "blue pages" consolidating the URLs referred to in that section. There are also an extensive table of contents and two indexes, one by the organizations within each branch of government and the other by the title of the listings on each site. The appendix gives Web pages for public–interest groups, universities, and libraries. This book is further enhanced by the publisher's commitment to post updates on its Web page. [R: BR, Nov/Dec 99, p. 84; BL, 1 Dec 99, p. 728; JAL, Nov 99, pp. 496-497]

—**Adrienne Antink Bendel**

P

285.   Kurian, George Thomas, and Jeffrey D. Schultz. **Political Market Place USA.** Phoenix, Ariz., Oryx Press, 1998. 345p. index. $65.00pa. ISBN 1-57356-226-2.

Many libraries will find this tool invaluable in locating addresses, names, facts, and organizations. Kurian is president of Kurian Reference Books in New York and brings to the table dozens of years of experience, not to mention his won voluminous political work. His co-compiler, Schultz, is also president of his own company (Schultz & Co., Inc.) and has taught political science and history at a number of colleges and universities. His previous works were two excellent encyclopedias on the Democratic and Republican Parties.

Political Market Place (PMP) is an annual tool that attempts to satisfy all things political. The first three chapters discuss the two major and third parties. Each section has a geographical listing of party headquarters and their chairs. Other chapters discuss political associations, think tanks, media consultants, political journals and newsletters, reference books, and important documents. A section on political statistics covers various state and national issues (e.g., referenda, term limits, and financial activities for the two major parties).

While certainly fulsome, there is no pretense at comprehensiveness. For example, in the section on organizations, there is no mention of the Women's Independent Forum. Neither *The Women's Quarterly* (Danielle Crittenden's magazine) nor any of the Rockford publications (e.g., *Family in America, Religion and Society Report, Chronicles: A Magazine of Culture*) are named in the magazine and newsletter section. But these oversights, while significant, do not vitiate what is an otherwise useful tool. [R: LJ, 1 May 99, pp. 69-70; BL, 1 May 99, p. 1636; Choice, Nov 99, p. 518; RUSQ, Fall 99, p. 99]—**Mark Y. Herring**

POLITICS AND GOVERNMENT

United States

Almanacs

C, P

286.   Lilley, William, III, Laurence J. DeFranco, and Mark F. Bernstein. **The Almanac of State Legislatures: Changing Patterns, 1990-1997.** 2d ed. Washington, D.C., Congressional Quarterly, 1998. 387p. maps. $135.00. ISBN 1-56802-434-7.

Synthesizing and updating information previously published in the 1st edition of *The Almanac of State Legislatures* (see ARBA 95, entry 710), *The State Atlas of Political and Cultural Diversity* (see ARBA 98, entry 329), and *State Legislative Elections* (see ARBA 99, entry 674), this work presents a vivid picture of the socioeconomic and demographic composition of state legislative districts in the United States for the period 1990 to 1997. Data are derived primarily from 1997 sources. The almanac begins with a brief introductory essay highlighting trends in rural and urban growth and the changing racial and ethnic populations throughout the United States. Three charts of selected legislative house districts in Chicago, Los Angeles, and Philadelphia provide statistics to support the descriptive analysis. What follows are detailed entries for each state. The entries begin with a well-written, concise essay that summarizes the changes in the political and demographic makeup of the state since the 1990 census. The essays provide an efficacious framework for placing the statistical data in proper context. Each entry also includes two-color maps showing the boundaries of state legislative districts color-coded according to population growth. Where appropriate, similar maps provide district breakdowns within metropolitan areas. The cartographic boundaries are easily discernible and well produced. Finally, the entries contain statistical charts intended to illustrate the shifting geo-demographic status of each district, broken down by ethnicity, income, and population. The editors properly acknowledge the underlying challenges to the manner in which the Census Bureau gathers data. These issues have been addressed by relying on a variety of legally mandated federal sources. Overall, this is an excellent resource for both students and researchers. This reviewer is looking forward to the post-2000 decennial census edition. Together with this edition, it will provide invaluable research tools that clearly delineate the changing demographic, political, and socioeconomic landscape at the state level as America enters the next millennium. [R: Choice, July/Aug 99, p. 1928]—**Robert V. Labaree**

Biography

C, P

287.   Foerstel, Karen. **Biographical Dictionary of Congressional Women.** Westport, Conn., Greenwood Press, 1999. 300p. illus. index. $65.00. ISBN 0-313-30290-1.

In the literature on women who have served in Congress, there is generally a direct correlation between the availability of information on that person and the amount of attention they received while in office. This biographical dictionary is a welcome research tool because it provides detailed information on all women who have been elected to Congress. The introductory chapter outlines the history of women in Congress and the challenges they face in getting elected and being accepted as equals in creating policy. The chapter is well written and concludes with two charts—a list of women who have chaired full House and Senate committees (one indication of who has wielded the most power among congressional women) and a chart showing the number of women who have served in each Congress since 1917. In the future, charts showing a list of congressional women by state and a chronology of service in the House and Senate could help enhance the presentation of data. Each biographical profile includes a description of the individual's political career, highlighting important public policy initiatives and, in many cases, placing the person's term in office in greater historical perspective. Personal anecdotes and excerpts from interviews are used to enhance the content of many profiles. A set of black-and-white photographs is included in the center of the book but is unnecessary. A selective bibliography and a name and subject index complete this work.

This is an accessible and informative research tool. The author steps beyond the dry writing style of most traditional biographical dictionaries by telling the story of each woman's rise to power in our nation's legislative branch and the personal challenges they had to overcome in becoming meaningful participants in our nation's legislative process. This work is especially useful to students. [R: LJ, 1 Sept 99, pp. 176-178]—**Robert V. Labaree**

Dictionaries and Encyclopedias

P

288.   Binning, William C., Larry E. Esterly, and Paul A. Sracic. **Encyclopedia of American Parties, Campaigns, and Elections.** Westport, Conn., Greenwood Press, 1999. 467p. index. $99.50. ISBN 0-313-30312-6.

The authors provide a comprehensive survey of key information on U.S. politics, politicians, parties, and elections in a short volume accessible to the general reader. Entries range from short biographies of the presidents and key congressional leaders to brief accounts of presidential elections from 1789 to 1996 to summaries of major Supreme Court rulings. Although the encyclopedia covers U.S. national politics since 1789, it gives more attention to recent personalities and issues. Inevitably in a volume designed to be of convenient size, some terms or people are given slight attention or omitted. For example, a curious omission is "impeachment." But the authors seem to have found a good balance between compactness and comprehensiveness in the selection of their entries.

This encyclopedia is recommended for public libraries, secondary schools, and university libraries. It is accessible to the general reader but provides details and bibliographies to the reader who wants additional information. [R: LJ, 1 Mar 99, p. 68]—**Frank L. Wilson**

C, P

289.   **Congress A to Z.** 3d ed. David R. Tarr and Ann O'Connor, eds. Washington, D.C., Congressional Quarterly, 1999. 592p. illus. index. (CQ's Ready Reference Encyclopedia of American Government). $95.00. ISBN 1-56802-388-X.

This volume, along with similar volumes on the presidency, the Supreme Court, and elections, makes up Congressional Quarterly's *Encyclopedia of American Government*. Congressional Quarterly is the most reliable and complete review of the U.S. government. This volume is an excellent example of their readable, accessible, comprehensive, and unbiased coverage of American politics. Entries range from specific events—such as the Teapot Dome scandal—to prominent past and current congressional leaders, rules and procedures, and specific issues. There are short, but excellent, entries on blacks, Hispanics, and women in Congress. A long entry on "Historic Milestones" provides a chronological listing and brief description of major developments in Congress since 1787.

This revision includes developments through early 1999. Entries are well organized and an index allows easy locating of issues or individuals. Many of the major entries include a listing of additional readings. There is also an extensive bibliography that includes scholarly works, political commentaries, and memoirs.

In addition to the encyclopedia entries, there are several appendixes. They include lists of past and present leaders, statistics on vetoes and expulsions, and figures on reelection of incumbents.

Congress A to Z is illustrated generously with photos, cartoons, tables, and figures. It is written at a level that general readers will find understandable, but includes information that will be useful also to specialists on American government. This is perhaps the best one-volume reference work on the U.S. Congress.—**Frank L. Wilson**

C, P

290.   **Encyclopedia of Women in American Politics.** Jeffrey D. Schultz and Laura van Assendelft, eds. Phoenix, Ariz., Oryx Press, 1999. 354p. illus. index. (The American Political Landscape Series). $99.00. ISBN 1-57356-131-2.

The preface to *Encyclopedia of Women in American Politics* states that it "attempts to be the most comprehensive single source on women in American politics." Other than perhaps the bibliographic compilations of Elizabeth M. Cox that concentrates on twentieth century women, this encyclopedia stands nearly alone. With the December 1999 publication of ABC-CLIO's *Encyclopedia of American Women in Politics*, a 2-volume work by Suzanne O'Dea Schenken, this is probably about to change. Hopefully the similarly titled encyclopedias will complement rather than duplicate each other.

Encyclopedia of Women in American Politics is the first title in the Oryx Press American Political Landscape Series. Schultz, a former college professor of history and political science, is editing several volumes in this series and van Assendelft is assistant professor of political science at Mary Baldwin College. More than 700 entries arranged dictionary style, comprise this encyclopedia. Entries are signed by one of 56 scholars from various U.S. colleges and universities. The introduction, arranged by historical periods, provides a scholarly overview of women in American politics from Colonial times to the present. Encyclopedia entries cover concepts, movements, issues, legislation, case law, and biographical information related to women in American politics. Entry titles include affirmative action, feminism and antifeminism, *Reed v. Reed* (1971), Elizabeth Cady Stanton, and one for the movie *Thelma and Louise*. Entry size ranges from a paragraph (biographical entries) to several pages and each ends with one or more bibliographic references. Generous cross-referencing and a thorough index enhance retrieval of specific topics. Four valuable appendixes conclude this volume. One covers speeches and documents, including the proposed Equal Rights Amendment to the U.S. Constitution. The tables appendix covers women members of Congress, cabinet members, and a list of First Ladies. Another appendix provides information for organizations, including addresses, URLs and e-mail addresses for various groups, PACs, and donor networks. The final appendix is a particularly useful timeline from 1848 to 1998.

The *Encyclopedia of Women in American Politics* is a valuable reference work that should be included in academic and medium- to large-sized public and high school library collections. This Oryx publication should be joined by other reference works covering the history, statistics, demographics, and biographies of the many women who have entered the political arena, both in the United States and internationally. [R: LJ, 15 Mar 99, p. 70; BL, 1 Mar 99, pp. 1248-1249; Choice, June 99, p. 1764; RUSQ, Fall 99, pp. 89-90]—**Linda D. Tietjen**

Directories

P

291.   Andriot, Laurie, comp. **The Internet Blue Pages: The Guide to Federal Government Web Sites.** 1999 ed. Medford, N.J., CyberAge Books/Information Today, 1999. 359p. index. $34.95pa. ISBN 0-910965-29-3.

This directory provides the Website addresses for more than 900 federal government offices. Each entry provides the site address, a brief description of materials on the Website, and the links available through the site. Entries are organized by federal department or agency. There is an alphabetic list of all agencies with their URL address. Unfortunately, this list does not cross-reference to the numbered, annotated entries in the main guide. The index allows searching by topic, agency, or program providing the entry number for relevant matches. There is a companion Website to the volume, allowing readers to get new listings, corrections, and updates online.

This resource will help readers gain access to the Website; however, the value of the Website depends on its own construction, maintenance, and creativity, and that varies widely. This work is recommended for press libraries and government relations offices as well as public and education libraries. [R: Choice, Oct 99, p. 301]
—**Frank L. Wilson**

Handbooks and Yearbooks

C, P, S

292.   **The Constitution and Its Amendments.** Roger K. Newman, ed. New York, Macmillan Library Reference/ Simon & Schuster Macmillan, 1999. 4v. illus. index. $225.00/set. ISBN 0-02-864858-7.

This illustrated, 4-volume introduction to the Constitution and its amendments is suitable for students studying the Constitution for the first time—regardless of age. After a chapter that provides the setting for the Constitutional Convention (1787), the work introduces persons and events critical to its success and concise essays clarify each article, including explanations of the intent of the founders and examples of application throughout the nation's history. Illustration, definitions of highlighted words, and enriching or explanatory sidebars all add to the accessibility of this important resource. For example, the 19th Amendment receives five pages of coverage. The exact wording of the amendment begins the chapter (with definitions as needed), along with a brief explanation of its meaning in layperson's terms. The explanation of the history of the amendment begins at Seneca Falls, New York, in 1948; explains several points of view; and reveals the tactics of both supporters and opponents, including jail time for women who picketed for the right to vote. The essay does not conclude with the passage of the amendment in 1920, but continues the discussion with information about those who were still denied the vote—women in territories, African Americans, and nonwhite immigrants.

The first three volumes cover the Constitution and the Bill of Rights. The final volume covers the remaining amendments. Each volume concludes with its own index; preceding the index to volume 4 is an inclusive glossary. This excellent set is recommended for all libraries servicing students grade 7 and up. [R: BL, 15 April 99, p. 1353; BR, Sept/Oct 99, p. 80; SLJ, Aug 99, p. 186]—**Vandelia L. VanMeter**

C, P

293.   **CQ's Politics in America 2000: The 106th Congress.** Philip D. Duncan and Brian Nutting, eds. Washington, D.C., Congressional Quarterly, 1999. 1564p. illus. maps. $98.95; 55.95pa. (with disc). ISBN 1-56802-470-3; 1-56802-471-1pa. ISSN 1064-6809.

This voluminous 10th edition of a biennial work produced by the publisher's editorial and reporting staff is an excellent resource for describing the men and women who make up the United States Congress. Although the publisher seeks to provide the best assessment of each member of Congress, the emphasis is not on where each politician stands on issues, but rather how his or her views are expressed and how effectively individual goals are accomplished.

This resource begins with an informative preface that outlines the current state of politics as well as an easy-to-read table of contents and an explanation of statistics section. Under the alphabetic listing of each state are the following three sections: the name and picture of the governor as well as relevant additional state and demographic information, including an outline of that state's congressional districts, pictures, and detailed background descriptions of each senator; and pictures and detailed descriptions of each representative. The text is supplemented with a useful index that indicates the page where members of Congress have been mentioned or described. A nice feature included with the publication is a CD-ROM with the full text in Adobe Acrobat format, which can be used with either Macintosh or Windows versions.

Although this resource is not the only publication covering the U.S. Congress, and there are other related publications such as *Congress and Its Members* (Congressional Quarterly) and various almanacs, this work is among those introductory and informative sources that most public, school, and university libraries should include within their reference collections largely because of its relatively inexpensive cost. This item is also likely to be considered a must-have resource for any number of businesses, special interest groups, lobbyists, and political consultants whose livelihood depends upon predicting or responding to the actions of Congress.

—**James M. Murray**

P, S

294.   **Federal Agency Profiles for Students.** Kelle S. Sisung, ed. Farmington Hills, Mich., Gale, 1999. 1070p. illus. index. $65.00. ISBN 0-7876-2795-X.

This anticipated volume provides a comprehensive overview of more than 175 federal agencies from each branch of government, including departments, government corporations, administrations, and commissions. In addition, more than 200 independent agencies are described. Agency profiles are arranged alphabetically according to the official name given in the *United States Government Manual* (1996/97 ed.; see ARBA 97, entry 604). Each profile contains information about the agency's mission or purpose and its organization, primary functions, and current programs. The editors have paid special attention to placing each agency in proper historical and political context. All the profiles include entries that outline the history of the agency and review important contemporary political issues that have empowered or constrained the agency's ability to carry out its mission. Profiles also include a brief entry describing possible future directions of the organization and its successes and failures based upon self-assessments of the organization. More profiles conclude with a description of agency resources, with public affairs contact numbers, e-mail and Internet addresses, a list of agency publications, and a brief bibliography for further reading. A select number of profiles may also include information on how individuals can become involved with the agency, "fast facts" about a specific agency function, or biographical sketches of key agency personnel.

The volume begins with a chronology of events in U.S. history and concludes with four brief appendixes, a glossary, and a subject index. Illustrations, photographs, and pie charts of agency budget allocations are used throughout the encyclopedia to enhance its textual presentation. The essays are well written and should be easily understood by most students. Although of limited value to scholars, this work succeeds in providing students with an in-depth understanding of the agencies that make up our system of government. This, and most likely future volumes in this series, should be available in every school and public library. [R: Choice, Oct 99, p. 314; BR, Sept/Oct 99, p. 81]—**Robert V. Labaree**

P, S

295.   **How Congress Works.** 3d ed. Washington, D.C., Congressional Quarterly, 1998. 184p. illus. index. $29.95pa. ISBN 1-56802-391-X.

This is the first revision of Congressional Quarterly's *How Congress Works* since 1991. Since then, much has changed in Congress and this volume captures and identifies those changes. However, its historical sweep allows the reader to recognize how much remains the same in this venerable political institution. It describes leadership in Congress, the legislative process, and the committee system. A reference section at the end provides useful information on party representation, leadership, and votes in Congress from 1789 to 1997. A useful addition is a section on Websites providing information on Congress on the Internet. Congressional Quarterly (CQ) is a reliable and thorough publisher on U.S. national politics. This volume continues CQ's tradition for useful, accurate, and accessible information on national politics. Information is presented clearly in nontechnical language. This volume is highly recommended for public libraries and school libraries at all levels.

—**Frank L. Wilson**

P

296.   Martin, Mart. **The Almanac of Women and Minorities in American Politics.** Boulder, Colo., Westview Press, 1999. 293p. index. $49.95. ISBN 0-8133-6870-7.

This almanac reconstructs the chronological histories of women and other minorities in the United States since its early history as a republic. The history begins with the first woman to cast a vote in the New World in 1655 and records minorities' interaction in U.S. politics until 1998.

The minorities include women, Afro-Americans, Hispanics, Asian Americans, native minorities, and gays and lesbians. Each of these groups has a chapter that begins with a brief chronology, political power defined through discussions of how each of the minorities achieved power through appointments to presidential cabinet, national party level, and congressional members. Statistics for voting percentages, ethnic representation, and first notables of the various minority groups are available. Academic libraries with a need for women and minority materials will find this almanac valuable to their collections. It contains information that is not readily available anywhere else. [R: Choice, Oct 99, p. 314]—**Kay M. Stebbins**

C, P, S

297.   **The United States Government Manual 1998/1999.** Lanham, Md., Bernan Associates, 1999. 869p. index. $41.00pa. ISBN 0-16-049690-X.

This manual is the official handbook of the U.S. federal government. In essence, the manual provides a detailed description of the legislative, judicial, and executive branches of government. For example, the section on the judicial branch is divided into 6 sections, namely the Supreme Court, the lower federal courts, special courts, the Administrative Office of the United States Courts, the Federal Judicial Center, and the United States Sentencing Commission. The researcher will find not only the purpose, nature, and function of these divisions but also a list of the positions and the personnel in those positions. Throughout this indispensable resource are additional sources of information, including office addresses, electronic access, and publications. In addition, all executive agencies are defined and described. The major departments are delineated here (e.g., Agriculture, Commerce, Defense, Interior, Justice, Labor, Transportation, and Treasury) as well as "independent establishments and government corporations." Some of the agencies under this last heading are the Central Intelligence Agency, Farm Credit Administration, Federal Labor Relations Authority, Federal Reserve System, Merit Systems, Protection Board, National Labor Relations Board, Nuclear Regulatory Commission, Office of Government Ethics, Social Security Administration, United States Commission on Civil Rights, and United States Postal System, to name only a few. There are other categories as well, including quasi-official agencies and multilateral organizations. There are two indexes—name and agency/subject. Every library should have a copy of this easy-to-use guide to the U.S. government.—**Michael A. Foley**

IDEOLOGIES

C, P

298. Gay, Kathlyn, and Martin K. Gay. **Encyclopedia of Political Anarchy.** Santa Barbara, Calif., ABC-CLIO, 1999. 242p. index. $60.00. ISBN 0-87436-982-7.

Most people will associate anarchism with terrorism, radicals, socialists, or communism, but the authors contend that they are not the same. Some anarchists used terrorism to make a point, but many groups publicly adopt some of the themes of anarchism to advance their particular radical goal. Using this book can help one differentiate between anarchism and other political movements. The 172 entries are in alphabetic order and are not arranged by broad subject categories. There is a detailed table of contents and index to help one find relevant entries. Events, political groups, themes, and movements are all covered, but most of the text is related to people. This is to be expected since it is individuals who are the most important aspect of this movement. Cross-references and citations for suggested readings are found at the end of the entries. Helpful Web addresses are also included. Quotations and extracts from other important writings are embedded in many of the entries. The glossary is much appreciated, saving the reader from having to search through other political science dictionaries. Photographs and a chronology of events would have increased the value of this reference tool. The appendix discusses the new field of Internet anarchism that is potentially very dangerous. There are no corresponding entries for anarchism as it might be utilized through journals, newspapers, television, or the radio. This title complements *The Encyclopedia of Revolutions and Revolutionaries: From Anarchism to Zhou Enlai* (see ARBA 97, entry 477), which is much broader in scope. The authors previously collaborated on *Heroes of Conscience: A Biographical Dictionary* (see ARBA 97, entry 22). This easy-to-read encyclopedia is recommended for the reference collections of public, academic, and school libraries. [R: LJ, July 99, pp. 80-83; Choice, Nov 99, p. 516; BR, Nov/Dec 99, p. 86]—**Daniel K. Blewett**

PUBLIC POLICY AND ADMINISTRATION

C, P

299. Hing, Bill Ong. **Immigration and the Law: A Dictionary.** Santa Barbara, Calif., ABC-CLIO, 1999. 400p. index. (Contemporary Legal Issues). $55.00. ISBN 1-57607-120-0.

ABC-CLIO's Contemporary Legal Issues series is designed for high school and college students seeking introductory information on U.S. legal issues. This volume focuses on the often-confusing issue of immigration law in the United States. The book begins with an introduction that addresses the history of immigration and explains how the laws and their amendments have created the complexities of current immigration procedures. It also discusses current laws and how family reunification, employment, labor certification, and the number of immigrants allowed into the United States a year come into play. The bulk of the book is arranged into A to Z entries that cover historical terms, laws, court cases, key people in immigration history, and basic terms (e.g., orphans, visa, picture bride). Each entry is one-half page to one page in length and all words contained within an entry that are provided their own entry are in bold typeface. The appendix that follows provides eight reproductions of government immigration documents including a form for employment eligibility verification; an application for naturalization; and 100 typical questions of the Department of Justice, Immigration, and Naturalization Service. An index concludes the volume.

This is a good introduction to immigration law for high school and undergraduate students. Anyone needing more information will need to consult more comprehensive legal sources. This work will be a valuable addition to high school and university libraries.—**Shannon M. Graff**

14 Psychology and Occultism

PSYCHOLOGY

Dictionaries and Encyclopedias

P

300. **Baker Encyclopedia of Psychology and Counseling.** 2d ed. David G. Benner and Peter C. Hill, eds. Grand Rapids, Mich., Baker Book House, 1999. 1276p. (Baker Reference Library). $59.99. ISBN 0-8010-2100-6.

This is the 2d edition of a work born out of an awareness of the need for a comprehensive treatment of psychology from a Christian point of view. Not only do articles present psychology in its own terms, but many also contain a biblical or theological perspective. This new edition gives more attention to pastoral care and counseling than the 1st edition, and includes a large number of new articles that explore issues of particular interest to clergy, Christian counselors, and mental health practitioners.

Included in this edition are articles covering psychological fields of specialization and professional organizations; people who have contributed to the field of psychology; systems and theories; human development; learning, cognition, and intelligence; sexuality, marriage, and family; social behavior; personality; psychopathology; and pastoral psychology and counseling. The signed articles are arranged alphabetically and most conclude with reference or reading lists. Article contributors include academicians and practitioners who specialize in psychology, psychiatry, social work, and pastoral care. Each was chosen for his or her involvement in the current discussion of the relationship between psychology and Christianity. Aids for use of the book include guide words at the top of each page, headings for articles and subdivisions of articles in bold typeface, and a category index. [R: Choice, Nov 99, p. 506]—**Dana McDougald**

Handbooks and Yearbooks

P, S

301. Boucher, C. Robin. **Students in Discord: Adolescents with Emotional and Behavioral Disorders.** Westport, Conn., Greenwood Press, 1999. 395p. index. (The Greenwood Educators' Reference Collection). $75.00. ISBN 0-313-30799-7.

Students in Discord fills a significant gap in mental health literature, made even more pressing by the recent violence in U.S. high schools. The book covers the psychological problems of students, with emphasis on the teenage years. Personality disorders in student behavior, eating, mood, anxiety, communication, learning, and other disorders are covered with sensitivity to adolescent development. Disorders are arranged into chapters where each is defined clearly, giving a research summary and history of the disorder, precursors of the disorder in the younger years, criteria used to identify a student with the disorder, and suggested educational strategies. The author also includes information on how these disorders may overlap. Actual student histories are often used to illustrate the diagnosis. For each disorder, the federal definitional guidelines are given.

Students in Discord would be a priority purchase for all schools whose social workers, counselors, special education, and classroom teachers would certainly find it useful. Public libraries would also find this book appropriate in their psychology sections both as a supplement to the DSM-IV and as a resource for parents.—**Carol D. Henry**

OCCULTISM

P

302.   Guiley, Rosemary Ellen. **The Encyclopedia of Witches and Witchcraft.** 2d ed. New York, Checkmark Books/Facts on File, 1999. 417p. illus. index. $50.00; $24.95pa. ISBN 0-8160-3849-X.

Guiley knows her witches. In the book's acknowledgements she thanks a "Who's Who" list of today's major leaders of Neo-Paganism (of which Witchcraft, or Wicca, is a denomination). Guiley is the author of more than 20 books, most dealing with aspects of Eastern and Western metaphysics. Her books are shining examples of professionalism in fields plagued by books that are poorly researched and written.

The book focuses on the magic and witchcraft in Western culture, covering classical to modern witchcraft. Classical witchcraft is a term often applied to the medieval conception of witches who worshipped Satan and performed vile deeds. The encyclopedia applies modern research to the concepts and cases of medieval witchcraft. Modern Neo-Pagan Wicca is a nature religion centering on the worship of a mother Goddess, her consort God, and the practice of self-empowering and transformative white magic. Another category of articles are on folk magic and include topics such as village wise women and Pennsylvania Dutch hex witches. Guiley also covers related religions such as Santeria and Vodoun (or Voodoo), which are usually treated by the media as inaccurately as it treats witchcraft.

The articles are arranged in alphabetic order. There are many *see also* references, although many more could be added. Most of the articles include a further reading list, and the book has an extensive bibliography. The index looks rather sparse, but is adequate to an encyclopedia that is already organized alphabetically.

The 2d edition adds new articles and updates many of those from the original 1989 edition (see ARBA 90, entry 755). New articles primarily deal with the modern religions and their developments since the earlier edition, although Guiley also reviewed new publications on classical witchcraft. Any encyclopedia deals with the problem of being out-of-date as soon as it is in print. For example, the wonderful Doreen Valiente, author of some of the most widely cherished Wiccan rituals, died in 1999 after the book went to press. Guiley might also want to consider if she publishes another edition adding an article about the dynamic Neo-Pagan Internet presence in newsgroups, mailing lists, and Web pages. *The Encyclopedia of Witches and Witchcraft* is highly recommended. It is a comprehensive source of accurate information concerning topics too often misunderstood. [R: LJ, 1 Oct 99, p. 80]—**Mary A. Axford**

15 Recreation and Sports

GENERAL WORKS

P

303. **Beyond the National Parks: A Recreation Guide to Public Lands in the West.** Mary E. Tisdale and Bibi Booth, eds. Washington, D.C., Smithsonian Institution Press, 1998. 395p. illus. maps. index. $19.95pa. ISBN 1-56098-566-6.

This book provides both a history and a guide to the 264 million acres of land that has been managed by the Bureau of Land Management (BLM) for the past 50 years. This land, which lies in 14 western states and several eastern states, belongs to U.S. citizens and is meant to be enjoyed by the public. Tourism to these beautiful areas generates $1 billion in revenue for the nation each year and provides such necessities as lumber, coal, grazing lands, and oil and gas. This work's goal is to highlight some of the most beautiful and popular of the areas and provide maps and descriptions in order to facilitate their use.

The book begins with an introduction explaining the role of the BLM. It then goes on to describe the many ways in which these public lands benefit U.S. citizens—by providing areas of recreation (e.g., camping, fishing, sports) and by providing a place to observe wildlife in their natural habitat. From there the book is divided up by state, with each trail, river, or canyon described in detail. Every site is given a small map; beautiful photographs; and information on its location, fee of admission, activities to be enjoyed, and anything else specific to the area. There are activity codes for each site indicating whether the area allows camping, fishing, hiking, hunting, horseback riding, wildlife and plant viewing, boating, or other special activities. There is an emphasis throughout the book on respecting the land and leaving it clean and in its natural condition. The book concludes with two appendixes that provide BLM state addresses and telephone numbers as well as contact information for other organizations mentioned in the work, such as the National Geographic Society and the National Audubon Society.

This guidebook is sure to provide readers with new information on exploring U.S. public lands. It will be of most value to public libraries in the western United States, where the majority of the featured sites are located.
—**Shannon M. Graff**

S

304. Hastings, Penny. **Sports for Her: A Reference Guide for Teenage Girls.** Westport, Conn., Greenwood Press, 1999. 254p. illus. index. $45.00. ISBN 0-313-30551-X.

As this book notes, one in three high school girls are involved in a sport and this number is growing each year. The number of athletics offered to young women is growing as well. The author of this work wrote this book in an attempt to get information about sports and their benefits out to young women. Besides the obvious benefit of promoting good health, sports also provide young women with self-confidence, socialization skills, leadership skills, and time management skills.

The top eight most popular sports among teenage girls are given their own chapters. These include basketball, field hockey, soccer, softball, swimming and diving, tennis, track and field, and volleyball. Another chapter titled "Other Sports to Try" includes less familiar sports, such as badminton and crew, and male-dominated sports, such as football and baseball. Each of these chapters provides practical advice on trying out for the team, equipment used, and most common injuries of the sport, among others. One of the most interesting chapters discusses the special issues that can arise from participating in athletics, such as eating disorders, over-involved parents, and problems with coaches. The book concludes with a list of resources and an index. This book will be a valuable addition to any middle or high school library.—**Shannon M. Graff**

P

305.   Sparano, Vin T. **Complete Outdoors Encyclopedia.** 4th ed. New York, St. Martin's Press, 1998. 830p. index. $39.95. ISBN 0-312-19190-1.

Now in its 4th edition, the *Complete Outdoors Encyclopedia* continues to be a reliable and up-to-date resource for the outdoor sportsman. The entries illustrate the new technologies and trends in outdoor recreation. This edition includes more than 1,300 illustrations and diagrams, 500 of which are new to this volume. Several new topics of interest are discussed, including kayaking and waterskiing, and more information is provided for sports that have found a wider audience (e.g., fly-fishing).

The book is divided into 11 chapters, which are further divided into more specific topics. The chapters cover topics such as hunting and shooting, game animals and birds, fishing, camping, survival, boating, archery, hunting dogs, and first aid. The author, a writer for *Outdoor Life* and the *Los Angeles Times*, has taken the updated information he has researched for these other publications and added it to this volume in one easy-to-use reference. Especially important are the new facts and procedures involved in first aid and survival. Many of these procedures are illustrated in the text for ease of understanding. The book concludes with a chapter titled "Outdoor Information Sources," which provides addresses and telephone numbers for U.S. Fish and Game Departments, U.S. National Parks and Forests, outdoor recreation organizations, and travel information. The book concludes with a subject index.

The update of this valuable resource will be an important purchase for any public library. Because it has not been updated since 1988, much of the information is new and there are many new outdoor activities included. [R: LJ, July 98, p. 100]—**Shannon M. Graff**

BASEBALL

P

306.   **Bill James presents ... STATS Minor League Handbook 1999.** 8th ed. Skokie, Ill., STATS Publishing, 1998. 420p. $19.95pa. ISBN 1-884064-57-4.

This is the 8th edition of what has become the standard guide to the year-by-year statistics for the hundreds of players and teams who compete each year in organized minor league baseball. For the true baseball fanatic, this guide is an indispensable source of information about players who are on their way up to, or down from, the major leagues or are only minor league players. Otherwise, this guide is of primary interest to those who follow the fortunes of a particular minor league team or league. Therefore, it can only be recommended for libraries with extensive baseball collections and for public libraries in cities with an active minor league team.

The excellent arrangement of this guide is designed to assist the most likely user who is apt to be interested in the career of a particular player. It begins with an extensive alphabetic listing (with career statistics) of every player who appeared in Double-A or Triple-A baseball in 1998; only players who also appeared in the major leagues are excluded, as they are included in *STATS Major League Handbook* (1998 ed.; STATS Publishing, 1997). From there a variety of other charts and tables are presented covering Class-A and rookie statistics and other individual and team statistics and records of all kinds. The most intriguing set of statistics is one that computes the major league equivalencies that, through a complex formula, suggest what a minor league player might have accomplished had he played in the major leagues in 1998. There is also an appendix that lists all current minor league teams by city with their major league team affiliation. This is a fine complement to the 2d edition of *The Encyclopedia of Minor League Baseball* (see ARBA 98, entry 729) that provides a historical compilation of statistical and other information about minor league baseball.—**Norman D. Stevens**

P

307.   Dickson, Paul. **The New Dickson Baseball Dictionary.** San Diego, Calif., Harcourt Brace Jovanovich, 1999. 579p. illus. $35.00; $20.00pa. ISBN 0-15-100380-7; 0-15-600580-8pa.

Dickson, a baseball fan and author of other books on the national pastime, has revised and updated the 1st edition of his book that was published in 1989 (see ARBA 90, entry 766). Unlike most dictionaries, this volume is entertaining to browse, even if one is not an avid baseball fan because no other sport has introduced so many words and phrases into our everyday language. Like the original edition, this reference work is filled with words and phrases associated with the game of baseball, and is written to satisfy an audience ranging from the little leaguer to the lover of language to the baseball fanatic. The entries, arranged alphabetically, provide definitions, etymology, the citation of a word's first use in print, and, if known, a term's first use outside of baseball. As appropriate, the entries also offer synonyms or signify whether a term is considered archaic or obsolete. As in the 1st edition, this volume provides a section on how to use the book and a bibliography. The new edition expands the number of terms from roughly 5,000 to 7,000, and is improved by the addition of a thesaurus, and a list of abbreviations and symbols commonly used in the game. Also included are hundreds of interesting reproductions of historic photographs and illustrations depicting the personalities and culture of the game.

The lingo of the "grand old game" is constantly changing. In addition to expanding the definitions of words and phrases included in the 1st edition, Dickson added terms that recently became associated with the game, such as "interleague play," "go yard," and the "400-400 club." This reviewer was able to find almost every baseball term imaginable in this absorbing work. However, being a loyal Red Sox fan, I was disappointed that the term "Pesky's pole" was missing. (For the record, Pesky's pole is the short right field foul pole in Boston's Fenway Park, named after Red Sox player Johnny Pesky, who hit more than one "cheap" home run barely 300 feet down the first base line.) Nevertheless, this fun, informative, and authoritative work is highly recommended for every general sports collection. [R: BL, 1 May 99, p. 1636; Choice, Sept 99, p. 114]—**David Selden**

P

308.   *The Sporting News* **Baseball Register.** 1999 ed. Mark Bonavita, Brendan Roberts, and John Duxbury, eds. St. Louis, Mo., Sporting News Publishing, 1999. 662p. $15.95pa. ISBN 0-89204-605-8.

The 1999 edition of *The Sporting News Baseball Register* belongs in any library if only because 1998 was such a remarkable baseball year: Mark McGwire's and Sammy Sosa's chase of Roger Maris' homerun record; David Wells' perfect gam and the New York Yankees run at the season record for team wins; rookie Kerry Wood's tie for the record of strikeouts in a 9-inning game (20); and the owner of that record, Roger Clemens, with a pitching triple crown (e.g., ERAs, strikeouts, victories), wins a record fifth Cy Young Award. One page explains the footnotes and abbreviations used with the statistical entries. Entries are in alphabetic order by last name, both 1998 minor and major league players. A separate section contains the career playing statistics of all 1999 major league managers. Entries give full names, with pronunciation guides for unusual or difficult names in most cases. A short introduction to explain how the statistics were gathered would have been helpful. At the end of the volume are a list of the 1998 statistical leaders and a list of the career statistics for this year's Hall of Fame inductees. This work is recommended for historical value alone.—**R. S. Lehmann**

P

309.   **Total Baseball: The Official Encyclopedia of Major League Baseball.** 6th ed. John Thorn and others, eds. New York, Total Sports; distr., Emeryville, Calif., Publishers Group West, 1999. 2538p. $59.95. ISBN 1-892129-03-5.

The publication of the *Macmillan Baseball Encyclopedia* in 1969 was a landmark event for baseball fans, particularly those of a statistical bent. Gathered for the first time in print was the cumulated statistical record of every professional who ever played the game. Subsequent editions updated the figures every few years, but the next publishing landmark was the 1st edition of *Total Baseball* in 1989. *Total Baseball* expanded the concept of a baseball encyclopedia in 2 ways. The statistics were expanded with the addition of many new complicated measures created from the traditional "counting" statistics compiled by Macmillan. Furthermore, the work was enlarged to include a greater preponderance of prose materials, essays on history, the players, and the game on and off the field. In 1995, Major League Baseball recognized the added value of *Total Baseball* and named it the game's official encyclopedia.

This 6th edition continues successfully in that vein. In the text section, established articles remain—team histories, baseball families, streaks and feats, awards and honors, black baseball, baseball in Japan, and so forth. These are supplemented by a new chronology of baseball records; essays on baseball in Korea, Taiwan, and Australia; and an analysis of home run records. The book jacket also touts the expansion of player biographies from 100 to 400, but this feature is merely an updated reinstatement of the 400 biographies originally published in the 1st edition.

The bulk of the work remains the pitcher and player statistical registers that are as complete, clearly arranged and accurate as ever. There are also rosters of all managers, coaches, umpires, team owners and officials, lists of all-time and year-by-year leaders, as well as a rundown of post-season play. Last year, statistical maven Bill

James and STATS Inc. came out with a wonderful 2-volume set—*STATS All-Time Major League Handbook* and *STATS All-Time Baseball Sourcebook*—(see ARBA 99 entry 715) with even more detailed historical statistics. But *Total Baseball* is as thorough a baseball encyclopedia as any library is likely to need. This volume is highly recommended for all libraries.—**John Maxymuk**

FOOTBALL

P

310.   **The Official National Football League 1999 Record & Fact Book.** New York, Workman Publishing, 1998. 488p. illus. $15.95pa. ISBN 0-7611-1319-3.

The 488-page *Official National Football League 1999 Record & Fact Book* lives up to its claim to being the "definitive source for NFL information"—complete 1998 statistical information is available for each team, as well as 1999 rosters and draft choices. It is also the premier source that many pro football television commentators rely on. It is the only record book authorized by the NFL that is distributed to news organizations around the world for their coverage of NFL games.

The book opens with a colorful collection of NFL team helmets and logos, followed by a 1999 weekly schedule for each team. Pages 27 to 152 contain 4-page sections on each team with management information, schedules, record holders, coaching history, 1998 team records and team and individual statistics, 1999 roster, and coaching staff. The 1998 season is reviewed in detail from pages 153 to 242, including preseason and regular season standings and results, game summaries, All-Pro teams, attendance records, and team and individual statistics.

Extras include NFL team Internet sites, tie-breaking procedures, an explanation of the NFL passer rating system, a discussion of instant replay, and 1999 draft lists. Perhaps the most interesting part covers less well-known accomplishments, such as the coldest NFL games, longest winning streaks, greatest comebacks, and career statistics for standout performers such as Warren Moon, Cris Carter, and Barry Sanders. Other sections include a chronology of the history of football, past standings as far back as 1920, all-time team-versus-team results, playoff and Super Bowl summaries, and AFC-NFC Pro Bowl results. A brief summary of rules is also included. The *1999 Record & Fact Book* is an indispensable and affordable source for any football fan or professional broadcaster.

—**Mark J. Crawford**

P

311.   **STATS Pro Football Handbook 1999.** Skokie, Ill., STATS Publishing, 1999. 522p. $19.95pa. ISBN 1-884064-63-9.

Already in its fifth year of publication, this is an impressive statistical resource for professional football. After a brief rundown of the final 1998 conference standings and playoff results, the major section of the book provides an alphabetic list of every player who participated in the 1998 National Football League (NFL) season. Each entry gives the player's vital statistics, position played, college draft placement, and a summary of statistics for each year played in the NFL. Many of the offensive and defensive players and all regular kickers and punters are then statistically profiled for their play in the 1998 season in a separate section. This analysis provides a breakdown in a variety of categories, allowing the user to gauge and compare individual performances and effectiveness in different situations, such as play on grass versus turf, home and away, in different formations, and by down played. An analysis of each team's offensive line play and a variety of leader board compilations complete the book.

It is hard to imagine a statistic on active players not covered by the compilers. The detailed situational analyses will be of particular interest to anyone with more than a passing interest in the game. This easy-to-use annual is a statistical treasure trove for fans and analysts alike.—**Barbara E. Kemp**

SOCCER

S

312.   Woog, Dan. **The Ultimate Soccer Encyclopedia.** Los Angeles, Calif., Lowell House, 1999. 144p. illus. maps. $9.95pa. ISBN 0-7373-0399-9.

Intended for young readers, this encyclopedia provides interesting tidbits of information about the game of soccer. It is not a comprehensive or in-depth examination of the game, but is more of a fun and entertaining introduction for young fans and players. Alphabetic entries of only a few sentences cover various players such as Mia Hamm, Thomas Dooley and, Tony Meola; rules and regulations; famous teams; and soccer terminology. Black-and-white photographs and educational maps enhance the work. Sidebars provide interesting facts and trivia, such as how Cobi Jones made a guest appearance on *Beverly Hills 90210* in 1994 and how much distance does an average soccer player cover during an average 90-minute game? (7 miles). Woog was the 1990 National Youth Coach of the Year and has written several other books about the sport, including *The Parent's Guide to Soccer* (Roxbury Park, 1999) and *The Ultimate Soccer Almanac* (Lowell House, 1998). This volume is recommended for juvenile reference and circulating collections.—**Cari Ringelheim**

16 Sociology

DISABLED

P

313.   Joffee, Elga. **A Practical Guide to the ADA and Visual Impairment.** New York, AFB Press, 1999. 159p. $39.95pa. ISBN 0-89128-318-8.

The purpose of this easy-to-read guidebook is to help "people and institutions design and carry out policies that improve the lives of people who are blind or visually impaired and those of their families, as well as the communities in which they live and work" (p. vii). The language of the book is understandable and identifies the different aspects of the law in an easy-to-follow way. There are four sections to the book. Within each section are helpful checklists, which are used as points for discussing the law and as guides for determining compliance with the law. Section 1 provides an overview of the Americans with Disabilities Act of 1990 (ADA), its five titles, and key points within each title. A discussion of visual impairment and accessibility issues, along with a chart that is a quick guide to getting help on the ADA, is included. Section 2 is designed as a customer service guide in accommodating the blind and visually impaired. Included are discussions on employees interacting with impaired customers, providing service in the areas of cash and credit transactions, and food services. Also discussed is the Americans with Disabilities Act Accessibility Guidelines for Buildings and Facilities (ADAAG) regarding environmental issues. Section 3 is on making the ADA work for your business or organization. It involves making accommodations for employees within the workplace; looking at services within the health care system; and providing service to customers within retail establishments, hotels and motels, dining, and food services.

Section 4 is an annotated list of several sources. There is a section on technical assistance, products and services that include contact and Website information, and a list of recommended readings. The text of the ADA; a section of excerpts from the ADAAG; and excerpts from the Accessible and Usable Buildings and Facilities, Revised 1998 ANSI Standards on Signage and Automatic Teller Machines (ICC/ANSI Standards A117.1) are also included. Several checklists used within the text of the chapters are reproduced at the end. They regard communication with blind and visually impaired individuals; accessibility under the ADA relating to communication barrier removal; accessible food services; employers' rights and responsibilities; and accommodating them as patients, customers, and hotel and motel guests. This is a useful book for all types of libraries.—**Jan S. Squire**

FAMILY, MARRIAGE, AND DIVORCE

P

314.   Carangelo, Lori. **The Ultimate Search Book: Worldwide Adoption and Vital Records.** 1998 ed. Bountiful, Utah, Heritage Quest, 1998. 293p. index. $39.95pa. ISBN 1-877677-85-X.

The author of this work is the president of Americans for Open Records (AmFOR), a group working to reverse or modify laws that keep adoption records unobtainable to adopted persons and birth parents. Portions of letters that she receives from people around the world who are searching for lost biological kin are included in each chapter of this book. Adoption-related newspaper accounts are also included. In spite of its obvious agenda, the book is a unique and valuable resource for anyone involved in or anticipating this type of search. Genealogists and others who may be looking for people with little information to go on will also find this volume useful.

Carangelo summarizes state laws and provides names and addresses of adoption search and support groups in each state as well as agency information for foreign countries. Low-cost strategies are outlined for finding each type of missing person, from runaway children to old war buddies. Detailed descriptions of searches, excerpts from searchers' letters, and reproductions of record types prepare the user for what she or he may encounter. This is a necessary purchase for public libraries.—**Glynys R. Thomas**

PHILANTHROPY

Directories

P

315.   **Guide to Grantseeking on the Web.** New York, Foundation Center, 1998. 392p. illus. $19.95pa. ISBN 0-87954-800-2.

Any guide to resources on the Web is by nature destined to almost immediate obsolescence. That said, readers can still use the information contained here, and update that information through more current Web resources.

The work opens with a basic introduction to the Foundation Center and an overview of functions and navigation through the Web, with the overall goal of providing an array of resources of potential use to grant seekers. Each of the nine chapters explores independent foundations, public charities, corporate giving, government resources, free and proprietary databases, online journals, interactive services, a guided tour of the Foundation Center's Website, and other useful sites. For most organization entries, snapshots of Web pages are presented along with the URL and a summary of the activities and resources available. In many cases, the history of the organization is also presented. Information is generally terse and to the point. Four appendixes detail procedures for Internet connectivity, the history of the Internet, a bibliography on grantseeking, and an Internet glossary.

Lack of indexes provides an obstacle to quick access of information, unless the reader already knows in which category to locate an organization. This resource is recommended for its breadth of information.

—**Edmund F. SantaVicca**

SOCIAL WELFARE AND SOCIAL WORK

C, P

316.   Barker, Robert L. **The Social Work Dictionary.** 4th ed. Washington DC, NASW Press, 1999. 584p. $34.95pa. ISBN 0-87101-298-7.

As with every profession, there is a need for a dictionary to standardize the terminology used in social work. Social workers face complexity and potential confusion in using professional terminology because of several factors: increasingly close ties to other professions with their own terminology (psychiatry, psychology, education); divisions within social work itself (policy makers, clinical practitioners); and divergent theoretical approaches to social work practice (behaviorist, cognitive, psychosocial). This volume is the standard social work dictionary, which first appeared in 1987, and clarifies much of the confusion concerning appropriate usage of social work.

This 4th edition, which is part of the National Association of Social Workers' special centennial project, adds almost 2,000 new entries to the previous edition, bringing the total to some 8,000 entries. The author's main goal for this volume "is to give the social worker an abbreviated interpretation of the words, concepts, organizations, historical events, and values that are relevant to the profession" (p. xiv). All diagnostic terms are based on the definitions provided by such accepted standard reference texts as the DSM (4th ed.; American Psychiatric Association, 1999) and the 10th edition of the *International Classification of Diseases* (World Health). The definitions cover a diverse number of entry types, including legislation, individuals, organizations, philosophies, trends concerning social work, and the broader subject of social welfare. The author has relied on the input of hundreds of his colleagues worldwide to make this work as inclusive and accurate as possible. A separate section of historical milestones in social work and social welfare follows the dictionary entries. Regrettably, some of the entries are inaccurate (in 1798 the U.S. government established the Marine Hospital Service, not the USPHS), and some major events are ignored (the 1879 creation of the National Board of Health). The book concludes with the NASW Code of Ethics and the addresses of state boards regulating social workers and NASW chapter offices. This volume is an invaluable reference tool, complementing the *Encyclopedia of Social Work* (19th ed.; see ARBA 96, entry 893) as a central resource for all health care, academic, and large public libraries.

—**Jonathon Erlen**

P

317. **Mercer Guide to Social Security and Medicare 1998.** 26th ed. By J. Robert Treanor, Dale R. Detlefs, and Robert J. Myers. Louisville, Ky., William M. Mercer; distr., Chicago, Independent Publishers Group, 1999. 200p. illus. index. $12.95pa. ISBN 1-880754-99-1.

All Americans should understand their rights and benefits under Social Security and Medicare, particularly as they approach retirement age when these programs typically become the major source of income and health care for the elderly. This excellent guide clearly explains these complex programs, covering how they were developed, what they do, how they are funded, and how to apply. Disability and survivor benefits are included, and supplement security income, plus many rules and regulations. The Medicare section discusses eligibility for parts A and B, what the individual pays, services covered, how the system works, and how to handle complaints. There is information on the new Medicare-Plus-Choice plans, Medicaid, and Medigap insurance, among others.

All material, including financial, is current to 1999. Through the question-and-answer technique, tables, and brief explanations, a great amount of information is available here. Many changes in Social Security and Medicare occur automatically or by legislation each year; this book is published annually to meet this need. This issue contains a short but thoughtful essay on the future of Social Security (pp. 167-171), summarizing the proposals on reform being debated today.—**Harriette M. Cluxton**

YOUTH AND CHILD DEVELOPMENT

P, S

318. **Raising Teenagers: The Best Resources To Help Yours Succeed.** John Ganz, ed. Issaquah, Wash., Resource Pathways, 1998. 256p. index. (Parenting Series). $24.95pa. ISBN 1-892148-04-8.

For parents, having been a teenager is not necessarily sufficient preparation for raising one, particularly in contemporary American culture. This guide provides assistance to those parents looking for help. It includes thorough descriptions and evaluations of books, media, and Internet sites dealing with both general approaches to raising teenagers and specific problems that teenagers and their parents might confront.

The book is arranged into six chapters: an introduction, "Understanding Adolescents" (with subsections for boys and girls), "Parent-Teen Relationships," "Critical Issues and Concerns," "General Overview of Raising Teenagers," and "Terrific Resources" for selected topics. Each chapter begins with an introductory overview of that chapter's subject, followed by the resource reviews. The chapter on critical issues has subsections on major social problems facing teenagers, including pregnancy, eating disorders, gangs, depression and suicide, substance abuse, divorce, and death. The chapter on "terrific resources" deals primarily with communicating values to one's children and cultivating parent-child relationships when dealing with difficult issues (e.g., substance abuse, sexuality, eating disorders). Entries for specific resources include bibliographic details, cost, and availability as well as paragraph-long descriptions and evaluations with ratings for overall quality and ease of use. Title, author, subject, media, and publisher indexes provide additional access to the entries. A directory of helpful organizations, broken down by topic, is appended.

Focusing on teenagers seems valid, given their unique social and developmental characteristics and the promise and peril we associate with that stage of life. However, it is also true that raising teenagers is part of a continuum of child rearing, and the way teenagers and their families deal with issues cannot help but be affected by the relationships and communication established during earlier years. Consequently, this guide legitimately could have, and possibly should have, included more works dealing with raising kids from the beginning. This caveat aside, Ganz has provided a thoughtful guide that is highly recommended for public libraries, counselors, and interested parents.—**Stephen H. Aby**

17 Statistics and Demography

DEMOGRAPHY

Handbooks and Yearbooks

P

319. **Demographic Yearbook, 1997.** 49th ed. New York, United Nations, 1999. 582p. $100.00. ISBN 92-1-051088-7.

One of the tasks of the United Nations is the making and keeping of records and estimates of the population of the world and all of its member nations. This volume is a 1997 revision in a series of similar volumes in the past, and supersedes them. It summarizes distributions by age and sex for each country, and for selected countries, over each fifth year beginning in 1950 through 1995. Preceded by explanatory information about the tables, the remainder of the book consists of the tabular data. Thus it is by its very nature a reference volume, a compendium of the population distribution by age and sex along with vital statistics of fertility and mortality. Updated as it is, it comprises the best data available and is a must for any reference library needing to be inclusive in demographics.—**Arthur R. Upgren**

STATISTICS

General Works

Dictionaries and Encyclopedias

C, P

320. **Cambridge Dictionary of Statistics.** By B. S. Everitt. New York, Cambridge University Press, 1998. 360p. $39.95. ISBN 0-521-59346-8.

This excellent dictionary provides concise definitions of statistical terms for those working in many disciplines who are users of statistics. Although all areas of statistics are covered, any choice of a specific term is dependent on the author. The author acknowledges that there is a difference in mathematical content and level among the definitions, but hopes that such differences will reflect the type of reader likely to turn to a specific definition. Those looking for students' t-tests, for example, will encounter relatively simple formulae, although those seeking information about spline functions will find the more extensive material required.

In content the dictionary contains 3,000 entries and short biographies of more than 100 important statisticians, all of whom are deceased. Ample cross-referencing is provided throughout the volume. The order of the entries may confuse some readers since the arrangement is letter-by-letter rather than word-by-word (e.g., "NOEL," an abbreviation preceding "N of 1 clinical trial").

For those readers who seek more extensive information about a topic than that provided here, the author has provided many entries with either a reference to one of the texts listed in the preliminaries or a more specific reference to a book or journal article. When entries for software are given, the appropriate address is provided.

The dictionary is well conceived and executed. The author has taken pains not only to provide concise and accurate information, but to ensure that users requiring more assistance are not frustrated in their search for information, either within the dictionary itself or beyond. This volume is useful for any reference collection and especially for those that serve higher educational institutions. [R: Choice, Feb 99, p. 1043]—**Robert H. Burger**

Handbooks and Yearbooks

P, S

321.   **Pocket World in Figures 1999.** 1998 ed. New York, John Wiley, 1998. 224p. $14.95pa. ISBN 0-471-29598-1.

This annual publication now has 62 major country profiles, including Russia and Ukraine. Each profile has a general section that includes information on the area, capital, and the unit of currency. A section on people includes data on population, population per square kilometer, average annual growth, the gross domestic product (GDP), the GDP per head, the GDP purchasing power, the origins of the GDP, and the components of GDP. There are also sections on the structure of employment; energy; inflation and finance; exchange rates; principal exports; principal imports; balance of payments, reserves, and aid; and family life. These profiles comprise almost the last two-thirds of the book.

The first third of the book consists of world rankings of 171 countries. To be included the country has to have a population of at least one million or a GNP of one billion U.S. dollars. The quality of the statistics varies from country to country. The data included are for the year ending December 31, 1996, unless otherwise noted. There are over 200 rankings, which include facts about the geography of the countries, the population, the economy, the quality of life, the economic growth (including inflation and debt, employment, banks, and stock markets), transportation, education, death rates, crime, and the environment. The book is relatively small (pocket size) and could get lost on the reference shelves. If purchased, it should circulate.—**Robert L. Turner Jr.**

United States

P, S

322.   **CQ's State Fact Finder 1998: Rankings Across America.** By Kendra A. Hovey and Harold A. Hovey. Washington, D.C., Congressional Quarterly, 1999. 406p. index. $79.95; $44.95pa. ISBN 1-56802-453-3; 1-56802-454-1pa. ISSN 1079-7149.

For anyone doing research that involves comparing the various states and Washington, D.C., or who may just wish for a convenient, up-to-date compendium of statistical data on a state-by-state basis, this volume will be quite welcome. It is the 5th edition, but it retains much of the arrangement found in its 4 predecessors, which will allow people having access to them to compare numbers over the years covered in the earlier editions. Each volume, as it is published, attempts to present the most recent figures the publisher can amass. For example, in this 1999 edition, the data for state health rankings are from 1998, but for AIDS cases they are from 1997. Nevertheless, it is estimated this edition consists of approximately 90 percent new data in comparison to the 1998 edition—a trend the publishers hope to maintain with each subsequent volume. The data are presented in 240 tables and are arranged under 12 general categories, such as population trends, health, crime, transportation, and taxation, among others. The tables also provide a numerical ranking for each state in the subject being treated so that one can see at a glance where a state ranks nationally. When available, each table also gives the national average and total for its particular subject. This publication is especially useful because it compiles statistical data not always readily available from standard sources, or if available, converts such data so that they can be used for meaningful comparisons within the context of this title. The source for the data presented in each table is carefully noted at the end of the section in which it appears along with any pertinent information about its usefulness or what to beware of when using it.

This volume is prefaced by a useful introduction that explains how best to make use of the data contained within, including some of the general questions it will help answer. It finishes with a final and convenient section that provides a state-by-state list of how each state ranks in all the categories listed by topic in the main section of the book. Thus, one can turn to the two pages for California and see at a glance that in 1997 California ranked number one in population, personal income, and number of prisoners, whereas it ranked number 40 in education spending per capita and number 50 in high school completion rates.

As fascinating as it is informative, this work belongs in any reference collection that wants to provide in one easy-to-use volume statistical data for students, researchers, or ordinary citizens.—**Paul H. Thomas**

S

323.   **State Rankings 1999: A Statistical View of the 50 United States.** 10th ed. Kathleen O'Leary Morgan and Scott Morgan, eds. Lawrence, Kans., Morgan Quitno Press, 1999. 569p. index. $49.95pa. ISBN 1-56692-332-8. ISSN 1057-3623.

If one is curious about where the U.S. Defense Department spends the most money (California), which state has the lowest crime rate (Vermont), or who is the top soybean producer in the United States (Illinois), this book is the source to consult. This book contains 569 tables of state comparisons—1 per page. The same rankings are reported twice—in an alphabetic list beginning with Alabama and ending with Wyoming and in an accompanying ranking list beginning with 1 and typically ending at 50. The District of Columbia is included where applicable. Running alongside both lists are the data on which the 1996 to 1998 rankings were based and each state's percentage. In a few cases, only percentages or data are reported. Sources, typically federal government publications, are given for each table. As a bonus, the publisher combined 24 negative variables (e.g., poverty rate) and 19 positive ones (e.g., books per capita in public libraries) to discover the country's most livable state. Minnesota won the distinction in 1998 and again in 1999. Each state's nickname, capital, population, area, song, flower, tree, and bird are included. *State Rankings 1999* makes for fascinating browsing. The work is highly recommended for middle and high school libraries.—**Pete Prunkl**

C, P, S

324.   **Statistical Abstract of the United States 1998.** 118th lib ed. By the U.S. Department of Commerce, the Economics and Statistics Administration, and the Bureau of the Census. Lanham, Md., Bernan Associates, 1998. 1020p. index. $50.00. ISBN 0-89059-123-7. ISSN 1063-1690.

This publication is one of the standard reference sources found in library collections and should need no introduction to anyone who has ever used a library's services. The volume under review is the library edition, meaning that it is hardbound and has larger print, making it easier for users to read (unless one finds reading a computer screen easier and wishes to resort to the CD-ROM version of this title).

Published continuously since 1878, this is the 118th edition of this venerable and indispensable title. As usual, its statistics are taken from a mix of government and private sources and, unless otherwise noted, cover the United States as presently constituted. (For data on specific states and metropolitan areas, one must consult other sources such as the *State and Metropolitan Area Data Book* [5th ed.; see ARBA 2000, entry 781] or *CQ's State Fact Finder* [1997 ed.; see ARBA 97, entry 817]).

This edition of *Statistical Abstract of the United States* consists of 1,487 tables containing statistics for the most recent year or period available by spring 1998. This edition contains 94 new tables that cover subjects ranging from the number of male sexual partners in lifetime, by selected characteristics 1995, to public library use of the Internet 1997, to age of driver and number of accidents 1996. Several of the new tables are the result of information taken from the National Survey of Family Growth. 88 tables were removed that appeared in the previous edition, making it a good idea to retain past editions of this title when possible.

As in past editions, the data are followed by several useful appendixes. They provide further sources for statistical information, on both a national and a state level, a list of metropolitan areas with their population estimates, a discussion of the limitation of the data listed in this book, and lists of the new and deleted tables. Given the importance of this publication, especially the inclusion of both the new tables and of newer data in general, this is a title that any reference collection will need to include on its shelves.—**Paul H. Thomas**

18 Women's Studies

BIOGRAPHY

P

325.   Adamson, Lynda G. **Notable Women in American History: A Guide to Recommended Biographies and Autobiographies.** Westport, Conn., Greenwood Press, 1999. 540p. index. $49.95. ISBN 0-313-29584-0.

There are 500 notable women from more than 100 different fields discussed in this volume. The three criteria for inclusion are that they "must have lived in the United States or one of its territories, and if born abroad after 1900, be a naturalized American citizen; have enriched life for other Americans in some way; and have a full-length biography or autobiography for either adults or mature young adults published since 1970 which is available by interlibrary loan" (pp. xi-xii). Adamson includes up to five citations to autobiographical monographs per person. The entries provide readers a tight, albeit short, summary of each women's life and are listed alphabetically. The appendixes include the women by date of birth (the earliest being Pocahontas in 1617); by occupation or main area of interest, such as activist, nurse, missionary, tribal leader; and by ethnicity, including African Americans, Asian Americans, Latino Americans, and Native Americans. This work is recommended as an excellent starting point for biographical research. [R: BL, 1 Dec 99, p. 726]—**Leslie R. Homzie**

CHRONOLOGY

C, P

326.   Franck, Irene M., and David M. Brownstone. **Illustrated History of Women.** Danbury, Conn., Grolier, 1999. 10v. illus. index. $295.00/set. ISBN 0-7172-7497-7.

The *Illustrated History of Women* is a comprehensive, well-written history of women from ancient times through the twentieth century. The text is enriched with illustrations, photographs, charts, sidebars, and many timelines and boxes. There is a set index in each of the 10 volumes. The reading level is appropriate for middle school and high school students.

The topics discussed in "HerStory" are religious battles, childbirth and midwives, education, women of power, women of medicine, scientists and inventors, slaves, art patrons, writers, and heroines and villains. Each of the volumes presents an overview of the period and a timeline for that period. A short bibliography and cross-references are provided and a cumulative index is provided in each of the volumes. This set is recommended for middle and high school libraries due to the reading levels and the limited bibliographies. [R: BR, Nov/Dec 99, pp. 88-89]—**Kay M. Stebbins**

HANDBOOKS AND
YEARBOOKS

P, S

327.   Harlan, Judith. **Feminism: A Reference Handbook.** Santa Barbara, Calif., ABC-CLIO, 1998. 308p. index. (Contemporary World Issues). $39.50. ISBN 0-87436-894-4.

Harlan has written on girls' self–esteem and on U.S.–Puerto Rican politics. In *Feminism: A Reference Handbook* she offers a broad overview of feminism in the United States from 1920 to today. This guide appropriately offers no surprises. It contains a brief history of feminism in the United States, a chronology, an attempt to define the basic tenets of feminism in all its broadness, biographical sketches of key people, and an extensive explanation of key issues.

Harlan defines feminist issues by asserting that there are two kinds of feminists: those who seek "access" for women and those who seek "control." She then names the primary areas feminists feel access and control are needed, including education, economics, politics, reproduction, sexuality, violence, and society in general. She touches on global feminist issues such as population control and genital mutilation.

A tiny slice of a pie chart displays the 1.9 percent of women representing the top earners at Fortune 500 companies. Such useful charts and statistical tables are included throughout this volume. An extensive section of organizations, books, Web pages, videotapes, and other media concludes the volume, along with an essential index. This reference could have used more imaginative photographic illustrations. Although visually dull, it offers a basic, general grounding in feminism and should be purchased by public, school, and academic libraries. [R: Choice, Dec 98, p. 668; BL, 1 Nov 98, p. 532]—**Glynys R. Thomas**

P, S

328.   Heinemann, Sue. **The New York Public Library Amazing Women in American History: A Book of Answers for Kids.** New York, John Wiley, 1998. 192p. illus. index. (New York Public Library Answer Books for Kids Series). $12.95pa. ISBN 0-471-19216-3.

A chronological history of women is presented in the latest reference text from the New York Public Library. The format is in questions and answers, with informative sidebars and numerous black-and-white photographs for kids grades 6 through 10. Women from political activism and slavery to fine arts and sports are explored. Notable women, such as Eleanor Roosevelt and Amelia Earhart, and less notable ones, such as Emma Goldman, Nelly Bly, and Ida B. Wells, are discussed. Their achievements and controversies are included in each of the women's stories.

There is a selected bibliography and a "New York Public Library's Recommended Reading List." This work is recommended for school libraries and public libraries for their women's studies collections or biography collections. [R: BR, Nov/Dec 98 , p. 83]—**Kay M. Stebbins**

Part III
HUMANITIES

19 Humanities in General

HUMANITIES IN
GENERAL

C

329.   **Walford's Guide to Reference Material, Volume 3: Generalia, Language and Literature, the Arts.**
7th ed. Anthony Chalcraft, Ray Prytherch, and Stephen Willis, eds. Lanham, Md., Bernan Associates, 1998.
1186p. index. $279.00. ISBN 1-85604-300-2.

Walford's guide has a long tradition and has been reviewed in ARBA many times. This is the 7th edition
of the work covering generalia, language, literature, and the arts, with several new libraries consulted, as mentioned
in the introduction (pp. ix–x). In the section on generalities there are 350 new items, "with every item checked
and, if necessary, revised" (p. ix). In the arts section there are 400 new entries and about the same number of new
entries in the language and literature section. In most cases, brief annotations are based on prefaces or introductions
to individual books covered in this guide and, in general, they are adequate. In comparison to the *Guide to Reference
Books* published by the American Library Association, Walford is more comprehensive, especially for European materials. Nevertheless, several items listed here are quite obsolete, but Walford is still the best resource
for general orientation.—**Bohdan S. Wynar**

20 Communication and Mass Media

GENERAL WORKS

P, S

330. **The Power of the Press.** Beth Levy and Denise M. Bonilla, eds. Bronx, N.Y., H. W. Wilson, 1999. 187p. index. (The Reference Shelf, v.71, no.1). $30.00pa. ISBN 0-8242-0962-1.

The Reference Shelf is a series of six books covering social issues in the United States and other countries that can be purchased separately or as a subscription. Five books are topical; the last of the series is a compilation of recent speeches. This first book in the series is a collection of critical articles, excerpts of books, and addresses about recent issues of importance in news reporting. The first chapter defines the press by exploring public perception of the media, the trend toward human-interest stories, news organizations as corporate entities, and the Internet as a news source. Next the book discusses the media's involvement in celebrity, or high-interest events, such as the O. J. Simpson trial, as well as the drive for journalists themselves to become celebrities. A chapter on ethics discusses the quality of investigating and reporting versus the need to "scoop" competitive news agencies. Subsequent chapters cover media scandals and their effects on the profession's credibility, and a look at freedom of the press as it exists in several countries. The contents are selective, but provide a good contemporary view of the profession, both its problems and its potential. The bibliography will lead readers to other sources and additional periodical articles. It is indexed for easy reference. School and public libraries may want this in both the reference and circulating collections.—**Jean Engler**

AUTHORSHIP

General Works

P

331. **The Writer's Handbook.** 2000 ed. Sylvia K. Burack, ed. Boston, Writer, 1999. 919p. index. $32.95. ISBN 0-87116-187-7.

For more than 60 years this handbook has served as a comprehensive resource for freelance writers seeking guidance on writing and marketing manuscripts (see ARBA 99, entry 832; ARBA 94, entry 999; ARBA 91, entry 945). Organized into 2 parts, the volume's strongest section continues to be section 1, with 110 chapters of how-to information from leading writers. The techniques, directed toward writing kinds of literature (e.g., poetry, mystery novels, greeting cards) and addressing specific audiences (e.g., young adults), remain enlightening, informative, and inspirational. The conversational interviews with eight famous writers (e.g., Doris Lessing) report on their experience and unique perspective as successful authors.

Part 2, resources for writers, offers 3,300 places to send manuscripts, along with useful listings of literary agents, writers' colonies, conferences, and arts councils. The articles market is divided into topical categories (e.g., travel, true crime) to aid the writer in locating a publisher. The brief descriptive entries are less informative than those found in *Writer's Market* (see entry 332). A glossary of key terms and an alphabetic index to the material in part 2 complete the volume. A detailed table of contents facilitates access to the volume's resources. The handbook is recommended for acquisition by public libraries. College and university libraries from institutions with writing programs should also consider its purchase.—**Sandra E. Belanger**

P

332.   **Writer's Market, 2000: 8,000 Editors Who Buy What You Write.** electronic ed. Kirsten C. Holm and Donya Dickerson, eds. Cincinnati, Ohio, F & W Publications, 1999. 1112p. index. $49.99pa. (with disc). ISBN 0-89879-916-3.

The latest edition of this must-have handbook for the writing market gives more information than ever before on how to get published. The three largest sections of the book are market listings of book publishers; consumer magazines; and trade, technical, and professional journals. Users will also find market listings for scriptwriting, syndicates, greeting cards, and contests and awards. Each listing contains information about the editorial focus of the market, how it prefers material to be submitted, payment information, and other helpful tips. The editors have also indicated whether or not markets will accept queries by e-mail.

This edition has been revised to include a list of 60 literary and 20 script agents. All of these agents have indicated a willingness to work with new, previously unpublished writers as well as more established authors. Most are members of the Association of Authors' Representatives (AAR) or the Writers Guild of America (WGA). As in previous editions the editors have included articles from professionals in the writing field with helpful tips and information on getting published. For example, the "Query Letter Clinic" showcases "good" and "bad" letters with comments straight from editors about what attracted and what distracted.

Seeing as how there is no user guide provided for the CD-ROM, it is recommended that users who are not computer savvy stick to the print version. Otherwise, users who have a general knowledge of navigating computer programs will have no problem installing and using the *Writer's Market* CD-ROM. Searching for the appropriate market for a writer's work is greatly improved on the CD-ROM as opposed to the print version. User's need only select specific criterion and their computer will select the most promising market opportunities along with all of the submission information provided in the print version. As an added bonus the CD-ROM also provides a submission tracker for writers to save time and stay organized. This work is highly recommended for all reference collections in university and public libraries. Serious writers should consider obtaining their own personal copies.

—**Cari Ringelheim**

Style Manuals

C, P, S

333.   Gibaldi, Joseph. **MLA Handbook for Writers of Research Papers.** 5th ed. New York, Modern Language Association of America, 1999. 332p. index. $14.50pa. ISBN 0-87352-975-8.

There were 7 years between the 3d and 4th (1995) editions of this classic style manual. Now the 5th edition has made its debut. As in previous editions, the handbook takes the reader through the mechanics of the research paper. It covers selection and narrowing a topic, outlining, note taking, spelling, punctuation, and formatting. It also covers the use of print and online library catalogs and indexes. The documentation and citation sections cover all types of sources, both print and nonprint. Section headings are in red and citation examples are in a different font, making them easy to locate and identify.

Although the information about print sources remains unchanged, this edition expands the coverage of electronic sources. What was called "Citing Online Databases" has become "Citing Electronic Publications" and has tripled in length. The section now includes instructions on citing information databases, online books and periodicals, and Websites including personal Web pages. There are also guidelines (as yet there are no agreed-upon standards) for works that will be submitted electronically.

Another valuable revision is the updated list of selected reference works by field. New titles and editions are included as well as online sources and CD-ROM products.

This new edition of a standard reference tool addresses the rapidly evolving needs of today's students and will once again prove its value in college and public libraries.—**Marlene M. Kuhl**

C, P

334.   Walker, Janice R., and Todd Taylor. **The Columbia Guide to Online Style.** New York, Columbia University Press, 1998. 218p. index. $17.50pa. ISBN 0-231-10788-9; 0-231-10789-7.

In cyberdom, there are no title pages, versos, or colophons—few of the familiar bibliographic signposts and conventions by which scholars and students have traditionally charted and documented the course of their research and writing. In fact, as Janice Walker and Todd Taylor discuss in their perceptive preface and introduction to *The Columbia Guide to Online Style*, the very notions of single authorship and linear discourse often fall by the wayside once that property is staked on the Web or other online venues. In the face of this complex and often inchoate new communications landscape, Walker and Taylor have made commendable strides toward establishing effective new standards for "ensuring scholarly integrity" in terms of both publishing and citing online academic research and correspondence. *The Columbia Guide* differs in a number of significant respects from the established style manual trinity—the MLA, Chicago, and APA. While the most recent editions of those venerable publications deal cautiously with some electronic sources, they unfortunately miss the precipitous rise of academic publishing on the Web in the last five years. In contrast, *The Columbia Guide* devotes a substantial chapter to WWW citation, as well as to a panoply of other electronic sources missed (or neglected) by the other manuals, including video games, graphic files, chat rooms, and other electronic ephemera. A bolder and generally less successful attempt is also made to establish standards and guidelines for academic Web authors (there is something slightly off in addressing standard publishing conventions in a hypertextual world). Perhaps the most notable innovation of *The Columbia Guide*—distinguishing it most from the other style guides—is its "element oriented" approach to style. Rather than prescribing a hard-and-fast, discipline-oriented citation style, *The Columbia Guide* attempts to define a core of essential bibliographic elements that can be applied to a variety of already established style guides and used in a wide variety of situations. While the MLA, APA, and Chicago manuals may eventually catch up to the realities of new scholarly media, it is unlikely that they will match Walker and Taylor's comprehensiveness, or their levelheaded grasp of what it means to do academic business in an increasingly online world. An essential addition to all libraries, portions of *The Columbia Guide* can be viewed online at http://www.columbia.edu/cu/cup/cgos/idx_basic.html. [R: LJ, 1 Sept 98, p. 175]—**Gary Handman**

21 Decorative Arts

COLLECTING

General Works

P

335. *Collector's Mart* **Magazine Price Guide to Limited Edition Collectibles, 1999.** Mary L. Sieber, ed. Iola, Wis., Krause Publications, 1998. 894p. illus. index. $17.95pa. ISBN 0-87341-646-5.

This book is the 4th edition of *Collector's Mart Magazine Price Guide to Limited Edition Collectibles.* The editors and staff have taken the information from the 3d edition, studied it, added to it, and updated it to create an incredible resource of nearly 60,000 prices that covers the broad spectrum of limited edition collectibles.

The goal of the book is to provide a guide listing thousands of secondary market (the market collectibles enter after they have left the original, primary point of retail sales) prices covering the gamut of limited edition collectibles including bells, cottages, dolls, figurines, ornaments, plates, prints, and steins. The book has been divided into categories that make it easy for readers to find the information relevant to the items they collect. An introduction precedes each section and summarizes many of the trends occurring in today's marketplace. Items within the listings are arranged alphabetically, first by company name, then by series name, and finally by the artist's last name. They are further organized chronologically by the year the collectible was issued, then alphabetically by the title of the piece. Folios at the top of each page mark each section and make flipping through the book quick and easy. Two indexes at the back of the book help readers locate items for which they may not have the necessary information.

This one-of-a-kind resource gives the reader almost 60,000 listings, with more than 200 photographs for easy identification. This book would be a help to those who are interested in collecting and seeing the market value of their collectibles.—**Barbara B. Goldstein**

P

336. Maloney, David J., Jr. **Maloney's Antiques & Collectibles Resource Directory.** 5th ed. Dubuque, Iowa, Antique Trader Books, 1999. 856p. $29.95pa. ISBN 1-58221-016-0. ISSN 1083-8449.

David J. Maloney, the author of this resource, is a nationally known appraiser, author, radio talk show guest, and lecturer. He is a full-time professional personal property appraiser, specializing in the valuation of antiques and collectibles.

Many people look at *Maloney's Antiques & Collectibles Resource Directory* as just a place to find a contact in order to buy or sell an item, but the book is much more than that. The book also provides valuable information on the legalities of buying and selling certain types of items as well as resources for learning more about fakes and reproductions. Readers will be able to find appraisers, repair services, matching services, suppliers of parts, and even auction services within the pages of this book. The best part of all this is that everything in *Maloney's* is also online in an easily searchable format.

In addition to thousands of new and updated listings and scores of new categories, the 5th edition of *Maloney's* includes the following important features: a greatly expanded cross-referencing system where readers are directed to the relevant categories that might contain information of interest; four important appendixes for educated and tested appraisers, auction services, general-interest periodicals, and repair firms; a redesigned and highly detailed index; and nearly 7,500 listings with Websites and more than 9,500 e-mail addresses. The goal of this book is to place as much information as possible at users' fingertips to allow them to make decisions based on knowledge and fact.

Prior to *Maloney's*, there was no organized method to capture, preserve, collate, and distribute collector resource information to efficiently keep the public accurately informed on a continuing basis. *Maloney's* is designed to overcome this shortfall through frequent updating and regular publication.

This is the reader's one-stop reference for contacting fellow collectors who might want to buy items they own. It also helps readers in identifying the recognized experts in thousands of collectibles categories and locating an appraiser or auction house that specializes in antiques and collectibles. Furthermore, it will help readers in seeking out and joining the most popular collector clubs and organizations, and subscribing to books and magazines devoted to the special areas of interest. It can also be used to find out where to get parts, have repairs done, and where to go to match a pattern.

Maloney's Antiques & Collectibles Resource Directory is the one book that savvy collectors, knowledgeable dealers, and professional appraisers and claims adjusters depend on as a basis for their research. Whether readers buy, sell, trade, or collect contemporary, traditional, or the most rare and unusual items, *Maloney's Directory* has the information they want and need.—**Barbara B. Goldstein**

Books

P

337.   **Huxford's Old Book Value Guide: 25,000 Listings of Old Books with Current Values.** 11th ed. Paducah, Ky., Collector Books, 1999. 442p. $19.95. ISBN 1-57432-119-6.

Not only does this book place values that an interested party would be willing to pay to obtain possession of nearly 25,000 books, it also lists scores of buyers along with the type of material each is interested in purchasing. These prices are taken from dealers' selling lists that have been issued within the past year.

Huxford's Old Book Value Guide places values on the more common holdings that many seem to accumulate. The majority of books listed in this guide are in the $10 to $40 range. The format of this guide is very simple: Listings are alphabetized first by the name of the author, translator, editor, or illustrator, and if more than one book is listed for a particular author, each title is listed alphabetically under his or her name. When pseudonyms are known, names have been cross-referenced. Dust jackets or wrappers are noted when present, and sizes (when given) are approximate. Condition is usually noted as well. If the condition is not stated, it is assumed to be very good. Dates within parentheses indicate the copyright dates while dates without parentheses are dates found on title pages or are the actual publication dates.

There is also a listing of book buyers according to the topic or theme of the book (i.e., art, aviation, bibliographies, civil war, farming, and so on). These topics are arranged alphabetically for ease of use. This book would prove worthwhile to those who have books they want to either learn the value of or sell.—**Barbara B. Goldstein**

Coins (and Paper Money)

P

338.   Bressett, Kenneth. **The Whitman Guide to Coin Collecting: A Beginner's Guide to the World of Coins.** New York, St. Martin's Press, 1999. 246p. illus. index. $11.95pa. ISBN 0-307-48008-9.

As the subtitle "A Beginner's Guide to the World of Coins" reveals, this guidebook is aimed at the beginning coin collector, and is designed to fill a need for basic information about how to get started in the coin collecting hobby and how to avoid costly mistakes. Guidebooks of this nature have appeared frequently, but many of them are out of print or out of date. The author's credentials are impressive; he is a former president of the American Numismatic Association and long-time coeditor of the renowned *Guide Book of United States Coins* (53d ed.; see ARBA 2000, entry 841) and the *Handbook of United States Coins* (see entry 339), also known respectively as "the red book" and "the blue book," the most trusted and most used references in the field of numismatics for decades.

The reader is introduced to coin collecting as a hobby. The book includes such information as where collectible coins can be obtained, sources for learning the history of coins, how to care for a collection, how coins are graded and priced, and information about special coins (e.g., commemorative issues, counterfeits, other interesting and collectible coinage). A chapter addressing an area that has generated more interest in recent years is devoted to coins as an investment and discusses when it is time to sell. A catalog chapter gives current values for all U.S. coins that sell for substantial premiums over their face value. Explanations are well written and the black-and-white illustrations are excellent. There are occasional errors, as where it is stated that "Barber design coins dated back to the late eighteenth century were still in circulation in the 1940s and '50s." Barber-designed coins were issued in the late nineteenth century, from 1892 to 1916, as shown in the catalog chapter of this book. The widespread interest in coins as collectibles and investments makes this book a welcome addition to any library.—**Larry Lobel**

P

339.   Yeoman, R. S. **Handbook of United States Coins, 2000.** 57th ed. Edited by Kenneth Bressett. New York, St. Martin's Press, 1999. 208p. illus. index. $7.95pa. ISBN 0-307-48006-2.

This book, informally called the "blue book," is published annually and lists the average prices paid by coin dealers by coin condition or grade; in effect, the wholesale prices for coins. This book is a useful guide to the collector who expects to sell coins to a dealer, although there is no guarantee that any dealer would pay the prices as listed. The prices are an average and are meant to be guidelines only.

The book covers U.S. coins and is chronologically arranged from 1616 to the present time. Photographs of each coin type accompany the entry and frequently details are highlighted to aid identification. Historical commentary adds richness to each entry. Each coin type is provided with complete mintage information, and prices are provided for a range of coin grades or conditions. Also included are listings for commemorative coins and gold, platinum, and silver bullion pieces.

This book is considered the standard reference wholesale price guide in the U.S. coin collecting market along with its companion volume, *A Guide Book of United States Coins* (53d ed.; see ARBA 2000, entry 841), which is the retail price guide. This book is recommended for public and college library collections.

—**Margaret F. Dominy**

22 Fine Arts

GENERAL WORKS

Directories

P, S

340. Walker, Sandra C., and Donald W. Beetham. **Image Buyers' Guide: An International Directory of Sources for Slides and Digital Images for Art and Architecture.** 7th ed. Englewood, Colo., Libraries Unlimited, 1999. 186p. index. (Visual Resources Series). $55.00pa. ISBN 1-56308-658-1.

Presentation software, image CD-ROMS, class Websites, and image databases are a few of the new formats that have changed the needs of curators, librarians, teachers, and scholars in their educational use of art and architecture images. Previously titled the *Slide Buyers' Guide*, the current edition marks a fresh direction for the scope of this reference work.

The new guide is well structured with a pleasing and thorough preface that explains the guide's history, methodology, arrangement, conventions, and evaluation procedures. The editors immediately acknowledge the most obvious drawback to any use of URL's in directory entries—the likelihood of change. In an attempt to keep current, the preface includes a URL for the guide's Website, and advises using the Website name as a constant that "can be located in a web index." Although it is confusing that the Website describes itself as "unofficial" when mentioned in the preface, it is clear that the Website is an extremely valuable resource. The Website contains working links to the entries.

The introduction provides a simple overview of the process of image buying that is extremely valuable for the novice. There is advice for inexperienced buyers, statements on slide quality standards, and clarification of copyright issues. The entries themselves include contact information, documentation and catalog information, product notes, purchasing procedures, and evaluations.

While evaluation help is welcome, some entries were assessed by only one committee member, or were assessed many years ago. Quality and consistency of evaluation seems like the main area where the guide could be improved. There is also the usual problem that all directories seem to have of some omitted fields in the entries due to lack of information from the vendor or resource.

This guide is an interesting resource and easy to use. The *Image Buyers' Guide* is highly recommended for those who use slides and digital images of art and architecture, and the staff that assist them to find the materials that they need. Even libraries with more general collections may want to consider this book as an addition to reference.

—**Sandra E. Fuentes**

Handbooks and Yearbooks

C, P

341. Vaughan, William. **Arts of the 19th Century: Volume 1, 1780 to 1850.** New York, Abrams, 1998. 625p. illus. index. $195.00. ISBN 0-8109-1982-6.

As the title suggests, this compilation is an attempt to show the arts of the first part of the nineteenth century. It includes not only two-dimensional paintings, but delves a little into sculpture, graphic art, furnishings, and architecture. The volume is huge, offering an abundance of illustrations that aptly cover the taste, flavor, and color of the era.

It is difficult reviewing an art book like this one. Because of this reviewer's deep love of the romanticism and style of nineteenth-century art, the book is held in high esteem simply because of its content. However, because of this personal admiration of all things of this century, I hold a more critical eye of the book's approach and presentation.

The various phases and styles of art during this time period are covered effectively by the narrative. A painting is often explained and categorized by its emotional offering, symbolism, and intent. A painting may be categorized as well by the application of coloring, shadowing, and technique of artistry, but this is not explained as fully.

Arts of the 19th Century includes painting, graphic art, sculpture, furniture and accessories, and architecture, but not theater, dance, music, functional art and design (e.g., bridges, tunnels, vehicles, appliances), and so on. The title *Arts of the 19th Century* suggests the era, not the region. France, England, Spain, the United States, and Italy are well represented. The rest of the world is not here at all, or only receives a footnote mention. The narrative is complete enough, but very dry. The art selected is an excellent representation, although as a whole hints of bias.

Finally, there is the physical book itself. As formatted, the figures are grouped together, which is fine for the majority of figures that have a figure number alongside for easy identification, but some do not. And in many cases, the figure is far away from where it is referenced in the text. Before each grouping of figures four of five captions are placed on a single page. This seems like a waste of space.

The book is 10 by 12½ inches—a nice size for showing details of the art, and the paper used is of a heavyweight, high quality to give a nice faithful reproduction of the pieces selected. But because the paper is of this heavier weight, and because there are more than 600 pages, the volume is extremely heavy and cumbersome to carry or place on the lap. If the captions had been placed on the same page of the pictures, it could have saved bulk and would have aided greatly in instantly identifying the piece.

Although it is clear that expense has been put into the text of the book, the cover and binding appear cheaply done. The cover is a black paper/cloth treatment around boards, and light-colored ink stamps the title, author, and publisher only on the spine. (There is nothing on the front or back to identify the book once the dust jacket is removed.) The fragility of the binding alone will send up red flags to libraries and librarians. After having opened the book less than a half dozen times, the endpaper has split in the back and the cover is now separated from the spine.

This volume is recommended as a reference book. The photographs and reproductions are superior, and the era is nicely covered. [R: Choice, Oct 99, p. 322]—**Joan Garner**

ARCHITECTURE

C, P

342. **Award Winning Architecture 1998/99: International Yearbook.** Frantisek D. Sedlacek, ed. New York, Prestel USA; distr., New York, Neues, 1998. 216p. illus. index. $49.95. ISBN 3-7913-1833-0.

Evaluating a meal from a photograph in a book is an exercise in futility. The aroma must be smelled and the food must be sampled between tongue and palate to determine taste and texture; it is an experience. Sampling architecture from a book is much the same. Good architecture represents a dynamic resolution of function and space, a juxtaposition poorly conveyed in small photographs. To be truly appreciated it, too, must be experienced. Having said that, however, the realities are such that, as a substitute for visiting 19 countries around the world, this book works very well. As Marcus Binney writes in the foreword, "The task of a book such as this…is to show whether world architecture is treading a wide and varied path full of surprises..." (p. 9). The book accomplishes its task and architecture is, indeed, full of surprises.

Each included project has received an award from a national architectural association. Of the 400 world-wide projects that received such awards, 100 were selected for inclusion in this volume, the 3d in the series that began in 1996. Projects are displayed on one or two pages, illustrated by multiple color and black-and-white photographs and accompanied by small site drawings, sections, or elevations, with accompanying details such as design team, structural team, contractors, areas of the project, and additional references. The book is indexed by project location, architect, and building type. The book is inspirational. The spectrum of projects included is broad and spectacular—both secular (residences, museums, hospitals, libraries, transportation facilities, and industrial buildings) and spiritual (synagogues, churches, and convents).

This book is more than a collection of structures; it is a sampling of innovative problem solving that affects populations. In the beginning of the book the editor laments the fact that recent architecture was falling into a boring series of similar solutions to diverse problems, banks appearing like housing projects and architecture reflecting neither site nor social conditions. The projects contained within this volume happily declare that the trend the editor observed may be over. The book is a volume that can easily be placed on the coffee table, but more effectively can be used as a reference to good architecture for those in the field or for students as an example of inventiveness and problem solving at its best.—**Craig A. Munsart**

PHOTOGRAPHY

C, P

343. McDarrah, Gloria S., Fred W. McDarrah, and Timothy S. McDarrah. **The Photography Encyclopedia.** New York, Schirmer Books/Simon & Schuster Macmillan, 1999. 689p. illus. index. $80.00. ISBN 0-02-865025-5.

The current interest in photography as an art can be seen in the great number of exhibitions, auctions, and books dealing with the medium. Long regarded as a stepchild of fine arts or thought of as a mechanical process requiring no artistic insight, the photograph has become in integral part of both the aesthetic and the commercial world of art. This excellent reference book offers information on the development of scientific techniques, from daguerreotype to video and digital imaging. Its major contribution lies in the short biographical sketches of photographers, from the pioneers in the field to the photomontage artists of the 1990s. Included are all the expected artists, from Julia Margaret Cameron and William Henry Fox Talbot to Dorothea Lange and Andy Warhol, but the attention, as well, to the less well-known photographers makes this an important reference tool. The accompanying black-and-white photographs are graphic examples of the art of those named and the addition of "photographers photographed" gives a human face to the name and the work. There are additional assets in this work; the sections on book reviews, booksellers, awards and prizes, films and magazines, and galleries and museums are all vital to the researcher in the field. Photography has come a long way from the camera obscura and this volume provides an excellent guide along this path. Treating the technical and the innovative, the people and the pictures, this encyclopedia makes a fine contribution to the literature for students, scholars, and amateurs. [R: C&RL News, June 99, p. 483; BL, 1 Sept 99, p. 183; Choice, Nov 99, p. 508]—**Paula Frosch**

P

344. **Photographer's Market, 1999: 2,000 Places to Sell Your Photographs.** Megan Lane, ed. Cincinnati, Ohio, Writer's Digest Books/F & W Publications, 1998. 630p. illus. index. $23.99pa. ISBN 0-89879-851-5. ISSN 0147-247X.

Photographer's Market retains its basic organization and purpose in this 1999 edition. As in earlier editions, it is aimed at the person who may be skilled in photography but inexperienced in the business world, one who is looking to move from the amateur to the professional level. The first 45 pages are devoted to such topics as creating a business plan, tax information, copyright information, specific information on dealing with international markets, and charging for one's work—information needed by people trying to succeed in the professional world. Following the 1st section are a series of chapters on various markets, such as consumer publications, trade publications, and stock photography agencies. A section titled "Resources" follows, with lists of helpful

Websites, photography workshops, and schools of photography. The main section of the book is titled "Markets." Each entry describes a particular outlet for photographic work, giving name, address, and telephone and fax numbers. Entries may also include information on what types of photographs the outlet purchases, how many each year, and what prices they pay.

Several new features appear in the 1999 edition. Perhaps most significantly, the editors have added a new index on international markets. Another addition is that of sidebars to several of the chapters on specific markets, in which practitioners in various fields write of their experiences and offer helpful hints. The new edition of *Photographer's Market* still provides useful information in a familiar format, with a few new twists.

—**Terry Ann Mood**

23 Language and Linguistics

GENERAL WORKS

C, P

345. Dalby, Andrew. **Dictionary of Languages: The Definitive Reference to More Than 400 Languages.** New York, Columbia University Press, 1998. 734p. maps. index. $50.00. ISBN 0-231-11568-7.

The book under review is an excellent survey of the languages of the world. There is no attempt at completeness, but the selection is wide enough to satisfy most searches for information. The numerically smallest languages covered are Bislama (a pidgin of the Western Pacific, about 60,000 speakers), Gaelic (in Scotland, 80,000), Kiribati (Micronesia, 70,000), Marshallese (Micronesia, 30,000), Ojibwa (U.S., Canada, 80,000), and Romansch (Switzerland, 65,000). Hawaiian seems to be the language with the smallest number of speakers (2,000) included in the book. The indication of the number of speakers is useful, although sometimes approximate; however reluctantly, one must accept the number, remembering the constant failures of governmental programs to revive the language. Some extinct languages are also covered, not only Akkadian or Latin, but also some like Sogdian. There are also sections on families of languages, such as Turkic or Afro-Asiatic, that contain more information about languages not mentioned individually. For instance, the "click languages" are summarily treated under the heading "Khoisan Languages."

The information given about the languages pertains mostly to their history, both linguistic (affiliation, cultural attributes) and political (periods of oppression, transplanted varieties, development of the standard variety); their geographic spread; and their scripts (with specimens). There is an indication of a few words (usually the first numerals), frequently compared with their counterparts in genetically related languages. If the language uses a script of its own, a short history of the script and illustration of its characters are given. Different alphabets are mentioned, and so are interesting orthographies. The book also provides interesting bits of information in separate boxes, making the work more readable and attractive. For instance, Makonde secret songs are mentioned on page 385.

One important component of the book is the maps indicating the location of practically all the languages mentioned. They are very informative and were obviously drawn for this book. The user of the book, however, must adjust to particulars. First, the maps indicate the contours of the land, the frontiers of states, the large rivers, a few cities, and the area where the language is spoken. Rivers and states are not mentioned by name. Second, while the maps are good, their printing does not always achieve the technical level of representing every minor detail. But these are mere trifling details; on the whole, the maps are immensely helpful.

For deeper study, the linguist will probably prefer the excellent surveys of the languages of the world in William Bright's *International Encyclopedia of Linguists* (see ARBA 93, entry 1050). But for the general public, this is the best source available, one that will offer, to the linguist as well, much interesting information. [R: LJ, 1 May 99, pp. 68-69; Choice, July/Aug 99, p. 1916; RUSQ, Fall 99, p. 88]—**L. Zgusta**

P, S

346.   Trask, R. L. **Key Concepts in Language and Linguistics.** New York, Routledge, 1999. 378p. index. (Key Concepts). $75.00; $18.99pa. ISBN 0-415-15741-2; 0-415-15742-0pa.

Key Concepts in Language and Linguistics is an accessible text for the layperson as well as the specialist. Trask makes the task of explaining such common terms as noun, adjective, and verb, and more esoteric concepts as syntagmatic relation and discourse analysis, both pleasurable and rewarding. The book appears to be the 5th in a series devoted to making current topics (cinema studies, popular music) more understandable to the lay reader.

The book's design is simple yet comprehensive. It is presented as an A to Z guide of the main terms and concepts used in the study of language and linguistics. Clear, readable definitions with multiple examples are provided for the following: terms used in grammatical analysis; branches of linguistics; critical approaches used in studying language; linguistic phenomena, such as code-switching and conversational implicature; and various forms of language from pidgin to standard discourse. Moreover, the entries for each topic trace its origin and mention the key individuals associated with the concept. Extensive cross-references and a lengthy bibliography complement this handy guide to language and linguistics.

One of the more enjoyable aspects of *Key Concepts in Language and Linguistics* is the engaging way in which Trask explains his key concepts. Although clearly demonstrating his mastery of linguistics and language, he succeeds in keeping a sense of humor throughout, even in the more complex sections of the book. Perhaps most helpful are the everyday examples he uses. In discussing connotation, for instance, he notes that "particularly emotive words like *foxhunting, lesbian, multinational*, and even *vegetarian* may produce connotations for different people that are almost wildly different." In addition, it is somewhat mind-boggling to learn that such languages as Basque and Finnish have a dozen or more case distinctions, while English and Romance languages like French and Spanish have only a few. One wonders how it is possible to learn such difficult languages without being born into them.

Trask has not only done his homework but convincingly demonstrates his extensive knowledge of Indo-European languages. This is a work that is both affordable and essential for anyone interested in the science of linguistics and in how language operates on a day-to-day basis. [R: BL, 1 May 99, pp. 1630-1632; Choice, Sept 99, p. 114]—**John B. Romeiser**

ENGLISH-LANGUAGE DICTIONARIES

General Usage

P, S

347.   **Cassell Concise Dictionary with CD-ROM.** rev. ed. Herndon, Va., Mansell/Cassell, 1998. Minimum system requirements: IBM or compatible PC. CD-ROM drive. Windows 95 or Windows NT 4.0. 256-color video adapter. Mouse. 1711p. $29.95 (with CD-ROM). ISBN 0-304-35003-6; 0-304-35015-X (CD-ROM).

Cassell is an English publisher that has published numerous dictionaries since 1891. The *Cassell Concise English Dictionary* was first published in 1989 (see ARBA 90, entry 995), revised and reprinted with amendments and additions in 1994, 1997, and 1998 respectively. The 1998 edition has both print and CD-ROM format and contains more than 250,000 entries and definitions—more words and phrases than any other concise dictionary. The coverage of this dictionary includes not only standard English but also scientific and technical terms. New words covered, such as *World Wide Web, Internet, e-mail*, and *cyberpet*, make this dictionary the most current when compared with other concise dictionaries. Being compiled by an English publisher, obviously this dictionary gives first the modern British spellings. North American alternatives are specified where applicable. To help readers choose the right word, this dictionary has more than 500 notes on correct usage. Another unique feature is its misspelling guide. If the reader sees an "x" in front of a word, he or she is informed that this is a misspelled word. Many people will enjoy the CD-ROM version of this dictionary. It gives readers more choices. One can search by headword, full text, idioms, style of use, area of study, origin, and crossword. For example, if one is interested in finding out how many words are from the French language, one need only to consult the origin feature to search and will receive a list of French words. The CD-ROM version also frees users from carrying around the 1,711-page print dictionary. This dictionary is a good reference tool for anyone who speaks or is learning to speak English. It is also a good replacement for the libraries with out-of-date reference materials.

—**Xiao (Shelley) Yan Zhang**

C, P

348.   **The Concise Oxford Dictionary.** 10th ed. Judy Pearsall, ed. New York, Oxford University Press, 1999. 1666p. $29.95. ISBN 0-19-860287-1.

This 1-volume dictionary from Oxford University Press is a recommended work. The best reason to recommend this edition is its organization. The dictionary's massive sibling, *The Oxford English Dictionary* (2d ed.; see ARBA 90, entry 1006), is considered the authoritative dictionary of the English language, but is difficult for the layperson to use. *The Oxford English Dictionary* (OED) is massive; definitions can last for pages and are full of information necessary to the linguist but which may otherwise confuse the average user. *The Concise Oxford Dictionary* is written, in contrast, for the remainder of the population. The definitions center on the "core" (most literal and central) use of the word in current English, and are written in clear, precise language. Meanings and sub-meanings are well organized, giving the reader a sense of the relationships between differing definitions of the same term. The origins and derivatives parts of the definition begin, respectively, with the word's "origin" and "derivatives," making it much simpler to understand than the comparable parts of the OED. Labels such as "formal," "archaic," "technical," "humorous," and "euphemistic" give a sense of how the word is currently used. The listings include some grammar guidelines and spelling variations.

The front matter includes a preface, introduction, guide to the use of the dictionary, abbreviations, and a note on trademarks and proprietary status. It is as well organized and written as the rest of the dictionary. Another notable quality of the dictionary is its currency. The 2d edition of the OED was published in 1989. Since then, revolutions in knowledge and knowledge access have taken place, and the 10th edition of *The Concise Oxford Dictionary* reflects the new vocabulary with such words as "webmaster," "wicca," "nanotechnology," and "html." This dictionary is highly recommended for any library or for personal use.—**Mary A. Axford**

P, S

349.   **Random House Webster's Basic Dictionary of American English.** New York, Random House, 1998. 524p. $10.95pa. ISBN 0-679-78005-X.

Random House Webster's Basic Dictionary of American English has targeted a rather specialized audience for this new version of its dictionary, but the work will almost certainly prove to be a valuable tool for a variety of individuals, including native speakers. Written primarily for beginning learners of English as a second or foreign language, this new dictionary will undoubtedly draw a large readership for both its excellent content and its highly readable format. Moreover, the dictionary is affordable for classroom and individual use.

One of the most exciting aspects of a new edition of a standard work like Webster's is the inclusion of newly minted words. This volume does not disappoint in this respect, including such recent issues as *digerati*, *dweeb*, *soccer mom* (which already appears to be outdated in many circles), and trendy but probably long-lasting abbreviations such as *ATM*, *PIN*, and *PCS*. However, even newer abbreviations spawned by technological leaps, like DVD, are missing and will surely be found in future editions. It was also helpful to include words related to unusual but significant cultural events in the United States, including the December 26–January harvest festival, Kwanzaa, celebrated in some communities by African Americans. Foreign words, most especially those related to popular ethnic cooking, figure prominently in this new dictionary, such as *fajitas*, *tortilla*, and *taco*. The accepted postal service abbreviations for the 50 states are also listed.

As the dictionary is intended for people who are learning American English as a second language, it offers a useful pronunciation guide based on the International Phonetic Alphabet. There is a relevant discussion of the differences between British and American standard English in which the editors note that the 2 languages differ mainly in their pronunciation and that they are actually quite similar considering the 400 years that have elapsed since they went their separate ways. The reader will also find abundant grammatical information, such as a list of intransitive verbs, irregular verb conjugations, and notations on whether nouns are considered "count" (i.e., can be preceded by "a" or "an") or "noncount."

Considering its relative brevity, *Random House Webster's Basic Dictionary of American English* offers a lot of useful information to anyone seeking to update and expand their knowledge of the language. It could also be a valuable reference work for K-12 and college users (both students and teachers), who will always benefit from a reminder of grammatical points and pronunciation rules.—**John B. Romeiser**

P, S
350.   **Webster's New World College Dictionary.** 4th ed. Michael Agnes, ed. New York, Macmillan General Reference/Simon & Schuster Macmillan, 1999. 1716p. illus. maps. index. $21.95. ISBN 0-02-863119-6.

This latest of the Webster's New World Dictionaries, the 4th edition of the *College Dictionary* is a revision of the 3d edition, originally published in 1988. It continues a line of dictionaries, published since 1951, committed to providing a guide to the vocabulary of general American usage. One therefore seeks and finds modern usage; American pronunciation; definitions written in a current style; American geographical etymology; and attention to American colloquialisms, slang, and idioms, all placed in a context of general English language and not narrowly limited to American colloquial language.

This medium-sized dictionary has 163,000 entries, about 7,500 of them new since the 3d edition. It is illustrated, including some new illustrations since the last edition and a few colored maps. Definitions are clear and concise. The type is small, but easier to read than in the 3rd edition. Perhaps some definitions are too concise: "central processing unit" is an inadequate definition of *cpu*. On the whole, current computer terminology, of the sort frequently needed by typical users of this kind of dictionary, is just adequately but certainly not excellently covered. *E-mail*, *PC*, and *byte* are included; *Unix*, *Y2K*, and *Pentium* are not. The "Reference Supplement" is both expanded and typographically spread out, in comparison to this section in the 3d edition. It contains 45 pages of population statistics (partially updated since 1988), English punctuation, U.S. political documents, meteorological data, chemical elements, and a new section on Mexico, among other things. Its contents are indexed at the end of the dictionary. Biographical and geographical entries are interfiled in the main section of the dictionary.

With its 163,000 entries, this dictionary may be compared in comprehensiveness to the *Oxford Dictionary and Thesaurus* (American ed.; see ARBA 98, entry 994). The later serves a slightly different purpose, with its inclusion of synonyms. It is now outdated by at least three years. In the Oxford dictionary the definitions and synonyms are integrated, but geographical and biographical entries are not. It lacks the etymology and illustrations present in the *New World Dictionary*.

This dictionary is inexpensive for its type and coverage and is apparently well bound. It is recommended for academic, high school, and public libraries, and is also desirable for home purchase and use.—**Florence W. Jones**

Juvenile

S
351.   **The Merriam-Webster and Garfield Dictionary.** Springfield, Mass., Merriam-Webster, 1999. 800p. illus. $12.95pa. ISBN 0-87779-626-2.

The Merriam-Webster and Garfield Dictionary is the most child-friendly dictionary to be published. This innovative dictionary actually encourages use by utilizing a cartoon character that appeals to children of all ages.

This dictionary features the cartoon cat Garfield, in collaboration with its creator Jim Davis, to highlight featured words in the dictionary. At the bottom of the pages that use the highlighted featured word is a comic strip illustrating that particular word's usage.

This dictionary, inspired by Jim Davis, is designed just like every other dictionary and includes a list of common English given names; a list of foreign words and phrases; a section on biographical, biblical, and mythological names; a section on geographical names; signs and symbols; a handbook of style section; and a section on documentation of sources. There is even a special list of wacky definitions that only Garfield could dream up. In the front is a section of explanatory notes, abbreviations used in the work, and a page devoted to pronunciation symbols. It is an extraordinary combination of both dictionary and comic book and is highly recommended.
—**Pamela J. Getchell**

S

352.   **Merriam-Webster's Intermediate Dictionary.** Springfield, Mass., Merriam-Webster, 1998. 943p. illus. $15.95. ISBN 0-87779-479-0.

This dictionary, of about 40,000 word entries, is intended for middle and junior high students. It is preceded by *Merriam-Webster's Elementary Dictionary* (Merriam-Webster, 1994) and followed by *Merriam-Webster's School Dictionary* (see entry 353). All three volumes are highly respected and widely used. For each entry in the main body of this work, syllabification is given, followed by variant spellings, phonetic pronunciation (the pronunciation key is found on each double-page spread), usage indication (e.g., slang, substandard), grammatical classification, and irregular plurals or tense formations when necessary. The definitions follow. They are clear, concise, and suited to the intended audience. As in other Webster dictionaries they are in chronological order. Separate entries are given for homographic words. A few basic words have synonym entries with definitions and usage pointers for each synonym. Some words with interesting origins are given a separate short paragraph called "Word History." There are about 300 "Word Histories" and an equal number of synonym entries. Brief etymologies or usage indicators are sometimes given, but there are no antonyms. The word coverage seems up-to-date. *Dork*, *Internet*, and *World Wide Web* are included, but not *search engine*. Many words considered obscene are absent; for example, *fornicate* is here but not its more frequently used synonyms. Running heads at the top of each page give both the first and last word on the page. Small black-and-white drawings are used to illustrate objects or animals. Special features include several mini-dictionaries at the back; a list of abbreviations, which includes chemical symbols; a biographical directory of more than 1,000 names with one-line identifications; a gazetteer of nearly 3,000 place-names with their pronunciations; and a short section of signs and symbols. The format is attractive, type size is suitable, and the binding is sturdy. This dictionary is highly recommended for students in grades six through nine.—**John T. Gillespie**

S

353.   **Merriam-Webster's School Dictionary.** Springfield, Mass., Merriam-Webster, 1999. 1158p. illus. $15.95. ISBN 0-87779-380-8.

Designed for high school students, this dictionary indicates the expertise of the staff of one of the preeminent dictionary makers in the United States. It compares well with the *Merriam-Webster's Collegiate Dictionary* (10th ed.; see ARBA 94, entry 1076), including about 75 percent of the same words. The definitions, while frequently shorter with few subsections, reflect a strong influence from that volume. The etymologies are also very similar, but with fewer abbreviations, making them easier to understand. The introductory material includes topics such as guidewords, pronunciation, function, form and meaning of words, cross-references, usage, synonyms, abbreviations, and pronunciation symbols. The pronunciation guide also appears on each two-page spread. General abbreviations; a biographical dictionary with historical, biblical, and mythological names; a geographical dictionary; and a brief article on style complete the book.

The back cover of the dictionary claims that it contains 85,000 entries and 91,000 definitions. Terms omitted from this volume that are present in the *Collegiate* volume would probably not be of pressing interest to the average high school student. There are no terms appearing in the *School Dictionary* that are not in the *Collegiate*. Terms such as *CD*, *RAM*, *ROM*, and *grass* as marijuana, are included, as are body parts relating to sexual functions, but not the slang words defined in the *Collegiate* volume.

Nearly every two-page spread includes at least one helpful drawing or chart. The pages have enough white space to be appealing and easy to read. This will be a good dictionary for senior high school students, libraries, and for some middle school students. Libraries and some high school students may also wish to consult the *Collegiate* in book or CD-ROM (see ARBA 98, entry 998) format.—**Betty Jo Buckingham**

Thesauri

S

354.   **The American Heritage Student Thesaurus.** By Paul Hellweg, Joyce LeBaron, and Susannah LeBaron. Westminster, Md., Houghton Mifflin, 1999. 378p. $17.00. ISBN 0-395-93026-X.

According to the cover, *The American Heritage Student Thesaurus* is meant for ages 12 to 16, in grades 7 to 10. A two-page introduction defines a thesaurus as a book of synonyms, or "a book of word choices." According to the authors, more than 6,000 words are listed as main entries, with approximately 100,000 synonyms in all. After explaining how to use the thesaurus, the editors invite readers' comments and questions and provide an address where they may be reached.

Each entry lists the part of speech of the word, followed by several synonyms and a sentence using the entry word. When a word has several uses, the most common are put first. Finally, the word's antonyms are listed. Occasionally, a blue box will give information about word groups. For example, the word *firework* is defined as "an explosive device set off to create bright lights and loud noises for amusement. Firework is a general term with no true synonyms." Then the box lists and describes some specific types of fireworks, such as pinwheel, Roman candle, serpent, skyrocket, and torpedo.

Certainly every writer, no matter what age, should learn to rely on a thesaurus. *The American Heritage Student Thesaurus* seems built to hold up well to classroom use. However, this volume's vocabulary level and content seem more suited to 5th through 7th graders than to those in higher grades.—**Kay O. Cornelius**

S

355.   **Scholastic Children's Thesaurus.** By John K. Bollard. Illustrated by Mike Reed. New York, Scholastic, 1998. 256p. illus. index. $15.95. ISBN 0-590-96785-1.

As an educational resource for young learners, this thesaurus is designed to improve vocabulary, language, and communication skills. It contains more than 500 entries and 2,700 synonyms. One distinguishing feature of this thesaurus is that definitions and example sentences are given to provide more in-depth understanding of the words and their synonyms. Information boxes provide additional data, such as parts of speech and differences in grammatical usage. Entries are also cross-referenced to direct readers to other groups of related synonyms. For example, the entry for "nice" points readers to also look at "friendly," "good," and "great."

The index lists all entry words and synonyms alphabetically, making it easy for users to locate a word they have in mind. Also included in the index for many of the entry words (which are listed in capital letters) are antonyms that are also listed in the thesaurus. This is a great learning tool for young readers and writers. The introduction provides instructions on how to use the thesaurus, but it would be beneficial for a parent or teacher to help children get started. [R: LJ, Dec 98, pp. 540-542; SLJ, Feb 99, pp. 132-134]—**Cari Ringelheim**

NON-ENGLISH-LANGUAGE DICTIONARIES

Chinese

C, P

356.   **Chinese-Pinyin-English Dictionary for Learners.** Wang Huan, ed. Boston, Cheng & Tsui, 1998. 1250p. $28.95pa. ISBN 0-88727-316-5.

This dictionary is exceptional in many ways. The main strength is its focus on learners. Students of the Chinese language are faced with the daunting task of learning to read and write characters, speak and understand, and most importantly for this volume, read transliterations in several styles. The Wade-Giles system, perfected in the nineteenth century, was joined by the French style, and most recently the Pinyin style created by the communist government. Being the most recent, it lacks many reference resources. This well-organized and complete dictionary goes far in correcting that problem. Compiled by teachers of Mandarin Chinese as well as the usual scholars, this 10-year project is extremely accessible and easy for the student to use. The 30,000 entries are presented with useful details. Each entry includes grammar usage and pronunciation, definitions in English and Chinese, sample sentences in Chinese characters, and additional notes. This dictionary is further enhanced by 2 indexes, 10 appendixes, and an overall guide. It is an excellent addition to any library.—**Linda L. Lam-Easton**

French

C, S

357.   Strutz, Henry. **Dictionary of French Slang and Colloquial Expressions.** Hauppauge, N.Y., Barron's Educational Series, 1999. 355p. $8.95pa. ISBN 0-7641-0345-8.

In the ever-changing world of language, slang is one of the most transitory and fleeting forms of communication. In one moment, a word changes from a standard usage to something completely different. New expressions rise and fall as each generation or group tries to distinguish itself from others. No longer does one need to try to discern current slang and colloquial expressions only in English, but in other languages as well. This work fits into that category quite well, with French slang in use currently. A student of French or current culture will find this an invaluable addition to the shelves, providing access to words and phrases ranging from humorous to earthy. The faint of heart are to be forewarned—all aspects of life and living are covered in detail, but then that too is part of an evolving language. For the price, any academic or public library will find this a useful addition to their collection of dictionaries on slang terms and colloquial expressions.—**Gregory Curtis**

Japanese

C, P, S

358.   **The Compact Nelson Japanese-English Character Dictionary.** By John H. Haig. North Clarendon, Vt., Tuttle, 1999. 779p. $27.95pa. ISBN 0-8048-2037-6.

This dictionary is an abridged edition of Andrew Nelson's award-winning *The Modern Reader's Japanese-English Character Dictionary.* The dictionary contains more than 3,000 main-entry kanji (Chinese characters) and more than 30,000 *jyukugo* (Chinese character compounds). Unlike an English dictionary, which arranges the entry words alphabetically, this dictionary, like any other kanji dictionary, lists kanji entries in the increasing order of the number of strokes of the radical (the left side of Chinese characters). This arrangement may inherently discourage anyone from looking up any kanji. But to assist the user, the author instructs precisely what radical of kanji the user should search for in order to look up any kanji. The user, who should already know how to read kanji but who does not know the English meaning of a word, can follow the instructions provided, but can also look a word up instead through the *on* (Chinese-derived) or *kun* (native) reading, a section about which is provided in the appendix. Many kanji entries are followed by useful *jyukugo* with an English translation but not by illustrative sentences. The dictionary includes 11 appendixes that contain information about radicals and explanations on how to find kanji and how to determine the radical. Since the number of Japanese words introduced to English-speaking people has been increasing, scholars, business people, or school libraries would benefit from having a Japanese-English dictionary that contains kanji. The brevity and lucidity of this dictionary make it recommendable. For greater comprehensiveness and wider coverage, *NTC's New Japanese-English Character Dictionary* (see ARBA 94, entry 1121) is preferable, if more expensive.—**Seiko Mieczkowski**

Russian

P, S

359.   **Random House Russian-English, English-Russian Dictionary.** By Howard H. Keller. New York, Random House, 1999. 565p. $25.00. ISBN 0-679-44964-7.

This bilingual dictionary is designed to provide accurate and up-to-date information in regard to the subject matter covered. The aim of this new dictionary is to cover as much current vocabulary as possible. There are 2 major sections in this publication, with about 64,000 entries: the Russian-English dictionary (pp. 1–251), and the English-Russian dictionary (pp. 253–563). In the front and back of the book are pronunciation guides for English and Russian, lists of abbreviations, and tables including irregular verbs. In both sections, all terms are entered in a single alphabetic listing. Some of the main entries contain compounds, phrases, and expressions that appear as boldface subentries that are preceded by a long dash. A number of main entries contain run-on derived words that are formed by adding a prefix or suffix. An explanatory note, gloss, or field label is given in parentheses if the meaning that is being translated is not self-evident. In the English-Russian section, the dictionary shows the pronunciation of English headwords, as a version of the International Phonetic Alphabet (IPA). In the Russian-English section, each Russian word is given in its basic form with the correct stress mark for that form. Comparing to the most popular analogous dictionary by K. Katzner, this publication is better adapted for Russian consumers, because it provides the pronunciation of English words and tables of irregular verbs. On the other hand, a glossary of geographical names and other proper nouns would be more helpful. Also, a number of set expressions and phrases could be expanded sufficiently. However, this dictionary is of valuable assistance to all Russians who would like to use up-to-date English.—**Ludmila N. Ilyina**

24 Literature

GENERAL WORKS

Bibliography

C, P

360. **The Comparative Reader: A Handlist of Basic Reading in Comparative Literature.** John T. Kirby, ed. New Haven, Conn., Chancery Press, 1998. 211p. (Comparative Studies, v.1). $26.95pa. ISBN 1-890657-01-8.

This book belongs in every library whose patrons include serious students and scholars of literature and rhetoric. *The Comparative Reader* consolidates bibliographies for the study of comparative literature by providing basic reading lists (modules) about the basic foundational texts in the field; about texts that examine the literature of one particular part of the world; and about ones that explore a particular school of literary criticism, era of rhetoric, or visual literacy (the figurative and plastic arts as well as film, television, and video). Each module gives bibliographic information for the most important 30 or 40 texts in a particular area, largely the kind of works that master's students taking written comprehensive exams would be expected to know. Compiled by leading scholars in the field (the majority of whom are colleagues of the editor at Purdue University), each of the 47 modules lists seminal works, the study of which would certainly advance most readers' understanding of the topic—from African literature, French literature, Indian literature, Japanese literature, and Spanish American literature to cultural studies, gay and lesbian studies, rhetoric, and semiotics. Kirby's introduction contextualizes issues of canonicity and multiculturalism in a thought-provoking manner. [R: Choice, Sept 98, p. 86]

—**G. Douglas Meyers**

C, P, S

361. Harner, James L. **Literary Research Guide: An Annotated Listing of Reference Sources in English Literary Studies.** 3d ed. New York, Modern Language Association of America, 1998. 772p. index. $37.50; $19.75pa. ISBN 0-87352-573-6; 0-87352-574-4pa.

This outstanding guide, intended for those seriously interested in English literature, has been considered a required purchase for library reference collections since 1990 (see ARBA 94, entry 1139; ARBA 91, entry 1097). Harner, an important scholar and bibliographer, delights in reviewing the strengths and weaknesses of various editions of important works as well as well-known titles that have been around for too long. Librarians will use his comments to make decisions about collection development as well as weeding collections. Indeed, many in academe will use the guide to discover sources that remained unknown to them throughout their graduate studies, including subject bibliographies, abstracts, surveys of research, genre histories, annals, and chronologies. Harner also points to works in progress, giving them the benefit of the doubt now but promising a reevaluation with the next edition (every three to four years).

This is clearly an important work in progress as well. There are 47 titles that have been reevaluated and removed, 560 entries are revised, and 60 new titles are added. This edition contains more than 1,200 entries, and the annotations refer to 1,331 additional books, articles, and electronic resources. For major reference sources, the author cites reviews (approximately 752) that add value to his annotations. And what annotations! Lay users benefit from reading descriptions of a source; scholars will delight in Harner's evaluative comments. It is helpful to read that more than one subscription reference set of long standing is considered "virtually useless" as a critical guide. Recommended works making the cut have their shortcomings as well. On and on they go, encouraging both scholar and serious student to read one entry after another, one section (there are 21 of them) after another. The discussion of database utilities (OCLC, RLIN) is helpful; the discussions of database vendors (Ovid Technologies, Wilsonline, Dialog) are discussions in progress. Pay attention as new editions are made available.

This guide is dense with information. All bibliographic citations are complete, and cross-references, indexes, organization, and pleasing topography contribute to the guide's reference value.—**Milton H. Crouch**

Dictionaries and Encyclopedias

C

362.   Ferber, Michael. **A Dictionary of Literary Symbols.** New York, Cambridge University Press, 1999. 263p. $69.95. ISBN 0-521-59128-7.

This book, the first of its kind and long overdue, describes traditional symbols used over many years by many authors. The descriptions are impressive. They explore the derivation of words used as symbols and elaborate on the probable reasons for their symbolism. The words are traced by means of citations and quotations from various writers through biblical and classical works to twentieth-century writings (primarily poetry).

The entries vary in length from approximately one-half of a page to several pages. Because the animal kingdom has been a source of symbols from the earliest literature to the present, for example, there is a one-half page entry for the generic word "beast" and separate entries of varying lengths for the words ape, ass, bat, deer, dog, leopard, lion, serpent, and so on. The author states in his introduction that he includes such words as "dawn, death, dream, nature, and certain other subjects not so much for what they have stood for as for what other things have stood for them." Hundreds of cross-references and quotations add to the body of the work.

The body of the work is preceded by a list of abbreviations. More than nine pages of authors cited, including their birth and death dates and the language or nation they represent, follow the body. A bibliography completes the book. An index is unnecessary, since all entries are arranged in alphabetic order.

Written by a professor of English and humanities, this scholarly work is highly recommended for all students of American and English literature faced with writing papers where they are expected to expound upon the symbolism found in a given poem or story. The author admits that the book was, in fact, inspired by such a student. Suggestions for researching symbols not found in this book are included in the author's introduction. This work will also be a valuable resource for literary scholars and practicing writers. They should be able to find it in any academic library.—**Lois Gilmer**

CHILDREN'S AND YOUNG ADULT LITERATURE

Children's Literature

Bibliography

S

363.   **Best Books for Children: Preschool Through Grade 6.** 6th ed. John T. Gillespie, ed. New Providence, N.J., R. R. Bowker, 1998. 1537p. index. $48.00. ISBN 0-8352-4099-1.

A bibliographic guide to a multitude of fiction and nonfiction books for preschool through sixth grade levels. The editor has aimed this guide to provide a list of books to satisfy both recreational and academic needs for young readers. In this sixth edition, there are more than 18,000 entries, of which over half are new. Each book listed has been recommended from sources such as *Booklist* and *School Library Journal*.

Entries are organized under major subject headings such as mathematics, fairy tales, and sports figures. In each listing, the guide provides basic bibliographic information, a brief synopsis, and review citations for books published between 1985 and March 1998. The editor has also noted any books that have been awarded Caldecott or Newbery medals. The four indexes—author, illustrator, book title, and subject/grade level—make locating specific entries very user-friendly. The preface also gives readers information about how to use the guide, including abbreviations that are utilized.

Readers need to keep in mind that certain types of books have been omitted from the bibliography, including reference books such as dictionaries and encyclopedias, and mass market series such as Nancy Drew and Hardy Boys books. Thus, this work is very extensive, but it is limited and may not contain listings for specific titles that readers may be looking for.—**Cari Ringelheim**

P, S

364.   Dole, Patricia Pearl. **Children's Books About Religion.** Englewood, Colo., Libraries Unlimited, 1999. 230p. index. $32.00. ISBN 1-56308-515-1.

When Dole set out to locate books on religion for children suitable for inclusion in public and school libraries, she found that she had to consult religious and mainstream publishers, church and public libraries, and bookstores. Limited sources within the library science profession were available, although Dole completed a master's degree project on the subject in the 1980s. In this resource, the author devotes sections to the world's major religions (including Native American religions), with subsections on major U.S. faiths and world religions.

Dole lists books on comparative religions, God, prayer, the Bible, biographies of religious leaders, and church history. Each book has an annotation of two to four sentences, and every section has a list called "Old and Noteworthy," most published in the 1980s. These have no annotation, but only the author, title, publisher, and date. She understands our discomfort with "didactic, saccharine, or doctrinaire material." Her lists include many series books, which is not negative because their authors take care to define and summarize, and the books are usually attractively packaged. Dole made unusually bad choices under the heading "Fundamentalism." Exceptionally awkward for the scanning librarian is Dole's omission of recommended age or grade levels; a selector must examine every review for this information. Once public and school librarians are inspired to select from the amount of religion-related books available, this book will provide a boost to publishers of quality religious books for children and a stimulus to authors. Dole states, "Since religion and spirituality are an integral part of every culture in the world, access to information on all types of faiths should be freely available to readers of all ages." Librarians should not suspend judgment when using this book, but choose it for a look at the many possibilities in an often-neglected subject area.—**Edna M. Boardman**

P, S

365.   **The Horn Book Guide Interactive.** [CD-ROM]. Westport, Conn., Heinemann, 1999. $35.00 (single user); $115.00 (network).

This CD-ROM is based on the *Horn Book Guide to Children's and Young Adult Books* (vol. 7, no. 2; see ARBA 98, entry 1078), which is published twice a year, and contains approximately 4,000 reviews per year. This product is a collection of all of the reviews published since 1990. Entries include the standard bibliographic information about the book (title, author or illustrator, series, publisher, page length, ISBN, and year). Also included in the entry are the genre, rating, grade level, and subjects. There are more than 29,000 short reviews that are descriptive and critical. The reviews also include notes about color and black-and-white illustrations or photographs. Also noted is whether or not an index, bibliography, or glossary is present. Searchable indexes are provided for all the elements present in the entry. Each book is rated on a six-point rating scale: outstanding and noteworthy, superior well above average, recommended satisfactory, recommended with minor flaws, marginal seriously flawed, and unacceptable.

The database is alphabetically arranged by the author's last name. Reviews can show up for individual books or books that are part of a series. Users are able to search multiple index fields by typing in text or selecting from a list of choices. Searches can be done by grade level (choose from those listed), author (enter last name), and genre (fiction or nonfiction). Searches by rating (1–6, 1 being the highest), review (choose from keywords), subject (type in subjects you want), title (type in title desired), year (choose from years listed), and full-text (allows for searching of all fields) are also available. There are clearly marked navigational buttons and a menu bar. Lists can be displayed that meet the search criteria, and records or portions of records can be marked for printing. This CD-ROM is aimed at the teacher or librarian and would be of benefit to school and public libraries, and those academic libraries that have a teacher education program that offers children's and young adult literature classes.—**Jan S. Squire**

P, S

366.   Lewis, Valerie V., and Walter M. Mayes. **Valerie & Walter's Best Books for Children: A Lively, Opinionated Guide.** New York, Avon Books, 1998. 708p. index. $15.00pa. ISBN 0-380-79438-1.

The publication of bibliographies of best books for children is, to be sure, not a new concept; however, these authors bring to their readers a somewhat different approach to this literature form, as indicated in their subtitle, *A Lively, Opinionated Guide.* The authors, recognized for their expertise in the world of children's literature, have compiled a list of 2,000 titles (slimmed down from an original list of 8,000) that they profess they "couldn't live without." To achieve their goal and to reach consensus on selections for inclusion, they combined their experiences as storytellers, read-aloud presenters, extensive reviewers of children¹s books, reactions from their listeners, and their own love of children¹s books. Acknowledging that most people are more apt to remember a title than an author's name, they entered each book alphabetically by title. The entries are grouped into age categories, including a list of recommended books for all ages and titles for the very young, and conclude with young adult selections. Their chatty, humorous comments accompanying each selection do, in fact, reflect their own biases. However, the resulting annotations make for enjoyable reading and may well pique the curiosity of the reader. Another helpful feature is their comprehensive, cross-referenced theme appendix, which appears to be thorough.

This "pooling of impressions" serves as an extensive and selective guide to both the oldies, such as Tolkien's *The Hobbit,* and books by current authors, such as the prolific and melodious writings of Jane Yolen. For anyone seeking to guide children toward becoming lifetime lovers of books and reading, this qualifies as a worthy purchase. Do not overlook reading the witty introduction; it sets the tone for what is to follow. [R: SLJ, Oct 98, p. 51]
—**Margaret Denman-West**

P, S

367.   Miller, Wanda J. **Teaching U.S. History Through Children's Literature: Post-World War II.** Englewood, Colo., Libraries Unlimited, 1998. 229p. illus. index. $27.50pa. ISBN 1-56308-581-X.

The purpose of this handbook is "to provide teachers with information to begin or expand their use of quality children's literature in the teaching of United States history" (p. xi). To that end the editor, herself a teacher, recommends specific titles for an entire class to read and discuss, offers brief information about the author, suggests group activities, lists discussion questions, and explains vocabulary terms. Additional suggestions are offered for small groups.

Individual chapters cover the Korean War, the Civil Rights movement, the Women's Rights movement, space exploration, the Vietnam War, multicultural heritage, and the Persian Gulf War. The chapter on multicultural heritage provides the most extensive bibliography and gives titles for second through ninth graders. The final chapter identifies professional resources and computer resources and offers ideas for teachers of social studies and English to use in evaluating students.

Unfortunately, the work does not explore the role that the school library media specialist can play in these collaborative efforts. Media specialists can use the annotated bibliographies to identify resources for the collection.
—**Phyllis J. Van Orden**

P, S

368.   Thiessen, Diane, Margaret Matthias, and Jacquelin Smith. **The Wonderful World of Mathematics: A Critically Annotated List of Children's Books in Mathematics.** 2d ed. Reston, Va., National Council of Teachers of Mathematics, 1998. 355p. index. $17.95pa. ISBN 0-87353-439-5.

Those with a phobia to mathematics and those who love math will appreciate this book. The title of the book may frighten some who do not love math but once inside, the reader finds a wonderful resource of mathematics topics and approximately 550 trade books related to the concept. Parents will have fun using the suggested titles with their children at home, teachers will have some helpful trade books to utilize with a math lesson, and librarians will have a guide to the best mathematics books in print.

In order to be included in this bibliography a book has to be in print and have math for a primary theme. The committee of reviewers arranged the books into topics and then gave them a rating on their usefulness in teaching the math concept. This is the 2d edition of this bibliography but 60 percent of the titles are new and the other 40 percent are still in print. Some of the sections list five or six books that may be out-of-print but are still considered exceptional titles. Textbooks and teacher workbooks were not included.

Each section of the book is arranged by topics that range from counting to measurement to geometry. The introduction of the math topic makes this book better than most bibliographies. It does not teach how to do the math concept, but it gives examples of how parents and teachers have used the books to successfully teach children about math. Some of the topics are unique and interesting, such as using quilts to teach geometry.

Once the topic is introduced, the trade books related to that concept are listed alphabetically by author. Each book is given a complete bibliographic citation, a grade level designation, a rating for its usefulness in teaching the topic, and a paragraph describing the book.

The format of the book is user-friendly with a good table of contents and indexes for author and title. Most of the suggested titles seem to be aimed at preschool and elementary school grades, but some of the picture books may be favorites of older students or adults, such as Jon Scieszka's *Math Curse*.—**Suzanne Julian**

Biography

P, S

369.   McElmeel, Sharron L. **100 Most Popular Children's Authors: Biographical Sketches and Bibliographies.** Englewood, Colo., Libraries Unlimited, 1999. 495p. illus. index. (Popular Authors Series). $48.00. ISBN 1-56308-646-8.

The compilation of this volume is based upon more than 3,000 teacher and student responses to a 1997 survey that attempted to identify the top 100 of the most important authors and illustrators of children's literature. Teachers, librarians, and students will find this easy-to-read volume useful in identifying and reading about popular authors' backgrounds and their works. Most of the books listed here are intended for an elementary or middle school audience. Please note that the author has also published a volume entitled *The 100 Most Popular Young Adult Authors: Biographical Sketches and Bibliographies* (see ARBA 98, entry 1102).

Entries are alphabetically arranged by the author's last name, and in some cases include a photograph. Each entry includes a birth and death date, an indication of the broad genre the author's work falls into, any books they have written in a series, and a biographical essay. Under the books and notes section of the entry is a bibliography (sometimes annotated) of the author's books on a certain subject, books in a series, and sources to consult for further information on the author. An appendix is included for photography credits and there are two indexes.

The genre index is alphabetically arranged and includes genres such as adventure fiction, biographies, contemporary realistic fiction, fantasy, historical fiction, humorous stories, mystery, nonfiction, poetry, and sports fiction. Underneath each genre the author is listed in alphabetic order by last name. Page numbers are not included. The general index is an alphabetic list that includes the author's name and titles of works mentioned in the author's biography. Page numbers are provided and the ones that reflect the main entry for an author are in bold typeface. Books listed in the bibliographies of each section and genres are not included in this index. [R: BL, 1 Sept 99, p. 182]—**Jan S. Squire**

P, S

370.   Murphy, Barbara Thrash. **Black Authors and Illustrators of Books for Children and Young Adults: A Biographical Dictionary.** New York, Garland, 1999. 513p. illus. index. (Garland Reference Library of the Humanities, v.21). $70.00. ISBN 0-8153-2004-3.

It is heartening to witness the growth of this work since its initial publication in 1987. Murphy does an admirable job of continuing the endeavors of the late Barbara Rollock in introducing children and educators to black authors and illustrators. Updating the more than 150 entries from the 2d edition and adding 121 new names to the book, this latest edition contains a total of 274 biographical sketches of modern and contemporary creators of children's books, along with selected bibliographies of their works. Black-and-white photographs (more than 120 new to this volume) accompany many of the sketches. Reproductions (again black-and-white) of a number of book jackets appear in an appendix. A second appendix lists chronologically awards and honor books, and a third contains a state-by-state directory of bookstores and distributors. The book also has two indexes—one for book titles and the other for authors and illustrators.

The biographies range in length from one paragraph to several pages and many were written by the illustrators and authors themselves, so the coverage is not consistent, nor does treatment reflect the importance of the individual. Even birth dates are left out of some of the entries. The biographies would be more useful if they followed a set format that contained similar information for each individual. In addition, the book could be made more attractive by integrating the covers into the biographies, rather than relegating them to an appendix. One hopes that future editions will remedy these rather minor shortcomings. However, in spite of the deficiencies, the book offers an abundance of valuable information to students and educators. It is a worthwhile purchase for school and public libraries.—**Barbara Ittner**

Quotation Books

P, S

371.   **Scholastic Treasury of Quotations for Children.** By Adrienne Betz. New York, Scholastic, 1998. 254p. $16.95. ISBN 0-590-27146-6.

Scholastic Treasury of Quotations for Children is an outstanding reference work for libraries and classroom use. A wonderful introduction to the concept of quotations, the book is targeted for a younger audience but is equally informative for adults. The book is divided into two main sections. The first section contains the quotations arranged by subjects. The second section has brief biographies of all the people quoted in the book and indicates the subject where they are quoted. The table of contents is arranged alphabetically by subject to help locate quotations about a specific topic. Some sections are highlighted in special boxes that contain more information about special quotations and the people who said them. There are cross-references at the end of some sections that point out similar topics containing related quotations.

Betz has provided an excellent introduction to the book. In it she explains the history of quotations and how books of quotations originated. Betz also discusses how one can use quotations in speaking and writing to introduce an idea; describe a person, place, or concept; add authority and support to opinions; borrow titles from old proverbs and literary works; twist a quotation to make a point; and use a favorite quotation to add style. The author selected quotations for this book because each says a lot in a few words. The goal was to create a balanced collection by including quotations that state clear and direct messages, present a variety of opinions, reflect knowledge and experiences of experts, and present famous statements from English and American literature and history.

Finally, Betz explains the difference between proverbs and quotations and provides several examples of books containing collections of proverbs. *Scholastic Treasury of Quotations for Children* is a compact, concise, and powerful resource book. It is a delightful browse and an equally serious study for those wanting quotations and information about quotations. It is a must-have for all school and public libraries. [R: SLJ, Feb 99, p. 132]
—**Mary L. Trenerry**

Young Adult Literature

P, S

372.   **Lives and Works: Young Adult Authors.** Danbury, Conn., Grolier, 1999. 8v. illus. index. $255.00/set. ISBN 0-7172-9227-4.

Lives and Works: Young Adult Authors is an eight-volume set of brief author biographies designed especially for the middle school student. The more than 250 authors profiled include both modern and classical writers ranging from William Shakespeare to Anne Frank to Francesca Lia Block. Each three- to four-page biography includes a picture; a quote from a major work; a brief overview of the author's life; a description and brief, critical analysis of the author's major works; a list of selected works by and about the author; and when available, a Web address. All eight volumes include a table of contents for the individual volume and a master index for all volumes. The master index has references to authors, titles, and subjects, which makes it useful for finding multiple books about a topic. Although the set is designed for the middle school reader to learn about individual authors, the design of the index should also prove useful for teachers and librarians looking for additional works on specific subjects.

The format of the volumes makes for easy, interesting reading but does not allow for any in-depth student research. The strength of the set lies in its up-to-date coverage of both modern and historical authors who are frequently read as part of the curriculum or for pleasure reading. [R: BL, 1 May 99, p. 1632; BR, Sept/Oct 99, p. 74]

—**Janet Hilbun**

FICTION

General Works

P, S

373.   Pearl, Nancy, with Martha Knappe and Joyce G. Saricks. **Now Read This: A Guide to Mainstream Fiction, 1978-1998.** Englewood, Colo., Libraries Unlimited, 1999. 432p. index. (Genreflecting Advisory Series). $65.00. ISBN 1-56308-659-X.

Readers' advisors or librarians who attempt to make suggestions to their patrons on what to read next will welcome this book. The compilers, who are librarians, library science students, and avid readers, after careful reading and animated discussion decided upon the "appeal characteristics" of mainstream fiction published between 1978 and 1998. According to them, "appeal characteristics" are those qualities that best describe a book's strengths and set it apart from other books. Mainstream fiction omits genre fiction like mysteries, romances, science fiction, westerns, and fantasy, and is limited to that which explores "aspects of human experiences: love, fear, despair, hatred, aging, and death as well as moral and ethical decisions and choices people make" (p. vii). *Now Read This* divides 1,000 titles into 4 categories based on their "appeal characteristics"—setting, story, characters, and language.

For each entry there is a bibliographic citation; a brief annotation; a listing of "second appeal," if applicable; subjects; and an indication if the book is recommended for discussion in book groups. Following this are two to four titles that might be read next.

Indexes include a title, a subject, and an author index. Bold typeface is used for title and author main entries. Because award-winning books are favored for inclusion, a list of book awards appears in the appendix. This volume, with its ease of use and carefully designed format, is not only appealing but invaluable to the readers' advisor who works with adults.—**Sara R. Mack**

Crime and Mystery

P, S

374.   Bleiler, Richard J. **Reference Guide to Mystery and Detective Fiction.** Englewood, Colo., Libraries Unlimited, 1999. 391p. index. (Reference Sources in the Humanities Series). $55.00. ISBN 1-56308-380-9.

This reference guide is a well-organized compilation of 749 entries, including Websites, on mystery and detective fiction. The introduction explains not only what has been included, but also precisely what has not—thrillers, westerns, adventure stories, true crime, and espionage.

The volume is organized by various types of bibliographies, including encyclopedias; readers' guides; genres (e.g., classic British, locked door, police detective); regional guides; magazine indexes; cataloging guides; media catalogs; and publishers. By far the largest category is that of more than 200 individual authors alphabetically arranged. Books that list awards, such as the Edgar and the Agatha, are mentioned. The "Directory of Dealers and Price Guides" is helpful for writers, and a selective listing of electronic sources is followed by addresses of journals and periodicals specializing in mystery writing as well as the addresses for professional organizations.

Each section is introduced by a scope note explaining what is covered and where the user may turn for more specific information. Following the bibliographic information on each work is a description of its intent, organization, content, and often an evaluative opinion. In the rare cases where the editor has not seen the work, it is so noted. An extensive index, by item number, ensures the finding of material. With this one volume, students and teachers will have all of the information needed to find any aspect of the genre. [R: LJ, 1 Oct 99, p. 78; Choice, Dec 99, p. 686; BL, 15 Dec 99, p. 804]—**Charlotte Lindgren**

P

375.   Riley, Dick, and Pam McAllister. **The Bedside, Bathtub, & Armchair Companion to Sherlock Holmes.** New York, Continuum Publishing, 1999. 216p. illus. $29.95; $19.95pa. ISBN 0-8264-1140-1; 0-8264-1116-9pa.

Sherlock Holmes fans will welcome this compendium of facts, trivia, and puzzles. The 60 capsules briefly provide information on the principal predicament and first publication of each of Conan Doyle's 56 short stories and 4 novels featuring Sherlock Holmes. Each capsule also includes notable features, quotations, or oddities and discrepancies. A 16-page biography of Arthur Conan Doyle details his life and interest in spiritualism. Other essays discuss the illustrators who determined Holmes' familiar appearance, actors who created his mannerisms, values of British money in the nineteenth century, life in Victorian England, crime, colonialism, the ranks of English society, Holmes' attitude toward women and drugs, and a glossary of Victorian terms.

Information is provided about many of the almost 400 Sherlock Holmes societies that exist worldwide and their Websites are provided. There are lists of popular mementos and collectibles. Parodies of the great detective are described as well. Black-and-white line drawings and engravings appear on almost every page, depicting actual people such as Doyle, James Bell (the inspiration for Holmes), and the various actors who played the roles of Watson and Holmes, along with cartoons and illustrations for the stories.

One need not be a serious scholar of Sherlock Holmes o enjoy browsing this volume, although the various puzzles presume a thorough knowledge of the mysteries. Even devoted followers will find much that is new in this companion.—**Charlotte Lindgren**

Historical Fiction

P, S

376.   Adamson, Lynda G. **American Historical Fiction: An Annotated Guide to Novels for Adults and Young Adults.** Phoenix, Ariz., Oryx Press, 1999. 405p. index. $45.50. ISBN 1-57356-067-7.

Adamson has compiled an annotated bibliography of 3,387 fiction titles covering U.S. history from before 1600 through the 1980s. For the purpose of the book, historical fiction is defined as a period earlier than which the reader is familiar. Although labeled for young adults as well as adults, only 25 percent of the titles are designated for the young adult audience of ninth grade or older. Most of these were chosen from lists in *School Library Journal* or *Booklist* and are noted with a diamond symbol. The volume will be more useful to adults seeking U.S. historical fiction or libraries building adult collections. It complements and expands the listings in *Dickinson's American Historical Fiction* (see ARBA 87, entry 1134), which the author originally sought to update. There is some duplication between the two books; however, Adamson includes more popular fiction. Vandelia L. VanMeter's *America in Historical Fiction* (see ARBA 98, entry 1114) will serve the young adult reader better. Titles for this volume were chosen from Library of Congress holdings and review journals since 1980. Copyright dates range from 1820 to 1989.

The titles are organized into 13 time periods and are listed alphabetically by author within each division. Titles are consecutively numbered, making referencing easy. If a title spans more than one era, it was placed in the period in which the book began. Entries provide expected bibliographic information: author; title; date of publication; recent reprint, if applicable; number of pages; setting; main character; genre; and awards. The descriptive annotations are brief and limited to one sentence.

The appendixes and indexes are a major strength of the book. The two appendixes are comprised of a list of award-winning books arranged alphabetically by award and an alphabetic list by author of titles suitable for the young adult audience. Five indexes—author, title, genre, geographic, and subject—provide extensive methods of locating titles. The 23 genre headings are defined in the preface. [R: LJ, Dec 98, p. 84; BR, Sept/Oct 99, p. 76]
—**Elaine Ezell**

P, S

377.   Adamson, Lynda G. **World Historical Fiction: An Annotated Guide to Novels for Adults and Young Adults.** Phoenix, Ariz., Oryx Press, 1999. 719p. index. $45.50. ISBN 1-57356-066-9.

More than 6,000 historical fiction titles set outside the United States are covered in this welcome tool for the readers' advisor. Espousing a reader-friendly definition of historical fiction, Adamson includes works that were contemporary when written but now belong to a bygone time, such as books by Jane Austen as well as books written more than 25 years after the specific time period setting. Each numbered entry (arranged geographically by time period and then alphabetically by author and title) provides bibliographical information, a concise descriptive annotation, and genre descriptors. Thirty-two genre descriptors, defined in the preface, are used. Books that may be suitable for young adult readers are indicated by a diamond-shaped symbol, but historical fiction written specifically for the young adult market is not included. Appendix 2 lists the books suitable for young adult readers and appendix 1 lists award-winning titles. There are also author, title, genre, subject, and place and time indexes. Some books in series have a parenthetical note to series title and number while on others the preceding books are mentioned in the annotation. Others have no series information noted, but the annotations include the character's name indicating a connection.

This does not provide all that a readers' advisor would like, such as cross-references to indicate that Victoria Holt, Jean Plaidy, and Philippa Carr were all one and the same or that the Angelique books by Anne Golon were originally published in the U.S. as being by Sergeanne Golon. Unfortunately, the early books in Winston Graham's Poldark series are excluded, perhaps because they are out-of-print, but they are still found in many libraries and it would have been nice to have them here, as later books in the series are listed. It would have been preferable in the case of series to include all titles regardless of the print status. This is an excellent addition to readers' advisory collections for public, secondary, and academic libraries as well as a good resource for teachers who use fiction in teaching world history. [R: LJ, 1 May 99, p. 68; Choice, May 99, p. 1590; BR, Sept/Oct 99, p. 76]

—**Diana Tixier Herald**

Romance

P, S
378.   Ramsdell, Kristin. **Romance Fiction: A Guide to the Genre.** Englewood, Colo., Libraries Unlimited, 1999. 435p. index. (Genreflecting Advisory Series). $45.00. ISBN 1-56308-335-3.

A glance at the title of this work might lead one to believe that it is a straightforward bibliography of romance fiction. It is instead a scholarly discussion and review of the literature, aimed principally at librarians who buy this literature and who must satisfy eager romance readers. In this 2d edition of the 1987 *Happily Ever After: A Guide to Reading Interests in Romance Fiction* (see ARBA 88, entry 1147), Ramsdell adds four chapters, including one on ethnic/multicultural romances and one devoted to the popular regency period romances; drops some chapters, including the one on young adult romances, which Ramsdell believes deserves its own book-length review; and revises all other chapters.

Ramsdell begins with a history of the genre, a discussion of its appeal, and some general hints to librarians on how to approach collection development in this area. She recommends that collection development librarians talk to colleagues and to regular readers of the genre, read reviews, and monitor circulation statistics. For those responsible for personnel allocation, she recommends designating a librarian to be responsible for collection building in this area.

The main body of the book is devoted to sections on subgenres of the field: contemporary romance; romantic mysteries; historical romances; regency period romances; alternative reality romance (e.g., vampire, time travel, fantasy); sagas; gay and lesbian romance; inspirational romance; and ethnic/multicultural romance. Each of these sections begins with a lengthy definition of the subgenre, followed by a discussion of its appeal. Hints on advising the reader follow, including such topics as what other subgenres a reader might find appealing and specific series that might be of interest. An annotated bibliography of selected authors rounds out each section.

Other material includes bibliographies of research material on the genre, including dissertations, a list of writers' organizations (e.g., Romance Writers of America), a list of awards, and a list of publishers in the area.

Romance Fiction is not meant to be used for a quick lookup question. For that, the librarian or the reader can use such tools as *What Do I Read Next: A Reader's Guide to Current Genre Fiction* (see ARBA 92, entry 1136) or the electronic product NoveList. This work is for the collection development librarian with a commitment to building a romance collection and the budget to support that commitment as well as for the scholar or student with an interest in the genre. [R: BL, 15 Sept 99, p. 301; Choice, Dec 99, p. 692]—**Terry Ann Mood**

Science Fiction,
Fantasy, and Horror

P

379.   **Fantasy and Horror: A Critical and Historical Guide to Literature, Illustration, Film, TV, Radio, and the Internet.** Neil Barron, ed. Lanham, Md., Scarecrow, 1999. 816p. index. $85.00. ISBN 0-8108-3596-7.

Because fantasy and horror are so closely related, this work is an extensive revision of two separate guides, *Horror Literature* (see ARBA 91, entry 1138) and *Fantasy Literature* (see ARBA 91, entry 1137). This guide directs readers and viewers to works of fantasy and horror, both commendable and historical. There is greater unity in this one–volume guide, whose scope is wider and now includes chapters on fantasy and horror poetry, teaching fantasy and horror literature, fantasy and horror comics, and a comprehensive guide to the most useful Internet sources.

The guide provides both critical interpretations and historical data pertaining to the fantasy and horror genres. Arranged chronologically, more than 2,300 works of fiction and poetry are discussed, each cross-referenced to other works of similar and contrasting themes. There are also lists identifying books in series, award-winning books, translations, and children's and young adult books. Readers, including librarians, should realize that this new guide is selective. In spite of its expanded size, the editor has necessarily limited the guide to include what he feels are the best works representing fantasy and horror. [R: LJ, Aug 99, p. 76; BL, 15 Nov 99, pp. 652-653]—**Cari Ringelheim**

P, S

380.   Fonseca, Anthony J., and June Michele Pulliam. **Hooked on Horror: A Guide to Reading Interests in Horror Fiction.** Englewood, Colo., Libraries Unlimited, 1999. 332p. index. (Genreflecting Advisory Series). $55.00. ISBN 1-56308-671-9.

This title in the Libraries Unlimited Genreflecting Advisory Series focuses on horror as its own genre rather than as a subgenre of fantasy. As the series title indicates, the purpose is to provide a readers' advisory tool for public librarians. High school and college librarians may find this title useful as patron reading choices and curriculum demands. It looks at books published from 1994 to 1998 that are still available either by purchase or library loan. It does not include young adult titles unless they are read by adults (e.g., Annette Klaus's *The Silver Kiss*).

The book is divided into 4 parts. The 1st introduces horror fiction as a genre. The 2d provides an annotated bibliography of horror short story collections by individual and multiple authors. The 3d part, the main section of the book, consists of an annotated bibliography of horror novels and films divided into chapters. The chapters cover ghosts and haunted houses; golems, mummies, and reanimated stalkers; vampires and werewolves; demonic possession, Satanism, black magic, witches, and warlocks; mythological monsters; telekinesis and hypnosis; small-town horror; maniacs and sociopaths; technohorror; rampant animals and other eco-monsters; psychological horror; splatterpunk; and comic horror. The 4th part focuses on ready-reference, criticism, and other helpful information such as cross-genre fiction, author bibliographies, periodicals, awards, publishers, and Internet sites. The entries are arranged alphabetically by author's last name within a chapter and cross-referenced among the chapters as needed. The book may be searched by the short story, subject, or author/title indexes. The gray and red cover with gargoyle type heads echoes the subject matter within. This is a good source for libraries that must develop their horror collections.—**Esther R. Sinofsky**

P, S

381.   Herald, Diana Tixier. **Fluent in Fantasy: A Guide to Reading Interests.** Englewood, Colo., Libraries Unlimited, 1999. 260p. index. (Genreflecting Advisory Series). $39.00. ISBN 1-56308-655-7.

Intended for readers, librarians, and booksellers, this volume tries to serve two audiences at once, readers searching for recommended fantasy books and those researching the genre. Books included were published between the nineteenth century and 1998. Using a format employed for other readers' guides (see ARBA 98, entry 1096, and ARBA 96, entry 1186), an introduction defining fantasy literature precedes chapters devoted to a subgenre (e.g., fairy tales, romance, time travel). Although the introduction neglects to explain the subgenres, each chapter offers a brief definition or explanation and titles chosen to represent the subgenre. Where available, bibliographic guides to the literature are noted. The annotations, which hint at the type of subgenre, are selective and chosen for annotating through an unnamed process. Keywords indicate terms employed in the subject index, while symbols identify award-winning and young adult titles. The author has continued the practice of recommending titles, but has neglected to state any criteria beyond personal choice.

Chapter 20, a compendium of resources, lists research tools (e.g., journals, publishers, biographical sources) useful in the pursuit of fantasy literature, with selective annotations. Librarians and researchers, the second audience, will appreciate the guide to research sources, related science fiction resources, and bibliographies. World Wide Web links mentioned throughout are updated at the author's homepage, a definite highlight. Three appendixes offer a glossary of common terminology, recommended young adult titles, and a recommended core collection. Author/title and subject indexes complete the volume. The first is useful for locating additional works by an author represented in different subgenres (e.g., Anne McCaffrey); however, some entries lead to award lists only (e.g., Jack Finney).

With her book designed to accompany forays into the book stacks, the author has made compromises in order to keep the volume relatively small. Most reprehensible is the intentional absence of publication information, a practice that severely limits the use of the guide for other purposes, such as collection development. This work is recommended for public libraries; the research resource section makes this worthy of consideration by academic libraries as well. [R: BL, 15 Nov 99, pp. 652-653]—**Sandra E. Belanger**

NATIONAL LITERATURE

American Literature

General Works

Bibliography

C, P
382. **Magill's Literary Annual 1999: Essay-Reviews of 200 Outstanding Books Published in the United States During 1998.** John D. Wilson, ed. Hackensack, N.J., Salem Press, 1999. 2v. index. $75.00/set. ISBN 0-89356-299-8.

Each year since 1954 Magill has published an annual of critical essays written by independent scholars and professors on 200 important books published in the United States the previous year. This 2-volume set contains articles on the outstanding books of 1998.

Following a publisher's note explaining philosophy and form, volume 1 lists the contents alphabetically by title and author, with an annotated list of the books divided into 31 categories ranging from fiction, biography, and history to economics, science, and psychology. Each essay is arranged in a set pattern consisting of title, author, publication information including number of pages and price, a brief synopsis, and, when relevant, locale, time period, and a list of the principal personages. In approximately 2,000 words, each signed article contains a discussion of the intent of the work, point of view, and the author's success in achieving his or her goal. Each ends with a source for further reading that consists of a bibliography of published reviews.

Volume 2 concludes with 4 cumulative indexes of the entire Magill series published since 1977. The reviews prior to that have been collected and published in a 12-volume *Survey of Contemporary Literature* (1977). The indexes are divided into biographical works by subject, including the contemporary biographies of people from Henry Adams and Jane Austen to Adolph Zukor, category (autobiography to women's issues), title, and author. In addition to enjoying the consistent quality of the articles, librarians and scholars will appreciate having 200 books selected as outstanding from among the thousands published during the year, although obviously they may question some of the choices or omissions.—**Charlotte Lindgren**

Biography

C

383.   Brennan, Elizabeth A., and Elizabeth C. Clarage. **Who's Who of Pulitzer Prize Winners.** Phoenix, Ariz., Oryx Press, 1999. 666p. illus. index. $69.00. ISBN 1-57356-111-8.

Who's Who of Pulitzer Prize Winners provides biographical information on the individuals who have been awarded Pulitzer Prizes as well as bibliographic information on the newspapers and publishers that have won the award. At their fullest, the biographical entries provide a picture of the winner; his or her birth date and place; the colleges at which the winner matriculated; the names of the winner's parents, spouse(s), and children (if any); the winner's career history; and the category of Pulitzer Prize that was awarded. Also provided are selective lists of other awards and of sources containing additional biographical information, a statement about the piece that won the prize, and (when relevant) the date of the winner's death. Entries for newspapers and publishers are briefer but provide the reason for which the prize was awarded and, in the case of newspapers, provide changes in name. In all, there are 1,175 entries for the 1,334 awards presented since 1917; data are current as of 1998.

There is much to praise about this work, but it is also a work that can be frustrating, for the body of the book is arranged by the category in which the Pulitzer Prize was awarded. In order to locate specific biographies, users must thus make use of one of the several indexes—newspaper and organization winners, individual winners, educational institutions, and chronology of prizes awarded. Winners who have Pulitzer Prizes in multiple categories—Norman Mailer, for example, has won the General Non-Fiction in 1969 and the Fiction in 1980—are listed in only one section; in Mailer's case, the entry is in "Fiction," with a cross-reference from "General Non-Fiction." There is no entry for Janet Cooke, whose fraudulent reporting necessitated her returning her prize for feature writing, but she is mentioned in the entry on Teresa S. Carpenter, who received the prize after Cooke returned it. Although not perfect, this volume brings together information that is not easily accessible elsewhere, and it belongs in academic libraries and larger public libraries. [R: LJ, 1 Sept 99, p. 176; BR, Sept/Oct 99, pp. 77-78]

—**Richard Bleiler**

Dictionaries and Encyclopedias

C, P

384.   **Encyclopedia of American Literature.** Steven R. Serafin and Alfred Bendixen, eds. New York, Continuum; distr., Farmington Hills, Mich., Gale, 1999. 1305p. index. $150.00. ISBN 0-8264-1052-9.

The editors of this satisfying new reference work, between them, have edited seven other literary reference sources. Here, their aim is to offer users topical essays on American literature as well as biographical information and critical comment on major and minor American writers, living or dead. The 70 topical essays are fully realized contributions to literary genres or themes dominating American literature. These essays serve to call attention to important critics, historians, film directors, and media personalities who, although not included in the encyclopedia, have made their own contributions to cultural life. Some of the topics covered are "The City and Literature," "Film and Literature," "Almanacs and Yearbooks," "The Slave Narrative," "Language and Dialect," and "Lesbian Literature." Each essay concludes with a secondary bibliography of books and articles.

Biographical and critical information on individual authors accounts for most of the encyclopedia's 1,100 entries and 1,282 pages of text. These discussions provide biographical information, but an author's primary themes and unique contributions to literary history are emphasized. Indeed, entries for current authors such as Bobbie Ann Mason and E. Annie Proulx concentrate on themes and unique contributions, not biographical background. Longer entries, those for Herman Melville and Walt Whitman, are made fresh by current critical commentary and genre associations. Many entries end with a selective bibliography citing both books and journal articles. Citations to books are incomplete, but librarians will be able to locate complete citations through electronic sources. Critical editions of major authors are not included, a serious oversight. One-volume secondary sources, biographies, and criticism account for most of the suggested readings.

The reference value of the encyclopedia is increased by an outstanding index that enables users to locate all references to any author mentioned within the encyclopedia, serving, among other things, to identify foreign authors whose work impacted the history of American literature. The cross-referencing system is easily followed, helping users to compare authors within genres. The encyclopedia is well produced, but could benefit from a more sturdy binding to help withstand heavy use by students.

This encyclopedia is the best 1-volume work on American writers presently available for purchase. Working with 300 contributors, the editors have perhaps achieved the stated objected: a useful reference work that "may itself be considered a lasting contribution to American literature." This reviewer is reminded of the *Cyclopaedia of American Literature* (William Rutter, 1880) by Evert and George Duyckinck, which remains a useful reference source for locating information on minor early writers. [R: LJ, 1 April 99, p. 85; BL, Aug 99, p. 2104]

—**Milton H. Crouch**

British Literature

General Works

Biography

C, P

385.　**An Encyclopedia of British Women Writers.** rev. ed. Paul Schlueter and June Schlueter, eds. New Brunswick, N.J., Rutgers University Press, 1998. 741p. index. $60.00; $28.00pa. ISBN 0-8135-2542-X; 0-8135-2543-8pa.

This ambitious and useful resource contains approximately 600 biographical entries on British women writers. The authors included are an interesting mixture of genres and time periods. Writers of various genres are well represented, such as Agatha Christie, Lynne Reid Banks, and Georgette Heyer. Not all entries are for women who wrote in England; for example, Anne Bradstreet, who is best known for her writings in colonial America, is presented here. Nor do all the writers exist in real life, such as Juliana Berners. The earliest writer found was Marie de France, born approximately 1140 C.E. The newest writer is Jeanette Winterson, born in 1959.

Each entry describes the author and her contributions to literature. A list of references helps the researcher find additional information. Some of the sources used for references include periodical sources and reference book sources. The entries range from a few paragraphs to four pages. The authors used a clever device to save space. The author is not referred to by name but instead by the first initial of her last name. For example, Eliza Acton is listed as "A" in her entry.

The book is easy to use with each author alphabetically listed by last name. Cross-references help the reader find the person when there may have been two or more variations to the name or written under a pseudonym. An index at the back of the book is also a quick way to access the entries on the author.

This is an updated version of a previous edition. There are 200 more entries and many of the existing entries have been updated. The coverage has been extended to cover women who resided in Great Britain, even though they may have been born elsewhere, and women who live in other parts of the British Commonwealth.

This one-volume reference work provides convenient and quick information on an impressive group of women writers. Even though the coverage falls somewhere between a dictionary and an encyclopedia entry, the entries are well written and concise. A chronological list of the authors covered in this work would have been an interesting and useful addition to the book. Perhaps the publisher will include it in the next revision of this work. [R: LJ, Dec 98, pp. 86, 88; BL, June 99, p. 1876; Choice, Nov 99, p. 506]—**Suzanne Julian**

Dictionaries and Encyclopedias

P, S

386.　Bruce, Christopher W. **The Arthurian Name Dictionary.** New York, Garland, 1999. 504p. (Garland Reference Library of the Humanities, v.2063). $125.00. ISBN 0-8153-2865-6.

Scholars and general readers alike will enjoy and profit from this comprehensive directory of major and minor items in the King Arthur legends. A longtime "aficionado" of the Arthurian world, Christopher Bruce, professor at Pennsylvania State University, treats each entry with thoroughness and "loving care."

Writing about the Round Table, for instance, Bruce states that this famous motif was first introduced by Wace in *Roman de Brut*, who wrote that the table had no "head." As it is later said in *The Grene Knight*, the king "made the Round Table for their behove, that none of them should sit above, but all should sit as one." The number of knights at the Round Table varies, according to which legend we choose to embrace. It ranges from 13, in the early Percival tradition, to 50, 60, 130, 150, and 250 in other traditions. In Layamon, the number rises to an astounding 1,600, and we are told that the table was portable, while another early writer (Beroul) claims that the table could "rotate like the earth." In dealing with the huge size of the table, some artists and writers have depicted it as a ring with inner places for servants and entertainers. Relative to the motif of the Holy Grail, some traditions trace the Round Table to the table used at the Last Supper, in the age of Joseph of Arimathea, who was supposed to have brought the Grail to England.

The treatment of the Round Table is indicative of the thoroughness and care that one finds throughout *The Arthurian Name Dictionary*. Similar care is seen in treatments of other major items, such as Excalibur, Lancelot, the Lady of the Lake, the Green Knight, Camelot, the Isle of Avalon, Merlin, Morgan Le Fay, the Fisher King, and the Dolorous Stroke, which created the Waste Land. The entries under "Arthur" occupy 10 double-column pages and touch on historicity, development of the legend, insignia, grave, relatives, battles, and numerous other matter, even "Arthur's cups and saucers," which are "natural rock basins on the side of the headland of Tintagel, on the coast of Cornwall" (p. 46).

It is clear that this "dictionary" was made for browsing, as well as for assistance in serious studies. Its sources number more than 250 in many languages, ranging from the earliest mention of Arthur as "Artorius" in the first-century Roman writings of Tacitus and Juvenal, down to the *Idylls of the King* by Alfred Lord Tennyson, the beginning of the modern era of Arthurian literature.

Bruce acknowledges the usefulness of other similar dictionaries, but adds that they tend to restrict themselves too much by using only texts in English, drawing primarily from Malory, or by centering too much on primary characters, to the exclusion of lesser but significant items. The job that Bruce has done here can only be described as masterful, and what he has created will entertain and inform readers for generations to come. The book is written in a lively, responsible style and is arranged in a manner that is consistently reader-friendly. There are occasional slips, such as calling Winchester "Wichester" (p. 430), but generally *The Arthurian Name Dictionary* is a welcome addition to the scholarship surrounding King Arthur. [R: Choice, Sept 99, p. 106; BL, Aug 99, p. 2103]

—**Peter Thorpe**

Australian and
New Zealand Literature

C, P

387.   **The MUP Encyclopaedia of Australian Science Fiction & Fantasy.** Paul Collins, Steven Paulsen, and Sean McMullen, eds. Victoria, Australia, Melbourne University Press; distr., Concord, Mass., Paul & Company Publishers, 1998. 188p. $39.95; $29.95pa. ISBN 0-522-84771-4; 0-522-84802-8pa.

The MUP Encyclopaedia of Australian Science Fiction and Fantasy was inspired to some extent by the successes of the much-honored 1993 *Encyclopedia of Science Fiction* (see ARBA 94, entry 1211) and the 1997 Encyclopedia of Fantasy (see ARBA 98, entry 1116). These volumes contained entries discussing Australia and its more significant writers, but they were of necessity broader focused and could not limit themselves to the works of one region. *The MUP Encyclopaedia*, on the other hand, concentrates almost exclusively on the Australian and New Zealand writers of science fiction and fantasy whose careers became active following 1950, including novelists as well as short story writers and writers for children in addition to writers for adults. *The MUP Encyclopaedia* also includes a number of thematic articles on subjects such as cinema, dark fantasy, early Australian science fiction and fantasy, magazines, and radio. In all, the volume contains approximately 1,200 signed entries with bibliographies; there are, alas, no illustrations and no index.

A number of critics have excoriated *The MUP Encyclopaedia*. An introductory statement of methodology by Paul Collins states, "It seems superfluous to go back beyond 1950, if only for the reason that most of the works would not be unobtainable and that, apart from being authoritative, such entries would add little to this work" (p. x). This has been used to indicate a lack of editorial commitment and understanding of the nature of literary history. The volume does indeed contain its share of errors and omissions—to say nothing of inadequate cross-references—but in condemning it outright, the critics have been too harsh. The volume is not perfect, but it marks the first time that a comprehensive attempt has been made at identifying and documenting a discrete body of literature and its writers. It is a volume that should be used with some caution, but it is nevertheless a volume that should be used. It belongs in the libraries of all institutions supporting research and studies in Australian literature and in contemporary science fiction and fantasy literature and its writers.—**Richard Bleiler**

C, P
388.   **The Oxford Companion to New Zealand Literature.** Roger Robinson and Nelson Wattie, eds. New York, Oxford University Press, 1998. 608p. $72.00. ISBN 0-19-558348-5.

Designed as a supplementary volume to the *Oxford History of New Zealand Literature* (see ARBA 92, entry 1239), this excellent guide goes well beyond its earlier companion. The earlier Oxford history, which covered only to 1986, is now outdated and provides only broad topical essays on various literary genres (e.g., the short story). This compact new volume deals more directly with 680 individual authors, 110 significant books or other pieces, and a wide range of other topics. Its broad approach provides entries for distinguished writers from other countries with an association, no matter how brief, with New Zealand. Other efforts, including articles on relationships to a number of other countries, have been made to place New Zealand literature in a broader cultural context. There is also good coverage of 125 Maori writers, texts, or topics, which was sadly lacking in the Oxford history. Although designed as a ready-reference source, with relatively brief entries, this Oxford companion is far more than that. The text is liberally sprinkled with cross-references so that almost every article immediately leads the reader to a series of related pieces that, as a whole, provide a broader perspective on an author, a journal, an organization, or a publisher. It is difficult not to follow those leads and the reader is richly rewarded by doing so. Best of all, virtually all of the entries are direct, honest, and critical. Although New Zealand literature is not widely studied in this country, this Oxford companion warrants a place in most college and university libraries and larger public libraries.—**Norman D. Stevens**

Russian Literature

C
389.   **Russian Literature in the Age of Pushkin and Gogol: Poetry and Drama.** Christine A. Rydel, ed. Farmington Hills, Mich., Gale, 1999. 449p. illus. index. (Dictionary of Literary Biography, v.205). $151.00. ISBN 0-7876-3099-3.

The handsome and durable Dictionary of Literary Biography Series (DLB) has only recently launched a Russian series that began with editor Marcus Levitt's volume on seventeenth- and eighteenth-century writers (see ARBA 96, entry 1261). This was followed by *Russian Literature of the Age of Pushkin and Gogol: Prose*, edited by Christine Rydel, a well-known specialist in Russian Romanticism. Rydel now completes her diptych with this volume on the poets of the "Golden Age of Russian Literature," an age that owes its glory far more to poetry than to prose.

Rydel's introduction sketches the historical and cultural context for the early decades of the nineteenth century, with particular attention to the debate over the meaning of "Romanticism," especially in its imported Russian setting. The 33 authors examined here range from giants (Aleksandr Pushkin, Mikhail Lermontov) to second-rank figures to obscure names such as Nestor Kukol'nik and Viktor Tepliakov. The handsomely illustrated essays, ranging from 5 to nearly 40 pages, are mostly by American and Russian literary specialists on their particular author. Russian drama during the period was relatively undeveloped and the few playwrights here are basically poets—with the exception of Aleksandr Griboedov. The best-known play of the time, Gogol's *Inspector-General*, finds no discussion here because Gogol is covered in the earlier volume on prose.

The articles follow the standard DLB format and include good critical bibliographies and reference to archival holdings. Also noteworthy is the "Checklist of Further Readings."—**D. Barton Johnson**

C
390.   **Russian Literature in the Age of Pushkin and Gogol: Prose.** Christine A. Rydel, ed. Farmington Hills, Mich., Gale, 1999. 432p. illus. index. (Dictionary of Literary Biography, v.198). $151.00. ISBN 0-7876-1853-5.

The impressive Dictionary of Literary Biography (DLB) series has only recently undertaken Russian literature. The Russian volumes commenced with *Early Modern Russian Writers, Late Seventeenth and Eighteenth Centuries*, edited by Marcus Levitt (vol. 150; see ARBA 96, entry 1261) and now moves on to early nineteenth-century prose. The subtitle is noteworthy because many of the period's major figures were poets. As a result,

Alexander Pushkin, the era's greatest writer, is absent from a volume that bears his name in its title. Presumably, there will soon be a DLB volume devoted to the golden age of Russian poetry, but meanwhile Pushkin's seminal prose writings are scanted.

Rydel, a specialist in Russian Romanticism, provides a succinct introduction where she lucidly sketches the historical and literary background. The 30 well-chosen figures (born circa 1800) range from writers such as Gogol, Aksakov, and Odoevsky to names such as Ivan Gagarin and Elena Gans. Also included are near-forgotten authors of the first Russian "bestsellers." Although a particular strength is the generous inclusion of critics, journalists, and editors, all of which were instrumental in establishing the role of literature for Russia's nascent reading public. Were it not for Vissarion Belinsky, Ivan Panaev, Makhail Pogodin, and Osip Senkovsky, Russian literature would have been much different. This is equally true for historians and philosophers, such as Timofei Granovsky and Nikolai Stankevich.

The handsomely illustrated essays, written mostly by American Slavists, average about a dozen pages. Each contains the author's bibliography (Russian and English translations) and concludes with a critical bibliography and archival sources. As in all DLB volumes, a cumulative series index is included. [R: Choice, April 99, p. 1435]
—**D. Barton Johnson**

POETRY

P, S

391.   **Index to Poetry for Children and Young People 1993-1997: A Title, Subject, Author, and First Line Index to Poetry in Collections for Children and Young People.** G. Meredith Blackburn III, comp. Bronx, N.Y., H. W. Wilson, 1999. 461p. $63.00. ISBN 0-8242-0939-7.

Initiated in 1942 as the *Index to Children's Poetry*, this stalwart guide, now in its sixth five-year supplement, will be welcomed in elementary and secondary school libraries, in academic curriculum centers, and perhaps in radio and television libraries. Professors and students of the literature for children and young people will also find it a useful addition to their own collections.

The 186 collections indexed here are appropriate for children in elementary school grades and intermediate and older students. The volume's broad scope includes new volumes by individual poets (e.g., Lee Bennett Hopkins) and selections from the works of older authors (e.g., Randall Jarrell). The four basic types of entries—title, subject, author, and reference from first line—facilitate searching for a poem after one becomes familiar with the alphabetic word-by-word arrangement. Fullest information is given in the title entry. Particularly helpful here is the means to distinguish between different poems bearing the same title. Following the boldfaced title is the first line of the poem, the poet's name, and the symbol for the book indexes. This worthy new supplement again brings children and poetry together.—**Charles R. Andrews**

25 Music

GENERAL WORKS

Biography

P

392. Jasen, David A., and Gene Jones. **Spreadin' Rhythm Around: Black Popular Songwriters, 1880-1930.** New York, Schirmer Books/Simon & Schuster Macmillan, 1998. 435p. illus. index. $29.95. ISBN 0-02-864742-4.

Two dozen individuals or songwriting teams are given rather comprehensive biographical entries here, starting with James Bland, the minstrel composer whose "Carry Me Back to Old Virginny" was until recently that region's state song, and continuing into the Harlem Renaissance with Eubie Blake and Noble Sissle, Henry Creamer and Turner Layton, James P. Johnson, and Fats Waller. This is the most recent and reliable treatment of the period. None of the figures are obscure or unimportant, although names (and tunes) might be less known to the novice. The coverage is lucid and fascinating in every regard, and this is a significantly rich source of data on this very important era in American music of ballads, blues, coon songs, musical theater, and publishing. Those who have read about ragtime will already know Jasen's name, and Gene Jones contributes information on the musical stage. Many of the illustrations (individuals and sheet music covers) have not been readily available previously. The back matter lists sources consulted in a brief, excellent bibliography. In addition to a general index, another is offered of song titles that will prove a most helpful reference feature. [R: LJ, 1 Sept 98, p. 172]

—**Dominique-René de Lerma**

Dictionaries and Encyclopedias

C, P

393. Boccagna, David L., comp. **Musical Terminology: A Practical Compendium in Four Languages.** Hillsdale, N.Y., Pendragon Press, 1999. 243p. $24.00pa. ISBN 1-57647-015-6.

This unusual combination of several types of specialized dictionaries is designed for performing musicians. English is not the language of choice for most composers in their instructions to performers on printed music, and it is vital for musicians to understand instructive terminology in the languages they are most commonly found—Italian, German, and French. The purpose of this dictionary is to provide musicians with translations of these terms in four languages. This pocket-size compendium can be invaluable to instrumentalists, conductors, teachers, students, and amateur music lovers who speak any of the languages.

Standard musical dictionaries provide definitions and explanations of the full range of musical terms, but it can be time-consuming and cumbersome to use these broader references when simply trying to find out how a composer wants a piece of music marked to "strepitoso" (to sound noisy). There have been cross-language dictionaries of musical terminology, such as the *Dictionary of Terms in Music: English-German, German-English. Wörterbuch Musik* (see ARBA 93 entry 1248), but the present volume may be the first multi-language translator of musical performance terminology. Thus, if an English-speaking conductor comes across the German term "ungezwungen" in his score, he can quickly determine that the music should be performed in an "easy going" manner.

A short introduction tells the interesting story of how this dictionary came to be compiled. This would make a useful and interesting addition to any music book collection.—**Larry Lobel**

C, P

394.   **The Hutchinson Concise Dictionary of Music.** Barrie Jones, ed. Chicago, Fitzroy Dearborn, 1999. 762p. $55.00. ISBN 1-57958-178-1.

This new entry in the crowded field of musical dictionaries has a strong pedigree, having been abridged from the 1995 *Hutchinson Encyclopedia of Music*, which itself descends from the highly regarded *New Everyman Dictionary of Music* (see ARBA 90, entry 1229). What distinguishes this latest entry into the field is its tight focus, defined in the introduction as "the core technical, biographical, organological (study of musical instruments) and other information vital to the comprehension and enjoyment of music." Thus, although it includes entries about musical genres and forms, biographies of composers, instruments and their makers, theorists and musicologists, and conductors, it excludes instrumental performers and singers, publishers, critics, teachers, and choreographers. Illustrations are limited to about 100 musical examples, and there is a 14-page appendix consisting of a chronology of the history of music, emphasizing composers and important works in the musical repertoire.

To this reviewer, some of the inclusions and exclusions seem inconsistent or arbitrary, but these deliberate limitations do keep the number of entries down to about 7,500 and allow for somewhat lengthier and more detailed descriptions than one finds in dictionaries that attempt to encompass the entire musical field. However, the narrow scope does result in the sacrifice of a pronunciation guide and a shortage of definitions of some terms used to define other terms (the definition of *a cappella* says it is characteristic of gospel music and doo-wop, neither of which has an entry). Nevertheless, this volume succeeds admirably in its stated goals and will serve its intended audience of concert–goers, compact disc collectors, radio listeners, and music students well. [R: Choice, Oct 99, p. 305]

—**Larry Lobel**

Directories

P

395.   **Schwann Spectrum: The Guide to Rock, Jazz, World ... And Beyond.** Woodland, Calif., Schwann Publications, 1999. 731p. $16.95pa. ISBN 1-57598-053-3.

Since their inception in the 1940s, the numerous incarnations, title changes, and spinoffs of what have been popularly called "Schwann catalogs" have become the preeminent authority for listing currently available recordings. In years gone by, just about every record store would have copies near the cash register, though nowadays e-commerce and a plethora of relevant Websites are regularly consulted as well.

The *Schwann Spectrum* has been published irregularly for the past decade, and is a testament to the continuing growth of the nonclassical music industry. The present volume claims to list all popular music recordings currently available in the United States on CD, LP, and cassette. The popular music field coverage is extensive, including rock, blues, country, folk, rap, dance, instrumental, and vocal pop. Also covered are jazz, television and cinema soundtracks, gospel and religious, international, and New Age. Most of the sections are arranged by artist or group name, except where other arrangements are more suitable, such as the international section being arranged alphabetically by country.

At the end of the volume is the labels section, with the full name of each record label or distributor for the abbreviations used throughout. Though the "How to Use" introduction says that addresses are furnished for each, this is not the case. The vast majority of listings just provide the name for the abbreviation and not the company's address. This obvious shortcoming may be somewhat alleviated by consulting other directories and Websites. Many record shops, who are a primary audience for this guide, will likely have a distribution network in place, and will not need to contact the record companies directly anyway.

Compared to previous editions, the number of LPs, CDs, and cassettes listed has more than doubled: There are approximately 158,000 entries displayed in the tiniest of typefaces. There are some minor format changes, including the integration of new releases into the main listings (previously, these had been separate). Also included are a few forgettable essays on contemporary music topics, and some reviews of recent recordings.

—**Richard W. Grefrath**

Discography

C, P

396.   Whitburn, Joel. **Joel Whitburn Presents a Century of Pop Music: Year-by-Year Top 40 Rankings of the Songs & Artists that Shaped a Century.** Menomonee Falls, Wis., Record Research, 1999. 242p. illus. $39.95pa. ISBN 0-89820-135-7.

A Century of Pop Music charts the top 40 songs for each year from 1900 to 1999 (incorrectly labeled as the twentieth century). Because no definitive chart of popular songs existed for 1900 to 1939, various surveys and sources were incorporated to compile charts for those years, such as *Talking Machine World*, Jim Walsh's columns in *Hobbies* magazine, and *Billboard* and *Variety* commentaries. From 1940 through 1999 all chart data are compiled exclusively from the following *Billboard* pop singles charts: Record Buying Guide, Best Sellers, Juke Box, Disk Jockey, Top 100, and Hot 100. This guide also notes the song's peak position and peak date from the chart where it attained its highest position. In the year-by-year section, before each 10-year division (i.e., 1900 to 1909, 1910 to 1919, and so on), an essay describes the era's news and popular music industry. Following the year-by-year section is an artist section where artists are listed alphabetically with their hits that appear in the year-by-year section. Interestingly, Bing Crosby has the most entries with 93 top 40 hits. This is followed by an alphabetic song title section. There are also charts of number 1 hits by decade and top 40 artists by half century and by decade. No index is provided but charts are easily browsed for pertinent information. This is a good purchase for music collections and enthusiasts.—**Cari Ringelheim**

Handbooks and Yearbooks

C, P

397.   Duckworth, William. **20/20: 20 New Sounds of the 20th Century.** New York, Schirmer Books/Simon & Schuster Macmillan, 1999. 214p. illus. index. $45.00pa. (with disc). ISBN 0-02-864864-1.

In this reference source Duckworth describes 20 selected composers and their works that have had profound impact upon twentieth-century music. Four criteria are used for selection: the compositions have made a difference in Duckworth's life, have been performed widely and steadily, are available on compact disc, and are likely to become monuments for decades to come. The book is about musical sounds of our time. He begins with 20 questions, such as "How do I begin to try to understand new music?" and "What is the avant-garde?" These are answered from a composer's perspective. Several times he states, "Let your ears be your guide." The essays are roughly in chronological order of the composition.

Many styles are explored, including the serial music of Arnold Schoenberg, the impressionism of Claude Debussy and Maurice Ravel, and the ragtime of Scott Joplin. Duckworth also exposes the use of dissonance by Igor Stravinsky and Olivier Messiaen; the minimalism of Terry Riley, Philip Glass, and Steve Reich; and the mysticism of Arvo Part. Articles on Charles Ives and Aaron Copland exhibit the use of folk and hymn tunes. Other American composers include George Gershwin and Alan Hovhaness, plus those who experiment with new structures or sound sources, such as Ben Johnston, John Cage, Alvin Lucier, Robert Ashley, Laurie Anderson, and Meredith Monk. Duckworth, a composer himself, describes the recorded composition, includes a few quotations by and about the composer, and presents a brief biography. He uses the translated English titles when possible throughout the narration. Each essay contains a photograph or drawing of the composer. For unfamiliar compositions, Duckworth writes an enticing essay. For more familiar works, he provides new insights. The 1st appendix is a long list of 86 works by 57 composers. The timeline of music, people, and events from 1813 to the present is useful, but has some misalignment, with 1960 as the date of President Kennedy's assassination. A bibliographic essay of further resources follows. The compact disc has 19 samples from 18 of the composers; Laurie Anderson and Steve Reich's works were unavailable. Duckworth succeeds in his objective to introduce students to the various styles pioneered in twentieth-century music.—**Ralph Hartsock**

C, P

398.   **Schwann Opus—, Winter 1997-98: Reference Guide to Classical Music.** Woodland, Calif., Valley Record Distributors, 1998. 1196p. $39.95pa./yr. ISBN 1-57598-043-6. ISSN 1066-2138.

Schwann Opus is a comprehensive reference guide for classical music recordings (see ARBA 91, entry 1293 for a review of the summer 1990 edition). This quarterly publication lists more than 45,000 currently available compact discs (CDs), cassette tapes, and laser discs. Lists provide complete descriptions of recordings, which are accessed in three sections—new releases (more than 2,300 in this issue), composers, and collections (e.g., instrumental, vocal, film soundtrack, and musical genre). Each list gives the album title as well as titles of musical selections on the recording, their key signatures and opus numbers, name of performing artist(s), name of recording company, format (whether CD or cassette), and other useful data to enable the reader to order recordings. A final section provides addresses and telephone numbers of the hundreds of labels from which recordings in the lists can be purchased.

Each issue of *Schwann Opus* has a handful of lengthy and well-written book and record reviews, but it is intended mainly as a finder's guide. For reviews and ratings of the majority of recordings one must consult other reference works, such as the *All Music Guide: The Expert's Guide to the Best Recordings . . .* (see ARBA 98, entry 1228) or the *BBC Music Magazine Top 1000 CDs Guide* (see ARBA 97, entry 1055). The criticisms of the companion to this work, the *Schwann Artist Issue*, voiced by another reviewer (see ARBA 90, entry 1236), apply equally to the work in question, but it remains an essential companion for the classical music aficionado.

—**Larry Lobel**

INSTRUMENTS

Guitar

P, S

399.   **The Complete Encyclopedia of the Guitar: The Definitive Guide to the World's Most Popular Instrument.** Terry Burrows, ed. New York, Schirmer Books/Simon & Schuster Macmillan, 1998. 224p. illus. index. $75.00. ISBN 0-02-865028-X.

Attractively designed and abundantly illustrated, this guide is a good introduction to the guitar, from early fretted and stringed instruments, such as the lute and the gittern, to the twentieth-century acoustic and electric guitars. Milestones in guitar development and design, such as the Fender Stratocaster, the National Style O, and the Gibson Les Paul, are also described. One chapter presents 16 guitar masters on 2-page spreads describing each player's career and preferred instrument(s) and lists a few "classic recordings." The black-and-white and full-color photographs of instruments and their players are not only large and numerous, but also well reproduced. Nearly one-half of the book is taken up by an A to Z list of 200 guitarists providing brief career profiles. A general index and a bibliography end the book.

The title of this guide is misleading—at 224 pages, it is neither complete nor encyclopedic. There are a number of books that treat the history of the guitar in far greater detail as well as books on individual guitar manufacturers such as Gibson and Martin. Nonetheless, this work is full of information and photographs that will delight the guitar aficionado.—**Lori D. Kranz**

P

400.   Gruhn, George, and Walter Carter. **Gruhn's Guide to Vintage Guitars: An Identification Guide for American Fretted Instruments.** 2d ed. San Francisco, Calif., Miller Freeman, 1999. 581p. illus. index. $27.95pa. ISBN 0-87930-422-7.

This is the 2d edition of a well-received guide written by the best-known vintage guitar dealer in the United States, located in Nashville, Tennessee. The guide is organized under maker and type of instrument. For each guitar the author describes in detail the production dates, shape and size, woods, pickups, bindings, neck and fingerboard, inlays, peg head, platings, finish, serial numbers, and identification keys. The guide is illustrated with 100 photos including close-ups of guitar detail. In addition to guitars, vintage basses, banjos, mandolins, and amps from selected manufacturers are covered. The 2d edition provides additional material on the very popular Fender and Gibson Tube amplifiers (considered the finest sound producers made by most players).

Gruhn's Guide is very important to instrument owners, because price can often change drastically over model years. Using the details supplied in this book, readers can determine the exact rarity of the model they have, and hence its value. No prices are given for instruments, but production serial number information is supplied in many cases. There is a good table of contents and a model index. The author has also supplied a brief two-page bibliography that is both general and manufacturer-specific. The reader will get a lot of information for a modest price in this 581-page volume. Instrument owners will be able to obtain a wealth of information on their specific models. Recommended for general reference collections in all libraries. [R: LJ, 15 Oct 99, p. 62]

—**Ralph Lee Scott**

Organ

C, P

401. **The Cambridge Companion to the Organ.** Nicholas Thistlethwaite and Geoffrey Webber, eds. New York, Cambridge University Press, 1998. 340p. illus. index. (Cambridge Companions to Music). $59.95. ISBN 0-521-57309-2.

The Cambridge Companions to Music series offers a concise and useful overview of several musical instruments and a selection of composers. This volume, *The Cambridge Companion to the Organ*, is comprised of 3 sections: "The Instrument," "The Player," and "Selected Repertoires." The section on the instrument examines the organ's history; construction; its sound, pitch, and tuning; its case; and current organ building trends. Section 2 deals with the fundamentals of playing the organ, performance practices, and organ music and its relation to the liturgy. The section dealing with repertoires is intentionally restricted because of the subject's great scope. However, the section is successful in concentrating on the major schools of organ literature, including Italian organ music to Frescobaldi, Iberian organ music before 1700, French classical organ school, English organ music to 1700, Catholic Germany and Austria (1648-1800), north German organ school, organ music of J. S. Bach, German organ music after 1800, French and Belgian organ music after 1800, British organ music after 1800, and North American organ music after 1800.

The chapters of *The Cambridge Companion to the Organ* are written by experts in the field; the majority of the authors are British, with only a few from the United States, Australia, or Italy. The volume is illustrated, contains an appendix titled "The Modes and Their Attributes According to Zarlino," has endnotes, is indexed, and has an excellent bibliography. The volume is well laid out and thorough in its coverage, although intentionally limited because of the instrument's long and expansive history. It certainly will be helpful to keyboard scholars as well as to organ students and teachers. *The Cambridge Companion to the Organ* should be included in reference divisions of music libraries.—**Robert Palmieri**

Piano

C, P

402. **The Cambridge Companion to the Piano.** David Rowland, ed. New York, Cambridge University Press, 1998. 244p. illus. index. (Cambridge Companions to Music). $64.95. ISBN 0-521-47470-1.

The Cambridge Companion to the Piano is comprised of 12 chapters by 9 British musical experts. The body of the title is divided into 2 parts. Part 1 focuses on the evolution of the instrument from early forms to the most recent developments and performance practice through this evolution. Part 2 is a discussion of the repertory of the instrument in social and stylistic contexts. Blues, jazz, and ragtime are even included. The title includes an index, a select bibliography, notes to each chapter, 38 musical examples, and 36 figures.

Actually, this book has been negatively reviewed for its lack of focus and editorial finesse (see *Times Literary Supplement*, April 9, 1999, p. 35 and *Independent*, February 1, 1999, p. 5). However, for this reviewer, two chapters redeem the title's blatant omissions. Chapter 5 is a survey of pianists on sound recordings, with the details of stylistic changes of the twentieth century noted, thereby make for fascinating reading. This information is difficult to find in one place. Chapter 6 contains a treatment of acoustics of the instrument, which makes for an accessible and enjoyable read.

Reviewers should keep in mind that this volume, like most of the titles in the Cambridge Companions to Music series, does not claim to be comprehensive. The editor states this in the introduction. However, as a supplement to a good basic collection on the topic, this title offers much.—**C. Michael Phillips**

MUSICAL FORMS

Blues

P

403.   **All Music Guide to the Blues: The Experts' Guide to the Best Blues Recordings.** 2d ed. Michael Erlewine and others, eds. San Francisco, Calif., Miller Freeman, 1999. 658p. index. (AMG All Music Guide Series). $22.95pa. ISBN 0-87930-548-7.

Primarily intended for consumers, the guide is encyclopedic in nature and could serve libraries well as a reference tool. While it is essentially a guide to the blues, the editors have included gospel singers and groups as well. Entries are arranged alphabetically by surname for individuals, and group name when appropriate. Some artists, like Harmonica Sam, are entered by their "first" name. This organization is somewhat awkward but not impossible to figure out. Each entry consists of a fairly complete biography, followed by an annotated discography of the artist's recordings. Evaluation symbols have been assigned to the recordings deemed as "essential" (an empty star) and "first purchase" (a filled-in star). Each recording is also rated overall with diamond symbols from one to five. Even those recordings deemed as inferior are listed to give the consumer a "Heads-Up" warning. All items are referred to as "Albums" regardless of format. The specific format of a recording is not given. Only the record label is listed. A section on various artists rounds out the alphabetical listing. Following this are several essays on various topics such as "Memphis Blues," "The Blues as Folklore," and "Focus on the Slide Guitar." The writing style is informal and very readable throughout. Recommended for most public libraries, music libraries, and academic libraries supporting blues, jazz, and gospel history courses. Useful for collection development as well.—**Roland C. Hansen**

P

404.   Dicaire, David. **Blues Singers: Biographies of 50 Legendary Artists of the Early 20th Century.** Jefferson, N.C., McFarland, 1999. 292p. index. $29.95pa. ISBN 0-7864-0606-2.

Dicaire has great enthusiasm for the blues, as evidenced in his lively essays on 50 blues musicians and singers born before 1940. The book is divided into five parts, four to cover each of the major blues regions—Mississippi Delta, Chicago, Texas, outside the Delta—plus one section on women who the author claims used a variety of styles rather than any one classic tradition. Each biography fills about six pages and is followed by a selected discography. Within each section, the musicians have been arranged by order of their birth (although in two cases this did not occur). The book ends with an appendix of "Recordings by Three or More Blues Singers" (presumably involving those in the book), a selected bibliography, and an index of people and recording companies mentioned. Photographs of the singers would have been a nice addition.

Blues Singers is a good and interesting introduction to blues greats. Readers wanting more blues history or music criticism will find it in Alan Lomax's *The Land Where the Blues Began* (Pantheon, 1993), Lawrence Cohn's *Nothing but the Blues* (Abbeville, 1993), Samuel Charters's *The Bluesmakers* (Da Capo, 1991), and in biographies of individual artists. In addition, a few of the great blues artists who qualify as composers can be found in the new 2-volume *International Dictionary of Black Composers* (see ARBA 2000, entry 1069).

The blues formed the basis for much of today's popular music. The contributions to American musical culture made by these pioneers are finally being recognized—in some cases, sadly, long after their deaths. One hopes that Dicaire will also publish a volume on blues artists born since 1940.—**Lori D. Kranz**

Choral

C, P

405.   Orr, N. Lee, and W. Dan Hardin. **Choral Music in Nineteenth-Century America: A Guide to the Sources.** Lanham, Md., Scarecrow, 1999. 135p. index. $25.00. ISBN 0-8108-3664-5.

Choral singing became increasingly popular in the United States during the nineteenth century, both in the churches and in secular settings. There is a substantial body of literature dealing with this topic, but bibliographic access to that literature has heretofore been limited. The authors, respectively a professor of music history and a librarian and organist at Georgia State University, have attempted to address that problem by compiling this initial bibliography. The entries are arranged topically and sub-arranged by main entry, beginning with comprehensive musical reference works and ending with studies of individual musicians and with histories of local churches that contain significant material on their choirs. Both published material (books and journal articles) and unpublished theses are included. Music scores and sound recordings are not covered. The citations employ standard bibliographic format, but they do not include annotations. There is an index of authors and main entries.

Although the authors admit that this is only the beginning of the task of documenting the literature of nineteenth-century choral music in the United States, and should be considered as a foundation for future work, not as definitive in itself, they have been able to bring together a great deal of valuable material that has previously been difficult to locate. This volume should prove useful to academic libraries supporting programs in music history and American studies.—**Paul B. Cors**

Classical

C, P

406.   Staines, Joe, and others. **Classical Music: The Rough Guide.** 2d ed. New York, Rough Guides/Penguin Books, 1998. 505p. illus. index. $23.95pa. ISBN 1-85828-257-8.

Classical Music: The Rough Guide introduces readers to classical music composers and their musical compositions. The body of the work contains an alphabetic listing of nearly 200 composers along with their major works. Each entry includes a brief biography of the composer, an overview of major compositions, and a discussion of the composer's most notable pieces. Entries also include a listing of CD recommendations with a description of the musical interpretation and the price.

The chronology of composers at the beginning of this work assists readers in finding contemporaries of their favorite composers. A glossary of musical terminology and an index to composers and their compositions are listed at the end. The index could have been left out considering that the work is already arranged alphabetically.

This work's strength is in bringing together both a mini-encyclopedia of composers and a selective review of CDs. For that reason, classical music listeners may find this a better selection than either *The Dictionary of Composers and Their Music: A Listener's Companion* (Wings Books, 1993) or *All Music Guide: The Best CDs, Albums, & Tapes* (2d ed.; see ARBA 95, entry 1256).—**Laura K. Blessing**

Country Music

C, P

407.   Goodman, David. **Modern Twang: An Alternative Country Music Guide & Directory.** Nashville, Tenn., Dowling Press, 1999. 439p. $22.00pa. ISBN 1-891847-03-1.

The first comprehensive guide to the "alternative country" music scene, this encyclopedia and guide is packed with information on the history of alternative country, various artists, record labels, publications, and addresses and Websites. Whether it is insurgent country, western swing, progressive bluegrass, cowpunk, or some other subtype, one is likely to find it in this book.

Modern Twang opens with an informative review of the alternative country field. About three-quarters of the book is devoted to an encyclopedic section of hundreds of alternative country performers. The entries are satisfyingly in-depth and present a chronological history of the performer followed by a complete discography. A browse through this section will turn up interesting names of performers from the rock and pop fields of the 1960s and the 1970s who have changed directions, such as Leon Russell and Mike Nesmith.

For those readers who are serious about this kind of music, other sections include books, articles, and reviews about alternative country; addresses and Websites for performers and record labels; a glossary of terms; venue guides; festivals; and radio and television programs around the world.

With the proliferation of alternative country artists in recent years, this book is a well-timed, comprehensive resource that covers both well-known and obscure performers. Alternative country and music history enthusiasts will want this book.—**Mark J. Crawford**

C, P

408.   **Joel Whitburn's Country Annual 1944-1997.** By Joel Whitburn. Menomonee Falls, Wis., Record Research, 1998. 700p. illus. $64.95. ISBN 0-89820-130-6.

This reference work draws on the rankings for country music from the trade magazine *Billboard*. The longest section is arranged by the years from 1944 through 1997, and documents the peak position of song titles. In later years, the peak position is subdivided for charts according to jukeboxes, disc jockeys, and best-sellers. The second section is an alphabetic listing, by song title, of every title to peak on *Billboard*'s country singles charts from 1944 through 1997. More indexes are given for top artists by decade and year. A final section has miscellaneous "chart facts and feats" such as "singles of longevity," "songs with longest titles," "songs with most charted versions," and "top country songwriters." At first glance this abundance of statistical riches for record researchers would lead to the business side of country music. Upon closer inspection, this annual provides great primary data for cultural studies from the impact of individual artist icons in American music, such as Elvis Presley and Hank Williams, to the ways that some songs become part of American consciousness. The annual deserves to be part of reference shelves in American studies, cultural studies, and music history collections.
—**Simon J. Bronner**

Jazz

P

409.   Carver, Reginald, and Lenny Bernstein. **Jazz Profiles: The Spirit of the Nineties.** New York, Billboard Books/Watson-Guptill, 1998. 304p. illus. index. $21.95. ISBN 0-8230-8338-1.

One of Carver's goals for this work was to profile today's top younger-generation jazz artists. Each profile contains a succinct biography, an interview, a brief discography, and a performance photograph, all of which is designed to give a natural, not contrived, view of the musician. Lenny Bernstein has 40 years' experience in photographing jazz performers; he provides some text from his experience. A second goal was to introduce 40 artists, ranging from Wynton and Branford Marsalis to Cindy Blackman and Kevin Mahogany. Carver subdivides these by trumpeters, saxophonists, trombonists, guitarists, pianists and organists, bassists, drummers, and vocalists. Most of the musicians interviewed were born in the 1950s or 1960s. Interviews are dated and thus provide a chronological framework. Carver, a practicing attorney, uses his oral skills well in documenting the lives of these jazz musicians.—**Ralph Hartsock**

Operatic

P

410.   Boyden, Matthew. **Opera: The Rough Guide.** 2d ed. Joe Staines and Jonathan Buckley, eds. New York, Rough Guides; distr., New York, Penguin Books, 1999. 715p. illus. index. $24.95pa. ISBN 1-85828-456-2.

The content, format, and reasonable editorial policy ensure that this book should have a long and useful life, although, because of its heavy emphasis on the discussion of available CD recordings of the operas included in the guide, it will need frequent revision. A review of the 1st edition can be found in ARBA 99, entry 1157. The book is divided into 8 historical chapters: the birth of opera; Baroque opera; the reformation of opera; the age of Romanticism; Verdi, Wagner, and their contemporaries; opera in transition; the era of modernism; and opera since World War II. Each chapter opens with a brief historical overview of the period covered. Then the composers to be discussed in the chapter are presented in roughly chronological order. Composer entries begin with a biographical sketch followed by detailed discussion of their operas. The opera entries begin with a statement of the date when the work was composed, the date of its first performance, the name of the librettist, and the source of the libretto. A synopsis of the opera is provided along with a historical and musical analysis of the work. An overview of recordings of the opera follows, then specific recordings on CD are ranked and discussed, usually in order of preference. The volume concludes with a directory of singers and a directory of conductors who are prominently featured in the book, a glossary of terms associated with opera and singing, and an index. Illustrations, usually portraits of composers or photos of CD covers, are scattered throughout the text.

An added attraction are 30 feature boxes of brief stories with titles like "Gluck versus Puccini," "Malibran's Desdemona," "Verdi in Rehearsal," and "Carmen the Bodice Ripper." Many readers will welcome the accounts of the 35 composers in the chapter on opera since World War II, because biographical information and accounts of their operas and recordings are not readily available.—**Dean H. Keller**

C, P
411.   Griffel, Margaret Ross. **Operas in English: A Dictionary.** Westport, Conn., Greenwood Press, 1999. 978p. index. $125.00. ISBN 0-313-25310-2.

This scholarly and interesting volume is now the standard reference work in its field. Its succinct preface gives informative surveys of opera in the United States, the British Isles, Canada, South Africa, Australia, and New Zealand. It traces the history of opera from its beginnings in the seventeenth century masque to its transition into musical comedy and musical drama. In opera, as in most art forms now, the lines between genres have crumbled.

The slant of the work is markedly American. Entries for American operas or musicals at times supply details of repeat performances, cast, and even evaluations. English operas do not receive the same attention. What most arouses the editor's warm appreciation is American musical comedy; her entries on the musical comedies to which she accords status comparable to that of operas are excellent for the 1970s, but she loses interest when they decline in the 1980s. Although she acknowledges the emergence of musical dramas like "Harvey Milk," she does not quite warm up to them and lists few before her cutoff point of 1996.

The work is thoroughly cross-indexed. By far the largest section is devoted to an alphabetic list of the operas in English, often giving brief story outlines and, in contemporary American operas, details of cast. There are other important indexes for composers and librettists (both usually with dates), authors and sources of the story, and a chronology of opera performances from 1634 through 1966.—**John B. Beston**

C, P
412.   Raeburn, Michael. **The Chronicle of Opera.** New York, Thames and Hudson, 1998. 256p. illus. index. $45.00. ISBN 0-500-01867-7.

This companion volume to Alan Kendall's *The Chronicle of Classical Music* (Thames and Hudson, 1994) is an oversized, handsomely illustrated chronology of 400 years of opera history. It is divided into 4 sections by time periods: 1589-1761 (Baroque Opera), 1762-1850 (Classical and Romantic Opera), 1851-1914 (International Opera), and 1915-1997 (The Age of Recording). Each section is preceded by an overview essay and followed by year-by-year coverage of important opera premieres and landmark productions with brief cast and background notes that sometimes include a plot annotation and mention of the work's reception. Both well-known and obscure operas are included (e.g., Tchaikovsky's lesser-known *Voevoda* and *Oprichnik* are covered). Scattered throughout the text are about 100 sidebars that give additional information on topics like famous opera houses; musical trends; and profiles of composers, singers, and specific operas. There are illustrations on every page: 320 in black and white and more than 100 in full color. They depict famous set designs, important scenes, original posters, opera houses, and pictures of important artists and composers. The work ends with an extensive reference section that contains a glossary of opera terms, biographies of 100 important singers, a discography of recommended recordings, a timeline of composers' productive periods, a list of opera premieres arranged by city, and a thorough index that includes references to the illustrations and sidebars. This is an outstanding reference work, particularly for supplying comparative material on opera developments in Europe and the United States. In larger collections, the purchase of two copies of this work might be considered—one for reference and the other for circulation.—**John T. Gillespie**

Popular

P

413. **All Roots Lead to Rock: Legends of Early Rock 'n' Roll.** Colin Escott, ed. New York, Schirmer Books/Macmillan Library Reference, 1999. 257p. illus. index. $24.95. ISBN 0-02-864866-8.

In *All Roots Lead to Rock*, Colin Escott presents a selection of liner notes that originally accompanied multi-CD sets from Bear Family Records. Since 1975, the Bear family from Germany has been in the business of producing high-quality, high-priced CD sets of individual musicians. Under the leadership of Richard Weize they have produced sets of such country performers as Jim Reeves and Hank Snow as well as such early rock and roll greats as Screamin' Jay Hawkins, Freddy Bell and the Bell Boys, Conway Twitty, and Frankie Lymon and the Teenagers. As the title indicates, Escott's collection traces the routes of today's rock and roll. The various selections demonstrate that rock and roll—or what would become rock and roll—emerged from different sections of the country. It came from the South of Smiley Lewis and the Mid-West of Julia Lee, from the Las Vegas act of Louis Prima and the African American traditions of Buddy and Ella Johnson, Charles Calhoun, Screamin' Jay Hawkins, and Frankie Lymon. It was black and white, north and south, and all American. So often liner notes appear in a CD set and are read only by the people who purchase those sets. Colin Escott has done a fine service by collecting these valuable essays and presenting them to a wider audience. Many of these selections present as good a biography as readers are likely to come across for lesser-known artists.—**Randy Roberts**

C, P

414. Helander, Brock. **The Rockin' '60s: The People Who Made the Music.** New York, Schirmer Books/ Macmillan Library Reference, 1999. 461p. illus. index. $20.00pa. ISBN 0-02-864873-0.

This reference is a critical and historical discography of rock and soul music in the 1960s, covering major musical artists who have contributed significantly to the development of contemporary popular music. In addition to musicians and singers there are also songwriters, FM radio pioneers, Motown Records founder Berry Gordy Jr., and others who have made significant contributions.

Helander, also author of *The Rock Who's Who* (1996) and *The Rockin 50s* (1998), provides, in the introduction, a brief history of popular music in the 1960s. The main text of the book is arranged alphabetically by either group name or last name of individual artists. Entries include birth and, when applicable, death dates; instrument(s) played by each artist; a narrative history of the group or individual; and an extensive discography that includes album title, record label, album catalog number, release year, and format the album was or is available in. A black-and-white photograph accompanies many of the entries. Appendixes include a bibliography and comprehensive index.

This well-researched, entertaining reference will satisfy a still-intense interest in the 1960s and the recording artists of that time, many who are still popular today. Students doing reports on the time period, as well as the general reader, will find this an essential source. [R: LJ, 15 Sept 99, p. 70]—**Dana McDougald**

C, P

415. Unterberger, Richie. **Music USA: The Rough Guide.** Jennifer Dempsey, ed. New York, Rough Guides; distr., New York, Penguin Books, 1999. 486p. illus. index. $23.95pa. ISBN 1-85828-421-X.

The *Rough Guides* are a well-thought-out series of handbooks to a variety of topics, including music and travel. The music guides include jazz and rock, and roots music. So it only seems logical that the publisher combined the two topics: a travel guide to musical sources.

There are 21 regions are covered, east to west, beginning with New York and ending with Hawaii. The shortest is Muscle Shoals (5 pages); the longest is New York (66 pages). Most of the text is a critical review of the history and development of the musical style of each area, stressing interaction within and without the region. Elements of jazz, folk, blues, rock, and soul are covered almost everywhere, but there are specifics of local domination, such as New York klezmer, San Francisco psychedelia, New Orleans jazz, Southwest swing, and Appalachia bluegrass.

The rest of the text, under each region, is an annotated listings guide to applicable festivals, radio stations, publications, record stores, books, videos, and museums. Two other components here are extremely useful: photographs (especially of record album covers) and commentaries on definitive recordings. There is an index to artists, record labels, and venues.

There is always room for improvement, and next time out the publishers need to add some maps for each region to pinpoint locations so the reader can visualize where, for example, Memphis is in relation to the rest of the Delta. Also, there is a distressing lack of Website addresses that can be useful in keeping the book up-to-date. Finally, many of the record recommendations come from Rhino. This company has done an excellent job of anthologizing American music (along with the Smithsonian-Folkways label). For the ardent collector, it may only be necessary to just buy them all.

This guide, of course, can only skim the surface, emphasizing the most influential and lasting music alone. But still, the chapter on Texas is a revelation in its scope of Tex-Mex music, western swing, blues, rock, folk, and honky-tonk. It is probably the most pervasive influence on American music, especially when Louisiana is added to the mix. This guide is highly recommended.—**Dean Tudor**

26 Mythology, Folklore, and Popular Culture

FOLKLORE

C, P

416.   Coughlan, Margaret N., comp. **Folklore from Africa to the United States: An Annotated Bibliography.** repr. ed. Washington, D.C., Library of Congress; repr., Detroit, Omnigraphics, 1999. 161p. illus. index. $40.00. ISBN 0-7808-0314-0.

This selective annotated bibliography, indexing works available in Library of Congress, was developed to promote understanding of African culture among Americans and Europeans. Many of the items listed were prepared in textbook formats, for government study, and to preserve purity of cultural roots. Arranged geographically by sections of Africa, the West Indies, and the United States, each geographic section begins with an abstract on the tribes, types of stories, and background, and is further broken down into subsections for adults and children. Missionaries, scholars, and others of a culture better known for its oral histories than for its written ones, capture prisms of cultural clarity as still lifes in writing. Most books are compiled research on certain aspects of African society, tradition, and folklore.

This annotated bibliography is an education on the subject of Africa and paints a colorful picture of a culture oozing with vibrancy and life worth preserving. Black-and-white illustrations, while adding atmosphere and validity to the bibliography, show diversity in art styles and forms. This volume is recommended for academic institutions supporting an African curriculum, for specific cultural and linguistic studies, and as an introduction to customs, mythology, legends, poetry, and language patterns of tribes mentioned.—**Kimberley D. Harris**

C, P

417.   Fritze, Ronald H. **Travel, Legend, and Lore: An Encyclopedia.** Santa Barbara, Calif., ABC-CLIO, 1998. 443p. illus. index. $75.00. ISBN 0-87436-759-X; 1-57607-127-8pa.

This eclectic gathering of real and imaginary destinations and people of yore makes fascinating reading for storytellers, educators, and secondary and college students. Fritze asserts that the focus of the entries is on the expectations of travelers before the twentieth century and that the aim is not to be exhaustive but to be comprehensive. Browsing through the encyclopedia takes the reader from the wanderings of Aeneas and other Greek and Trojan heroes to the wagon trains of the American west. It is populated with entries on people and creatures, such as assassins, circuit riders, Gogs and Magogs, Margery Kempe, and St. Christopher. Along with these legendary names nestle commentaries on places such as the Great Sea of Darkness, the Holy Land, the Indian Ocean, and Timbuktu as well as things like the Alexandrian library and museum, the Grand Tour, Griffins, crossing-the-lines ceremonies, and El Dorado.

The entries are of varied length, but each is concluded with cross-references and suggestions for further reading. Imaginary ancient and historic persons, places, and things are alphabetically arranged within the encyclopedia. A bibliography and comprehensive index follow the main body of entries. Various photographs and sketches break the pages of text. The well-written entries are well researched with commentary on the research by the author. The only complaint is that the first part of each entry is a definition presented as a sentence fragment that may be quite complex in structure, but still jarring when first read.—**Gail de Vos**

C, P

418.   Snodgrass, Mary Ellen. **Encyclopedia of Fable.** Santa Barbara, Calif., ABC-CLIO, 1998. 451p. illus. index. (ABC-CLIO Literary Companion). $65.00. ISBN 1-57607-026-3.

This volume represents an ambitious attempt to embrace all aspects of the fable (and major subgenres) as it has developed throughout the ages. Snodgrass defines fables as "witty, comic, and disturbingly accurate morality tales" (p. xiii) illustrating human foibles, national embarrassment, and cultural downfalls through comparing humans to animals. The subgenres identified and discussed by the author include cruelty jokes, exemplary tales, pourquoi stories, and the art of storytelling. "As a character builder, [the fable] has given the parent, preacher, teacher, and political exhorter just the right story to lighten a spiritual load or ease a ticklish situation" (p. xvi).

Organized by alphabetic entries, the book contains articles of various lengths on the different aspects of fable and its relatives. The average entry is three to six pages of well-written and insightful documented text followed by cross-references as well as reference sources including Internet addresses. Large photographs and illustrations dot the volume and add to the understanding of this vast topic. The entries are followed by several appendixes "to assist the student, writer, scholar, and classroom teacher." The first, a timeline of fable, begins at 2300–2200 B.C.E. with a listing of an anonymous Babylonian fable, *The Tamarisk and the Palm*, and retires with several books of fables and animal tales published in 1995. Snodgrass also provides a comprehensive listing of major authors of fable and fable-based literature, films based on fables (such as the 1994 releases *Thumbelina* and *The Lion King*), the major sources of fable, primary sources of texts, audiovisual and Internet material, and a bibliography with Internet resources.

Extensive entries explore the cultural history of Hispanic, Christian, Latin, and Native American fables among other cultures and eras. Several famous characters are also given their own entries, including Brer Rabbit and Reynard the Fox. Readers will discover not only the historical background of the fables, including their publishing history, but will also be led to literary connections both classical and contemporary. From the ancient Greeks to Chaucer to George Orwell's *Animal Farm* and Richard Adams's *Watership Down*, the book canvasses and encompasses all manners of animal tales. These entries also include public reactions to the texts and discussions of audiovisual interpretations. Space is dedicated to the art of storytelling as well as to various internationally acclaimed contemporary tellers from the United States, the United Kingdom, Australia, and Canada. There are surprising, but ultimately logical, entries in this volume, such as articles on tricksters, illustrators, Robert Louis Stevenson, Jacquetta Hopkins Hawkes, and Anansi. This is a fascinating and thorough discussion of fables in their widest sense. [R: LJ, 1 Feb 99, p. 78; Choice, May 99, p. 1594; BL, 1 May 99, pp. 1614-1616; SLJ, Aug 99, p. 187]

—**Gail de Vos**

P

419.   Van Scott, Miriam. **Encyclopedia of Hell.** New York, St. Martin's Press, 1998. 308p. illus. $16.95pa. ISBN 0-312-24442-8.

The *Encyclopedia of Hell* is an explanation of the underworld, offering depictions of Hell utilizing a wide range of genres including myth, religion, literature, theater, art, music, film, television, and pop culture. Sources for this work include African legends, Asian folktales, and familiar infernal chronicles from Western lore. The encyclopedia's broad range is both its strength and its weakness. Within the volume one can make connections between ideas of Western and non-Western concepts of Hell. However, the publication also contains an unevenness and cursory treatment that will be frustrating to users. Miriam Van Scott created a reference book with many short articles about Hell and the afterlife from various cultural traditions that vary in depth of scholarship. Most of the literature categories contain useful basic information, such as on Blake and Dante, while other genres such as popular culture are sketchy (e.g., tattoos). With entries ranging from Virgil's *Aeneid* to the 1994 noir film *Dark Angel: The Ascent*, the reader is led through a cultural historical journey of Hell. Folklore and its disciplinary relations seem to be avoided, but they create an integral part of thematic areas in this volume, such as the supernatural; magic; alchemy; witches and witchcraft; devil and demons; gods and goddesses; mysterious creatures and lands in myth and legend; creation myths, beliefs, and customs; psychology and paranormal; and rites of passage. All entries are organized alphabetically. Because of the gamut of entries and no index, specific searching is cumbersome. The illustrations, especially graphs and tables, are very useful. This work could provide inspiration for writers, and is recommended for individuals interested in browsing. Appropriate in public libraries and colleges. [R: LJ, 1 Sept 98, p. 175; BL, 15 Feb 99, p. 1088]—**Magda Želinská-Ferl**

MYTHOLOGY

P, S

420.   Dixon-Kennedy, Mike. **Encyclopedia of Greco-Roman Mythology.** Santa Barbara, Calif., ABC-CLIO, 1998. 370p. index. $65.00. ISBN 1-57607-094-8; 1-57607-129-4pa.

Although there is no shortage of good encyclopedias of Greek and Roman mythology, this new one is deserving of a place on school and public library shelves. It is a straightforward alphabetic list of all of the gods, people, and places described in the works of the standard classical authors. The brief entries are of varying lengths—from one short sentence to a page or more—depending on the importance of the subject. To simplify matters, Dixon-Kennedy provides no citations but, instead, states that the information is derived primarily from Homer's *Odyssey* and *Iliad*, Virgil's *Aeneid*, and Robert Graves' *The Greek Myths*. That covers just about everyone and every place, and, as Dixon-Kennedy points out, there is a wide range of readily available sources that can be used to obtain additional information. There is a good nine-page bibliography that helps identify those sources. There is also a brief chronology of the history of ancient Greece and Rome, a chronological listing of Roman emperors, and an index. Other works, such as Michael Grant and John Hazel's *Who's Who in Classical Mythology* (ARBA 94, entry 1393), provide similar information and, for the most part, the older standard texts, such as *Bulfinch's Mythology* (Random House), are as useful as newer publications. Despite recent cultural changes, classical mythology remains an educational staple that requires tools that provide basic information. This is an excellent supplemental text that may be, for many smaller libraries, perfectly adequate as a primary source of such information. [R: BL, 15 Feb 99, p. 1088; Choice, June 99, p. 1756]—**Norman D. Stevens**

POPULAR CULTURE

P, S

421.   Marks, Diana F. **Let's Celebrate Today: Calendars, Events, and Holidays.** Englewood, Colo., Teacher Ideas Press/Libraries Unlimited, 1998. 337p. illus. index. $35.00pa. ISBN 1-56308-558-5.

Let's Celebrate Today: Calendars, Events, and Holidays is a teacher and librarian resource that takes each day of the year and lists important events and birthdays of famous persons for that day. At the beginning of each month, a history of the month's name is given. Month-long events and special days are listed. Following several of each day's individual entries for both events and birthdays, the author suggests activities that can be done with students. Some Website addresses and telephone numbers of organizations to contact for further information are also included. The book contains a table of contents, strategies for using the book, a bibliography, and an index. One interesting inclusion in the book is an introduction to time with calendars listing dates of major holidays for Christians, Jews, Muslims, and Hindus. Although other books have been written that contain much of the same information, this new entry into the field is interesting and should prove useful, especially because of its currency. [R: BR, May/June 99, p. 87]—**Janet Hilbun**

C, P

422.   **War and American Popular Culture: A Historical Encyclopedia.** M. Paul Holsinger, ed. Westport, Conn., Greenwood Press, 1999. 479p. index. $89.50. ISBN 0-313-29908-0.

The editor of this work, M. Paul Holsinger, is a professor of history at Illinois State University and founder of the World War II area of the Popular Culture Association. He has authored or edited a number of works about America's wars and popular culture, especially about World War II. This title, however, covers several hundred years of American history, beginning with the early battle between the European colonizers and the Native American tribes. Although all subsequent wars are covered, particularly large sections of the book deal with the popular culture of the American Revolution, the Civil War, the Indian Wars west of the Mississippi, World War II, and Vietnam. Each segment of the book contains half-page entries that describe works of fiction that were selected as significant representations of popular culture that deal with the nation's various wars. Novels, short stories, poems, songs, plays, films, radio and television programs, as well as paintings, cartoons, toys, comic books, and posters, are all included. There are also articles about some of the writers, songwriters, and other artists who created them. There are almost 500 entries in all. Each entry concludes with one or two bibliographic entries for more information.

As always in a compilation like this, it is almost as interesting to consider the entries omitted as those included. After some review of the possibilities, the author concludes that his definition of popular culture is any work "embraced by the people" (preface). Within this definition, the author also stresses new materials, as they are more readily available for use and because "Americans today are far more attuned to the modern era than they are to the past" (preface). *War and American Popular Culture* is a practical reference tool that conveniently identifies and describes a broad range of resources that reflect how American culture has viewed and portrayed our history replete with wars. In addition to serving as a resource guide for instructors who seek popular culture material, the book could be simply read or browsed through by those interested in American history or some aspect of popular culture such as war movies or Civil War songs. [R: BL, 15 April 99, p. 1550; Choice, July/Aug 99, p. 1930; SLJ, Aug 99, p. 182]—**Henry E. York**

27   Performing Arts

GENERAL WORKS

Biography

P
423.   Lentz, Harris M., III. **Obituaries in the Performing Arts, 1998: Film, Television, Radio, Theatre, Dance, Music, Cartoons, and Pop Culture.** Jefferson, N.C., McFarland, 1999. 245p. illus. $25.00pa. ISBN 0-7864-0748-4. ISSN 1087-9617.

This is a single source for obituaries in film, television, theater, music, and popular literature. It gives essential data of date, place, and cause of death for 566 people, with 380 photographs. Names are filed by the form in which they are best known: Harry Caray (Harry Carabin), Grandpa Jones (Louis Jones), and Sheri Lewis (Sheri Hurwitz). Lentz is a veteran writer of obituaries; all of these are written in the style typical of obituaries. He covers a wide range of individuals, from Russian composer Alfred Schnittke to film composer John Addison. If the person was an actor, Lentz presents as complete a filmography as possible, as in the cases of Sonny Bono, Lloyd Bridges, and E. G. Marshall. For actor Jack Lord, Lentz lists his numerous television programs. Several songs are listed for Frank Sinatra. He includes wrestler Junkyard Dog, runner Florence Joyner, and football player Ray Nitschke, all of whom made film appearances or were considered to be in the entertainment industry. Most articles include citations to major newspapers, such at *The New York Times* and *The Los Angeles Times*, or magazines, such as *Time* and *Newsweek*. For some entries, no citations are given because Lentz provides the only obituary readily accessible.—**Ralph Hartsock**

FILM, TELEVISION, AND VIDEO

Biography

C, P
424.   Andrew, Geoff. **Stranger Than Paradise: Maverick Film-Makers in Recent American Cinema.** New York, Limelight Editions, 1998. 374p. illus. index. $38.00. ISBN 0-87910-277-2.

As Hollywood movies have increasingly become big-budget extravaganzas with spectacular special effects and highly paid megastars, the coterie of so-called independent filmmakers has flourished. Ignoring market surveys and target groups, the "indies" (as they like to be called) emphasize originality and freshness in themes, characters, and techniques. Andrew, well-known author and film critic in England, analyzed more than 200 of cinema's most famous directors worldwide in his *Film Handbook* (see ARBA 91, entry 1386). Now he turns his attention to the indies, some of whom, such as Spike Lee and Quentin Tarantino, have achieved notoriety, while most have not.

Major chapters are devoted to 10 filmmakers, including David Lynch, Todd Haynes, and Steven Soderbergh, along with an excellent essay on the history of independent cinema. Acknowledging that maverick filmmakers have always been around the motion picture industry, Andrew examines how the achievements of early outsiders such as Orson Welles and John Cassavetes relate to the current wave of independent filmmakers. He is especially good at explaining the qualities that go together to make important independent films. His insightful analysis of the Coen brothers' acclaimed film *Fargo* suggests how the relatively unknown actors, low budget, and quirky plot were successfully transformed into an engrossing film with memorable performances. He lends a light and entertaining tone to the book by picking up on the comic elements of the films.

This will nicely complement the best film-by-film reference book on the subject, *VideoHound's Independent Film Guide* (2d ed.; see ARBA 2000, entry 1169). This volume is recommended for academic libraries and cinema collections.—**Richard W. Grefrath**

Dictionaries and Encyclopedias

C, P

425.   Hischak, Thomas S. **The American Musical Film Song Encyclopedia.** Westport, Conn., Greenwood Press, 1999. 521p. index. $69.50. ISBN 0-313-30737-7.

Hischak's *The American Musical Film Song Encyclopedia* is an ambitious, carefully executed, and generally successful attempt to do for movie musicals what the author's excellent *The American Musical Theatre Song Encyclopedia* (see ARBA 96, entry 1416) did for Broadway. The author provides valuable information on more than 1,700 songs from 500 notable Hollywood musicals, from the birth of talkies to filmed rock operas. For the purposes of this work, musicals are defined as "having at least three songs sung by characters in the movie." Songs in films that originated on Broadway or Tin Pan Alley are excluded—an unfortunate but probably necessary editorial decision.

Hischak largely limits his selection to U.S. movies, including animated works but excluding shorts. Each alphabetically listed entry includes lyric and songwriting credits and performing credits, along with a short but lively overview that provides the plot context for the song and other interesting background. Revelations abound on almost every page. Who would have thought, for example, that the old Dixieland chestnut "Do You Know What It Means to Miss New Orleans" was written for the 1947 film *New Orleans!*? In addition to the information in the body of the encyclopedia, the author has thoughtfully provided a number of other useful indexes and appendixes, including a listing of alternative song titles, songs from other sources, best–song Oscars, and a bibliography of works on film musicals and film songwriting. There is also an essential alphabetic list of musicals cited in the body of the work (with songs cited) and a general index. This is an essential addition to music, film studies, and popular culture collections. [R: Choice, Sept 99, p. 110; BL, June 99, p. 1870]—**Gary Handman**

C, P

426.   Katz, Ephraim. **The Film Encyclopedia.** 3d ed. New York, HarperCollins, 1998. 1506p. $28.00pa. ISBN 0-06-273492-X.

The tradition of Katz has been well maintained by new editors Klein and Nolen. No entries have been eliminated from the earlier editions nor have other cosmetic changes, such as photographs, been added. It still adheres to Katz's original intent to compile "the most comprehensive one volume encyclopedia on World cinema ever published in the English language."

Entries are presented in alphabetic order and there is still no index. Each entry, however, does contain cross-references to help readers locate other entries that contain related or complementary information. Those cross-references are noted with the use of small capitals.

If the entry is biographic, "FILMS" indicates that what follows is a fairly complete list of credits in a professional capacity or for the function specified (e.g., director, screenplay writer, and so on). If the entry contains "FILMS INCLUDED," the entry is only a partial listing. When it is not apparent, the national origin of a film or the country where the film was produced is given after the title in parentheses and abbreviated.

A slash separating titles in the credits indicates an alternative title, either in the original language produced or in a second or third language for an international distribution. A slash used with country designation indicates film production done in two or more countries that are also noted. Dates following titles are usually the year of first release for a general screening.

Some credits, where a single film is given, usually give the production in the country of origin. Original titles are listed for pictures in the English, French, Spanish, Italian, and German languages. Titles produced in less familiar languages (i.e., Swedish, Japanese, Russian) are given when released in the United States or United Kingdom. If no record of release in an English-speaking country is known, the title given in a lesser-known language is a literal translation or the English rendition of an untranslatable title.

As has been noted in earlier reviews of earlier editions, there are still some failings that continue. Some "rockumentaries" are not listed nor are the rock groups or individual artists appearing in them. For example, The Who's "Tommy" or Elton John, who appeared in the movie, is not listed. Additionally, musicians who appear under a pseudonym are not cross-referenced (e.g., Ice-T, Ice-Cube, and so on).

Nonetheless, this compendium is still a most useful and necessary acquisition for a library or film buff's collection. The new editors have done a reasonable job in maintaining a credible publication, including new entries and updating those already included.—**Daniel C. Barkley**

P, S
427.   Lenburg, Jeff. **The Encyclopedia of Animated Cartoons.** 2d ed. New York, Checkmark Books/Facts on File, 1999. 576p. illus. index. $24.95pa. ISBN 0-8160-3832-5.

This 2d edition of a classic work is sure to be a popular item in school, public, and academic libraries. Lenburg has produced a monumental resource chronicling the history and development of a unique art form. Perhaps the most valuable part of the book is the introduction entitled "A Nutshell History of the American Animated Cartoon," which traces the origins of animation from Winsor McCay to *The Simpsons*. The use of the word "American" in the introduction is significant; students of Japanese anime will not find a great deal of information in Lenburg's work. His information is divided into detailed descriptions of every animated silent and sound cartoon, every animated feature film, and every animated television series or special. The more than 2,200 entries provide complete information on creators, directors, release dates, awards received, and—crucial to the success of any animated film—the voice talents behind the characters. Lenburg clearly demonstrates the social and political significance of animated films, showing how they are able to make statements in a few drawings that would take thousands of words in text. His book is also a treasure-trove of trivia where readers can find out such esoteric information as Beavis and Butt-head's first names; what animal provided the inspiration for Betty Boop; and what happened to such forgotten characters as Clint Clobber, Fanny Zilch, and Honey Halfwitch. Not only is this book a great reference, it is a lot of fun to read.—**Joseph L. Carlson**

Filmography

P
428.   Fetrow, Alan G. **Feature Films, 1950-1959: A United States Filmography.** Jefferson, N.C., McFarland, 1999. 712p. index. $72.50. ISBN 0-7864-0427-2.

Many changes in the movie industry during the 1950s were promoted by the need to compete with the ubiquitous box appearing in more and more living rooms. Censorship rules were stretched, science fiction and films about teens were on the rise, and westerns and serials declined. This filmography, listing 3,075 U.S. movies, reflects such changes.

Alphabetically arranged entries include title, production company, release year, full cast and credits, songs, running time, video availability, plot synopsis, and production notes. Character names are included for Oscar winners or nominees, top-grossing films, and for nonfictional characters. Cross-references are made to alternate titles. A list of award-winning films and a brief bibliography precede an extensive name index, enhancing access to the movie listing.

The author has published two other volumes documenting American films back to 1927. Hopefully, he will continue this chronological documentation of the U.S. film industry. [R: Choice, Sept 99, p. 110; BL, June 99, p. 1878]—**Anita Zutis**

P

429.   **TLA Film and Video Guide: The Discerning Film Lover's Guide 2000-2001.** David Bleiler, ed. New York, St. Martin's Press, 1999. 756p. illus. index. $18.95pa. ISBN 0-312-24330-8.

As implied in the subtitle, the compilers of this selective guide to films and videos set out to advise users on the quality of the titles they include. Bleiler is the video columnist for the *Philadelphila Daily News* and he emphasizes that this is a critical survey for cinema lovers, not a comprehensive viewing list. It covers more than 9,500 films, with special focus on independent and international movies and the best of mainstream feature films.

This is a more readable product than one finds in many video guides. The layout is spacious, with nice margins around each entry. Arrangement is alphabetic by title, with the title clearly shown in large, bold print. Each entry includes year of release, running time, country of origin, directory, a short critical review, a rating on a four-star scale, and the film's main actors. All reviews have cost and format information (e.g., VHS, DVD, letterbox) for prospective film purchasers. Almost all the titles are available from the TLA Entertainment Group, the enterprise that lends its initials to the title of the book. An order form and citation for the group's Website make up the final page. Six indexes round out the volume: countries of origin, genres, directors filmographies, stars filmographies, authors and screenwriters, and themes. And finally, there are lists of "TLA Bests" for 1990 to 1998 and "Awards" for 1970 to 1998.

This successful and moderately priced directory will help film lovers make viewing choices among the better movies of the twentieth century. Libraries that support users in film studies programs should find this a popular reference tool.—**Berniece M. Owen**

Videography

C, P, S

430.   Frank, Sam. **Buyer's Guide to Fifty Years of TV on Video.** Buffalo, N.Y., Prometheus Books, 1999. 1498p. index. $22.95pa. ISBN 1-57392-226-9.

This comprehensive directory was written and compiled with the help of many individuals and sources. It covers television series, television movies, and documentaries. The directory aims to be more than just a list of available shows; it was written to give the reader the edge so that they can in assembling the best possible library of favorite and forgotten shows, movies, and miniseries based on content and visual quality. The author provides helpful commentary throughout the book, indicating places where he is stating his personal opinions, observations, and preferences.

The main section of the directory lists shows in alphabetic order. Entries include several elements—an episode title, network, original air dates, cast members and character names, running times, the author's content ratings from "bomb" to "excellent," and format availability of the show. The author also includes comments and memorable highlights from the show or episode that stood out to him, such as whether it is recommended for children or family viewing, available in color or black-and-white, or closed-captioned. Availability in laser disc, pricing, MPAA ratings for movies and television series, and cross-references to several other well-known television directories are also provided. The author points out that several of these "standard" sources do contain inaccuracies. Entries also contain warning labels for shows concerning content, credits for each show, Nielson rankings, Emmy Awards, and other awards.

There are informative and helpful sections of this book. All of the shows listed are available for purchase, so an alphabetic list of mail and telephone order companies is provided with commentary on what is available from each, ease and time frame of purchase and arrival, and the quality of those purchases. There is a section on recommended family shows that Frank categorizes, from adventure to westerns. His introduction is quite informative and contains many components. He provides explanations for his rating scales, shows how to care for video tapes, discusses the different timings there can be for shows, and details the variations of picture quality there can be based on dubbing from original or copies of different formats. The book gives brief histories on the "fourth network" and the "golden age of television" and includes a detailed section on the history of kinescopes, videotape, and color television. The author includes a section on 180 shows that he would like to see made available for purchase as well as a trivia quiz section, a bibliography, and a name index.

An alphabetic running head in the entries section would help with locating items in the directory because entries can go on for several pages. Also, bolding the episode titles instead of enclosing them in quotation marks might also help with identification. Despite these minor suggested changes, this book is highly recommended for those academic, school, and public libraries that are building a collection of television shows and movies and for all general reference collections. [R: LJ, 1 Sept 98, p. 170]—**Jan S. Squire**

P
431.   Mayo, Mike. **VideoHound's War Movies: Classic Conflict on Film.** Farmington Hills, Visible Ink Press/Gale, 1999. 368p. illus. index. $19.95pa. ISBN 1-57859-089-2.
     This is an engagingly written and liberally illustrated discussion of 201 war films. The book strives to be representative rather than exhaustive; for instance, there are some John Wayne films here, but not all (no *Back to Bataan* or *Flying Tigers*). The chapters include "American Wars" (*The Alamo, The Red Badge of Courage*), "British Wars" (*Beau Geste, Braveheart, Zulu*), "French Wars" (*The Battle of Algiers, Waterloo*), "Japanese Wars" (*Seven Samurai, Yojimbo*), and "Russian Wars" (*Alexander Nevsky, Doctor Zhivago*). The major chapters are "Word War I" (*All Quiet on the Western Front, The Blue Max*), "Between the World Wars" (*For Whom the Bell Tolls*), "World War II: Europe and North Africa" (*The Dirty Dozen, Where Eagles Dare*), "World War II: Pacific" (*Battle Cry*), "World War II: Documentaries" (*Battle of Midway*), "World War II: The Holocaust" (*The Last Metro, Life is Beautiful*), "World War II: Homefront" (*Since You Went Away*), "World War II: POWs" (*Bridge on the River Kwai*), "World War II: The Resistance" (*Casablanca*), "Korean War" (*Pork Chop Hill*), "Vietnam War" (*Platoon*), and "Coming Home" (*The Best Years of Our Lives*).
     Each film receives two pages of treatment, including an intelligent annotated plot summary; a black-and-white photograph; a cast list; and lists of the writers, cinematographers, producers, and others. There is also a list of awards, the rating, running time, and formats on which the film is currently available. Somewhat surprisingly, considering the book's popular nature, it has an extensive indexing that makes it usable for reference purposes. These include a title index, a cast index, a directory index, a writer index, a cinematographer index, a composer index, and a category index.
     The heart of the book, however, is the annotations and plot summaries, which are intelligent and engaging. Mayo is no hero worshipper or uncritical lover of war movies. For instance, he properly notes the rather disturbing lack of concern in *The Dirty Dozen* over the killing of the civilians in the chateau. However, Mayo is not a censor or a moralist; he simply notes the tendency in films of the time to include such violence and states that "the morality is dubious, but the movie sure is fun."
     The book is current, covering *Saving Private Ryan* and other recent films along with the classics. Each film section includes a significant quote or two from the film, and occasionally also some fact of historical interest. There is a short list of thematically similar films on the opening page of each review. Mayo has packed a lot of information into this engaging volume, and its reasonable price makes it a great buy for both individuals and reference departments.—**Bill Miller**

THEATER

C, P
432.   Lounsbury, Warren C., and Norman C. Boulanger. **Theatre Backstage from A to Z.** 4th ed. Seattle, Wash., University of Washington Press, 1998. 231p. illus. $27.50 spiralbound. ISBN 0-295-97717-5.
     First published in 1967, this 4th edition updates theater terms and definitions particularly to include technological advancements in the area of automated lighting and their controls, trusses, and rigging. It also updates computer applications in theater and explains the basic atmosphere of backstage (scenery, construction, stage appliances). Along with the terms and definitions are appendixes of manufacturers and distributors, bibliographies, periodicals, and pertinent Websites.
     This is a good basic book for backstage goings-on. The coverage is complete and illustrations are adequate. However, in reviewing its contents, one cannot help but feel—to spite the updates incorporated into this edition—that the book is pretty much confined to representing the stage of 1967 and before. Any indication of advanced technology and its application to the stage after the 1960s is sporadic and minimal. Realizing that many backstage techniques and operations of a hundred years ago (or earlier) are still utilized, the amount of

page space used to cover the making of an archaic thunder machine, for example, and other old-time devices seems unnecessary in a book of this sort. The explanation of color, color gels for lighting, and texturing techniques also seems insufficient when explained in black-and-white, not color.

Theatre Backstage from A to Z is a good starting point, but readers would be more impressed if further thought was given to this edition. When taking the effort to revise an edition, it is just as essential and appropriate to remove the old as it is to update it with the new and more valuable.—**Joan Garner**

28 Philosophy and Religion

PHILOSOPHY

Dictionaries and Encyclopedias

C, P

433.   **The Cambridge Dictionary of Philosophy.** 2d ed. Robert Audi, ed. New York, Cambridge University Press, 1999. 1001p. $74.95; $29.95pa. ISBN 0-521-63136-X; 0521-63722-8pa.

With the revision of this work (originally reviewed in ARBA 97, entry 1159) into a new edition, it becomes only stronger as a reference work and more worthy of inclusion on the library shelf. This 2d edition includes more than 400 new entries by 50 additional contemporary philosophers. It also expands the coverage of developing fields, such as applied ethics and philosophy of the mind, while at the same time expanding on non-Western and non-European philosophy. A large selection of entries is devoted to African, Arabic, Islamic, Japanese, Jewish, Korean, and Latin American philosophy. This inclusion is especially gratifying with the world becoming smaller all the time. Inclusion of the non-Western philosophies further exemplifies the breadth of discussion currently undertaken in philosophy.

Entries, as the preface to the 1st edition indicates, fall between brief descriptions of the concept and that of an encyclopedic entry consisting of background context and bibliographic information. Each entry attempts to express the nature and content of the concept while illuminating salient related side avenues of the entry. The target of this volume is the well-versed reader in other fields who may need access to definitions of concepts in the field of philosophy to enhance their understanding. A number of philosophers are included in the entries, not as much to define and discuss their biographical information, but to more fully explore the developments of philosophical thought throughout its development as a field of intellectual inquiry. Various related fields and subfields are also included. Some examples include the philosophy of history, computer and artificial intelligence, political philosophy, and the philosophy of science. Modern philosophers are selectively included in the 2d edition, again weighted toward writers whom many nonphilosophers may want to look up.—**Gregory Curtis**

C, P

434.   **Dictionary of Existentialism.** Haim Gordon, ed. Westport, Conn., Greenwood Press, 1999. 539p. index. $99.50. ISBN 0-313-27404-5.

Some 65 specialists in the field have contributed a series of signed essays arranged in dictionary format, with the primary goal being to provide a key reference tool for scholars and students who are seeking information on particular thinkers, writers, terms, and ideas that have been developed in or linked to existentialism. Entries range in length, with more depth given to significant names and concepts. Each of the entries includes extensive cross-referencing as well as a brief bibliography of primary and secondary sources, as appropriate.

In most cases, topical concepts are discussed as they relate to major and minor thinkers; and where contrasting perspectives of uses are evident, these are explained. By consulting main entries and cross-references, the reader comes to understand the influence that many writers had on each other and the currents of exchange of ideas. A selected bibliography, index, and list of contributors supplement the text. This will be a solid addition to the philosophy section of any reference collection, and a handsome complement to general and subject-specific encyclopedias. [R: Choice, Dec 99, p. 686]—**Edmund F. SantaVicca**

P, S

435.   **Ethics and Values.** Danbury, Conn., Grolier, 1999. 8v. illus. index. $265.00/set. ISBN 0-7172-9274-6.

This work is aimed at providing clear, unbiased information about ethical issues and concerns. It is oriented to students of all ages, but is particularly relevant for intermediate and high school levels. It contains more than 200 entries that reflect a broad range of issues related to ethics, morals, and values. A sample of the topics included is abortion, addition, animal rights, anti-Semitism, capital punishment, censorship, cults, discrimination, euthanasia, child abuse, corruption, Nazism, pornography, gun control, genocide, the Holocaust, racism, and sexism.

The entries are arranged alphabetically. Most are only two pages long, with one black-and-white photograph as illustration. The photographs are well chosen and interesting. The articles are subdivided into shorter sections, which makes for easier reading. The type is large and presented in two-column format. Each volume has an index to the entire set; however, individual entries do not include bibliographic information. There is a one-page listing of references ("further reading") in the last volume that focuses on ethics in general rather than on specific topics included.

Individual articles are not signed. There is a list of contributors hidden on the back of the title page of each volume, with no indication of their qualifications or positions. The authority of the work appears to rest on the reputation of the publisher. However, the information included does clarify and present a balanced, objective, easy-to-understand introduction to complex moral and ethical issues. The set is a useful starting point for discussion and work with students on many important, critical issues that impact today's society. It is recommended for children's and young adult collections in public libraries, as well as for intermediate and high school library collections. [R: BL, 15 Nov 98, p. 612]—**Susan J. Freiband**

RELIGION

General Works

Biography

C, P

436.   Melton, J. Gordon. **Religious Leaders of America: A Biographical Guide to Founders and Leaders of Religious Bodies, Churches, and Spiritual Groups in North America.** 2d ed. Farmington Hills, Mich., Gale, 1999. 724p. index. $99.00. ISBN 0-8103-8878-2. ISSN 1057-2961.

Until now a researcher needing a biography of a current religious leader was required to check many different sources. This volume makes the search much simpler. It includes the biographies of 1,200 Americans and Canadians who have had an influence in North American religious life since 1865.

Whereas earlier works were usually limited to Christian figures, the author of this work has chosen to include leaders from Protestant, Roman Catholic, Jewish, Islamic, Eastern, and metaphysical groups (e.g., Humanists, Agnostics, Atheists), as well as some foreign contemporary leaders. Furthermore, Melton made an effort to include women, African Americans, and North American Indians who were omitted from earlier works.

According to the introduction, in order to select the persons to profile, Melton chose leaders of major older religious bodies of America, leaders of ecumenical bodies, founders of newer and smaller religious traditions, and those who are self-proclaimed nonreligious.

In addition to the main body of the work, which contains the profiles of the religious leaders arranged alphabetically according to surname, there is a "List of Profiled Leaders" that gives a quick overview of the persons included, a "Religious Affiliation Appendix," and a "Master Name and Keyword Index."

Each entry contains the name by which the individual is best known, birth date and place (if applicable), affiliation and occupation, and a brief biography encompassing the individual's life and beliefs. Finally, there are bibliographic citations for publications by or about the person. Each entry is numbered for easy reference in the master index. This 2d edition (see ARBA 92, entry 1402, for a review of the 1st edition) is a valuable biographical work for public, academic, and religious libraries.—**Sara R. Mack**

Dictionaries and Encyclopedias

P, S

437.   **The Encyclopedia of World Religions.** Robert S. Ellwood and Gregory D. Alles, eds. New York, Facts on File, 1998. 390p. illus. index. $29.95. ISBN 0-8160-3504-0.

This brief 1-volume encyclopedia is written for young adults in grades 6 through 12. It contains nearly 500 entries covering ancient, modern, and "new" religions as well as symbols, ideas and concepts, general terms, and past and present personages. The work is minimally illustrated with halftone prints, drawings, maps, tables, and charts. A topical outline grouping all entries under 16 main headings, a 3-page selected bibliography of print and electronic texts, and an 8-page index are included at the back of the work.

The text, in two-column format, is clear and easy to read. All the traditional world religions are included, and each is supplemented with an additional entry addressing its status in America. Christianity, however, receives the greatest coverage (80 entries). Judaism (54), Hinduism (54), and Buddhism (30) are represented with fewer entries. Islam is represented by a mere 20 entries. Woefully weak coverage is devoted to Confucianism, Jainism, Shintoism, Sikhism, and Taoism; none of these exceeds five entries. Only eight new religions were included and all except Scientology were founded prior to the twentieth century. All entries for religions and denominations are generally subdivided under history, beliefs or teachings, practices, organizations, and significance. Entry keywords and running headers are presented in uppercase letters. Cross-references are indicated by words within the text appearing in small capital letters.

The stated purpose of this encyclopedia is "to help readers find information on the world's religious traditions that is simple and interesting to read." The editors have not adequately accomplished that goal. Each bold typeface entry keyword is followed immediately by a definitional clause (rather than a sentence) that is frequently so simplistic or reductional as not to be helpful at all. The remainder of the essay, however, generally supplies enough extra information to derive some sense of the meaning of the term. The encyclopedia covers a broad range of topics, albeit in a fairly cursory and idiosyncratic fashion. The index serves as an important aid to locating topics not addressed by a unique entry, but the listing—in three-column format—appears in a considerably reduced typeface and thus is difficult to read. The predominance of Judeo-Christian topics is specious in that the tradition is held in low esteem; for example, Jesus Christ and Christianity are no more unique than any other religious leader or religion. Biases are displayed in other ways as well. The entry for "Church and State" addresses only the American situation; it does not cover affairs in other parts of the world. "Evangelical and Fundamentalist Christianity" is addressed in a single entry, yet Liberal Christianity or Liberalism is not identified at all. Muslim prohibitions regarding meat are not mentioned in the "Diet and Religion" entry. The entry for "Christianity in America" focuses on Roman Catholicism and Eastern Orthodoxy, but not on Protestantism; the latter is contained in a different entry. Very few illustrations are included in this work but some, such as for the Buddhist bodhi, tree are indecipherable. Halftone prints are included for Gandhi, Martin Luther King, and Malcolm X, but not for Aquainas, Confucius, Luther, Muhammad, and many others. Guru and syncretism are not defined and it is not self-evident why two entries (Pentecostal Christianity and Pentecostalism) were needed to address the charismatic traditions. David Levinson's *Religion: A Cross-Cultural Encyclopedia* (see ARBA 97, entry 1178), with somewhat fewer entries, is a preferred work even for young adults, and *The HarperCollins Dictionary of Religion* (1995), edited by Jonathan Z. Smith, is the definitive scholarly work for the subject. [R: BL, 1 Sept 98, pp. 156-158; SLJ, Nov 98, p. 151]—**Glenn R. Wittig**

P

438.   **Merriam-Webster's Encyclopedia of World Religions.** Wendy Doniger, ed. Springfield, Mass., Merriam-Webster, 1999. 1181p. illus. $49.95. ISBN 0-87779-044-2.

This 1-volume encyclopedia is a product of the University of Chicago faculty and alumni. Most of the contributing editors and the consulting editor have earned degrees from or work for the university. The volume is functional and convenient in its format. Containing 3,500 entries and 30 longer articles, it serves the needs of the quick informational check and the in-depth beginning study. The bibliography, illustration, pronunciation guide, maps, and intricate cross-referencing system all add to the value of this text. The audience is the general reader, not the scholar, and it does well in providing information for the curious reader. [R: BL, 15 Dec 99, pp. 799-800]—**Linda L. Lam-Easton**

Handbooks and Yearbooks

C, P

439.   Lewis, James R. **Cults in America: A Reference Handbook.** Santa Barbara, Calif., ABC-CLIO, 1998. 232p. index. (Contemporary World Issues Series). $45.00. ISBN 1-57607-031-X.

This reference work is part of the series that addresses often controversial, vital issues in today's society. It provides a balanced view of alternative and controversial religions that are sometimes referred to as cults. Sensational news reports of cults periodically dominate the national news—the recent incidents of Heaven's Gate, the UFO group in San Diego (1997) and the Branch Davidians in Waco (1993) are two examples of highly complex and controversial cults. The fascinating history of cults and sects in America often chronicles the emergence of charismatic leaders, brainwashing and mind control debates, communes, murders, and tax evasion. This reference work is well-organized into chapters that provide a logical presentation of a lot of information, including a historical overview of cults and alternative religions in the United States. There is also a chronology beginning in 1740 of key names and events and important court decisions as well as facts and data and a directory of organizations and Websites. This last section is fully annotated and provides cult information with more than two dozen URLs of Websites as well as some e-mail contacts. A comprehensive and useful index is provided, as is an extensive list of sources, including books, articles, and videotapes. Readers will most likely proceed directly to the 46 entries in the "Controversial Groups and Movements" chapter; some of the especially interesting ones are on Santeria, the Hare Krishna movement, Satanism, Erhard Seminars Training (EST), Voodoo, and the Church of Scientology. This reference work can be used by students, parents, and psychologists. It is highly recommended for all libraries, but especially those serving undergraduate students and the general public. [R: LJ, 1 Feb 99, pp. 76-78]—**Edward Erazo**

P, S

440.   Smart, Ninian. **The World's Religions.** 2d ed. New York, Cambridge University Press, 1998. 608p. illus. index. $27.95pa. ISBN 0-521-63748-1.

Revised and updated, this work unravels the world's religions from a historical perspective that takes the reader from early beginnings to the modern world. Divided into 2 major parts, the 1st traces the development of religions through the fifteenth century, with separate chapters on South Asia; China; Japan; Southeast Asia; the Pacific; the Americas; Ancient Near East; Persia and Central Asia; Greece and Rome; classical African religions; and the manifestations of Christianity, Judaism, and Islam in medieval times.

The 2d part covers cultural transformation from 1500 to the present, and is more focused on the evolution of religions and cultural values. Religions are described through their symbols, rituals, followers, architecture, and art. The volume is heavily illustrated with black-and-white photographs and images, with a few color plates. The work opens with an introduction that touts the value of comparative study of religion, and concludes with a glossary, bibliography, and full index.

Students and others who need a basic overview of various religions should find the volume useful for its cultural approach. Those needing more in-depth information can consult religious encyclopedias. *The World's Religions* is recommended as a basic introduction, and quite possibly for the circulating as well as reference collection.

—**Edmund F. SantaVicca**

Bible Studies

Dictionaries and Encyclopedias

C, P

441.   **The Dictionary of Biblical Imagery.** Leland Ryken and others, eds. Downers Grove, Ill., InterVarsity Press, 1998. 1058p. index. $39.99. ISBN 0-8308-1451-5.

Much of the Bible is taken up with story (of ancient Israel in the Old Testament and of Jesus and the early church in the New Testament) and poetry (primarily the Book of Psalms). The stories, poems, and even the nonliterary writings, such as the letters of Paul, are full of images. God is described as a warrior, Israel as an unfaithful wife, and the adversaries of God and his people are portrayed as beasts. Although this aspect of the Bible is not completely ignored in previous Bible dictionaries and encyclopedias, this is the first one to deal specifically with the imagery in the Bible. The more than 150 contributors include both biblical and literary scholars, many of whom are quite at home in both fields.

Among the alphabetically arranged articles are ones on each book of the Bible; typical characters (e.g., hero/heroine, villain, pilgrim), locations (e.g., city, countryside, sea), and motifs (e.g., quest, rags to riches, crime and punishment); and images (e.g., blindness, drought, fruitfulness). In addition, there are survey articles on rhetorical devices: "Character Types," "Plot Motifs," and "Rhetorical Patterns." Often there is interplay among images in Bible passages, and the cross-references within and at the end of articles, the subject index, and the scripture index tie these together well. One could wish for a bit more bibliography; the majority of articles do not have one.

The articles are well written and will inform readers about not only the images and messages of the biblical writings, but also the world and cultural mindset in which they arose. This work is recommended for academic, public, and church libraries.—**Craig W. Beard**

C, P
442.   **The Illustrated Bible Dictionary.** J. D. Douglas, ed. Downers Grove, Ill., InterVarsity Press, 1998. 3v. illus. maps. index. $79.99/set. ISBN 0-8308-1460-4.

As the title implies, this 3-volume book is a dictionary of the Bible. However, given its size and breadth, it could just as easily pass for an encyclopedia. In total, the book is about 2,000 pages long and covers an enormous number of topics.

The cover of the book declares, "A superb three-part dictionary of the Bible filled with pictures, maps, and diagrams, most in full color." This brief, rather subjective description appears to be quite accurate. With respect to the "superb" part of the description, the definitions and articles contained in the book appear to be quite accurate and very detailed. The editors have done a great job of reducing the individual articles to their most essential pieces. In fact, if the book suffers from any chronic faults, it would be its brevity. Abbreviations are used extensively throughout the work, sometimes to an almost absurd degree. For example, directional words are never spelled out. N, W, S, and E are used for North, West, South, and East. One gets the impression that one of the primary goals of the editors was to make the book as small as possible. There is irony here in that this book is anything but small. It is three large, rather substantial volumes. The extensive use of abbreviations and scholarly detail makes the dictionary a little difficult to use for younger readers, although the binding may give one the impression that it is a juvenile reference work. Each volume is bound in 9-by-11-inch glossy covers, each a different primary color.

However, the dictionary was written by some of the finest conservative evangelical scholars in the world. As such it is highly recommended for every library collection that may serve researchers with serious questions about the Bible, its theology, its literature, and its history. Make no mistake, this is a serious reference work, very much at home in a serious adult reference department.—**Richard A. Leiter**

Handbooks and Yearbooks

C, P
443.   **Zondervan Handbook to the Bible.** 3d ed. Grand Rapids, Mich., Zondervan Publishing/HarperCollins, 1999. 815p. illus. maps. $39.99. ISBN 0-310-23095-0.

This volume is a revised and expanded edition of the best-selling *Eerdmans Handbook to the Bible* (1st ed.; see ARBA 74, entry 1187). It retains the arrangement of the previous edition: an introduction to the Bible and its study (part 1); a section each on the Old Testament (part 2) and New Testament (part 3), with books arranged in canonical order, outlined, and commented upon; and a reference index (part 4). The introduction is comprised of articles written by some of the 69 contributors. Other articles written by these scholars are strategically placed throughout parts 2 and 3, the text of which was written by Pat Alexander. Among these articles are character portraits (absent from the previous editions), introductions to specific types of biblical literature, and historical sketches of contemporary civilizations. Also, like its predecessors, the handbook is profusely illustrated with maps, timelines, and pictures of artifacts, among other things. Few, if any, similar works approach the quantity and quality of illustrations.

The sections on the Old and New Testaments is revised and many of the 119 articles are either newly written or thoroughly rewritten for this edition. Some of the articles made the transition unchanged. The same is true of the illustrations; they are a combination of old and new. Most of the changes, which resulted in an increase of 135 pages, were indeed improvements. Unfortunately, a few features that were not retained, such as the charts illustrating weights, measures, and coins of biblical times, will be missed.

Not only was the content itself revised and expanded, so was the list of contributors. The number of scholars was expanded from 32 to 69. Several names appear in the list of contributors of both this and the previous edition (e.g., Alan Millard, Howard Marshall, Dick France). Among the new names are, for the first time, about a dozen women, including Katharine Dell, Grace Emmerson, and Claire Powell. Thorough yet concise coverage, appropriate and appealing illustrations, timeliness, and great attention to detail—which, sadly, cannot be said about enough reference works—make this a highly desirable acquisition for congregational, school, public, and undergraduate academic libraries.—**Craig W. Beard**

Christianity

Almanacs

C, P

444.   **Our Sunday Visitor's Catholic Almanac, 2000.** Matthew Bunson, ed. Huntington, Ind., Our Sunday Visitor, 1999. 607p. index. $28.95; $23.95pa. ISBN 0-87973-905-3; 0-87973-904-5pa. ISSN 0069-1208.

The range of Catholic data in this 2000 edition impressively adds to the content and style of the previous editions of the *Catholic Almanac* (1994 ed.; see ARBA 95, entry 1471). It includes revisions and updating of standard sections (e.g., doctrine and dogma, Catholic communications, ecumenism and interreligious dialogue, U.S. Catholic history, the Church in the world); new sections, including an annual review of key Church events and reports; and a special supplement, the philosophy of the Jubilee Holy Year 2000 and its significance for American Catholics. The multiple entries give a fine overview of the structure and teachings of the largest Christian denomination in the world at the start of the Christian third millennium. They are composed from canonical texts and authoritative writings and succeed in projecting evolving developments in the life of the Church (e.g., contra longstanding tradition, cremation in extreme situations may be tolerated if the doctrine of the resurrection of the dead is not tampered). However, the authenticity of self-impression reveals insiders' judgment calls, gerrymandering, and flaws. On the latter, for example, Judaism teaches that the weekly Sabbath is more solemn than Rosh Hashanah, the Passover feast begins on Nisan 15 not 14, and the "Ten Words" are integral but not the sum of the Mosaic Covenant. The up-to-date reports are also a testimony of the diversity and richness of the Church and its mandate—to celebrate Christ's presence in history. In sum, this is a compelling invitation to learn about a dynamic faith community.—**Zev Garber**

Dictionaries and Encyclopedias

P

445.   **Dictionary of the Presbyterian & Reformed Tradition in America.** D. G. Hart and Mark A. Noll, eds. Downers Grove, Ill., InterVarsity Press, 1999. 286p. $16.99pa. ISBN 0-8308-1453-1.

A reference book with an attitude, this work is explicit about its perspective and is an excellent example of repackaging information for a specialized audience. The editors, respected church historians with excellent reputations, have put together an extension of the publisher's acclaimed *Dictionary of Christianity in America* (see ARBA 91, entry 1444) and have pointed it specifically at the Presbyterian community, stating that the fundamental aim "has been to represent the diversity of efforts to propagate, defend and preserve the Reformed tradition in the United States and Canada" (p. vii). This translates into a more comprehensive coverage of evangelically oriented segments of the general Presbyterian community than has been possible in existing works, such as *The Encyclopedia of the Reformed Faith* (see ARBA 93, entry 1422). An introductory essay, "The Presbyterians: A People, a History & an Identity," underscores this perspective. In addition to a nuanced theological difference, there is a difference in the scope of entries—the focus is on biographical entries and those for various denominational groups. However, contrary to the advertised content, one misses entries for renewal movements (e.g., Presbyterians for Renewal, Presbyterian Coalition), for "A Brief Confession of Faith," or for gender issues—suggesting minimal updating since 1990. Although many of the 400 or more entries are taken from the parent work, they are so identified only if they have been modified in some way. Other entries have been written originally for this work. All entries are signed and include bibliographic references, but there is no index for locating embedded proper names. This work will have greatest appeal to institutions needing information of value to conservative Presbyterians.—**Donald G. Davis Jr.**

C, P

446.   **Encyclopedia of Christianity, Volume 1 (A-D).** Erwin Fahlbusch and others, eds. Leiden, the Netherlands, Brill and Grand Rapids, Mich., William B. Eerdmans, 1999. 893p. $100.00. ISBN 0-8028-2413-7.

The end of the millennium and a desire to provide a serious, scholarly reference work on Christianity are the motivations for production of this work, which is in reality a translation into English, with additions described below, of the fine German work,*Evangelisches Kirchenlexicon* (Vandenhoeck and Ruprecht, 1968). There are 4 more volume to come in the next 5 years, making 1,700 dictionary-type entries total, all written and signed by scholars, mostly from Europe and Germany. A suitable number of additional entries on Christianity of interest to British, American, and other English-speakers have been added, and the already extensive bibliographies at the ends of the articles have had English-language citations added.

Intended for use in academic and public libraries, the work invites comparison with the *Oxford Dictionary of the Christian Church* (3d ed.; see ARBA 98, entry 1389) and *New Schaff-Herzog Encyclopedia of Religious Knowledge* (Baker, 1949). The former, with its English-speakers and Anglo-American emphasis of the subject is a much shorter work (one volume), with shorter entries and shorter bibliographies, compared to the work under review, which emphasizes Continental Christianity and has longer entries and bibliographies. A huge effort has been made here to infuse the work with globalization, with articles on Christianity on different continents and in most countries of the world, and articles on worldwide and ecumenical bodies.

The pluses of the work are numerous. First is the provision of statistical information on Christianity's adherents all over the world, from the resources of David Barrett, a noted demographer of Christianity and author of the 1982 *World Christian Encyclopedia*. Second, the spirit of the work is even-handed and ecumenical, although the starting point is a Western Christian Protestant viewpoint. Roman Catholic, Protestant, Anglican, and Orthodox interpretations are provided. Third, articles on ecumenical bodies are provided. Fourth, current sociocultural contexts are provided in the articles on other world religions, secular philosophies, cultural trends, and political and economical forces. Fifth, historical contexts are provided in articles on historical and theological topics. Sixth, there are biographical entries, although not nearly as many as in the *Oxford Dictionary of the Christian Church*. Seventh, the bibliographic references for further reading are extensive and include both books and periodical articles.

Drawbacks have been noted by other reviewers. These include a complete lack of any illustrations and some inaccuracies in articles on U.S. religious groups. This reviewer notes that in comparison to the entry on Congregationalism the entry for Christian Science seems a bit brief. We have only the one volume so far, so there are maddening cross-references to articles in volumes yet to come, such as under "Campus Crusade for Christ *see* Student Work or Youth Work." The reviewer sees no entry for the African Methodist Episcopal Church, nor a cross-reference. The reader must be clever enough to think to look under "Black Church." There are articles on quite secular topics, such as bourgeois society and birth control, but not one on bioethics. This volume has no index; presumably the index will be for the work as a whole and not be available until the whole set is published, a decided disadvantage, particularly as more volumes appear. Think of this as a companion volume to the *Oxford Dictionary of the Christian Church*, particularly good for materials on Western, continental Christianity, less good for Anglo-American topics, with better attention than most such works to the state of Christianity in countries around the world. [R: LJ, 15 Feb 99, pp. 140-142; BL, 1 Mar 99, pp. 1247-1248; Choice, Oct 99, p. 304]—**Agnes H. Widder**

C, P

447.   **Encyclopedia of the Vatican and Papacy.** Frank J. Coppa, ed. Westport, Conn., Greenwood Press, 1999. 483p. index. $99.50. ISBN 0-313-28917-4.

The Vatican and Papacy remain both the most familiar and the least understandable institutions of the worldwide Roman Catholic Church. To make the executive, legislative, and judiciary branches of the near one billion strong church accessible to the educated public requires a certain amount of scholarly effort. Coppa and the contributors of this work ably provide capsule-size entries on important events, ideologies, and persons examined within church teachings and against outside influences that clearly shows the interweaving of the Vatican and Papacy with the course of Western civilization in general and European history in particular. Although the emphasis is on Vatican diplomacy and history from the Renaissance through the 1990s, due recognition is given to influential pre-Renaissance issues (e.g., heresy, schism) as well as papal policy on current theology and morality, including liberation theology and biomedical ethics. A valuable feature is background information on all popes, anti-popes, and 21 church councils from Nicea (325) to Vatican Council II (1965). Arguably, certain topics generate controversy (e.g., Pope Pius XII, Vatican on Zionism) but for the most part plausible evaluations are generally presented. In sum, this is a source of verified information on Vatican matters that will prove beneficial to students and scholars alike. [R: LJ, 15 Nov 98, pp. 60-61; BL, Aug 99, pp. 2107-2108; Choice, Oct 99, p. 304]

—**Zev Garber**

Judaism

C, P

448.   Solomon, Norman. **Historical Dictionary of Judaism.** Lanham, Md., Scarecrow, 1998. 521p. (Historical Dictionaries of Religions, Philosophies, and Movements, no.19). $60.00. ISBN 0-8108-3497-9.

This book is an excellent addition to Scarecrow's volumes of historical dictionaries. Like other volumes in the series, the entries are arranged alphabetically and, in this instance, cover all aspects of Judaism from Ortho-dox to Reconstructionist. Key articles on liturgy, festivals, and beliefs are identified as such, and each is given added depth through numerous cross-references to other topics in the text as well as books in the bibliography. The bibliography is more than 40 pages long and mainly topical in format. Topics include poetry, music and art, Kabbalah and mysticism, Holocaust theology, and women in Judaism. There are up-to-date sections on Jewish texts available on CD-ROM and on Jewish sources on the Internet. Appendixes include the 613 Commandments of Mitzvot and excerpts from the several platforms defining the Reform movement. British rabbi and scholar Norman Solomon has compiled a wonderful book that can be used for research or browsing by both laypersons and scholars. [R: Choice, May 99, p. 1594]—**Deborah Hammer**

Part IV
SCIENCE
AND
TECHNOLOGY

29 Science and Technology in General

BIBLIOGRAPHY

C, P

449. Hurt, C. D. **Information Sources in Science and Technology.** 3d ed. Englewood, Colo., Libraries Unlimited, 1998. 346p. index. (Library and Information Science Text Series). $55.00; $45.00pa. ISBN 1-56308-528-3; 1-56308-531-3pa.

Society has come a long way in both science and technology since the turn of the century. In 1900, medicine, for example, was overrun with homeopaths and mountebanks in surfeit. Cars had not yet been born, and computers were not even a figment of anyone's imagination. Indeed, not one dollar had been spent on computers by businesses in 1965, whereas more than a billion was spent last year.

With the 3d edition of this notable work, Hurt takes away the pain of source-hunting in this area by updating his work substantially. More than half of the previous sources have been dropped. Unless the source was a "classic," it has been dropped from this edition. This change, Hurt felt, grew out of necessity—the rapid expansion of both science and technology required a serious updating. But the outline of the work is still intact: multidisciplinary works, biological sources, math and the physical sciences, engineering and computer technology, and the health sciences. Websites abound throughout the work, making it as up-to-date as possible. The usual title and subject indexes close out the work. Because the updating is so extensive, libraries with the 2d edition will want this one, too. They will want to keep the previous editions as well. [R: BL, 1 Dec 98, p. 698]—**Mark Y. Herring**

BIOGRAPHY

C, P, S

450. Haven, Kendall, and Donna Clark. **100 Most Popular Scientists for Young Adults: Biographical Sketches and Professional Paths.** Englewood, Colo., Libraries Unlimited, 1999. 526p. illus. index. (Profiles and Pathways Series). $56.00. ISBN 1-56308-674-3.

This 1-volume resource focuses on uncovering the "early intentions and plans and the early life events that shaped" the lives of the scientists discussed. Each 5-page entry contains 6 sections: Career Highlights, Important Contributions, Career Path, Key Dates, Advice, and References. The advice section explains in the scientist's own words, "how to start a successful career in that field of science" (p. xv). Some entries include a black-and-white photograph of the scientist. The appendix provides Internet references and a list of scientists by field of specialization. The 100 scientists include some of the ones most frequently researched by students in grades 5 through 10 (e.g., Isaac Asimov, Robert Bakkar, Robert Ballard, Luther Burbank, Rachel Carson, Albert Einstein, Enrico Fermi, Dian Fossey, Edwin Hubble, Bill Nye, Sally Ride, and Carl Sagan). The entries are arranged alphabetically by last name, but the table of contents and page guide words, instead of listing last name first to make scanning for a name easier, the names are listed first name then last name, making the reader work a little harder to scan the last names. The emphasis on the scientist's career makes this a useful research tool.—**Esther R. Sinofsky**

DICTIONARIES AND ENCYCLOPEDIAS

P, S

451.   **The Facts on File Encyclopedia of Science.** Sharon Brimblecombe, Diana Gallannaugh, and Catherine Thompson, eds. New York, Facts on File, 1999. 2v. illus. $125.00/set. ISBN 0-8160-4008-7.

This 2-volume set was first published in 1998 in England as the *Hutchinson Encyclopedia of Science*. Intended for academic use as well as for the general reader, the encyclopedia is well designed for both quick fact lookup and browsing. The alphabetically arranged entries, more than 10,000 in all, are broad ranging and generally short. Interspersed among them are well-chosen quotations, offbeat facts, and the kind of mnemonic phrases that make memorizing so much easier (e.g., "To remember the order of the planets: My Very Educated Mother Just Served Us Nine Pies" [p. 586]). Also included are short essays on various topics of current interest, such as El Niño, the millennium bug, and cloning as well as topics of perennial interest, such as evolution, dinosaurs, and astronomy; brief biographies of scientists (with a European emphasis); chronologies of the major scientific fields; and seven appendixes covering scientific discoveries, inventions, Nobel Prize winners, the Greek alphabet, and Roman numerals. There are also several Websites featured; some URLs are inevitably already out of date. There is no index, but one is not needed because the reader is guided to related articles by a symbol within the text of the entries. The typography is excellent, with highlighted sections set off in gray. The illustrations consist of clear drawings and less clear photographs, all in black and white. *The Facts on File Encyclopedia of Science* is a handsome resource appropriate for home, school, and public libraries. [R: LJ, 1 May 99, p. 69; BL, 1 Sept 99, pp. 179-180; Choice, Nov 99, p. 510; BR, Nov/Dec 99, p. 85]—**Hope Yelich**

C, P

452.   **The Facts on File Encyclopedia of Science, Technology, and Society.** By Rudi Volti. New York, Facts on File, 1999. 3v. illus. index. $225.00/set. ISBN 0-8160-3123-1.

This book offers about 900 alphabetically arranged articles on a wide variety of topics in science and technology (including agriculture and biotechnology) and some medicine. The articles, which are between 400 and 2,500 words, give brief definitions and explanations of the topics, with emphasis on societal context, applications, and influences. Topics are chosen for their practical or intellectual significance for contemporary society and to some extent for past societies (e.g., "Crossbow," "Phlogiston"). There are treatments of inventions and technological processes; natural or artificial substances; concepts and phenomena; and organizations, programs, and social problems. There are smaller numbers of articles on events, scientific methods and activities, scientific instruments, and disciplines and subjects. Medicine is treated sparsely. Smallpox eradication is included, but there are no articles on cholera, malaria, schistosomiasis, or yellow fever.

This work was written by Volti with the advice of an editorial board. There are 95 contributors featured who are responsible for about 45 percent of the articles. The rest are by Volti. Sometimes one or two references to further reading are included with the articles and are collected in a bibliography in volume 3. The work is well indexed, making subjects and personal names within the articles accessible. The index appears in each of the three volumes.

The articles are well written, accurate, and interesting, and the topics are well chosen. The further reading lists are scanty. If the index had been printed just once, there would have been more space for further reading. [R: LJ, 1 April 99, p. 86; BL, 15 April 99, p. 1546; Choice, Sept 99, p. 116; BR, Sept/Oct 99, p. 79; RUSQ, Fall 99, pp. 91-92]—**Frederic F. Burchsted**

C, P, S

453.   **McGraw-Hill Concise Encyclopedia of Science & Technology.** 4th ed. Sybil P. Parker, ed. New York, McGraw-Hill, 1998. 2318p. illus. index. $150.00. ISBN 0-07-052659-1.

This volume is the 4th edition of a single-volume version of the 20-volume *McGraw-Hill Encyclopedia of Science and Technology* and is edited by the staff of its parent volume. It includes 7,800 alphabetically arranged entries that have been edited from the parent source to provide "helpful knowledge without extensive detail." During editing proportional lengths of entries were maintained. All articles are cross-referenced to related entries and subjects. Text entries are often accompanied by color-enhanced line drawings, black-and-white photographs, and pertinent graphs and tables. The authors of articles are cited in the entry and a list of authors and their affiliations is given in the front matter.

Appendixes include a bibliography by subject, tables of physical constants, supporting data for math and science conversions, fundamental particles, geologic time, 3 tables of data about telescopes, and a biography of 1,200 scientists mentioned in the text. This is followed by a comprehensive index. The index, cross-references, and alphabetic entries all serve to make the volume very user-friendly.

Although touted by the publisher as being useful to the general reader, some entries, because of their inherently complex nature, may be less than informative to those without some knowledge of the field; for instance, those entries that include differential equations in their definitions. The meaning of other entries would be clearer with some background. The entry for *Anisomyaria* reads, "an order containing seven superfamilies of marine and brackish bivalves with byssal attachment."

Other single-volume science references are written at a more introductory level, such as the *DK Ultimate Visual Dictionary of Science* (see ARBA 99, entry 1311) or the *DK Science Encyclopedia* (rev. ed.; see ARBA 99, entry 1310). This comprehensive and technically written volume would be more useful to upper secondary or college students and supporting libraries or homes. It is often suggested that a home reference library should contain an almanac, atlas, dictionary, thesaurus, book of quotations, and a single-volume science reference. The *McGraw-Hill Concise Encyclopedia of Science and Technology* could serve well as a science reference for many homes or libraries.—**Craig A. Munsart**

C, P, S

454.   **Van Nostrand's Scientific Encyclopedia.** 8th ed. [CD-ROM]. Douglas M. Considine and Glenn D. Considine, eds. New York, John Wiley, 1999. Minimum system requirements: IBM or compatible 386. CD-ROM drive. Windows 3.1. 4MB RAM. 1MB hard disk space. SVGA monitor. $235.00. ISBN 0-471-29323-7.

Comprehensive yet complicated, this latest edition of a standard scientific encyclopedia provides a number of enhancements that users will appreciate. Among these are the ability to customize searching with comprehensive search criteria; links to cross-references that allow easy back and forward movement between articles; search and retrieval software that allows the user to add notes, create bookmarks, and make additional links; 500 tables and charts; and more than 3,500 photographs, illustrations, and diagrams that enhance the entries. In total, there are some 7,000 entries written by more than 250 subject experts.

The encyclopedia covers six major categories of scientific endeavor: earth and space sciences, life sciences, energy and environmental sciences, materials sciences, physics and chemistry, and mathematics and information sciences. Updates and revisions have been made throughout these six categories, including such topics as AIDS, genetics, satellites, television, anorexia, and obesity. The CD-ROM provides a variety of search options, from simple to complex, and the user is provided a series of explanations on effective use of search engines, navigation, image viewing, and printing.

Some may find the multiple search options a bit confusing, and others may be frustrated by the preponderance of black-and-white illustrations over color. However, the encyclopedia still remains an authoritative source of basic information in the sciences. High school, public, and college libraries should consider adding this as part of a ready-reference collection. [R: BR, Nov/Dec 99, p. 91; Choice, Dec 99, p. 696]—**Edmund F. SantaVicca**

HANDBOOKS AND YEARBOOKS

P, S

455.   **Scientific American Science Desk Reference.** New York, John Wiley, 1999. 690p. illus. index. $39.95. ISBN 0-471-35675-1.

The editors of *Scientific American Magazine* have produced a ready-reference for science buffs (and the naturally curious). Arranged thematically, there are chapters on measurement; mathematics; chemistry; physics; astronomy; earth science; environment and ecology; biology; the animal kingdom; the plant kingdom; the human body; health and diseases; computer science; technology; and discoveries, inventions, and prizes. Each chapter follows the same structure (except the final chapter on discoveries): a subject overview, chronology, biographies of important figures, glossary of key vocabulary used within the chapter, and a bibliography for further reading. The volume concludes with a comprehensive index.

Aids to the coverage of each topic include tables, charts, diagrams, and illustrations. Sidebars provide further aids such as factual tidbits, quizzes, and mnemonic aids. Cross-references are self-contained within each chapter. URLs, with descriptions of the Websites, are interspersed throughout the text, offering endless sources of information on topics covered. The amount of information found in this easy-to-use reference makes it a good choice for either secondary school or public libraries, as well as a delightful and useful home reference.

—**Dana McDougald**

30 Agricultural Sciences

FOOD SCIENCES AND TECHNOLOGY

Dictionaries and Encyclopedias

P

456.   Reavley, Nicola. **The New Encyclopedia of Vitamins, Minerals, Supplements, & Herbs.** New York, M. Evans, 1998. 792p. index. $19.95pa. ISBN 0-87131-897-0.

The Encyclopedia of Vitamins, Minerals, Supplements, & Herbs is a gold mine of information on what the human body needs to fuel itself to maintain optimal health. The American public is inundated with new "miracle" vitamins and supplements that promise to enhance our health and longevity. It is nearly impossible for the layperson to keep up with the latest discoveries in how nutrition and health are related. This easy-to-use volume will provide many answers to commonly asked questions about nutrition.

The book begins with a question-and-answer section that features many common concerns among consumers, such as "Is it possible to get enough vitamins and minerals from food?" "Are vitamin and mineral supplements necessary?" and "Who might need supplements?" It is then broken down into chapters, including "Vitamins," "Minerals," "Other Nutrients," and "Herbal Medicines." Each vitamin, mineral, or supplement is listed alphabetically in its chapter, and a "quick guide" describes its role in fueling the body, sources of the nutrient, and daily recommendations, among other facts. The last section, "Health Problems," discusses the role of nutrients in fighting such health concerns as cancer, HIV/AIDS, insomnia, and many more. The book concludes with a glossary, list of references, and comprehensive index.

This book is extremely user-friendly and contains a lot of information that readers will be seeking on the subject of vitamins and nutrition and how they relate to human health. It is written for the layperson seeking quick information; however, the entries are interesting enough that many users will probably find themselves reading up on more than what originally they were looking for. This volume will be a valuable addition to the reference shelves of any public library.—**Shannon M. Graff**

Handbooks and Yearbooks

P

457.   Rinzler, Carol Ann. **The New Complete Book of Food: A Nutritional, Medical, and Culinary Guide.** New York, Facts on File, 1999. 440p. index. $40.00. ISBN 0-8160-3987-9.

The New Complete Book of Food: A Nutritional, Medical, and Culinary Guide provides multiple facts about many common foods. It gives basic nutritional information on fat, protein, fiber, and other levels, along with vitamin and mineral contributions and energy value. This information is presented two different formats—with a profile ranking of low, moderate, or high and in a more detailed format with easy-to-follow educational information. Individual food entries go beyond other nutrition works to provide tips on the most nutritious ways to serve, what to look for when buying, and storage and preparation. There is also information on what happens when foods are cooked and how other kinds of processing affect foods, such as canning, drying, and freezing. One of the most important and useful parts of this guide is the information it provides about medical uses and benefits (such as cancer and heart disease prevention), adverse effects associated with specific foods, and food and drug interactions that are possible with certain foods. Important diet information is also provided: first it is noted in the individual entries what diets may restrict or exclude a food, and second, an appendix charts what foods are high in nutrients for specific diets. A bibliography of sources and an index conclude the work. This is a good basic reference for nutritionists and anyone interested in streamlining their diets for their specific health needs.—**Cari Ringelheim**

31 Biological Sciences

BIOLOGY

Dictionaries and Encyclopedias

C, P

458. **Encyclopedia of Genetics.** Jeffrey A. Knight, ed. Hackensack, N.J., Salem Press, 1999. 2v. illus. index. $200.00/set. ISBN 0-89356-978-X.

This timely 2-volume set on genetics is written in a language that can provide the general reader with an overview of genetics and its related glossary. Mostly this source emphasizes human genetics. Many contributing authors from academia and research institutes put their thoughts together to publish this reference text. The public or school libraries might find this text useful in explaining the various areas in this field of study. Although the encyclopedia is alphabetic in scope it includes 8 related areas; 11 essays on bacteria genetics: topics on classical transmission genetics; developmental genetics; genetic engineering and biotechnology; human genetics; surveys on immunogenetics; molecular genetics discussions; and centers on population genetics. The appendixes include a timeline of major developments in genetics, a biographical dictionary of important geneticists, a glossary, a bibliography, and an index. In addition, this easy-to-read set contains more than 200 photographs, charts, graphs, and illustrations that can further illuminate the complex nature of genetics. Each article has the standard format, such as field of study, significance, key terms, *see also* references, and further reading. It is interesting to find concepts such as fragile X syndrome, knockout genes, gene therapy, and molecular medicine included in this encyclopedia. This is a good starting point for locating introductory information on genetics, but more supplemental readings will be required for more in-depth research findings. [R: Choice, Oct 99, p. 310; SLJ, Aug 99, p. 184]
—Polin P. Lei

C, P

459. **The Facts on File Dictionary of Biology.** 3d ed. Robert Hine, ed. New York, Checkmark Books/Facts on File, 1999. 361p. $17.95pa. ISBN 0-8160-3908-9.

As the revised, updated, and expanded edition of an established reference work, this dictionary retains the basic format of previous editions, with some 3,300 alphabetically arranged headwords. Appendixes giving succinct diagrams of the animal and plant kingdoms and amino acid structures have been added. Definitions, usually encyclopedic in scope (one or two paragraphs) are clearly written for the intelligent layperson and are fairly nontechnical. Many cross-references are provided. Entries have been revised and updated when needed. A few illustrations of chemical or cellular structures have been included.

The Facts on File Dictionary of Biology remains a good basic dictionary for school and public library use, particularly where budgets are limited and works such as the *McGraw-Hill Dictionary of Scientific and Technical Terms* (5th ed.; see ARBA 95, entry 1493) and the *Concise Encyclopedia Biology* (see ARBA 97, entry 1266) are not readily available.**—Jonathan F. Husband**

BOTANY

General Works

Dictionaries and Encyclopedias

C, P

460.   Holliday, Paul. **A Dictionary of Plant Pathology.** 2d ed. New York, Cambridge University Press, 1998. 536p. $155.00. ISBN 0-521-59453-7.

This is a comprehensive list of major and many minor plant pathogens. More than 500 genera of fungi and 800 viruses, bacteria, mollicutes, nematodes, and viroids are described. Entries are also included for diseases and disorders, crops and their pathology, fungicides, taxonomic groups, terminology, toxins, vectors, and past plant pathologists. More than 11,000 entries are included.

The author claims that this 2d edition represents a major revision in that cross-references have been increased and new journal references have been added. The use of common names has also been expanded for those readers unfamiliar with scientific names. An important note is that mycorrhizae are omitted with one exception. A list of approximately 175 major textbooks dealing with plant pathology and related areas is included. Abbreviations and conventions are listed.

Many of the actual entries include literature citations for those readers wanting further information. Most of these citations consist only of the author(s) name and a date so readers will have to do some hunting to find the referenced sources.

This book will be valuable primarily to plant pathologists, mycologists, virologists, and others dealing with microbes and the diseases they cause. It is strictly a dictionary, and will be of no use for diagnosing diseases or studying their etiology and life cycles. However, it will be useful for naming conventions and clarification of meanings when writing scientific papers. [R: Choice, May 99, p. 1596]—**Michael G. Messina**

Flowering Plants

P

461.   Grimshaw, John. **The Gardener's Atlas: The Origins, Discovery, and Cultivation of the World's Most Popular Garden Plants.** Willowdale, Ont., Firefly Books, 1998. 224p. illus. maps. index. $29.95. ISBN 1-55209-226-7.

Many gardeners probably do not stop and think of the origins of the flowers they tend so carefully. Yet flowers, in addition to being beautiful, have fascinating histories. Grimshaw, a noted botanist, has selected 20 families of plants and reviews their origins and how they were carried to new areas of the world—ultimately becoming the flowers we enjoy today.

Among those plants Grimshaw includes are narcissus, begonias, gentians, pinks, daisies, heather, geraniums, iris, peas, lilies, oleanders, orchids, poppies, primroses, buttercups, roses, camellias, pansies, and ferns. The text is liberally supplemented with 300 color photographs and illustrations and 50 maps. In addition, there are supplemental articles on such subjects as the gardens of Islam and the medieval garden. Sidebars on botanists and on various aspects of flowers and gardens combine to make this an appealing book to browse through.

The work is not comprehensive, thus limiting its reference value. It is, however, a good source of information on the origins of the included plants. With its reasonable cost, libraries might consider buying a copy for reference and one to circulate. [R: LJ, 1 Nov 98, p. 118]—**January Adams**

P, S

462.   Hood, Susan. **National Audubon Society First Field Guide: Wildflowers.** New York, Scholastic, 1998. illus. index. $17.95. ISBN 0-590-05464-3.

As anyone who has seen them classifying and trading Pokemon cards can attest, children are natural classifiers, even to the extent of understanding evolutionary relationships and fine distinctions between similar types. So a series of field guides to the natural world expressly for children is a great idea, if done well. This volume, in a series that includes guides to birds, insects, and rocks and minerals, improves on a similar effort sponsored by the

Audubon Society in the early 1980s. Those tiny softcover books, the Audubon Society Beginner Guides, published by Random House in 1982, were perhaps too simple for all but the youngest children. This new effort is much more ambitious. It combines an introductory look at plant anatomy, physiology, and ecology with a beginner's field guide to the most common flowers of North America.

Much of the introductory section is in question-and-answer format, with two-page spreads answering questions such as "What is a fruit?" or "What is the purpose of a flower's color?" The answers are given with colorful illustrations of both common everyday plants and some of the less familiar oddities of nature that are guaranteed to capture children's interest.

The field guide section has 1-page write-ups on 50 of the most common North American wildflowers, plus on the facing page smaller photographs and descriptions of 2 to 3 flowers that either look similar or are closely related. The one flaw is in organization. The main flowers are grouped by color, although the reader is never alerted to this fact. The author has developed a novel identification system based on flower silhouettes, and although a silhouette symbol is included with each flower, no effort is made to group flowers of the same shape. The best way to use this field guide is just to page through the 100 pages of flower photographs, looking for the plant in question. Because the pictures throughout the volume are exquisite, and the choice of flowers is a good sampling of the wildflowers most likely to be found across North America, this system actually works fairly well. Anyone who becomes truly interested in wildflower identification will need a more complete regional or national guidebook, but this volume is a wonderful introduction to the hobby for both children and adults.—**Carol L. Noll**

Trees and Shrubs

P

463.   **500 Popular Shrubs and Trees for American Gardeners.** Loretta Barnard, ed. Hauppauge, N.Y., Barron's Educational Series, 1998. 288p. illus. index. $12.95pa. ISBN 0-7641-1178-7.

Editor Barnard and her 3 consultants have adapted *500 Popular Shrubs and Trees for Australian Gardeners* for amateur, contiguous North American gardeners. A helpful hardiness zone map includes 11 zones from 1 (below 50 degrees Fahrenheit) through 11 (above 40 degrees Fahrenheit). Use this work with caution. While advising amateurs planning their first gardens to consider native or exotic plants, attracting birds, and cultivating shrubs and trees, only basics are mentioned. Beginners are urged to consult their agricultural extension agents or nurseries. Ponder each entire discussion from the opening genera statement, to cultivation, and through the species description that concludes with the hardiness zone range. All the genera from Abelia to Ziziphus give two or three labeled, colored photographs on each page. A reference table including scientific name, tree or shrub, zone, height at 5 and 20 years, deciduous or evergreen, and uses is followed by an index that includes popular and scientific names. This volume is part of the Barron's Educational Series. Readers many want to proceed to the more scholarly *Dirr's Hardy Trees and Shrubs: An Illustrated Encyclopedia*, by Michael A. Dirr (see ARBA 98, entry 1456); *Hillier Gardener's Guide to Trees & Shrubs*, edited by John Kelly (R D Association, 1997); and *Plants That Merit Attention, Volume II: Shrubs*, by Janet Meakin Poor and Nancy Peterson (see ARBA 97, entry 1285). This work is recommended for high schools, public libraries, and garden stores.—**Helen M. Barber**

NATURAL HISTORY

C, P

464.   **Encyclopedia of Animal Rights and Animal Welfare.** Marc Bekoff and Carron A. Meaney, eds. Westport, Conn., Greenwood Press, 1998. 446p. illus. index. $59.95. ISBN 0-313-29977-3.

This reference work offers an overview of the issues on the use and abuse of animals along with the ways in which different groups are tackling the issue of animal welfare and animal rights. A multidisciplinary collection of contributors from disciplines such as biology, psychology, education, law, and theology have been tapped to provide an essay that discusses the central theme from different perspectives.

Other than the vague manner in which Bekoff indicates how the topics were chosen, the essays cover a wide array of topics pertaining to the subject matter and include animals living in highly controlled laboratory environments to those living in the wild. Each essay is well written and provides a good introduction to the topic.

The entries are arranged in alphabetic order, vary in length from one to two pages, and each ends with a bibliography and the author's name. Some of the larger topics have been subdivided into smaller sections written by different contributors. Cross-references are used throughout to lead readers to other relevant topics. Also included are a chronology, an annotated directory of organizations involved in animal welfare or who provide educational materials, an index, and information about the contributors to this resource. Another plus is the well-written foreword by Jane Goodall. Few illustrations are included, although some black-and-white photographs are used.

This work makes an excellent addition to the literature on animal rights and animal welfare. This is a definite purchase for academic libraries, although public libraries may find it useful. [R: Choice, Nov 98, p. 496; LJ, 15 April 98, p. 68; BL, 15 Sept 98, p. 260; SLJ, Feb 99, p. 132; RUSQ, Spring 99, p. 301]—**Julia Perez**

P, S

465.   Schmidt, Diane. **A Guide to Field Guides: Identifying the Natural History of North America.** Englewood, Colo., Libraries Unlimited, 1999. 304p. index. (Reference Sources in Science and Technology Series). $65.00. ISBN 1-56308-707-3.

Vacationers, hikers, bird-watchers, and others have long relied on the compact field guide to help them identify and describe features of the natural world. Large numbers of these guides have been produced, creating a potential use for a bibliographic guide to these works. Schmidt's guide provides descriptions of over 1,300 such titles, mostly published since 1980. Only guides that treat North American subjects and can commonly be found in bookstores and libraries are included here, though the author maintains a free Website with considerably more titles that are either more specialized or international in scope. Subjects of the guides range from the expected birds, flowers, and trees to more unusual topics like astronomy and weather, geology, and man-made objects (e.g., windmills and barns). The entries are quite brief and contain no evaluation, but they present sufficient information to judge the depth and approach of each title. The titles are grouped according to type of organism or other subject, then arranged by geographic region.

Schmidt has gathered a significant number and range of guides, though some evaluative comments would allow easier selection between similar titles. The author makes no pretense of this work being comprehensive, yet the sections on astronomy and geology seem a bit thin—excellent series such as the Roadside Geology books (Mountain Press) are not included. The reference usefulness would also have been augmented by a geographic index that would provide more specific locations than the simple division into eastern and western North America found in the text. These minor criticisms aside, this work offers a good starting point for seekers of appropriate guides to take into the field. [R: BL, 1 Dec 99, pp. 733-735]—**Christopher W. Nolan**

ZOOLOGY

General Works

C, P, S

466.   **Animals: A Macmillan Illustrated Encyclopedia.** Philip Whitfield, ed. New York, Macmillan Library Reference/Simon & Schuster Macmillan, 1999. 3v. illus. index. $120.00/set. ISBN 0-02-865420-X.

The 1st edition of this encyclopedia, published in 1984, covered mammals, reptiles, birds, amphibians, and fishes in one volume. This edition packages the same information (even the foreword and introduction are the same) in a 3-volume set. More than 2,000 animals are covered in brief field guide entries, organized by taxonomic category of order, family, genus, and species. Each entry includes information on the animal's size, breeding patterns, feeding habits, habitat and range, behaviors, common and scientific names, and conservation status. As in the previous edition, beautiful color illustrations accompany each entry.

Each volume contains a glossary, an alphabetic index and a classification list. Volume 3 has a list of threatened species, world zoos and aquariums, and conservation organizations. A bibliography is also included. New to this edition is an essay on classification and evolution and the presentation of the cladistic method of taxonomy. Unlike the brief species information that is accessible to upper elementary school students, the classification and cladogram explanations are written for an older audience. Libraries owning the older edition should not feel compelled to replace it with this one just for the added information.

Other titles on the topic, although not covering as many species, do provide more in-depth coverage of individual animals. For example, the *Great Book of Animals* (Courage Books, 1997) has double-paged spreads with beautiful illustrations for more than 700 animals. This set would be a good choice for libraries needing to replace a quick reference title or a worn older edition.—**Marlene M. Kuhl**

S

467.   Nagel, Rob. **Endangered Species.** Farmington Hills, Mich., U*X*L/Gale, 1999. 3v. illus. maps. index. $84.00/set. ISBN 0-7876-1875-6.

This is a nicely laid-out book for middle school students. The general overviews and species accounts are easy to understand. The book covers 200 endangered species from a broad taxonomic range: mammals, birds, reptiles, amphibians, fish, mollusks, insects, arachnids, crustaceans, and plants. There are 3 volumes. The 1st covers mammals; the 2d covers arachnids, birds, crustaceans, insects, and mollusks; and the 3d covers amphibians, fish, plants, and reptiles. Each volume has the same helpful glossary; introductory sections; a further research section with books, journals, and Internet addresses; and an index, making it easy to navigate between books or to review general information.

The introductory sections are titled "Reader's Guide"; "Endangerment and Its Causes: An Overview"; "Endangered Species Fact Boxes and Classification: An Explanation"; "International Union for Conservation of Nature and Natural Resources (IUCN–The World Conservation Union)"; and "Endangered Species Act." Within each book, sections are organized by class and within class. Accounts are alphabetic by common name.

Each species account contains the common and scientific names of the species, classification information, current status in the wild according to the International Union for Conservation of Nature and Natural Resources and the United States Fish and Wildlife Service, the country where the species currently lives, and locator maps with the range. Each account has 3 sections: "Description of Biology," "Habitat and Current Distribution," and "History and Conservation Measures." Most entries have color or black-and-white photographs. This is a good purchase for any school library. [R: BL, 15 April 99, pp. 1544-1546; BR, Sept/Oct 99, p. 70; SLJ, Aug 99, p. 186]

—**Constance Rinaldo**

Birds

P, S

468.   Bird, David M. **The Bird Almanac: The Ultimate Guide to Essential Facts and Figures of the World's Birds.** Willowdale, Ont., Firefly Books, 1999. 460p. $19.95pa. ISBN 1-55209-323-9.

This handbook provides a concise, but remarkably inclusive, reference to the world of birds, bird-watchers, and ornithologists. Nearly half of the volume is devoted to an updated world checklist of bird species, with notations of range and, where applicable, conservation status. Traditional taxonomic organization of birds is compared with the latest DNA-based arrangement of orders and families. Basic avian biology is reviewed with anatomical tables and drawings, including, for example, plumage and molt, skeletal systems, and digestive tract. Data on avian reproduction include incubation periods, clutch sizes, and sex ratios. Again, there are helpful diagrams when necessary (e.g., embryonic development of the egg). Survival data and avian diseases are reviewed briefly with management and conservation figures. A substantial "who's who" in bird biology gives very short biographical comments on more than 200 ornithologists from John J. Audubon to the present. For backyard bird-watchers there are tables on bird box dimensions, attractive plantings for birds, and of course detailed listings on bird feeding. Birders will also find useful lists of a wide variety of ornithological resources, from journal and Internet addresses to videos and CDs of birdsong. The handbook concludes with a glossary of terms from avian biology. This handy guide will be a useful reference, especially for enthusiastic amateurs. [R: LJ, 15 June 99, p. 68]—**Charles Leck**

Domestic Animals

P

469.   **Barron's Encyclopedia of Dog Breeds.** By D. Caroline Coile. Hauppauge, N.Y., Barron's Educational Series, 1998. 328p. illus. index. $26.95. ISBN 0-7641-5097-9.

The *Encyclopedia of Dog Breeds* covers 150 breeds of dogs. This book is divided by groups—"The Sporting Group," "The Hound Group," "The Working Group," "The Terrier Group," "The Toy Group," "The Non-Sporting Group," and "The Herding Group"—and is preceded by a section called "The Right Dog." This section includes some practical advice to consider when choosing a dog, and how to use the Breed Profiles that cover each breed.

Each group is introduced by a short paragraph that gives an overview of the dog breeds in that group. Each breed that is covered has a short history of that breed and insights into the temperament, upkeep, health, and form and function of that breed. There is a boxed sidebar that gives some standards of the breed as well as an "At a Glance" guide that gives insight into that breed's energy level, ease of training, watchdog ability, and other pertinent information that should factor into any decision when choosing a family dog.

In the back of this book are definitions of medical conditions, a guide to hereditary health problems, and a glossary, as well as a section on dog anatomy. This delightful reference book is highly recommended for any public library's reference collection or anyone considering acquiring a dog.—**Pamela J. Getchell**

Mammals

C, P, S

470.   Forsyth, Adrian. **Mammals of North America: Temperate and Arctic Regions.** Willowdale, Ont., Firefly Books, 1999. 350p. illus. maps. index. $40.00. ISBN 1-55209-409-X.

The author of this beautifully done resource is well qualified to write on the more than 35 species of North American mammals explored within the book's pages. Forsyth is a specialist in animal behavior and rainforest ecology as well as a researcher for the Smithsonian Institution. He has first divided the animals into taxonomic classification and then grouped them into order and further into family. Each family receives about 10 pages of thorough description. Each animal is represented with photographs and a map that indicates where they live. A sidebar follows that provides information on the animal's proper name and its meaning, a physical description, the weight and height of the animal, its gestation period and number of offspring, its life span, its diet, and its predators. The description that follows features such topics as why certain animals act as they do and how human intervention affects their habitat and therefore their population. Interspersed throughout the text are magnificent photographs of the animals in their natural habitat. An extensive bibliography and thorough index conclude the work.

Mammals of North America is much more than a field guide. It allows readers insight into the lives and history of the animals featured. With its beautiful photographs and well-written text it will be welcome in both school and public libraries.—**Shannon M. Graff**

C, P, S

471.   Nowak, Ronald M. **Walker's Mammals of the World.** 6th ed. Baltimore, Md., Johns Hopkins University Press, 1999. 2v. illus. index. $99.95/set. ISBN 0-8018-5789-9.

Since the 1st edition of *Walker's Mammals of the World* was published in 1964, it has been considered by many to be the most comprehensive reference work on mammals ever written. The 6th edition continues that tradition. A comparison of the latest edition to the 5th edition (see ARBA 93, entry 1572), finds a 25 percent increase in text length, 95 percent of previous generic accounts significantly modified, and 81 new generic accounts added. A goal of the work since the beginning has been to provide a quality photograph of a living representative of every genus of mammal. The black-and-white photographs are excellent in quality. Each genus entry contains information on the number of species known, key literature references, physical description, comparison of characteristics of representative species, description of habitat, general behavior, breeding and care of young, and information on the species' endangered status. This edition takes great care in noting whether a species is endangered or in decline based on the International Union for Conservation of Nature's (IUCN) list of threatened animals. Close to one-half of all of the world's living mammal species are in serious to critical decline.

The high quality of scholarship of this work is evidenced not only in the careful descriptions of each genus, but also in the extensive 172-page bibliography of references. The only other reference work on mammals that approaches the excellence of this set is *Grzimek's Encyclopedia of Mammals* (see ARBA 91, entry 1593). Grzimek's work is nearly as comprehensive as Walker's, and includes color photographs and more information on behavior, ecology, and conservation, but with a much higher price tag. As there has been a significant amount of additional and revised material added since the 5th edition, this latest edition of *Walker's Mammals of the World* is recommended for every academic and public library.—**Elaine F. Jurries**

Marine Animals

P, S

472.   Parker, Steve, and Jane Parker. **The Encyclopedia of Sharks.** Willowdale, Ont., Firefly Books, 1999. 192p. illus. index. $24.95pa. ISBN 1-55209-324-7.

The sinister image of a shark rising from the waters with its sharp-toothed jaws wide open strikes a universal chord of terror in all of us. Because we are both repulsed and fascinated by this magnificent group of sea-dwellers, there is no shortage of books about sharks. *The Encyclopedia of Sharks* joins the ranks of numerous overviews of sharks and their relatives.

This is not an encyclopedia in the traditional sense. Rather it is a loosely compiled narrative of shark lore and information, with an emphasis on color photographs. Chapter headings such as "Super Killers," "Who's Afraid of Sharks," "Sharks in War," "Shark Kith and Kin," "Shark Sizes and Numbers," "From Shallows to the Deep," and "The Survival Suite" are not particularly useful in directing one to specific information. This is a book for the recreational reader, not the serious researcher, and is most suitable for the circulating collection of school and public libraries where the demand for general shark books is high. [R: LJ, 15 Sept 99, p. 71]

—**Elaine F. Jurries**

P, S

473.   **Sharks.** 2d ed. John D. Stevens, ed. New York, Checkmark Books/Facts on File, 1999. 240p. illus. maps. index. $39.95. ISBN 0-8160-3990-9.

Sharks have become cultural icons, much like dinosaurs. The public is fascinated with strange, primitive, and menacing beasts; and scientists have found many clever ways to use this interest to teach physiology, ecology, and evolution. This book is a superb example of how quality science can be presented attractively and effectively. Most libraries have dozens of shark books on their shelves, and this one should join them. It is profusely and beautifully illustrated with color diagrams and photographs, and the text is readable and highly informative.

This book contains the contributions of almost two dozen shark experts, from paleontologists to marine photographers. It is edited so well that the prose flows smoothly between chapters and sections. The first third of the book is devoted to the origin of sharks, their classification, shark physiology and behavior, and shark ecology. The systematic section is especially important, since general readers rarely see the details of a formal classification. One of the basic premises of the book is that the first step in predicting a shark's behavior is knowing what kind of shark it is. And that mistaken identity provokes most shark scares. The diversity of shark adaptations is very impressive, and the authors use this extraordinary variety to dispel many myths about sharks. Only some, for example, must keep moving in order to breathe, and some nourish their unborn young with placentas analogous to our own. The middle third of the book covers "encounters" with sharks around the world. The reader learns that shark attacks are horrible but relatively rare compared to so many other hazards in the water. The last section of the book is an eclectic set of myths, stories, and observations of sharks. Here is where readers see that people are far more of a threat to sharks than they are to people. Sharks are used for meat, fertilizer, biochemicals, abrasives, cosmetics, paint base, and even corneal transplants. Several species of sharks now face extinction because of overexploitation. The book ends with a short guide to shark resources, including reference books, Websites, and a list of institutions with shark exhibits.—**Mark A. Wilson**

32 Engineering

CHEMICAL ENGINEERING

P, S

474. **Chemical Elements: From Carbon to Krypton.** By David E. Newton. Lawrence W. Baker, ed. Farmington Hills, Mich., U*X*L/Gale, 1999. 3v. illus. $84.00/set. ISBN 0-7876-2844-1.

This young person's guide (high school level) to the chemical elements is thoughtfully designed and attractively produced. Entries are alphabetic by element name, and there is a table of contents by atomic number as well as one by periodic group. Each volume includes the same timeline of the discovery of the elements, glossary, index to the set, and bibliography that includes Websites as well.

Entries are self-contained, and technical terms are explained within them, although that can lead to slight misstatements. For example, the entry for argon defines fractional distillation as the process of letting liquid air slowly warm up, but fractional distillation is a more general term that includes separations of components in any temperature range. Each profusely illustrated entry contains the atomic symbol; atomic number; mass; periodic family; the pronunciation of the element's name; the history of knowledge; and use of the element, physical, and chemical properties, occurrence in nature, isotopes, extraction processes, compounds of the elements, health effects, and more. There are plentiful cross-references and informative sidebars. Each entry also gives a simple shell diagram for the electronic energy levels, but because the meaning of this diagram is not explained it may be simply puzzling. An explanation would also help the reader to understand what is meant by the periodic group into which the element is placed and to understand the periodic table itself, which is printed on the front and back endpapers of each volume. This is my only real quibble about the set, which would be a useful resource in any public or school library.

Finally, the subtitle is a bit of a mystery. Possibly carbon is there as the element forming the largest number of chemical compounds, but krypton is not quite the element forming the fewest compounds, since helium, neon, and argon form no stable compounds at all. [R: BL, 1 May 99, pp. 1606-1608; BR, Sept/Oct 99, p. 79; SLJ, Aug 99, pp. 186-187]—**Robert Michaelson**

ENVIRONMENTAL ENGINEERING

P

475. Woodside, Gayle. **Environmental Health, and Safety Portable Handbook.** New York, McGraw-Hill, 1998. 279p. index. $49.95 flexibinding. ISBN 0-07-071848-2.

This handbook is especially designed for environmental and health safety professionals and covers environmental, occupational health, safety, and regulatory issues, as well as EHS (Environmental Health and Safety) management techniques and audit and inspection guidelines. Features include checklists, figures, equations, and pages left blank for relevant notes. It is not designed to be a replacement for technical EHS books such as Lewis's *Hazardous Chemicals Desk Reference* (4th ed.; see ARBA 98, entry 1635).

It is not recommended for purchase by any library, as it is intended for use in the field. However, this is an important issue and a better purchase would be Gayle Woodside's *Environmental Safety and Health Engineering* (Wiley, 1997) or the *Standard Handbook of Environmental Engineering* (CRC, 1999).—**Susan B. Ardis**

33 Health Sciences

GENERAL WORKS

Dictionaries and Encyclopedias

P, S
476. Hirschfelder, Arlene B. **Encyclopedia of Smoking and Tobacco.** Phoenix, Ariz., Oryx Press, 1999. 411p. illus. index. $65.00. ISBN 1-57356-202-5.

Consider that each day in the United States alone 3,000 young people under the age of 20 become established smokers, and each year more than 400,000 individuals die from tobacco-related diseases such as lung cancer and heart disease. A book that summarizes information on smoking and tobacco in a way that could be helpful to any interested reader is timely. The book is arranged on topics from A to Z. For example, "A" has *addiction* and *advertising*, "C" has *chewing tobacco* and *Cuba*, "N" has *Native Americans*, "S" has *Surgeon General's Report*, and "Z" has *Zyban* (a smoking-cessation pharmaceutical). Beyond the encyclopedia are essays on relevant topics, such as "Women, Tobacco, and Health," "Warning Labels As a Legal Protection for the Tobacco Industry," and "Surgeon General's Reports from 1964-1998." Appendixes include "Workplace and Smoking: Selected Landmark Cases," and a chronology starting with Christopher Columbus in 1492. This well-written and interesting book could be usefully placed in many locations, including libraries, health workers' offices, and educational institutions.
—**Marquita Hill**

P
477. Sharma, Rajendra. **The Family Encyclopedia of Health: The Complete Family Reference Guide to Alternative & Orthodox Medical Diagnosis, Treatment, & Preventive Healthcare.** Rockport, Mass., Element Books, 1998. 692p. illus. index. $24.95pa. ISBN 1-86204-426-0.

The Family Encyclopedia of Health is the most thorough resource to date that integrates discussion of alternative therapies within articles on common health concerns and their recommended Western medical treatments. The author is affiliated with the Hale Clinic, a British organization that promotes alternative health care practice. British and European health systems have moved more quickly than U.S. health care to accept and blend alternative therapies into mainstream medical practice. As a result, much of the advice given in this resource is not commonly accepted practice in the United States, and qualified practitioners of some of the recommended alternative modalities may be scarce in this country. Some U.S. libraries may find this work unsuitable for purchase if they strongly emphasize scientific or evidence-based medical information in their collections because only anecdotal evidence is available for many therapies discussed in this work.

However, this reference has many strengths. It is the first work on complementary or alternative care that discusses alternative practice side by side with Western medical practice, allowing the reader to evaluate the pros and cons of both therapies. As well, the multicultural approach of the work helps to ground the theories or rationales behind alternative therapies within the culture of origin. The work also explains the therapies in a clear and forthright manner that is suitable for its intended audience of health care consumers. The resource includes a contents list for a basic alternative medicine chest and recommends providers of the listed preparations. This work is generously illustrated, with diagrams of anatomy and procedures including, for example, a detailed topography of the eye used in iridology. There is an interesting glossary that includes many terms not found in medical dictionaries. The encyclopedia follows an arrangement that subdivides the book into 3 sections. Part 1 contains articles on sexuality, fertility and conception, and pregnancy and childbirth, then addresses health throughout periods of the life span. Part 2 addresses nutrition topics, diagnosis, alternative therapies, and drugs. And finally, part 3 includes a glossary, a recommended readings list, and an address list for alternative medicine information and practitioners. A thorough index provides access to the three parts of the encyclopedia by topic. [R: LJ, July 99, p. 84; Choice, Dec 99, p. 696]—**Lynne M. Fox**

Handbooks and Yearbooks

P

478.   **Health Care State Rankings 1999: Health Care in the 50 United States.** 7th ed. Kathleen O'Leary Morgan and Scott Morgan, eds. Lawrence, Kans., Morgan Quitno Press, 1999. 512p. index. $49.95pa. ISBN 1-56692-333-6.

This health state ranking source on the 50 states provides answers to health questions relating to birth, death, incidence of disease, reproductive health, facilities, abortions, insurance and finance, health providers, and physical fitness. The data in more than 500 tables are collected from government agencies and private sectors. This 7th edition is an updated version with a few deletions, additions, and unchanged data. The birth and reproductive health section has 58 tables, including topics such as teenage birthrate, rate of Cesarean delivery, and birth by midwives, among others. There are 17 tables on legal abortions and 119 tables on different causes of death. The section on facilities lists nursing home occupancy rate, Medicare and Medicaid services, community hospital data, and office and clinic visits. Insurance and finance tables provide ranking of health expenditures on prescription drugs, home health care, nursing homes, dental care, physician services, and more. Incidence of disease includes AIDS, cancer, Lyme disease, sexually transmitted diseases, E-Coli, and the like. The "Providers" section gives dental, chiropractic, and different specialty rankings. The "Physical Fitness" section provides ranking of activities such as swimming, golf, tennis, running, beer consumption, wine consumption, mental health, and car safety seats. Each table lists the rank of the states from highest to lowest, and an alphabetic list of states with the ranking is provided. The District of Columbia is placed at the bottom of the listing. There are no analyses of counties, which might be even more convenient to data-seekers who are looking for in-depth research data. Each table includes the source of the data and footnotes to assist users in locating additional information on their search. The 1st edition of this title (see ARBA 94, entry 1816) included bibliographic references, but this 1999 edition has a separate page on the sources for the table data but no bibliography. For libraries with patrons looking for answers to unique health questions, this is a worthwhile purchase.—**Polin P. Lei**

C, P

479.   **The Merck Manual of Medical Information.** home ed. Robert Berkow, Mark H. Beers, and Andrew J. Fletcher, eds. New York, McGraw-Hill, 1997. 1509p. illus. index. $29.95. ISBN 0-911910-87-5.

For a hundred years, *The Merck Manual* has been the doctor's bible. Finally, here is a rewriting in everyday language, a translation of the professionals' reference book to be consulted by today's increasingly literate searchers for medical information. It is in no way paternalistic, but maintains a neutral attitude, uses medical terminology, and is not a "how to" self-care manual. Almost all of the content of *The Merck Manual* is given, except for drug dosages, microscopic slide interpretations, and so on, for which the layperson must depend on the professionals.

The home edition enables the patient and family to learn about human disorders and to understand their biological bases, diagnosis, treatment, and even prognosis, as understood by practitioners of orthodox medicine. A tremendous amount of medical information has been carefully arranged into briefly introduced sections, such as blood disorders. The first chapter under each section often covers the biology of the organ, system, or type of disorder (e.g., infections). Following chapters are more specific, such as abscesses under the skin. A pattern of symptoms, diagnosis, treatment options, and outcomes are often used. Cross-references are indicated by small red symbols in the text, repeated at the bottom of the page, with the location of related topics. There are some general sections on topics such as on death and dying. Additional information often appears in sidebars. Original illustrations have been digitized and sparingly colorized, making them easy to understand. The table of contents is detailed, and the index is extensive. There are several appendixes, such as lists of common medical terms and the generic and trade names of often-prescribed drugs.

This is a definitive, authoritative, easy-to-use current medical reference for laypeople, and should be considered for all hospital libraries, consumer health centers, public libraries, and many individual collections. It is presented from the medical viewpoint and compared to books like the *Mayo Clinic Family Health Book* (Morrow, 1996), this is more concise in statement and inclusive in essential information. It is also directed toward helping the user comprehend the basic nature of diseases and disorders and what the treatments and outcomes may be. The reader should be well prepared for more intelligent interaction with his or her doctors after consulting this excellent book.—**Harriette M. Cluxton**

MEDICINE

General Works

C, P

480.   **Consumer Issues in Health Care Sourcebook.** Bellenir Karen, ed. Detroit, Omnigraphics, 1999. 618p. index. (Health Reference Series, v.35). $78.00. ISBN 0-7808-0221-7.

In this era of managed health care, it is critical that consumers keep themselves well informed about health issues that affect them. To meet the demand for more information, many books have been published to guide consumers in making good decisions about their health care. This sourcebook is another in the Health Reference Series published by Omnigraphics aimed at educating the layperson.

The book is arranged in seven broad categories covering the gamut of health care issues: health care fundamentals, physicians and hospitals, medications, cautions for health care consumers, managing common health risks in the home, caring for chronically or terminally ill patients and making end-of-life decisions, and a section on resources. Within each part, there are chapters that thoroughly cover the aspects within that section. For example, in the section on physicians and hospitals, there are chapters that describe the types of health care providers, how to check up on a doctor, how to talk to doctors, questions to ask prior to surgery, hospital hints, and a guide to mental health services. Most of the chapters contain sources of additional information. The indexing is excellent.

Among the many other books on this topic, *Health Care Choices for Today's Consumer: Guide to Quality and Cost* by Marc Miller (John Wiley, 1997) has similar coverage to this book. The layout and organization of the information in Miller's book is more pleasing to the eye than the volume at hand, and thus more readable. Aside from the difference in style, the information itself is essentially the same in both books. Both public and academic libraries will want to have a copy of either or both of these fine books in their collection for readers who are interested in self-education on health issues. [R: BL, 1 Dec 98, p. 698; RUSQ, Spring 99, p. 299]

—**Elaine F. Jurries**

P

481.   Dashe, Alfred M. **The Man's Health Sourcebook.** 2d ed. Lincolnwood, Ill., National Textbook, 1999. 288p. illus. index. $17.95pa. ISBN 0-7373-0109-0.

As the title implies, this text discusses men's health issues and should be read by both men and women, just as the author recommends. It includes a preface, introduction, glossary, index, illustrations, and tables. Unfortunately the reference section is limited and Internet and Web addresses are not provided.

In the preface and introduction the author explores recent trends and issues relevant to today's health care system. This includes the author's opinions in regard to the current status, insights, and future trends as seen from the eyes of a practicing physician. Both of these sections are informative and beneficial as they describe the sociological and health care changes taking place in our world.

The main body of the text is divided into two sections. The first section is a general overview of issues such as healthy living, how to choose a physician, and when to call a doctor. This section should be reassuring for those individuals who are either evasive or procrastinate when it is time to visit their physician. In fact, men who have not had a recent physical exam may find this text to be a motivator to take the first step.

The second section provides an overview of selected medical issues relevant to males. Topics include a basic review of the male anatomy, cardiovascular system, respiratory system, skin and hair, gastrointestinal system, endocrine system, male sexuality, male sexual health, the aging process, substance abuse, and mental health. At the end of each topic the author provides the reader with a useful summary of topic highlights.

Within the text are several tables, charts, and illustrations. The tables and charts are presented in a clear and concise manner. Although the illustrations are black-and-white, they are relevant, effective, and correspond with the text. Medical terminology is included and is either defined within the text or in the glossary.

This text contains information that can be of benefit to both sexes. It can be used as a general reference source and in conjunction with a physician's physical examination. A text of this nature is a valuable source of information and would be appropriately available in a variety of environments, including private physician offices, clinics, and home and school libraries.—**Paul M. Murphy III**

Alternative Medicine

C, P

482. **Alternative Medicine Sourcebook.** Allan R. Cook, ed. Detroit, Omnigraphics, 1999. 737p. index. (Health Reference Series). $78.00. ISBN 0-7808-0200-4.

Like the other books in Omnigraphics' Health Reference Series, this work is presented in a format to help the reader understand the basics and the breadth of a particular health issue. The *Alternative Medicine Sourcebook* is designed to help the layperson understand the issues and controversies surrounding alternative and complementary medicine. It presents an overview of the major families of therapies, and includes in-depth descriptions of some of the most common practices, such as Rolfing, aromatherapy, acupuncture, homeopathy, and reflexology.

The book is divided into 9 parts: the issues of alternative medicine; alternative systems of medical practice; "bioelectromagnetics"; diet, nutrition, and lifestyle changes; herbal medicine; manual healing; mind and body control; pharmacological and biological treatments; and additional help and information. A typical essay on an alternative medicine topic includes a brief history, a description of the practice, an objective analysis of the effectiveness of the practice, and any scientific studies that have been conducted on the particular form of alternative medicine. Many of the essays also contain a list of additional references and sources of information. There are few illustrations to aid in presenting the material. A more colorful and visually appealing work with similar information is *The Encyclopedia of Alternative Medicine* (see ARBA 97, entry 1345). As a starting point to introduce readers to alternative medicine practices, this book will be a great addition to the reference collection of every type of library.—**Elaine F. Jurries**

C, P

483. Cassileth, Barrie R. **The Alternative Medicine Handbook: The Complete Reference Guide to Alternative and Complementary Therapies.** New York, W. W. Norton, 1998. 340p. illus. index. $19.95pa. ISBN 0-393-31816-8.

This is an excellent, balanced overview of the numerous alternative and complementary medical therapies that are being practiced today. The author defines "alternative" as a therapy that is used instead of Western mainstream medicine, and "complementary" as a therapy that serves a supplementary role in conventional care. Alternative therapies tend to be unproven and may or may not be harmful. Complementary therapies, usually used alongside conventional treatment, are generally noninvasive and helpful. With great objectivity, the author describes the background, goals, benefits, and risks of each therapy, neither recommending nor condemning any of them.

The book is composed of 7 parts, each part representing a broad category of alternative or complementary medicine. The 7 parts are routes to health and spiritual fulfillment, dietary and herbal remedies, using the mind for emotional relief and physical strength, alternative biological treatments, reducing pain and stress through bodywork, enhancing well-being through the senses, and restoring health with external energy forces. Within each part, 6 to 12 individual therapies are thoroughly described. The description of each therapy contains the following information: what it is, what practitioners say it does, beliefs on which it is based, research evidence to date, what it can do, and where to get it. Among the 54 therapies discussed are acupuncture, homeopathy, Native American healing, Chinese medicine, fasting and juice therapies, macrobiotics, biofeedback, biological dentistry, oxygen therapies, craniosacral therapy, rolfing, aromatherapy, humor therapy, shamanism, and therapeutic touch.

Although there are numerous alternative medicine handbooks on the market, some of which border on the fantastical, this book stands out because it is balanced, rational, and objective. It deserves a place on the reference shelf of both academic and public libraries.—**Elaine F. Jurries**

C, P

484.　Goldberg, Burton. **Alternative Medicine Guide to Heart Disease, Stroke, & High Blood Pressure.** Tiburon, Calif., Future Medicine Publishing, 1998. 293p. illus. index. $18.95pa. ISBN 1-887299-10-6.

As increasing numbers of people are turning to alternative methods for the prevention and healing of various illnesses, and are seeking information in guides such as this one. As part of a series published in conjunction with the *Alternative Medicine Digest*, this guide is divided into three main sections treating heart disease, stroke, and high blood pressure. In an introductory statement, the author points out that the book is on alternative methods, and many are not understood or endorsed by the traditional medical community. While he urges readers to discuss the treatments prescribed with their doctors and not to use the book as a substitute for the advice and care of a physician, he also points out that the traditional medical community (including pharmaceutical companies, physicians' trade groups, insurance companies, and some government agencies) is somewhat of a monopoly and has an investment in keeping non-patentable, expensive treatments from the public.

In each of the three areas covered in the guide, the causes of the problem are clearly discussed, along with the self-care options available for prevention related to diet, exercise, and lifestyle changes. The main text describes various alternative therapies, citing both individual cases and research studies that are well documented in standard medical and scientific journals. Accompanying the text are excellent illustrations and diagrams, particularly useful for seeing how certain problems appear in the cardiovascular system. An added feature of the guide is the use of icons in the margins to give further information in smaller print. A small caution sign, for example, alerts the reader to certain risks or contraindications. In addition to the list of citations from footnotes in the text, an index and a list of organizations are found in the appendix. This highly informative, very readable guide should be an excellent introduction to alternative treatments for those with heart problems. The fact that most of the material comes from physicians with traditional training who have turned to alternative methods should be a plus for those who are somewhat fearful of trying something new.—**Lucille Whalen**

C, P

485.　**The Illustrated Encyclopedia of Body-Mind Disciplines.** Nancy Allison, ed. New York, Rosen Publishing, 1999. 448p. illus. index. $79.95. ISBN 0-8239-2546-3.

The United States has been experiencing a spiritual awakening in the 1990s that involves linking mind, body, and spirit in an attempt to find greater peace of mind and physical well-being. Many of the techniques used in body-mind disciplines have been practiced for centuries in various parts of the world. *The Illustrated Encyclopedia of Body-Mind Disciplines* describes in detail more than 100 different practices that help link the physical body with the sensing, feeling, and intuitive facilities of the mind.

The book begins by giving short definitions of the techniques covered. After a short introduction to the history and theory behind body-mind disciplines, the book is divided into chapters that supply 5- to 10-page entries on very specific techniques. The chapters include topics such as alternative health models (e.g., holistic, shamanism), sensory therapy (e.g., aromatherapy, light therapy), massage, acupuncture, martial arts, meditation, and body-oriented therapies (psychodrama, rebirthing), among others. The entries are thoroughly described and include the history and theory behind the technique. Many entries include photographs, and all include resources and suggestions for further reading. The work concludes with a name/subject index.

The encyclopedia will be a valuable inclusion in any health, public, or university library. The topic is timely and the entries offer enough information to help readers grasp the idea behind the subject. [R: LJ, July 99, p. 83; BL, 1 Sept 99, pp. 180-181]—**Shannon M. Graff**

Pediatrics

C, P

486.　**American Academy of Pediatrics Guide to Your Child's Nutrition: Making Peace at the Table and Building Healthy Eating Habits for Life.** William H. Dietz and Loraine Stern, eds. New York, Villard/Random House, 1999. 234p. index. $23.00. ISBN 0-375-50187-8.

This helpful guide for parents and other caretakers gives advice on working with the picky eater and myriad other issues involving the nutrition of children from infancy through adolescence. Written in a narrative style with many case studies of common problems, this book is entertaining reading as well as full of authoritative advice from the doctors of the American Academy of Pediatrics. The first five chapters are an overview of nutrition for children through all the stages of their early life. Many of the questions that parents ask their doctors are discussed. For example, breast-feeding and what to order a child when eating out are both discussed here. Chapters on nutrition basics; outside influences (e.g., television, grandparents, childcare providers); eating disorders; alternative diets and supplements; and allergies round out this useful book.

There are a number of other books that address the topic of children's nutrition. An equally authoritative work, *The Yale Guide to Children's Nutrition* (see ARBA 98, entry 1555), contains essentially the same information, with the addition of 100 pages of recipes designed to entice children to eat better. *Mom's Guide to Your Kid's Nutrition* (Alpha Books, 1997) is a popular rendition of advice on children's nutrition.

This guide is a worthy addition to the nutrition collection of all public libraries. Academic libraries that have an education, nutrition, nursing, or medical program will also find it useful.—**Elaine F. Jurries**

Poisoning

P, S

487.   Turkington, Carol. **The Poisons and Antidotes Sourcebook.** New York, Checkmark Books/Facts on File, 1999. 408p. index. $35.00. ISBN 0-8160-3959-3.

The Poisons and Antidotes Sourcebook is designed to inform readers about dangerous materials that may be within their own home without their knowledge of their dangers or of how to treat them in case of deadly contact. The book includes information on such common items as household poisons; insecticides and fertilizers; poisonous spiders and snakes; drugs; and poison ivy and other toxic plants. Part 1 of the work contains tips on what to do in a poison emergency, how to make one's home safe, food poisoning, and what poisons are associated with what symptoms. The book then is arranged into A to Z entries. These entries explain what the poison is, the symptoms that will occur, and treatment. The book is extensively cross-referenced. At the end of the work are several appendixes that provide hotline telephone numbers in case of emergency, newsletters, organizations, regional poison control centers, and Websites for more information. A glossary, reference section, and index conclude the work. The information provided in this guide is both in-depth and valuable. The work will be useful in both personal libraries and public reference collections.—**Shannon M. Graff**

Specific Diseases and Conditions

Alzheimer's Disease

P

488.   **Alzheimer's Disease Sourcebook.** 2d ed. Karen Bellenir, ed. Detroit, Omnigraphics, 1999. 524p. index. (Health Reference Series, v.26). $78.00. ISBN 0-7808-0223-3.

This new edition of the *Alzheimer's, Stroke, and 29 Other Neurological Disorders Sourcebook* (see ARBA 94, entry 1862) is actually a very different book. The 1st edition provided mainly descriptive information about a wide range of neurological diseases; this 2d edition narrows its focus to diseases producing dementia. It is not only more current but also provides more practical assistance to those who fear these diseases or who must deal with an afflicted loved one. The wide-ranging information included is reprinted, like that in its predecessor, but is drawn not only from U.S. government agencies but also from medical journals and organizations, such as the Alzheimer's Association. The initial section summarizes what is known about Alzheimer's and its occurrence. What used to be called senility is far from universal; only 5 to 6 percent of elderly people suffer from Alzheimer's or related dementias. An overview of warning signs and diagnostic information help the consumer understand what are and what are not signs of a serious problem. Another section covers other diseases of the aged causing dementia, such as Huntington's Disease and Multi-Infarct Dementia, which is the result of a series of strokes causing brain damage. Parts 3, 4, and 5 of this work cover recent developments in prevention and treatment research, information on long-term care of patients, and guides to where those caring for an Alzheimer's patient can find assistance (including directories of federal, state, community, and other assistance programs), and a bibliography. Compilations of reprinted articles can be uneven in style and possibly in currency. Nonetheless, this book provides a wealth of useful information not otherwise available in one place. This resource is recommended for all types of libraries.—**Marit S. MacArthur**

Blood and Circulatory Disorders

P
489.   **Blood and Circulatory Disorders Sourcebook.** Linda M. Shin and Karen Bellenir, eds. Detroit, Omnigraphics, 1999. 554p. index. (Health Reference Series, v.39). $78.00. ISBN 0-7808-0203-9.

This volume is a recent publication in a series of books that bring together and index reprints of articles originally published by government health agencies and private disease-related organizations. Omnigraphics has produced more than 45 of these volumes, on topics ranging from AIDS to learning disabilities. The target audience is patients and their families as well as health professionals who are involved with patient education. In all cases articles are clear and easy to understand, written in lay terminology and often providing illustrations. Some are in question and answer form, which is particularly handy for patient education purposes. The 51 chapters include material on specific blood problems, such as anemia, leukemia and bleeding disorders, and articles on diseases of the circulatory system, such as aneurysms, hypertension, and atherosclerosis. A final section discusses blood transfusions and their risks, autologous transfusion, and progress toward safety of the blood supply. There are a glossary of blood-related terms and a list of private and government agency resources for patients that gives addresses, telephone numbers, e-mail addresses, and Websites. Most articles are fairly recent, with copyright dates of 1995 or later.—**Carol L. Noll**

Burns

P
490.   **Burns Sourcebook.** Allan R. Cook, ed. Detroit, Omnigraphics, 1999. 604p. illus. index. (Health Reference Series). $78.00. ISBN 0-7808-0204-7.

Annually, some 1.25 million burns are reported to medical personnel in the United States, including 5,500 burn fatalities, making burn injuries one of the nation's leading causes of accidental death. This latest volume in the Health Reference Series from Omnigraphics is an important resource for both health professionals and the general public in dealing with the problems created by burn injuries. Drawing from governmental, medical, and scientific literature, the editors provide a lot of knowledge pertaining to the prevention and the appropriate handling of a wide variety of burns.

This book is divided into 7 easy-to-use sections. Beginning with burn statistics, the following segments discuss the types and degrees of burns, the variety of treatment protocols, issues of rehabilitation and living with the long-term effects of burns, preventive measures to safeguard homes and businesses from burn hazards, and emergency and first-aid procedures for burn victims. A final brief section lists some of the major additional societal and institutional burn resources that are available. Illustrations and bibliographies provide additional useful information throughout this volume, which also includes a comprehensive index.

Burns are a serious public health problem in the United States. This key reference guide is an invaluable addition to all health care and public libraries in confronting this ongoing health issue.—**Jonathon Erlen**

Diabetes

P
491.   **Diabetes Sourcebook.** 2d ed. Karen Bellenir, ed. Detroit, Omnigraphics, 1999. 688p. illus. index. (Health Reference Series, v.3). $78.00. ISBN 0-7808-0224-1.

This giant comprehensive volume is designed as an overview for laypersons to help them recognize the risk factors associated with diabetes, to identify symptoms, and to acquire the proper medical care. Of the 16 million Americans who suffer the illness, there are still 8 million people who remain undiagnosed. Medical professionals recommend that all adults age 45 and older should be tested for diabetes, and high-risk people under

45 should be tested as well. Based on these sheer numbers alone, this book serves a unique purpose for those people who are diabetic or for those who are high-risk candidates.

The new edition takes into account the changes in diabetic care since the first edition in 1994. According to the preface, the new volume contains 95 percent revised or new material. The 67 chapters of the book are divided into 8 parts. The parts of the book focus on broad areas of interest whereas the chapters relate to single topics. Part 1, "Diabetes Prevalence," offers statistical information about diabetes in the United States. Part 2, "Types of Diabetes and Related Disorders," describes the risk factors and symptoms for the major types of diabetes and related disorders. Part 3, "Diabetes Management," provides practical suggestions for managing the disease and reducing complications. Part 4, "The Role of Diet and Exercise in Diabetes Management," examines the relationship between diabetes management and the lifestyle factors of diet and exercise. Part 5, "Insulin and Other Diabetes Medicines," provides information about the different types of insulin, other medications, and drug interactions of special concern to diabetics. Part 6, "Complications of Diabetes," explains the major complications of diabetes, describes how they develop and provides treatment information. Part 7, "Research Initiatives," reports on diabetes research and the path toward further investigation. Part 8, "Additional Help and Information," provides a diabetes dictionary, sources for cookbooks and recipes, a bibliography of diabetes information, financial help sources, and a directory of diabetes organizations.

A comprehensive index provides easy access to information in the book. Material for this volume was collected from a wide array of government and private agencies. Copyrighted articles from a variety of sources have been reprinted throughout the book. In the commitment to provide ongoing coverage of important medical developments in the field of diabetes, the editors ask the readers to share their medical concerns for the next volume. This comprehensive book is an excellent addition for high school, academic, medical, and public libraries serving clientele with a broad range of medical concerns about diabetes. This volume is highly recommended.

—**Betty J. Morris**

Endocrine and Metabolic Disorders

P

492.   **Endocrine and Metabolic Disorders Sourcebook.** Linda M. Shin, ed. Detroit, Omnigraphics, 1999. 574p. index. (Health Reference Series, v.36). $78.00. ISBN 0-7808-0207-1.

Presently there are 44 titles on various medical topics in Omnigraphics' Health Reference Series. Because of the success of this series, Omnigraphics intends to expand the series to 58 volumes in 1999. *Endocrine and Metabolic Disorders Sourcebook* follows a similar format of the other sourcebooks. Generally the sourcebooks are written in easy-to-read text and are designed for consumers seeking health-related information on certain medical disorders. These sourcebooks intend to be comprehensive in scope, but supplementary sources will still need to be acquired for any in-depth clinical information on disorder.

There are a total of 58 chapters in the volume at hand. Part 1 begins with an introduction to the endocrine system and human metabolism. The other 5 parts contain information on the glands and their disorders. Part 2 lists pancreatic and diabetic disorders, with nutritional recommendations and exercise control. Part 3 is on adrenal gland disorders and has only 4 chapters. Part 4 is on pituitary and growth disorders and includes a chapter on acromegaly. Part 5 is on thyroid and parathyroid disorders, which is extremely useful for a percentage of the general public. Part 6 provides information on other disorders of endocrine and metabolic functioning, such as hypercalcemia, PKU, FMEN1, galactosemia, and more. There are a few illustrations and charts to illustrate growth rate and locations of glands. Although some Websites are included for certain organizations and associations, it would be useful if more appropriate links were inserted, such as PDQ, NCI, or NIDDM for the electronic-savvy readers. Some chapters give suggested readings, other resources, or references. The index at the end is thorough, and readers will have no problem in locating "the information on the glands of the endocrine system, its components, the hormones it regulates, and the metabolic consequences of various disorders." Omnigraphics has produced another needed resource for health information consumers.—**Polin P. Lei**

Sexually Transmitted Diseases

P, S
493.   Marr, Lisa. **Sexually Transmitted Diseases: A Physician Tells You What You Need to Know.** Baltimore, Md., Johns Hopkins University Press, 1998. 341p. index. $39.95; $16.95pa. ISBN 0-8018-6042-3; 0-8018-6043-1pa.

This text addresses a topic that is of increasing importance and yet is still considered by many to be taboo. The book has two primary components. Part 1 discusses what readers need to know about sexually transmitted diseases (STDs) and part 2 is called the "Encyclopedia of STDs." This approach is beneficial because part 1 provides readers with an overview of what they should know regarding anatomy, symptoms, STD examinations, communication skills, and safe sex. Part 2 is a natural transition as it explains the STDs, including STD signs and symptoms, treatment options, and statistics.

The medical terminology and statistics will not be overly complex for the adult reader to understand. The illustrations are easy to interpret and they correspond directly to the contents of the book. The resources, a glossary of terms, and references are provided in the latter portion of the text. Contact information, including telephone numbers, mailing address, and Website, has been included when possible.

This text provides valuable information that has been presented in a professional and concise manner. Although it could be included in any medical library, it could easily complement a number of libraries (i.e., public, home, health care clinic) as a source of valuable information. It may also be useful as a reference resource for individuals involved in teaching courses that discuss sexually transmitted diseases.—**Paul M. Murphy III**

Sleep Disorders

P
494.   **Sleep Disorders Sourcebook.** Jenifer Swanson, ed. Detroit, Omnigraphics, 1999. 439p. index. (Health Reference Series). $78.00. ISBN 0-7808-0234-9.

This text, which is part of Omnigraphics' Health Reference Series, contains more than 400 pages of useful information relating to sleep. The book is divided into 6 parts and contains 53 chapters.

Part 1, "Understanding Sleep Requirements and the Cost of Sleep Deprivation," discusses topics such as why we need sleep and power napping. Part 2 contains 11 chapters that explore "Sleep Through the Lifespan." Topics include "What Is Sudden Infant Death Syndrome" (SIDS), "Common Bedtime Trauma," and "Sleep in Older Persons." Part 3 discusses major sleep disorders. The 15 chapters cover topics such as sleep apnea, snoring, narcolepsy, insomnia, and sleepwalking. Part 4, "Sleep Medications," focuses on medications that may be used to either enhance or facilitate sleep. Four chapters are dedicated to medications such as Melatonin, benzodiazepines, and over-the-counter options. Part 5 has 9 chapters that focus on "Sleep and Other Disorders." This section of the book explores the effects and relation between sleep and coexisting illnesses. Part 6, the last 4 chapters of the book, provides the reader with a glossary of terms and an extensive list of references. The inside of the front and back covers of this book lists a complete catalog of the Health Reference Series. This text will complement any home or medical library. It is user-friendly and ideal for the adult reader.—**Paul M. Murphy III**

Sports Medicine

C, P
495.   **Sports Injuries Sourcebook.** By Heather E. Aldred. Detroit, Omnigraphics, 1999. 606p. index. (Health Reference Series). $78.00. ISBN 0-7808-0218-7.

This new volume in the Omnigraphics Health Reference Series describes the causes, treatments, and rehabilitation of common sports injuries and also provides information about injury prevention in many different sporting activities. Concerns of special groups (i.e., young athletes, senior citizens, and women) are also addressed.

The book's 46 chapters are arranged in 5 parts: understanding common injuries, injury prevention during training, injury prevention for specific sports, rehabilitation and treatment, and a final section with a glossary and directory of organizational resources. The subject index is fairly comprehensive, as is the table of contents.

Sport Injuries Sourcebook provides basic information for the layperson. It is not intended to be a comprehensive resource for diagnosis and treatment. Although the editors state their concern for providing current information in revised and updated volumes, it should be noted that many of the references cited in this book were originally published before 1996. There is also one glaring error: Indiana University is in Bloomington; Indiana State University is in Terre Haute. In health care, information over three to five years old is often obsolete. Public libraries and undergraduate academic libraries will find this book useful for its nontechnical language.—**Vicki J. Killion**

PHARMACY AND PHARMACEUTICAL SCIENCES

P

496.   Garrison, Robert, Jr., and Michael Mannion. **Pharmacist's Guide to Over-the-Counter and Natural Remedies.** Garden City Park, N.Y., Avery Publishing, 1999. 368p. index. $6.95pa. ISBN 0-89529-850-3.

The purpose of this book is to give important information on over-the-counter (OTC) and natural remedies and to explain how they can be used beneficially for treating conditions not requiring prescription drugs. The information provided is clearly and concisely written for understanding by the majority of readers. This book is divided into 2 main sections. Part 1 lists "fifty common herbs and their potential interactions with regular drugs" alphabetically and other broad general information on these remedies, such as what type of labeling information to look for, the units of measurement, and "vitamin and mineral intakes." Part 2 is an alphabetic list of common conditions. Each entry describes the condition, the OTC remedies, the natural remedies, and if there are specific precautions to note. Appendix A is a list of organizations to contact for further information on any of the conditions or remedies listed. Appendix B is a personal medical form, which includes a place to list all medications, making it easier for someone to note if there might be interactions among medications, OTCs, and natural remedies. There is a list of references for further reading and an alphabetic index of all conditions and natural remedies. Cross-references are included in the index. This book is highly recommended for all library collections because more people are looking for alternative treatments.—**Betsy J. Kraus**

P

497.   Kuhn, Cynthia, Scott Swartzwelder, and Wilkie Wilson. **Buzzed: The Straight Facts About the Most Used and Abused Drugs from Alcohol to Ecstasy.** New York, W. W. Norton, 1998. 317p. illus. index. $14.95pa. ISBN 0-393-31732-3.

Drug education is often incomplete. We tell our young people to "Just Say No," and cite horror stories of relatively rare cocaine deaths and marijuana "addiction." In addition, many of the drugs that young people encounter go by names we do not know or are themselves arcane and little known outside the youth scene. This excellent resource lays out the plain unvarnished facts in language that high school and college students can understand. Part 1 examines broad categories of drugs: alcohol, caffeine, herbal drugs, entactogens, hallucinogens, inhalants, marijuana, nicotine, opiates, sedatives, steroids, and stimulants. It describes how each is introduced into the system (e.g., ingest, inhale, inject), the effects on the body, common terms used for the substance, overdose, interactions with other drugs, and, where applicable, the different effects of different forms. Each substance is thoroughly examined with no inflated scare tactics. Part 2 covers the basics of brain function and drug function in general as well as legal issues. A bibliography is appended and an excellent glossary of slang terms is provided. This resource will be useful for public library reference departments, but be sure to buy several circulating copies too.

—**Susan B. Hagloch**

P

498.   Mindell, Earl, and Virginia Hopkins. **Prescription Alternatives: Hundreds of Safe, Natural, Prescription-Free Remedies to Restore and Maintain Your Health.** 2d ed. Lincolnwood, Ill., National Textbook, 1998. 562p. index. $19.95pa. ISBN 0-87983-989-9.

Written in clear, understandable language, the theme of this work is to be aware of alternative ways of treating medical disorders rather than becoming part of what the author suggests is the "drug treadmill." The source is organized into 2 parts. Part 1 consists of laying the foundation for good health, and part 2 considers prescription drugs and their natural alternatives. Such areas as being aware of the pill-popping mindset; how to avoid prescription drug abuse; the interaction of drugs with food, drink, supplements, and other drugs; and how to read drug labels and information inserts are some of the issues that are considered in part 1.

Part 2, which makes up the majority of the work, considers various types of medical problems, the drugs that are usually prescribed to alleviate the problem, and the alternative remedies to prescription drugs. Each of these medical problems is arranged in a chapter-by-chapter format. For example, chapters on diabetes drugs and their natural alternatives and drugs for pain relief and their natural alternatives are present. Other medical areas considered are digestive tract problems, insomnia, eye diseases, osteoporosis, cold, cough, and asthma. For each medical area considered, general information regarding the malady, prescription drugs given for the malady, along with their side effects and natural alternatives for treating the disease, are given. All of this information is written for a layperson in an informal style and does not follow the conventional type of reference book. More than 1,000 simple, safe, nature-based remedies are presented, along with explanations on how to monitor the body as one switches from drugs to natural health. A list of recommended readings, a list of references reflecting each of the chapters presented, and a subject index complete the work. This work is recommended for all high school, public, and college libraries. Persons interested in this topic may wish to purchase the guide for their own home libraries.—**George H. Bell**

34 High Technology

GENERAL WORKS

C

499. Dillon, Patrick M., and David C. Leonard. **Multimedia and the Web from A to Z.** 2d ed. Phoenix, Ariz., Oryx Press, 1998. 355p. $39.95pa. ISBN 1-57356-132-0.

Acknowledging the impact that the World Wide Web is having on the field of multimedia, the authors decided to revise and enlarge the previous edition of *Multimedia Technology from A to Z* (see ARBA 96, entry 1750). Almost 500 new terms have been added, most of which originated from the language of the Internet, as reflected in the title change. Most of the definitions for the more than 1,000 terms in the 1st edition were rewritten to reflect the relationship to the Web. The authors' desire is to establish a professional vocabulary for the field of multimedia; thus, they focus on terms used by the major disciplines that contribute to the industry.

The terms cover a wide range of topics. Familiar terms, such as *JPEG, cookie,* and *search engine* are defined as well as perhaps less familiar terms such as *Neuro-Baby* and *double buffering.* However, this dictionary includes more than just computer jargon. There are terms reflecting the publishing, recording, and video industries, such as *art director, refresh rate, footage,* and *fair use.* The paragraph-length definitions are clearly written and understandable to the informed layperson. Often the authors include a statement as to how a particular technology impacted the field of multimedia. Italicized words within the definitions are defined elsewhere and serve as cross-references. The authors also include a list of acronyms and their meanings as well as an annotated bibliography of selected books, scholarly articles, magazines, trade journals, and electronic publication collections to help guide the reader to additional sources of information.

This dictionary is geared toward the practitioner and serves its purpose well. Oftentimes, books about technology are dated the minute they are published, but the authors' style of writing keeps the material fresh. This book is recommended for academic and large public libraries. [R: BL, 15 Nov 98, p. 610; BR, Mar/April 99, p. 72]—**Teresa U. Berry**

COMPUTING

C, P, S

500. Levine, John, Margaret Levine Young, Doug Muder, and Alison Barrows. **Windows 98: The Complete Reference.** New York, Osborne/McGraw-Hill, 1998. 1001p. illus. index. $39.99pa. (with disc). ISBN 0-07-882343-9.

The authors promise much, beginning with the book's title. At 1,001 pages plus a CD-ROM and updates and supplements at a companion Website, this "package deal" fulfills that promise. *Windows 98: The Complete Reference* will provide answers to most questions regarding the installation, customization, and, most importantly, the day-to-day use of the Windows 98 operating system. Featured authors John Levine and Margaret Levine Young have made practically a cottage industry writing "for dummies" and other computer books that are used worldwide and have been translated into several languages. So when the authors say they intend their book to be useful for beginners through experienced users, they can be believed. Topics range from very basic (icons, the desktop, taskbars) through advanced concepts, such as LAN configurations, network security, and editing the registry.

Windows 98: The Complete Reference is extremely well organized and thoroughly indexed, as befits a book intended primarily for reference use rather than cover-to-cover reading. The book's table of contents alone is an impressive 23 pages. An introduction tells readers how to use the book and its companion CD-ROM most effectively and explains the book's graphic and textual conventions.

The body consists of narrative, tables, charts, and annotated screen prints. A question-and-answer format is also used. The exclusive use of black-and-white print may help ensure this book's reasonable price, but use of color, at least for the screen prints, would really enhance this book's eye appeal and perhaps make it seem less intimidating at first glance. A comprehensive glossary and a detailed index conclude the book.

Windows 98: The Complete Reference is highly recommended for either reference or circulating collections of public, high school, and academic libraries. Companies and individuals currently using or thinking of using Windows 98 should also consider its purchase.—**Linda D. Tietjen**

INTERNET

S

501.   Gralla, Preston. **Online Kids: A Young Surfer's Guide to Cyberspace.** rev. ed. New York, John Wiley, 1999. 276p. index. $14.95pa. ISBN 0-471-25312-X.

This is the revision of the widely reviewed and widely acquired 1996 edition of the same title. Like the original edition, the more recent effort introduces the young reader (and the reader's parents) to the world of cyberspace. This is not a book filled with unintelligible jargon and technical information. It provides the basics within the context of entertaining, yet informative articles and annotations.

The chapters cover a wide range of topics within the parameters of cyberspace. For instance, one chapter speaks of what cyberspace is and defines its various capabilities, including chat, downloading software, and video or sound clips. But it is not a "how to" guide. Another chapter discusses equipment requirements, but does not delve into detail beyond the basics. It appears the book is written with the assumption that an adult will guide any child embarking into Internet explorations. With adult supervision in mind, an entire chapter is devoted to online etiquette and a child's safety on the Internet. There is discussion on the site blocking software available, plus how various services provide for protecting children.

The best parts of the book are the chapters devoted to Websites. They are chosen with children in mind, but many are equally as interesting to adults. Each entry includes the address of the site, plus brief annotations describing what is on the site. For quick reference, there is the "Usefulness Index" and the "Coolness Index." According to the introduction, the author's children rated each site. Some of these entries did have drawbacks. Not all of them were readily available unless one is a subscriber to a service such as America on Line (AOL) or CompuServe. Also, a random check showed that some sites are no longer active. But then, that is a problem of the medium. No book of this type will be completely accurate.

Like the well-received, earlier edition, this book achieves exactly what it is designed to do. It provides the young reader a well-organized, well-presented, and informational introduction to the cyberworld.

—**Phillip P. Powell**

P, S

502.   Polly, Jean Armour. **The Internet Kids & Family Yellow Pages.** 3d ed. New York, McGraw-Hill, 1999. 744p. illus. index. $34.99pa. ISBN 0-07-211849-0.

The 3d edition of these yellow pages is a directory of 4,000 educational or entertainment-oriented Internet sites for children in grades K-8. The arrangement is alphabetic by broad subject headings. An index is provided for those who wish to locate a Web page by specific topic. An electronic CD-ROM version of the yellow pages is furnished with keyword search capability to enable direct access to listed Websites. Special features include a short list of the 100 best sites on the net, a list of Websites for countries of the world, and a "net files" section to illustrate how the Internet can be browsed to locate trivia. The audience for these yellow pages seems to be apprehensive parents with little direct knowledge of the Internet who fear that their children will access inappropriate material while surfing the Web. The compiler, Jean Armour Polly, a former librarian and self-titled "net mom," assures parents that she has personally reviewed each Website to verify that it is "family friendly" and free of any offensive content. Perhaps her distaste for controversy explains why a good number of sites in these yellow pages come under the heading of fun and games. For example, there is a generous list of links to commercial Disney Online sites, which may not be surprising considering that Polly works for the corporation as a private consultant. So great is her maternal concern that she includes advertisements for "net-mom"-endorsed products that parents may purchase to guarantee the safety of their kids on the Internet.

All good intentions aside, currency is the unavoidable problem with all Web directories in print format. To compensate for this weakness, the author directs us to her personal homepage for free updates to track changes to Web addresses listed in the yellow pages. While consulting her Web page for updates, however, one cannot fail to notice the "net-mom" bookstore link where one can purchase the new 4th edition of her yellow pages through Amazon.com just in time for the millennium. For reference staff who use the Internet on a daily basis in public and school libraries to satisfy the information needs of young patrons, these yellow pages will contain no surprises because the educational sites identified by Polly are already well known by librarians and are usually accessible as bookmarks or links on most library homepages.—**David G. Nowak**

C, P, S

503.   Reese, Jean. **Internet Books for Educators, Parents, and Students.** Englewood, Colo., Libraries Unlimited, 1999. 299p. index. $32.50pa. ISBN 1-56308-697-2.

A useful and relative inexpensive guide to resources that explicate and teach the Internet and its various functions, this volume includes somewhat lengthy (500 to 1,000 words) reviews of books pertinent to the topic. The volume is divided into 6 major sections: General Internet Books; Internet Books for Educators and Librarians; Internet Books for Parents, Children, and Students; Internet Books for Curriculum Development; The Internet in Juvenile Fiction; and Internet Books for Web Page Design and Creation. Within each section, entries are arranged alphabetically by title, followed by author's name, publication information, date, Web address, name of pages, series title, ISBN, type of binding, cost, software information (when available), and an annotation.

As thorough and information-laden as the volume is, it cannot overcome the problems inherent in its scope—namely, that much of the information contained in the books reviewed is already out-of-date. In some cases, newer editions might exist, but there is no guarantee. This work is recommended for astute librarians who are capable of transcending the limitations of the information, and for collections that might not have more recent guides to the Internet.—**Edmund F. SantaVicca**

P

504.   Schlein, Alan M. **Find It Online: The Complete Guide to Online Research.** 2d ed. Tempe, Ariz., Facts on Demand Press; distr., Lanham, Md., National Book Network, 1999. 506p. index. $19.95pa. ISBN 1-889150-06-1.

The 2d edition of *Find it Online: The Complete Guide to Online Research* is intended to aid those with basic knowledge of the Internet with the tools to research effectively on the World Wide Web. It will help users narrow information searches, find specific background information, access government and business resources, and check on the accuracy of online information.

The book begins by getting readers familiar with Internet terminology and explaining how the terms relate to one another. The following chapters discuss such topics as the various search engines and how to use them; how to use and access more specialized tools (e.g., discussion rooms, mapping tools, newsgroups); how to save results; and how to access government sources, public records, news resources, and business resources. There are special chapters on managing and filtering information as well as the issue of privacy and protection on the Web. Chapter 12 is especially useful to beginning Internet users because it takes the reader through a series of searches and leads them to the right results. The last half of the book consists of indexes, which serve as a kind of directory to government sites, private and public sites, and different Website profiles. A list of contributors, a glossary, and an index conclude the volume.

This book will serve many library patrons that are new to the Internet and particularly to researching on the Internet. Its clarification of Internet-specific terms and no-nonsense approach make it beneficial for both the circulating and reference collections. [R: Choice, Sept 99, p. 104]—**Shannon M. Graff**

TELECOMMUNICATIONS

Dictionaries and Encyclopedias

C, P

505.   Newton, Harry. **Newton's Telecom Dictionary: The Official Dictionary of Telecommunications &** **the Internet.** 15th ed. New York, Miller Freeman; distr., Emeryville, Calif., Publishers Group West, 1999. 953p. $32.95pa. ISBN 1-57820-031-8.

The author bills this work as "the official dictionary of telecommunications and the Internet." He pretty much hits the mark. Harry Newton has an MBA from Harvard, 29 years of experience in the telecommunications industry, and has founded a host of leading monthly industry magazines: *Call Center*, *Computer Telephony*, *Imaging*, *LAN* (now *Network*), *Teleconnect*, and *Telecom Gear*. He is in the process of starting another new magazine, *Technology Investor Magazine* (http://www.TechnologyInvestor.com). The 1st edition of this work appeared in 1989 and the current offering is the 15th edition. The 16th will appear in early January 2000. Now some 1,400 pages in length and 5 and a half pounds in weight, *Newton's* is the virtual industry bible, used by engineers, corporate executives, lawyers, accountants, marketing, sales, and advertising staff among many others. In fact, anyone who works in telecom, networking, or the Internet could benefit by the information in *Newton's*.

The dictionary starts out with an essay on recent trends in the industry, followed by an essay on where Newton thinks the industry will go in the next century. The dictionary section contains around 20,000 defined terms, making it the largest dictionary of its kind by far in the world. The entries are excellent and often very detailed— important definitions are actually essays. A typical example is the listing for the new Internet Protocol (IPv6), which will be installed worldwide to everyone's joy on January 1, 2000. Newton gives two long paragraphs describing the essential upgrade features of IPv6. The alphabetic main sequence of the dictionary is preceded by a numbers section. Embedded in the numbers section is a small telecommunications chronology that lists important events that happened from 1453 (Gutenberg) to 2002 (Eurobills). Newton ends the volume with an appendix of organizations, interest groups, publications, international calling codes, plugs, and connectors.

Few will want to be without this up-to-date volume, which also has the keen insight of a leading force in the telecommunications industry. Like many books now on the market, this volume has a Website, but unfortunately it suffers from a typo in the book. The site is http://www.HarryNewton.com, not http://www.Harry_Newton.com as listed on page ix. Do not expect too much from the site, however, for it consists largely of positive reviews of the book. This is a hefty paperback book, both in terms of weight and price, but well worth both.—**Ralph Lee Scott**

35 Physical Sciences and Mathematics

PHYSICAL SCIENCES

General Works

C

506.   **CRC Handbook of Chemistry and Physics 1999-2000: A Ready-Reference Book of Chemical and Physical Data.** 80th ed. David R. Lide, ed. Boca Raton, Fla., CRC Press, 1999. 1v. (various paging). index. $99.95. ISBN 0-8493-0480-6.

The venerable *CRC Handbook of Chemistry and Physics*, first published in 1913 and now appearing in its 80th edition, has long been a cornerstone of science reference collections. Information is drawn from numerous publications, indicated in the "References" section accompanying each table. The handbook has been updated in each edition since its inception, and the new edition has added tables on stratospheric chemical kinetics, high and low temperature properties of water, gas diffusion and solubility of salts in water, and other topics. One table has been eliminated and the contents of several others have been incorporated into other tables. "Tables Removed from CRC Handbook of Chemistry and Physics, 71st through 79th Editions" (CHEMINFO Chemical Information Sources, Indiana University; http://www.indiana.edu/~cheminfo/crc_xtabs_71-79.html) details the disposition of tables appearing in earlier editions but re-titled, removed, or incorporated into other tables in the 80th edition. [R: BL, 1 Dec 98, p. 689; Choice, Dec 99, p. 694]—**Frederic F. Burchsted**

Chemistry

Dictionaries and Encyclopedias

S

507.   **The Facts on File Dictionary of Chemistry.** 3d ed. John Daintith, ed. New York, Checkmark Books/ Facts on File, 1999. 266p. $17.95pa. ISBN 0-8160-3910-0.

Produced for use in schools, this dictionary, first published in 1980 (see ARBA 82, entry 1436), has been revised and extended. It now contains more than 3,000 entries covering the terminology of modern chemistry; some 250 new terms have been added. Line drawings interspersed throughout the text serve to illustrate chemical structures. Useful tables in the appendix include the chemical elements, the Greek alphabet, fundamental constants, elementary particles, and the periodic table.

Arranged in alphabetic order, each page includes guide words. Entry words are in bold typeface, and each entry is separated by a generous space. Type size is sufficient enough to allow for easy reading. Features include cross-references and *see* references. Definitions are presented in a clear and concise style that is accessible to the beginning chemistry student or layperson, and are frequently enhanced with formulas, the above-mentioned line drawings, and practical applications. This is an affordable and useful reference that will be welcome in both secondary school and public libraries.—**Dana McDougald**

C, P, S

508.   Hunt, Andrew. **Dictionary of Chemistry.** Chicago, Fitzroy Dearborn, 1999. 365p. $40.00. ISBN 1-57958-140-4.

This dictionary, first published in the United Kingdom in 1998 under the title *The Complete A-Z Chemistry Handbook*, is a wonderful learning tool. Alphabetically arranged entries begin with one-sentence definitions, followed by expanded explanations, equations, examples (including in many cases worked numerical examples), tables, diagrams, and illustrations. Cross-references are indicated by words in italics.

Coverage includes both basic and applied chemistry, with entries for general subjects such as chemotherapy and spectroscopy as well as specific technical terms such as amphoteric oxides, delocalized electrons, and oximes. Where appropriate, such as in the entries for chemotherapy and thermochemistry, there is an historical overview of the subject. The entries are informative and clearly written and include information on why the defined topic is important. For example, immiscible liquids are useful in solvent extraction (a cross-reference). This chemistry dictionary will be especially useful for libraries serving undergraduates, but it is also highly recommended for high school and public libraries, and would even be useful for libraries serving graduate students. [R: LJ, 15 Nov 99, p. 61]—**Robert Michaelson**

Handbooks and Yearbooks

C, S

509.   Newton, David E. **Chemistry.** Phoenix, Ariz., Oryx Press, 1999. 294p. illus. index. (Oryx Frontiers of Science Series). $44.95. ISBN 1-57356-160-6.

This volume provides readers with an overview of developments in the fields of chemistry and chemical engineering from 1996 to 1998. The author summarizes about two dozen research studies, covering areas such as buckyballs, reactions at the atomic scale, protein folding, nerve cell growth, and chlorofluorocarbon (CFC) disposal. The topics were selected because they appeared in science journals designed for the general reader, such as *Scientific American* and *Science News*. Readers will need to have a basic knowledge of chemistry to understand the text. Since the author intended to provide only a brief synopsis of each topic, the references at the end of each summary are valuable sources of additional information.

The rest of the book has more general information about the field of chemistry. Newton includes a chapter on controversial issues such as pollution, ozone depletion, greenhouse effect, chemical weapons, and food quality protection and a chapter with excerpts from congressional hearings on these controversies. The biography section provides brief biographies of important chemical researchers in recent years, so the names may not be familiar. There are also sections on the future of chemistry, career information, organizations and associations, a glossary, and an index. Newton also includes a section of statistics on various aspects of the chemical industry and a good list of print and electronic information sources.

Even though Newton gives the reader a good overview of recent advances in chemistry, the organization of the book is a bit confusing. The biographical section separates the chapter on social issues from the congressional hearings on the same topics. Although it may not be the intention, Newton's book is a source of career information. He gives a nice overview of the fields of chemistry and chemical engineering, the kinds of people who work in these fields, and several good information sources. Students considering a science career will find his book very useful. Recommended for high school and undergraduate students.—**Teresa U. Berry**

Earth and Planetary Sciences

General Works

P, S

510.   Newson, Lesley. **The Atlas of the World's Worst Natural Disasters.** New York, DK Publishing, 1998. 159p. illus. maps. index. $50.00. ISBN 0-670-88330-1.

This book will convince anyone that the world can be a cold, cruel, dangerous place and that civilization does indeed exist only by "geological consent." The diagrams, photographs, and maps are spectacularly horrific and will be a jolt to anyone perusing this book in a quiet library far from nature's wrath.

The atlas is divided into two parts. The 1st and longest is a fully illustrated catalog of the woes visited upon us by our dynamic planet. This section begins with geological hazards, primarily earthquakes and volcanoes, with good but brief introductions to the physical mechanisms behind tremors and eruptions. Particular events are highlighted in text boxes, giving details of timing, magnitudes, damage, and casualties. Weather-related disasters (e.g., hurricanes, cyclones, blizzards) follow, with the same type of coverage and detail. The least cohesive portion is titled "Patterns of Chaos," which is a catch-all term for floods, droughts, fires, avalanches, landslides, mass extinctions, and patterns of global climate change. These are interesting but could have been placed in the geological and weather chapters. This would have provided more integration between natural systems and human catastrophes. The last descriptions cover biological hazards, from pests to disease epidemics. Here is the new frontier for cataclysms in the new century, particularly with the globalization of obscure and deadly tropical viruses.

The 2d part of the book is a gazetteer with maps covering most of the world. Each map is annotated with locations of natural disasters, numbered so that they can be looked up on an extensive descriptive list. The book ends with a short glossary of prominent terms and an index.—**Mark A. Wilson**

Astronomy and Space Sciences

C, P

511.   Angelo, Joseph A., Jr. **The Dictionary of Space Technology.** 2d ed. New York, Facts on File, 1999. 487p. illus. $50.00. ISBN 0-8160-3073-1.

The introduction to the 1st edition of this work, published in 1982, calls attention to the recently completed 1st space shuttle mission. Obviously, an updated edition has been long overdue, especially in such a highly volatile discipline. The work follows the standard Facts on File two-column format, and has grown from 380 to 487 pages. There are approximately 3,000 definitions and 135 black-and-white photographs and line drawings. The definitions range from one sentence to highly technical, extending for more than a page and involving calculus and advanced scientific concepts. The placement of illustrations is generally appropriate, though the captions do not always indicate the corresponding definitions. For example, a group portrait of the Challenger crew does not include "Challenger" in the caption, and one must turn the page for the Challenger article. Definitions include recently declassified information, including the Russian space program, and are reasonably current. The discussion of "Mars Surveyor '98" refers to future launches that actually occurred in December 1998 and January 1999, and the SOHO (Solar and Heliospheric Observatory) article does not mention all the technical difficulties this project has experienced in recent months. Longer definitions usually have one or two cross-references. The work includes some slang definitions, including "bird" (a rocket, missile, satellite, or spacecraft) and "barbecue mode" (the slow roll of an aerospace vehicle to equalize the external temperature). More astronomical terminology might be appropriate, such as "right ascension" and "declination" (the standard coordinates for locating astronomical objects). Most appropriate for libraries serving a knowledgeable clientele. [R: BL, June 99, pp. 1874-1876; Choice, Oct 99, p. 308]—**Richard S. Watts**

P

512.   Dickinson, Terence. **The Universe and Beyond.** 3d ed. Willowdale, Ont., Firefly Books, 1999. 168p. illus. index. $40.00; $29.95pa. ISBN 1-55209-377-8; 1-55209-361-1pa.

This impressive volume provides an excellent overview of the heavens for the general reader. What sets it apart from a multitude of other books of its type is a lively, informative text and dozens of stunning photographs and illustrations. It is a delight to read and a delight for the eye. The arrangement is fairly standard, starting with the solar system and moving on to stars, galaxies, and beyond. Additional topics include cosmology, the search for extraterrestrial life, and telescopes. Like other introductory works, it emphasizes findings and photographs from recent space explorations. Substantially updated from the previous edition, this volume contains approximately 25 percent new information and 50 percent new images. Although it may not be considered a reference book as such, it does have many tables of numerical data, a bibliography, and an index at the back. This work is highly recommended for the public and home library.—**Robert A. Seal**

P, S

513.   **Innovations in Astronomy.** Santa Barbara, Calif., ABC-CLIO, 1999. 328p. illus. index. (Innovations in Science). $50.00. ISBN 1-57607-114-6.

This book is part of a series whose apparent mission is to present a patchwork of information within various scientific disciplines. It contains an assortment of chapters on the field of astronomy. There are seven chapters. The overview chapter is the only chapter that is signed; however, there are no credentials provided for this author. Through 23 pages, the overview takes the reader on a tour of the various subdisciplines of astronomy; a bit of history, including related space programs milestones; and astronomical instrumentation. It is presented at the level of the interested layperson.

The remainder of the chapters are essentially lists. Chapter 2, "Chronology," lists by year the important advances of astronomy, beginning in 1903. Chapter 3 is a list of brief biographical sketches. Chapter 4 is a directory of organizations, observatories, and facilities. Conspicuously missing is anything about McDonald Observatory of the University of Texas, which has one of the largest land-based optical telescopes. The information here seems out-of-date. For information of this kind, the current volume of the *Astronomical Almanac* published by the U.S. Naval Observatory is reliable. Chapter 5 is a list of astronomy resources, some of which are certainly classics but may no longer be in print. Chapter 6 is a list of Websites. Unfortunately, the Internet changes so rapidly that many sites listed were out-of-date before it was printed. Chapter 7 is a dictionary.

A book like this that tries to bring together many different aspects of a discipline might be appropriate for school libraries where students just need a summary of a discipline for class projects or career information. [R: LJ, 1 Oct 99, pp. 80-82]—**Margaret F. Dominy**

P, S

514.   Moore, Patrick. **Atlas of the Universe.** New York, Cambridge University Press, 1998. 288p. illus. maps. index. $39.95. ISBN 0-521-64210-8.

This handsome revision of a classic atlas contains little text from the original edition (1970). The volume reflects contemporary developments in the field of astronomy and related sciences and disciplines, ranging from the generalities of the universe and the solar system to the specifics of each planet, the Sun, the stars, and the various constellations that comprise the borders of outer space. A brief overview chapter opens the work, presenting the history of telescopes, observatories, rockets, and the arrival of man in space. This is followed by detailed discussions of individual phenomena and objects, accompanied by a wealth of color photographs and images. Sidebars are included for many of the articles and explanations, enhancing the discussion through the presentation of statistics or other relevant data. A concluding section presents information on buying a telescope and creating a home observatory. A glossary and index supplement the main text. This volume is highly recommended for its scope, treatment, and readability. Considering the cost, this volume should easily find a place in the atlas collection of any library. [R: LJ, 15 Feb 99, p. 143]—**Edmund F. SantaVicca**

P, S

515.   **Space Exploration.** Christopher Mari, ed. Bronx, N.Y., H. W. Wilson, 1999. 157p. index. (The Reference Shelf, v.71, no.2). $30.00pa. ISBN 0-8242-0963-X.

This title follows the traditional format of the venerable H.W. Wilson series The Reference Shelf, now in its 71st volume. It contains 25 articles drawn from periodicals such as *Time*, the *New Yorker*, *Astronomy*, and *Aviation Week and Space Technology*, as well as the *New York Times*, covering 5 major space exploration topics. These are as follows: John Glenn's return to space, the exploration of Mars, the International Space Station, private enterprise and space exploration, and new technologies and discoveries. There are also numerous abstracts of additional articles concerned with these topics. Mari generally does a good job of balancing both sides of controversial topics. Was Senator John Glenn's recent mission in the space shuttle a blatant NASA publicity stunt, or was it the triumphant conclusion to an illustrious career with important implications for geriatric research? Is the International Space Station a necessary step for further exploration of the solar system, or is it an enormous waste of tax dollars, having no real scientific value, used to prop up the aerospace industry in key congressional districts while rescuing Russia's industry from oblivion? Unfortunately, in such a rapidly advancing area, events such as the late 1999 loss of the Mars Climate Orbiter and the extended grounding of the shuttle fleet because of wiring problems quickly overtake speculations in the articles. Many libraries have standing orders to this series. Public, high school, and undergraduate libraries without such standing orders should acquire this title if local interest warrants doing so, with the realization that much of the material will date itself rapidly.—**Richard S. Watts**

C, P

516.   **The Universe Revealed.** Pam Spence, ed. New York, Cambridge University Press, 1998. 192p. illus. index. $39.95. ISBN 0-521-64239-6.

Assembling an introductory book on the entire universe must be a daunting task these days. Our perspectives on the solar system; stellar evolution; the formation of galaxies; and the origin of time, space, and matter have dramatically changed in just the past decade. The authors of this book succeed spectacularly and give readers a text that is up-to-date, beautifully illustrated, and a model of scientific clarity. School-age children as well as curious adults will find the book highly informative and challenging.

The Universe Revealed is divided into 6 sections, each with color-coded pages. The theme is first to place us in our physical context in the cosmos, starting with the solar system. Each planet is discussed in clear prose, with the latest spacecraft images and colorful block diagrams as illustrations. The authors present standard planetological information (size, orbital and rotation statistics, surface temperatures, and the like), with a few unsolved mysteries, such as the magnetic field of Mercury and the origin of Pluto. The best chapter is on Mars because of the inclusion of the recent Pathfinder images and data. There is a good essay about the "Martian fossils" controversy centered around a meteorite recovered in Antarctica in 1984 and found to be a rock blasted from the surface of Mars. The chapter on Earth is followed by two pages on global warming, which is a timely and useful addition, even if it is unduly alarmist in tone. The end of the solar system section includes short discussions of gravity, light, and the existence of other planetary systems. These provide essential concepts for the following sections on stars and galaxies, which are well supported by dozens of Hubble images and explanatory diagrams.

The section on cosmology provides the only disappointment in this book. Any simple explanation of the Big Bang Theory may be ultimately doomed to fail, and this one certainly does. A few glossary pages are just not enough to convey the depth of the ideas and the extensive evidence that supports them. Readers may be intrigued by the illustrations enough to look for more details elsewhere.

The final section of the book is a brief discussion of "skywatching," followed by simple but useful star and moon maps. After scanning the text and gazing at the marvelous illustrations, it would be a cold reader indeed who did not want to gaze that very evening at the night sky. This book is highly recommended for everyone who reads.—**Mark A. Wilson**

P, S

517.   Vanin, Gabriele. **Cosmic Phenomena.** Willowdale, Ont., Firefly Books, 1999. 167p. illus. index. $35.00. ISBN 1-55209-423-5.

For those with an interest in astronomy or the natural wonders of the universe, this book should provide more than adequate information and stimulation. The work is divided into 3 major sections: "Great Comets," "Meteor Showers," and "Eclipses." Each of the sections follows the same format, discussing the phenomena in historical perspective and identifying the great comets, meteor showers, and eclipses of history. This is followed by a section treating the origin and nature of the phenomena, providing a better understanding of how these phenomena have developed. Additional sections are provided that are unique to each phenomenon (e.g., observing comets, lunar eclipses, solar eclipses). More than 300 impressive color photographs and illustrations enhance the text throughout. Some are full-page, whereas others are snapshots. A bibliography and index supplement the text.

High school and college students as well as armchair astronomers will appreciate the readability of the text; the historical treatments; and the in-depth discussions of the more famous and noteworthy comets, meteors, and other natural phenomena. The author uses a commonsense approach to the topic, and provides an excellent learning and reference tool.—**Edmund F. SantaVicca**

Geology

C, P, S

518.   **Geology.** James A. Woodhead, ed. Englewood Cliffs, N.J., Salem Press, 1999. 2v. illus. index. (Magill's Choice). $95.00/set. ISBN 0-89356-522-9.

For the small public or school library, it is often difficult to provide useful coverage of a subject as complex and diverse as geology. The editors of Magill's Survey of Science: Earth Science Series have responded by selecting from their 6-volume work 87 articles on all aspects of earth science. These cameo articles, which tend to be from 8 to 10 pages in length, provide the reader with current information on topics ranging from archaeological geology, permafrost, and minerals to volcanoes and the origins of oil and gas. Each entry provides a summary of the topic, ways in which the topic is studied and how the resulting information is put to use, and context that describes the role played by the topic. The well-selected, brief, annotated bibliography provides sources of additional information. At the beginning of each article there are a definition of the topic and definitions of principal terms that will be discussed in the article. Each article is signed and one can go to the beginning of volume 1 to identify the author's affiliation.

The articles are arranged alphabetically by title. For the reader wishing to locate related topics easily, a list of subject categories is provided in the appendix. A glossary is also provided, which includes a wide variety of terms. The comprehensive index leads the reader to specific items. In a number of cases, the index term leads only to the glossary, which is understandable given that this book represents approximately one-third of the parent work.

This reference book, intended for high school students and college undergraduates, provides a well-written, up-to-date series of articles, each complete in itself, that cover the fundamentals of geology and its subdisciplines. An added bonus is that it is well written and a pleasure to read. [R: LJ, 15 June 99, p. 72; Choice, Sept 99, p. 114; RUSQ, Fall 99, p. 92]—**Ann E. Prentice**

Mineralogy

P, S

519.   **Cambridge Guide to Minerals, Rocks, and Fossils.** rev. ed. By A. C. Bishop, A. R. Woolley, and W. R. Hamilton. New York, Cambridge University Press, 1999. 336p. illus. index. $14.95pa. ISBN 0-521-77881-6.

The preface of this book states that its updated data conform to standards of the International Mineralogical Association (IMA). Seventeen new plates have been added to this revised edition. The main introduction includes safety instructions, a basic equipment essentials list, and general instructions for care and storage of specimens. The introduction to each major section (minerals, rocks, and fossils) gives the history and geography of each broad category. The minerals section defines minerals, their symmetry, references axes, form, and aggregates. It also provides a chemical chart, brief descriptions of physical and chemical properties, and where specific minerals are located. Rocks are categorized by their main features: mineralogy, color index, texture, structure, field relationships, and intrusions. Meteorites and tektites are included. The fossils section was developed in conjunction with The Natural History Museum in London. Its scope includes the most common and widespread specimens—those not requiring special training or equipment to see. A bibliography, geological time scale, comprehensive index, and conversion table are included. This book contains similar information and color graphics to that which is presented in the Eye Witness children's science series, but this handbook has been developed in fact sheet format for young adults and adults. This work is recommended for public and high school libraries.—**Kimberley D. Harris**

Volcanology

S

520.   Lentz, Harris M., III. **The Volcano Registry: Names, Locations, Descriptions, and History for Over 1500 Sites.** Jefferson, N.C., McFarland, 1999. 190p. index. $29.95. ISBN 0-7864-0732-8.

This volume catalogs more than 1,500 of the world's volcanoes, both named and unnamed, including some mountains that have been claimed as volcanoes, but are not. Each entry includes the name of the volcano, its geographic location, its latitude and longitude, and its physical characteristics. In some cases, a brief summation is given of its eruptive history. It is prefaced by a pleasantly discursive introduction, and concludes with appendixes to extraterrestrial volcanoes, a brief summary of some common language terms applied to volcanoes, and a bibliography.

The Volcano Registry is a simplified version of the standard reference in the field, *Volcanoes of the World* by Tom Simkin and Lee Siebert (2d ed.; see ARBA 96, entry 1818). This latter work is far more detailed in many respects (including maps, illustrations, tabular summations of data, references cited, and details of eruptive history), and will provide a more complete reference source to volcanic activity in the last 10,000 years.

—**Bruce H. Tiffney**

Physics

P, S

521.   **The Cassell Dictionary of Physics.** By Percy Harrison. London, Cassell; distr., New York, Continuum Publishing, 1998. 216p. illus. $27.95. ISBN 0-304-35034-6.

Offering clear and concise definitions and explanations of hundreds of terms used in physics and related subjects, this dictionary is a small gem. It provides students in high school and college with easy-to-understand entries on terms from mainstream physics, inorganic chemistry, quantum theory, mathematics, astronomy, and computer technology. Many entries also include relevant formulas and illustrations. Although the work does not provide depth of coverage, it does succeed in providing a source for quick definitions to aid in understanding academic texts.

The work is arranged in a logical alphabetic arrangement with cross-references to related articles included within entries. *See* references to preferred terms are also included in the alphabetic listing. Most definitions are only one or two sentences long, while major entries may contain several paragraphs. It should be noted that there is no index. In addition, no pronunciations are given with the entries, leaving the reader to guess at the correct pronunciation of many terms. Several appendixes, some useful, others less so, are included: SI units, SI prefixes, SI conversion factors, common measures, physical concepts in SI units, fundamental constants, electromagnetic spectrum, periodic table of the elements, elementary particles, the solar system, common differential coefficients and integrals, and the Greek alphabet.

Although this dictionary will definitely see use in the library, it does not cover its expressed fields completely. For example, terms such as "dark matter," "variance," and "skew" are omitted, while other related terms are included. Although the periodic table of elements is included, the elements themselves are not included in the body of the work and there are no cross-references from the symbols for the elements to their actual names. With these weaknesses noted, libraries that need an inexpensive and current dictionary of physics should consider the work for inclusion in their collections.—**Gregory A. Crawford**

C, S

522.   **The Facts on File Dictionary of Physics.** 3d ed. John Daintith and John Clark, eds. New York, Checkmark Books/Facts on File, 1999. 250p. $17.95pa. ISBN 0-8160-3912-7.

This ready-reference dictionary has been substantially updated since its original publication in 1980 and revision in 1989 (see ARBA 89, entry 1677). The comprehensive coverage includes 2,400 entries, which range in length from a sentence to more than 300 words. Black-and-white drawings and tables are interspersed throughout the main body and enhance the text. Both *see* and *see also* references are used extensively in the dictionary. Words and phrases are italicized within an entry when they have an entry of their own. This is a particularly useful feature to the reader. Five appendixes supplement the main body: chemical elements, periodical table, symbols for physical quantities, conversion factors for various measurements, and the Greek alphabet. This is a useful handbook for high school and college, but is not suitable for in-depth research.—**Elaine Ezell**

MATHEMATICS

C, P, S

523. **CRC Concise Encyclopedia of Mathematics.** By Eric W. Weisstein. Boca Raton, Fla., Chapman & Hall/CRC Press, 1999. 1969p. $65.00. ISBN 0-8493-9640-9.

This work attempts to define the field of mathematics, no small feat and no small work at nearly 200 pages. Definitions tend to be concise, usually not much longer than a column page. For clarity, an illustration is often included. Mathematical rigor is maintained in the definitions. For some of the longer entries, references are provided. The cross-referencing is generous to both internal entries and Internet sites.

Of particular interest is the effort to relate the mathematical topic to recognizable everyday life through copious examples. This makes for very appealing reading. Mathematicians, scientists, engineers, and students will find this book useful and a delight to use. The book is also available on CD-ROM. This encyclopedia is highly recommended for academic, public, and school libraries. [R: Choice, June 99, p. 1761]

—**Margaret F. Dominy**

36 Resource Sciences

ENVIRONMENTAL SCIENCE

Handbooks and Yearbooks

P, S

524. Katz, William B. **The ABCs of Environmental Science.** Rockville, Md., Government Institutes, 1998. 155p. index. $39.00pa. ISBN 0-86587-627-4.

Directed to people of any age with little or no scientific background, Katz's book is enjoyable reading on environmental issues that are in the media today. Although definitely not a textbook, it will be a useful introductory reference for students in high school or college environmental science classes. The book is written in simple, clear, concise language with specific scientific terms in italics the first time they are used. These words are then compiled into a glossary, which follows the text. The book is divided into 4 parts: "Matter, Energy, and Population Growth," "World's Resources," "Pollution," and "Our Planet's Future." The 22 chapters are short, with less than 10 pages each. Chapters are divided into subtopics; for example, "Minerals—A Nonrenewable Resource" covers the Earth's crust, minerals in demand, mineral distribution, cost of minerals, and environmental impact of mineral production. Each chapter is summarized in a "What You Should Remember" box at the end of the chapter. Topics within the chapters range in length from one paragraph to a page. They do not provide detailed discussion of the particular topic but do clearly explain the issue or scientific principle in plain English. Katz explains how the environment works and the impact humans have on it. He stresses renewable and nonrenewable resources and measures we can and need to take to preserve the environment. Graphs and basic black-and-white clip art illustrate the text. A thorough index is provided.—**Elaine Ezell**

37 Transportation

GROUND

P, S
525. Bennett, Jim. **The Complete Motorcycle Book: A Consumer's Guide.** 2d ed. New York, Facts on File, 1999. 258p. illus. index. $27.95; $14.95pa. ISBN 0-8160-3853-8; 0-8160-3854-6pa.

A new edition four years after an original publication can be suspect, but not in this instance. Not only is there new information on trends (the rapidly growing number of women riders, for example), new models (including imported ones), prices, and a new section on exotic bikes, but there is even more material in the sections on safety scattered throughout the book. In this reviewer's opinion, the most notable contribution of this volume is the commonsense approach to all aspects of safety, from health to protective clothing and headgear, skill levels, group riding, and many other factors that novices and experienced riders alike need to take into consideration. This, added to basic and sensible chapters on whether to buy a motorcycle in the first place through the selection process (new or used, domestic or imported, what type) and maintenance, makes Bennett's book a useful and effective one. There is even a brief chapter on road driving aimed at car drivers. This book is highly recommended for public and community colleges in particular.—**Walter C. Allen**

P
526. Jensen, Todd A. **Automotive Web Sites.** Jefferson, N.C., McFarland, 1999. 175p. index. $25.00pa. ISBN 0-7864-0741-7.

Following a brief preface on the scope of the volume and an introduction on searching the Web for automotive topics, the body of the work consists of 17 sections on various areas relating to automobiles. Topics include aftermarket, automobile buying resources, eZines and publications, and women's groups. Entries are alphabetical within each section. They give full names and acronyms and full Web addresses, along with descriptions of the scope and content of each site. References are numbered sequentially through the entire book, from 1 to 714. The index refers to these numbers, not pages. Presumably, the work will need to be revised fairly frequently to keep up with all the additions and closings. But at the modest price of the 1st edition, it should not be too hard for libraries to keep up with. This should be very useful for hobbyists as well as public and engineering libraries.
—**Walter C. Allen**

Author/Title Index

Reference is to entry number.

Subject Index

Reference is to entry number.

BIOLOGY
Facts on file dict of biology, 3d ed, 459
Guide to field gds, 465

BIRDS
Animals, 466
Bird almanac, 468

BLIND - DEAF
Practical gd to the ADA & visual impairment, 313

BLOOD - DISEASES
Blood & circulatory disorders sourcebk, 489

BLUES (MUSIC)
All music gd to the blues, 2d ed, 403
Blues singers, 404

BOATING
Complete outdoors ency, 4th ed, 305

BONAPARTE, NAPOLEON
Napoleon, 219

BOOK COLLECTING
Huxford's old bk value gd, 11th ed, 337

BOTANY
Dictionary of plant pathology, 2d ed, 460
Guide to field gds, 465

BULGARIA
Bulgaria, 49

BURNS
Burns sourcebk, 490

BUSINESS - BIOGRAPHY
American business leaders [CD-ROM], 62
Business leaders for students, 63

BUSINESS - DICTIONARIES & ENCYCLOPEDIAS
Encyclopedia of African American business hist, 64
Lexicon of labor, 92
Wall Street dict, 76

BUSINESS - DIRECTORIES
Toll-free phone bk USA 1999, 3d ed, 25

BUSINESS - EDUCATION
Best 80 business schools, 2000 ed, 126

BUSINESS - HANDBOOKS
Sexual harassment in America, 272

BUSINESS - QUOTATIONS
Wiley bk of business quotations, 68

CABLE TELEVISION - CAREERS
Career opportunities in TV, cable, video, & multimedia,
    4th ed, 85

CAMEROON
Cameroon, rev ed, 39

CAMPING
Beyond the natl parks, 303
Complete outdoors ency, 4th ed, 305

CANADA
Historical dict of Canada, 211
Quebec, 47

CANADA - ECONOMIC CONDITIONS
Encyclopedia of North American hist, 241

CANADIANS
Canadian who's who 1999 [CD-ROM], 14
Canadian who's who 1999, v.34, 13
Encyclopedia of Canada's peoples, 134

CAPITAL PUNISHMENT
Capital punishment in the US, 266

CAREERS
America's top jobs for college graduates, 3d ed, 88
Career exploration on the Internet, 84
Career opportunities in TV, cable, video, & multimedia,
    4th ed, 85
Career opportunities in the sports industry, 2d ed, 89
Career opportunities in theater & the performing arts, 2d
    ed, 90
Complete gd to environmental careers in the 21st century,
    86
Job hunter's sourcebk, 4th ed, 91
National job hotline dir, 87

CARIBBEAN AREA
Economic survey of Latin America & the Caribbean
    1997-98, 50th ed, 83

CARTOGRAPHY
Southeast in early maps, 3d ed, 179

CASTRO, FIDEL
Castro & the Cuban Revolution, 212

CATHOLIC CHURCH
Encyclopedia of the Vatican & Papacy, 447
Our Sunday Visitor's Catholic almanac, 2000, 444

CD-ROM BOOKS
Directory of law-related CD-ROMs 1999, 256
Genealogy on CD-ROM, 168

CD-ROMS
American business leaders [CD-ROM], 62

Atlas of the official records of the Civil War [CD-ROM], 193
Barron's profiles of American colleges, 1999 ed [CD-ROM], 107
Campaigns of the Civil War & the Navy in the Civil War [CD-ROM], 201
Canadian who's who 1999 [CD-ROM], 14
Civil War CD-ROM II [CD-ROM], 202
Encyclopaedia Britannica CD-ROM 1999, multimedia ed [CD-ROM], 17
Encyclopedia Americana on CD-ROM [CD-ROM], 18
Encyclopedia of world biog on CD-ROM [CD-ROM], 9
Horn Bk gd interactive [CD-ROM], 365
New millennium world atlas deluxe [CD-ROM], 183
Southern histl society papers [CD-ROM], 204
Van Nostrand's scientific ency, 8th ed [CD-ROM], 454
World Bk: millennium 2000, deluxe ed [CD-ROM], 21
World Bk multimedia ency: Macintosh ed [CD-ROM], 22

CELEBRITIES
Obituaries in the performing arts, 1998, 423

CENSORSHIP
Censorship in America, 275
100 banned bks, 276

CENTRAL AMERICA. *See also* **LATIN AMERICA**
Peoples of the Americas, 136
Social panorama of Latin America, 1997 ed, 59

CHEMICAL ELEMENTS
Chemical elements, 474

CHEMISTRY
Chemistry, 509
CRC hndbk of chemistry & physics 1999-2000, 80th ed, 506
Dictionary of chemistry, 508
Facts on file dict of chemistry, 3d ed, 507

CHILDREN'S ATLASES
National Geographic beginner's world atlas, 181
National Geographic US atlas for young explorers, 182

CHILDREN'S ENCYCLOPEDIAS & DICTIONARIES
Junior worldmark ency of world cultures, 135
Merriam-Webster & Garfield dict, 351
Merriam-Webster's intermediate dict, 352
Merriam-Webster's school dict, 353
New bk of knowledge, 1999 deluxe lib ed, 19

CHILDREN'S LITERATURE
Best bks for children, 6th ed, 363
Children's bks about religion, 364
Horn Bk gd interactive [CD-ROM], 365
Strong souls singing: African American bks for our daughters & our sisters, 143
Valerie & Walter's best bks for children, 366
Wonderful world of mathematics, 2d ed, 368

CHILDREN'S LITERATURE - BIOGRAPHY
Black authors & illustrators of bks for children & YAs, 370
100 most popular children's authors, 369

CHILDREN'S LITERATURE - TECHNIQUE
Teaching US hist through children's lit, 367

CHILDREN'S NONFICTION
Guide to ref materials for school lib media centers, 5th ed, 274

CHILDREN'S ONLINE INFORMATION SOURCES
Online kids: a young surfer's gd to cyberspace, rev ed, 501

CHILDREN'S REFERENCE BOOKS
Fiesta! 2, 31
National Geographic beginner's world atlas, 181
National Geographic US atlas for young explorers, 182
New bk of knowledge, 1999 deluxe lib ed, 19
Scholastic children's thesaurus, 355
Scholastic treasury of quotations for children, 371

CHINA
Encyclopedia of China, 43

CHINA - HISTORY
China during the cultural revolution, 1966-76, 207
Dictionary of contemporary Chinese military hist, 208
Dictionary of the politics of the People's Republic of China, 42

CHINESE LANGUAGE DICTIONARIES - ENGLISH
Chinese-Pinyin-English dict for learners, 356

CHRISTIAN - DICTIONARIES
Dictionary of the Presbyterian & reformed tradition in America, 445

CHRISTIAN EDUCATION
Christian colleges & universities 1999, 109

CHRISTIANITY
Encyclopedia of Christianity, v.1 (A-D), 446

CITIES & TOWNS
Encyclopedia of world cities, 33

CLIMATOLOGY
Atlas of the world's worst natural disasters, 510

COINS
Handbook of US coins, 2000, 57th ed, 339
Whitman gd to coin collecting, 338

COLLECTIBLES
Collector's Mart mag price gd to ltd ed collectibles, 1999, 335
Maloney's antiques & collectibles resource dir, 5th ed, 336

COLLECTION DEVELOPMENT (LIBRARIES)
Guide to ref materials for school lib media centers, 5th ed, 274

COLLEGE CHOICE
Barron's profiles of American colleges, 1999 ed [CD-ROM], 107

Best 80 business schools, 2000 ed, 126
Best graduate programs: engineering, 2d ed, 108
Best 331 colleges, 2000 ed, 112
Graduate school, 127
Princeton Review African American student's gd to college,
    1999 ed, 129

COLOMBIA
Culture & customs of Colombia, 60

COMMERCIAL CATALOGS
Catalog of catalogs 6, 71

COMMODITIES
CRB commodity yrbk 1998, 69

COMPARATIVE LITERATURE
Comparative reader, 360

COMPOSERS
Schwann opus, winter 1997-99: ref gd to classical music,
    398
Spreadin' rhythm around: black popular songwriters,
    1880-1930, 392

COMPUTER SOFTWARE
Genealogy sftwr gd, 169
Windows 98: the complete ref, 500

**CONSTITUTIONAL AMENDMENTS - UNITED
    STATES**
Constitution & its amendments, 292

CONSUMER GUIDES
Catalog of catalogs 6, 71
Consumer issues in health care sourcebk, 480
Consumer sourcebk, 12th ed, 72
Toll-free phone bk USA 1999, 3d ed, 25

CONSUMER PROTECTION
Consumer fraud, 73

CORPORATE LAW
Laws of the US: corps, 262

COST & STANDARD OF LIVING
Value of a dollar 1860-1999, 2d ed, 67

COUNSELING. *See also* **PSYCHOLOGY**
Baker ency of psychology & counseling, 2d ed, 300

COUNTRY MUSIC
Joel Whitburn's country annual 1994-97, 408
Modern twang: an alternative country music gd & dir, 407

CRETE (GREECE)
Crete, 55

CRIME
Crime state rankings 1999, 6th ed, 267
Hate crimes, 265

CRIMINALS
Mafia ency, 2d ed, 199

CROATIA
Croatia, 50

CUBAN REVOLUTION
Castro & the Cuban Revolution, 212

CULTS (RELIGIOUS)
Cults in America, 439

CULTURES
Lands & peoples, 32

DATABASE SEARCHING
Find it online, 2d ed, 504

DEATH PENALTY
Death penalty, 261

DEMOGRAPHICS
Demographic yrbk, 1997, 49th ed, 319

DETECTIVE & MYSTERY STORIES
Bedside, bathtub, & armchair companion to Sherlock
    Holmes, 375
Reference gd to mystery & detective fiction, 374

DIABETES
Diabetes sourcebk, 2d ed, 491

DICTIONARIES - ENGLISH LANGUAGE
Cassell concise dict with CD-ROM, rev ed [CD-ROM], 347
Concise Oxford dict, 10th ed, 348
Merriam-Webster & Garfield dict, 351
Merriam-Webster's intermediate dict, 352
Merriam-Webster's school dict, 353
Random House Webster's basic dict of American English,
    349

DIGITAL IMAGES
Image buyers gd, 7th ed, 340

DIRECTORIES
Genealogist's address bk, 4th ed, 170
Guide to American dirs, 14th ed, 24

DISTANCE EDUCATION
Barron's gd to distance learning, 102
Distance learning funding sourcebk, 4th ed, 103

DIVORCE
Laws of the US: divorce, 263

DOGS
Barron's ency of dog breeds, 469

DOMINICAN AMERICANS
Dominican Americans, 151

DOYLE, ARTHUR CONAN, SIR
Bedside, bathtub, & armchair companion to Sherlock
    Holmes, 375

DRUG ABUSE
Buzzed: the straight facts about the most used & abused
    drugs from alcohol to ecstasy, 497

DRUGS
Pharmacists gd to over-the-counter & natural remedies, 496
Prescription alternatives, 2d ed, 498

ECONOMIC DEVELOPMENT
Social panorama of Latin America, 1997 ed, 59

ECONOMICS. *See also* **BANKS & BANKING;**
    BUSINESS; FINANCE
Dictionary of free-market economics, 65
Economic survey of Latin America & the Caribbean
    1997-98, 50th ed, 83
New Palgrave dict of economics & the law, 66
Pocket world in figures 1999, 321
Value of a dollar 1860-1999, 2d ed, 67
World dvlpmt indicators, 1998, 81

EDUCATION
Historical dict of American educ, 97

EDUCATION - DIRECTORIES
Best 331 colleges, 2000 ed, 112
College blue bk, 27th ed, 110
Funding sources for K-12 educ 1999, 2d ed, 106
Guide to American educl dirs, 8th ed, 99
Higher educ dir, 1999, 114
Princeton Review gd to performing arts programs, 100

EDUCATION, ELEMENTARY
Internet resource dir for K-12 teachers & librarians,
    1999/2000 ed, 105
Uncle Sam's K-12 Web, 104

EDUCATION, HIGHER
Barron's gd to distance learning, 102
Barron's profiles of American colleges, 1999 ed [CD-ROM],
    107
Best 80 business schools, 2000 ed, 126
Best 331 colleges, 2000 ed, 112
Christian colleges & universities 1999, 109
College blue bk, 27th ed, 110
College Board college costs & financial aid hndbk 2000,
    20th ed, 123
College Board college hndbk 2000, 37th ed, 124
College Board scholarship hndbk 2000, 3d ed, 125
Colleges that encourage character dvlpmt, 111
Princeton Review African American student's gd to college,
    1999 ed, 129
Princeton Review student athletes gd to college, 130

EDUCATION - HIGHER - GRADUATE WORK
Graduate school, 127
Graduate study in psychology 1998-99, 32d ed, 113

Money for grad students in the humanities 1998-2000, 2d
    ed, 121

EDUCATION - INTERNATIONAL PROGRAMS
International exchange locator, 1998 ed, 131
Peterson's summer study abroad 1999, 132

EDUCATION, MULTICULTURAL
Encyclopedia of multicultural educ, 98

EDUCATION, SECONDARY
Internet resource dir for K-12 teachers & librarians,
    1999/2000 ed, 105

EDUCATION - STATISTICS
Education stats on the US 1999, 101

EDUCATIONAL FUND-RAISING
Teacher's gd to winning grants, 115

EGYPT
Daily life of the ancient Egyptians, 232
Gods of ancient Egypt, 206

ELECTIONS - UNITED STATES
Almanac of state legislatures, 2d ed, 286
Encyclopedia of American parties, campaigns, & elections,
    288

ELECTRONIC PUBLISHING
Columbia gd to online style, 334

EMIGRATION & IMMIGRATION
American immigration, 200
Immigration & the law, 299

ENCYCLOPEDIAS & DICTIONARIES. *See also*
    CHILDREN'S ENCYCLOPEDIAS &
    DICTIONARIES
DK concise ency, 16
Encyclopaedia Britannica CD-ROM 1999, multimedia ed
    [CD-ROM], 17
Encyclopedia Americana on CD-ROM [CD-ROM], 18
New bk of knowledge, 1999 deluxe lib ed, 19
World Bk: millennium 2000, deluxe ed [CD-ROM], 21
World Bk ency, 1999 ed, 20
World Bk multimedia ency: Macintosh ed [CD-ROM], 22

ENDANGERED SPECIES
Endangered species, 467

ENGINEERING
Best graduate programs: engineering, 2d ed, 108

ENGLISH LANGUAGE - DICTIONARIES
Cassell concise dict with CD-ROM, rev ed [CD-ROM],
    347
Concise Oxford dict, 10th ed, 348
Merriam-Webster & Garfield dict, 889
Merriam-Webster's intermediate dict, 890
Merriam-Webster's school dict, 353

Random House Webster's basic dict of American English, 349

Webster's new world college dict, 4th ed, 350

ENGLISH LANGUAGE - DICTIONARIES - CHINESE
Chinese-Pinyin-English dict for learners, 356

ENGLISH LANGUAGE - DICTIONARIES - FRENCH
Dictionary of French slang & colloquial expressions, 357

ENGLISH LANGUAGE - DICTIONARIES - JAPANESE
Compact Nelson Japanese-English character dict, 358

ENGLISH LANGUAGE - DICTIONARIES - RUSSIAN
Random House Russian-English, English-Russian dict, 359

ENGLISH LANGUAGE - SYNONYMS & ANTONYMS
American Heritage student thesaurus, 354
Scholastic children's thesaurus, 355

ENVIRONMENTAL ENGINEERING
Environmental health, & safety portable hndbk, 475

ENVIRONMENTAL LAW
ABCs of environmental regulation, 269

ENVIRONMENTAL SCIENCE
ABCs of environmental sci, 524
Complete gd to environmental careers in the 21st century, 86

ETHICS
Ethics & values, 435

ETHNIC GROUPS. *See also* **MINORITIES**
Macmillan ency of Native American tribes, 2d ed, 154

ETHNOLOGY
Encyclopedia of Canada's peoples, 134

ETIQUETTE
Do's & don'ts around the world: Asia, 41

EUROPE - HISTORY
Daily life in medieval Europe, 214
Hutchinson ency of the Renaissance, 213

EXECUTIVE DEPARTMENTS. UNITED STATES
Federal agency profiles for students, 294

EXISTENTIALISM
Dictionary of existentialism, 434

EXPLORERS
Explorers: from ancient times to the space age, 184
Explorers & discoverers, v.7, 185

FABLES
Encyclopedia of fable, 418

FANTASY FICTION
Fantasy & horror, 379
Fluent in fantasy: a gd to reading interests, 381
MUP ency of Australian sci fiction & fantasy, 387

FEMINISM
Feminism, 327

FICTION
American histl fiction, 376
Fantasy & horror, 379
Fluent in fantasy, 381
Now read this: a gd to mainstream fiction, 1978-98, 373
Reference gd to mystery & detective fiction, 374
World histl fiction, 377

FILIPINO AMERICANS
Filipino Americans, 141

FINANCE
International dict of personal finance, 75

FINANCIAL AID & SCHOLARSHIPS. *See also* **GRANTS-IN-AID**
College Board college costs & financial aid hndbk 2000, 20th ed, 123
College Board scholarship hndbk 2000, 3d ed, 125
College student's gd to merit & other no-need funding 1998-2000, 117
Financial aid for research & creative activities abroad, 1999-2001, 118
Financial aid for study & training abroad 1999-2001, 119
Financial aid for vets, military personnel, & their dependents 1998-2000, 120
How to find out about financial aid & funding, 116
Money for grad students in the humanities 1998-2000, 2d ed, 121
Money for graduate students in the social scis 1998-2000, 2d ed, 122

FINANCIAL STATISTICS
International financial stats yrbk 1999, 79

FISHING
Complete outdoors ency, 4th ed, 305

FLAGS
Flags, 176

FLORIDA
Sunshine state almanac & bk of Fla.-related stuff, 37

FLOWERS
Gardener's atlas, 461
National Audubon Society 1st field gd: wildflowers, 462

FOLKLORE
Encyclopedia of fable, 418
Folklore from Africa to the US, repr ed, 416
Travel, legend, & lore, 417

FOOD SCIENCES
New complete bk of food, 457

FOOTBALL
Official Natl Football League 99 record & fact bk, 310
STATS pro football hndbk 1999, 311

FOREIGN STUDY
Peterson's summer study abroad 1999, 132

FORMER YUGOSLAV REPUBLICS
Bibliography of sources on the region of Former Yugoslavia, 52
Conflict in the Former Yugoslavia, 231

FRANCE - HISTORY
Authorized press in Vichy & German-occupied France, 1940-44, 218
Napoleon, 219

FREE ENTERPRISE
Dictionary of free-market economics, 65

FRENCH GUIANA
French Guiana, 58

FRENCH LANGUAGE - DICTIONARIES
Dictionary of French slang & colloquial expressions, 357

FRENCH PERIODICALS
Authorized press in Vichy & German-occupied France, 1940-44, 218

FUNDRAISING
Teacher's gd to winning grants, 115

GARFIELD (FICTITIOUS CHARACTER)
Merriam-Webster & Garfield dict, 351

GAYS
Almanac of women & minorities in American pol, 296

GENEALOGY
County locator, 171
Finding a place called home, 175
Genealogical ency of the Colonial Americas, 167
Genealogist's address bk, 4th ed, 170
Instant info on the Internet, 173
They became Americans: finding naturalization records & ethnic origins, 174

GENEALOGY - DIRECTORIES
Cyndi's list: a comprehensive list of 40,000 genealogy sites on the Internet, 172
Genealogy on CD-ROM, 168
Genealogy sftwr gd, 169

GENETICS
Encyclopedia of genetics, 458

GEOGRAPHY
Columbia gazetteer of the world, 188
Dictionary of geography, 187
Encyclopedia of world cities, 33
Merriam-Webster's geographical dict, 3d ed, 186
National Geographic desk ref, 189

GEOLOGY
Cambridge gd to minerals, rocks, & fossils, rev ed, 519
Geology, 518

GERMANY
History of Germany, 221

GOVERNMENT INFORMATION
County locator, 171

GRANTS-IN-AID. *See also* **FINANCIAL AID & SCHOLARSHIPS**
Grants register 2000, 18th ed, 128
Guide to grantseeking on the Web, 315

GREAT BRITAIN
Britain 1999, 50th ed, 53
Encyclopedia of Britain, 54

GREAT BRITAIN - HISTORY
Blackwell ency of Anglo-Saxon England, 228
Hutchinson illus ency of British hist, 229
Medieval England, 230

GREECE
Crete, 55
Macedonian empire, 222

GUERRILLA WARFARE
Encyclopedia of guerrilla warfare, 282

GUITARS
Complete ency of the guitar, 399
Gruhn's gd to vintage guitars, 2d ed, 400

GUN CONTROL
People for & against gun control, 264

HATE CRIMES
Hate crimes, 265

HEALTH CARE. *See also* **MEDICINE**
Health care state rankings 1999, 7th ed, 478

HEART DISEASE
Alternative medicine gd to heart disease, stroke, & high blood pressure, 484

HELL
Encyclopedia of hell, 419

HISPANIC AMERICANS
Hispanic-American experience on file, 166